Library of Congress Cataloging-in-Publication Data

Thompson, John M.
Understanding prajñā: Sengzhao's "wild words"
and the search for wisdom / John M. Thompson.
p. cm. — (American university studies. Series VII,
Theology and religion; v. 256)
Includes bibliographical references and index.
1. Sengzhao, 384–414. 2. Wisdom (Buddhism). I. Title.
BQ984.E527T46   294.3'42042092—dc22   2006028266
ISBN 978-0-8204-8826-4
ISSN 0740-0446

Bibliographic information published by **Die Deutsche Bibliothek**.
Die Deutsche Bibliothek lists this publication in the "Deutsche
Nationalbibliografie"; detailed bibliographic data is available
on the Internet at http://dnb.ddb.de/.

The paper in this book meets the guidelines for permanence and durability
of the Committee on Production Guidelines for Book Longevity
of the Council of Library Resources.

© 2008 Peter Lang Publishing, Inc., New York
29 Broadway, 18th floor, New York, NY 10006
www.peterlang.com

Printed in the United States of America

Understanding *Prajñā*

american
university
studies

Series VII
Theology and Religion

Vol. 256

PETER LANG
New York • Washington, D.C./Baltimore • Bern
Frankfurt am Main • Berlin • Brussels • Vienna • Oxford

John M. Thompson

Understanding *Prajñā*

Sengzhao's "Wild Words" and the Search for Wisdom

PETER LANG
New York • Washington, D.C./Baltimore • Bern
Frankfurt am Main • Berlin • Brussels • Vienna • Oxford

For my wife Cathy,
whose love has shown me the meaning of life.
"Maid of Athens, *s'agapo*."

For my older daughter Julia,
who in her seven odd years on this planet has taught me
more about Dao than any other teacher I have had.

For my younger daughter Sophia,
who reminds me that Wisdom continues to be reborn
in this world—we only have to be open to receiving it.

CONTENTS

PREFACE

It is customary in prefaces for authors to relate the untold story behind their work, to "fess up" to what has motivated the study in the first place. This is a valuable tradition from which I have no intention of breaking. My interest in Sengzhao (374–414) is part and parcel of a long-standing fascination with hermeneutics and interpretation in general. That question of "meaning" has plagued me for much of my life. How is it that we are able to comprehend a bewildering array of phenomena—marks on a page or screen, gestures of hand and body, intonations of voice, subtle shadings of light and color—and proclaim its "meaning"? The fact is that we all do this at every waking moment. We live in a world (or "worlds") pregnant with meaning, even when we judge it all "meaningless." As a scholar of religion and philosophy I am continually confronting worlds of meaning and trying to help my students comprehend what often appears to them to be meaningless.

My struggles with hermeneutics began in earnest when I was an undergraduate concentrating in Western philosophy but, like Sengzhao, I found myself drawn to Daoist and Buddhist perspectives. It was only when I went to seminary, however, that I finally studied those traditions in a systematic fashion. This led to a dramatic shift in my own thinking. In a class on Chinese Religion and Philosophy in particular I found myself continually facing the same old questions of meaning and understanding but in a new fashion. Although I had read parts of the *Zhuangzi* before, I was unprepared for the effect of reading the first two chapters in their entirety. From then on I knew that I could never "do philosophy" in quite the same way. A few weeks later when reading Sengzhao in the same class I became even more excited, for here was someone doing the "Zhuangzi thing" but in a Buddhist fashion. I made a mental note to investigate Sengzhao's writings further in the future. This intention lay dormant for some time only to resurface during my first year of doctoral study in Berkeley when I came across a copy of Liebenthal's translation of the *Zhaolun* in the library of the Graduate Theological Union. In a bout of typical graduate student foolishness, I read it from cover to cover during the winter break and decided I would try to do something on this intriguing if obscure thinker.

Dao moves in mysterious ways and my chance was given to me in the form of a Buddhist Text seminar in spring of 1996 that was devoted to reading and translating the *Zhaolun*. My most vivid memory of that seminar comes *not* from a discussion during class time or any discovery I made doing research but a pre-class chat with my fellow students. One of my friends simply looked at me, gestured to the Chinese manuscript in front of him and said, "This just doesn't make any sense." He was right, of course, but what I realized then was that that was precisely Sengzhao's point: the writings of the *Zhaolun* do not make sense from a sober, analytic perspective. Sengzhao is the Buddhist Zhuangzi—his "sense" is "nonsense." It is up to us to figure out what this "nonsense" means, and this study is my best effort to do so.

Most of the material here is new, although I have recycled some of it from previous incarnations. Certain sections come from my work as a participant on a panel on the *Zhaolun* presented at the Western Regional meeting of the AAR in spring of 1997. Other parts come from a paper on "wild words" that I delivered at the national meeting of the AAR in November of 1999 and another paper reviewing research on the *Zhaolun* that I presented at the 11th International Conference on Chinese Philosophy in summer of 1999. My work was greatly facilitated by two dissertation grants awarded to me by the Rocky Foundation in 1998 and 1999. During the summer of 1999 I was also awarded a Numata Fellowship to study at Ryukoku University in Kyoto, where I did a great deal of the translation work. During this time I was also privileged to sit in on the weekly meetings of the Ryukoku University Translation Center presided over by Meiji Yamada and his colleagues. This first-hand experience of such an important interpretive enterprise remains one of the highlights of my academic life and continues to have an influence on my work.

As a translator and interpreter, I often find myself looking for inspiration and guidance in those figures I study. There is no doubt that I have found such inspiration in Sengzhao. In addition to Sengzhao, however, I have also looked to his predecessor in Chang'an, Shi Daoan (312–385). Daoan, as I note in this study, established the Chang'an translation bureau and set in place much of the institutional structures that allowed **Kumārajīva** and his followers (including Sengzhao) to produce so many fine translations of Buddhist texts. Daoan, like **Kumārajīva** and Sengzhao, was deeply concerned with hermeneutic issues and devoted most of his life to them. For Daoan, such concerns were deeply bound up with his religious vocation. Indeed, according to his biography in the *Gaosengzhuan*, Daoan was a devotee of Maitreya, the future Buddha who resides in Tusita Heaven awaiting his rebirth in our world. Maitreya was, and still is, the patron of translators and exegetes, and he has the power to inspire those who turn to him with doctrinal problems. Daoan and his followers even vowed before an image of Maitreya to be reborn in his presence to gain further guidance. While I have not followed Daoan formally here, there is no doubt that I, too, have looked to Maitreya for guidance; he is, in some sense, Hermes in Buddhist guise (or perhaps Hermes is Maitreya in Greek garb?). All of us who translate and interpret carry out the work of these figures and invoke them constantly. May they continue to grace us with their presence. I must admit, though, that my more Zhuangzian side hopes Maitreya will appear to me most often in his humorous persona, jolly old Budai (Hotei), the "hemp bag bonze" or, as I prefer to say, "the cool fat Buddha." Translation and interpretation are serious work, but we shouldn't take ourselves too seriously while we do it. We will never find Dao if we insist on remaining heavy-laden.

Williamsburg, Virginia   **John M. Thompson**
February, 2007

ACKNOWLEDGMENTS

Although we speak of books as being created by specific authors the truth is books are communal creations, the products of many hands. This is certainly the case with the present volume, and I think it is only fair to acknowledge those who helped usher this book along. First, I must offer sincere thanks to the members of my dissertation committee who patiently endured the early (and far-too wordy) drafts from which this book derives: Ronald Y. Nakasone (Graduate Theological Union), Judith Berling (Graduate Theological Union), Edmond Yee (Pacific Lutheran Theological Seminary) and Whalen Lai (University of California at Davis). As time has passed I have come to realize the extent to which their individual and collective scholarly talents surpass my own, and I remain honored and humbled by their support of my efforts. Second, I need to thank Heidi Burns, Senior Editor at Peter Lang Publishing, Richard Atkins, Production Liaison, and Jackie Pavlovic, Production Supervisor, who (along with their staff) have overseen the lengthy process of transforming my manuscript to full-fledged book. In addition, I must thank several people at Christopher Newport University: Ken Rose and Lori Underwood, my colleagues in the department of Philosophy and Religious Studies who helped steer me to Peter Lang in the first place; Dick Summerville, CNU's outgoing Provost, and Douglas Gordan, Dean of the College of Liberal Arts and Sciences, both of whom generously provided funds for this book's preparation.

Finally I would like to thank my family and friends for their constant support and affection; academic life is often frustrating but you make it infinitely easier to bear.

May you all be showered with immeasurable merit, may you enjoy rebirth in the presence of all Buddhas in the 10 Realms, and may you quickly attain *anuttara-samyak-sambodhi*!

ABBREVIATIONS

DNZ   Nakano Tatsue, ed., **Dai Nihon zokuzōkyō** 大日名續藏經 (Kyoto: Zōkyō shoin, 1905–1912). This has been reprinted as Xu zangjing 續藏經 (Taibei: Xinwenfeng, 1968–1970).

SBBY   Sibu beiyao 四部備要 (Shanghai: Zhonghua shuju, 1927–1935).

T   J. Takakusu and K. Watanabe, eds., Taish shinshu **daizōkyō** 大正新修大藏經 (Tokyō: Taishō issaikyō kankōkai, 1924–1932).

INTRODUCTION:
SENGZHAO'S QUEST
FOR UNDERSTANDING AND
OUR ATTEMPT TO UNDERSTAND HIM

Someone asked a Zen-Master, "What is the ultimate nature of reality?"
The Master replied, "Ask that post over there." The man responded, "Master,
I don't understand!" The Master said, "Neither do I."

—Raymond M. Smullyan, The Tao is Silent

During the early fifth century C.E. in Chang'an, the capital of the Eastern Jin
dynasty, a young scholar-monk was caught up in a hermeneutical crisis. Sengzhao
(374–414), a disciple of **Kumārajīva**, the renowned Kuchean **Mādhyamika** master who had been appointed *guoshi* ("National Preceptor") by Emperor Yao Xing
(r. 394–416), was struggling to understand the Buddhist notion of *prajñā*. His
was not a new problem. During the previous two centuries various literati[1] had
been wrestling with *prajñā* based upon their readings of the *Prajñāpāramitā*
sūtras. Although we are still unsure of the details of these so-called "*prajñā*
schools," we do know that their members were all wrestling with the teachings of *śūnyatā* ("emptiness"), the Two Truths (*paramārtha satya* and *samvṛti*
satya), as well as the sort of "knowing" such teachings call for.[2] There were
many different views here and some scholar-monks attempted to sort out the
various texts and opinions. Sengzhao was familiar with these debates but had
an advantage his predecessors lacked: a genuine **Mādhyamika** master to explain
Buddhist teachings. Under **Kumārajīva's** guidance Sengzhao arrived at an understanding of Buddhism from which he was able to assess earlier positions.

Sengzhao articulated his understanding in a series of four essays (*Wu bu-qian, Bu zhenkong, Panruo wuzhi, Niepan wuming*—henceforth "Things Do Not Shift," "Emptiness of the Not-real," "*Prajñā* is Not-knowing," and "Nirvana is nameless") which were collected posthumously and entitled the *Zhaolun*. In these essays Sengzhao expounds on the major issues of **Mahāyāna** with which Chinese Buddhists were struggling. Of these essays, "*Prajñā* is Not-knowing" is the most intriguing. It is the first essay Sengzhao wrote, it met with **Kumārajīva**'s enthusiastic approval, and circulated widely among learned Buddhists of the day. "*Prajñā* is Not-knowing" is the essay wherein it is easiest to see Sengzhao's understanding of Buddhism as it develops, yet this same essay also created misunderstanding for those who read it.

Liu Yimin (354–410) was one of the literati who was taken with Sengzhao's treatise but puzzled as well.[3] He wrote to Sengzhao asking for clarification on various points, even arguing with him on certain issues. Sengzhao, in turn, wrote a reply to Yimin in which he answers Liu's objections and reiterates his position. These letters have been preserved and appended to "*Prajñā* is Not-knowing." For simplicity's sake I treat these letters as a single text entitled "The Correspondence." Together "*Prajñā* is Not-knowing" and "The Correspondence" reveal a great deal about the thought and practice in China during the early fifth century and the place of Buddhism in that context.

In "*Prajñā* is Not-knowing" Sengzhao lays out what *prajñā*, the "Sagely Wisdom" of the Buddhas and Bodhisattvas, is and how it functions by explaining key passages from Buddhist scriptures. He also addresses misunderstandings and attempts to clarify his points by answering various possible "objections." The correspondence between Sengzhao and Liu Yimin continues this clarification process. From a contemporary academic perspective we would say that the essay and the correspondence both revolve around matters of hermeneutics. That is, in "*Prajñā* is Not-knowing" Sengzhao is working to understand Buddhist teachings and to correct previous misunderstandings, and his exchange with Liu Yimin tries to correct further misunderstandings. Sengzhao makes his hermeneutic concerns clear in the essay's opening lines: "*Prajñā*, void and 'dark,' is perhaps the beginning and end of the Three Vehicles. It is truly One, lacking all duality. [Yet] discussions of different teachings [of *prajñā*] have caused confusion for a long time."[4] By trying to adjudicate between these interpretations of *prajñā*, Sengzhao's essay "*Prajñā* is Not-knowing" and his correspondence with Liu Yimin together provide some of the most important examples of hermeneutic thinking in early Chinese Buddhism.

Yet if Sengzhao was wrestling with problems of understanding during the Jin dynasty (317–420), then it is even more the case for those of us in the present studying his work. Sengzhao was a monk who lived some 1500 years ago whom we only know through texts. Some of these texts (those written by him and his commentators) are in Classical Chinese, a language that can no longer be spoken. Others of these texts are scholarly books and articles written in various contemporary languages (e.g. Japanese, Chinese, French, and English). Our situation, thus, differs considerably from Sengzhao's, for we are trying to understand him across a vast cultural and historical distance mediated by previous scholars who may not have understood Sengzhao themselves. Our problem is how to bridge this great distance via texts that often say different or even contradictory things. Nonetheless, our concerns with understanding and interpreting, like Sengzhao's, are hermeneutic as well. This study then, is *explicitly hermeneutical* in that we are seeking to understand Sengzhao and our own process of understanding him.

This distinction between *hermeneutic* and *hermeneutical* calls for some elaboration. The universal nature of hermeneutics as a fundamental characteristic of human being means that, broadly speaking, all of our daily deliberations and efforts to make sense of things are hermeneutic. For the most part, however, when I use the term "hermeneutic" I mean it in its narrower, more specialized sense as referring to various attempts to understand and interpret a text. Of course, those engaged in such interpretive struggles do not always do so in a self-conscious way. The more deliberative exercise of hermeneutics requires a some critical distance and usually arises only as a tradition matures or perhaps in moments of crisis. Often as well this critical hermeneutics develops as part of an on-going discourse on interpretation, one in which a tradition recognizes problems and issues at stake in textual understanding. Such a critical hermeneutics is theoretically oriented, and tends to be formulated on the basis of an overall theory of understanding. For the purposes of this study I refer to this latter, more circumspective approach to interpretation as *hermeneutical*.[5] This distinction between *hermeneutic* and *hermeneutical*, though, is subtle and really is more a difference in degree rather than kind.

Any effort to interpret a text forces an interpreter to become aware of the initial differences between her world and that of the text, to question her assumptions, and to revise her understanding. As this process of give and take continues she may begin to reflect on the theoretical basis of her attempts to understand, perhaps even becoming open to multiple interpretations. In such instances the interpreter is moving into a hermeneutical understanding. As we shall see, this striving for a fully hermeneutical understanding has parallels in Chinese and Buddhist traditions, and seems to be the type of understanding of *prajñā* to which Sengzhao's texts call us.

In Chapter One, I review of hermeneutics in Western, Chinese and Buddhist contexts. What I show is that the long-standing concern for finding and preserving meaning that lies at the heart of the hermeneutic enterprise spans cultures–it is a universal human concern. After briefly tracing the history of hermeneutics in the West, especially in the work of Martin Heidegger, Hans-Georg Gadamer and Paul Ricoeur, I then turn to Chinese and Buddhist hermeneutics. In China hermeneutics center on understanding Dao whereas in Buddhism, hermeneutics focus on understanding the Dharma. I argue that both traditions have similar overriding concerns although there are important differences between them that we should note. I finish the chapter by pausing to consider some important questions that we need to be mindful of as we engage in our study: the idea of meaning as intention, postmodern criticisms of hermeneutics, and the problems surrounding Orientalism and its legacy within scholarship.

Chapter Two picks up with these basic hermeneutic concerns, focusing specifically on interpretive problems surrounding *prajñā*. I begin by looking at some common misunderstandings of *prajñā* before launching into a brief examination of *prajñā* as understood in India and China before Sengzhao's day. It quickly becomes apparent that *prajñā* is not a simple concept but had multiple definitions and conflicting interpretations over time and across traditions. These differences and conflicts became even more acute as Buddhism entered China in the early centuries of the Common Era and underwent a large-scale transformation. Translation was a major part of this transformation and we see problems arising again and again. It is in this context that the mysterious "*prajñā* schools" of early Chinese Buddhism arose. Although it is difficult to sort out the key features (tenets, histories, proponents, etc.) of these "schools," they clearly come down to differing interpretations of *prajñā*. Indeed, I argue that Sengzhao's writings are his responses to these conflicting views, in which he is trying to adjudicate among these varying notions of *prajñā* under the tutelage of his master **Kumārajīva**.

It is in Chapter Three that I actually begin a detailed examination of "*Prajñā* is Not-knowing." After some considerations of Sengzhao's own context and important influences upon him I give an overview of the treatise's structure and function. I then engage in a close reading of Sengzhao's words, centering on the special language of *prajñā* that he uses, a type of discourse

I term "wild words." "Wild words" work differently than ordinary discourse and I demonstrate their distinctive working in five ways: allusion, "chain arguments," paradox, metaphorical playing, and puns. All five of these ways of using language form distinct yet interrelated moves within Sengzhao's rhetorical repertoire and I argue that we cannot make sense of them rationally. Instead, they require a different kind of reading. "Wild words" do not inform us of what *prajñā* is but transform our minds into the Mind of *prajñā*. At the end of this chapter I elaborate on the ideas behind "wild words" by drawing parallels to the findings of other scholars. I close this chapter by examining some important questions about "wild words" and their relationship to Sengzhao's other writings, claims of ineffability, and possible influence of "wild words" on later *Chan* and *Zen* traditions.

Chapter Four follows the lines laid out in Chapter Three, except the focus changes to "The Correspondence." I begin by tracing the context and influences on Liu Yimin, whose life on Lushan, one of China's holy mountains, differed considerably from Sengzhao's life in Chang'an. I then give an overview of both letters before plunging into a close reading of them. My reading focuses especially on Liu's concerns and assumptions as they reflect his ascetic Pure Land devotion as well as the way Sengzhao in his reply to Liu once again makes use of "wild words." I make it clear in my discussion that these letters reveal a profound misunderstanding rooted in the fact that both thinkers are members of different interpretive communities.

In Chapter Five I reflect in a more self-conscious fashion on my findings in the attempt to assess what *we* can say about *prajñā*. I return to the questions I raise at the end of Chapter One about intention, postmodern critiques and Orientalism, and examine my own study in light of these concerns. I then turn to what bearing Sengzhao and Liu's exchange may have on contemporary issues in religious and philosophic studies surrounding the field of "mysticism." "Mysticism" is even more complex than *prajñā*, but after a brief tracing of academic scholarship on "mysticism" thus far, I turn to what Sengzhao and Liu have to say about *prajñā* and see what light (if any) they shed on the subject. I suggest that we consider both Sengzhao and Liu to be different types of "mystics" who have much in common with mystics of other traditions even as they also reveal great differences. I then reflect again on what *prajñā* is, or more accurately, what we can say about it based on our readings of Sengzhao and Liu Yimin.

The final chapter of this study, my conclusion, comprises a short summary of my main points with some philosophical reflections on what the term "understanding" actually means and what it means to "understand" *prajñā* through Sengzhao's writings. In this section I reflect how complex and ambiguous the concept of "understanding" is, what Heidegger, Gadamer and Ricoeur mean by "understanding," and in light of these considerations, what we can say about "misunderstanding." It is obvious that the exchange between Sengzhao and Liu Yimin is a misunderstanding but as I point out, what this "misunderstanding" entails and how it differs from "understanding" is difficult to determine. Ultimately a misunderstanding "misses" something and, I argue, it misses the "other", or rather, it misses *meeting* the other on common ground. Lastly, I close this section by suggesting that there may be parallels between the transformative understanding that arises out of hermeneutic engagement and the being-knowing of *prajñā*. Sengzhao calls us to understand *prajñā* through his words. To interpret Sengzhao is to strive for the Sagely "not-knowing knowing" of *prajñā* itself.

One could say that I use a "hermeneutic approach" in this study. This description seems simple enough but in actuality it tells us very little. "Hermeneutics" is an amorphous field of study and there are literally as many types of "hermeneutics" as there are methods of inquiry. My study of Sengzhao and his work on *prajñā* relies heavily on Western hermeneutic theory, specifically the philosophical hermeneutics associated with twentieth century European thinkers such as Heidegger, Gadamer and Ricoeur. All three of these thinkers, though they often have different concerns, nonetheless share much in common in that their work consistently grapples with problems of Western thought in light of the decline of modernity.[6] I believe that insights arising from philosophical hermeneutics help us understand Sengzhao's efforts within his context and shed light on our interpretive situation vis-à-vis Sengzhao's works. It also, I think, will become apparent that philosophical hermeneutics' concerns with close attention to texts, constant questioning of our initial assumptions and how we appropriate meaning in light of our own situation is shared by Buddhist and Chinese traditions.

It may be helpful at this point for me to explain some of the more technical aspects of my study that will likely be only of concern for Sinologists and other philological specialists. Throughout this work I use pinyin romanization for Chinese terms and Hepburn romanization for Japanese terms, as these have become fairly standard. The Chinese passages I cite are all my translations. In my footnotes I provide alternative English translations for comparative purposes. The versions of Non-Buddhist Chinese texts I use come from the *Sibu beiyao* (SBBY). In my citations I generally note author (if known), title, *ce* ("volume"), *juan* ("roll") and/or *pian* ("section"), and page. I do this mainly for ease and conformity. The SBBY is an authoritative collection of Chinese texts but by no means the only one. In my citations I also distinguish between the SBBY versions of "original" texts such as the *Analects* and *Daode jing* from later commentaries on these texts, even though the SBBY groups "originals" and commentaries together. Some might argue that this is an artificial distinction since Chinese texts have come down to us *through* their commentaries rather than as a separate, "pure" transmission. Nonetheless I find this distinction helpful, particularly when citing the allusions to and quotations from "original" works that Sengzhao makes. Generally I also italicize all technical Chinese and Sanskrit terms with the exception of certain common terms such as Buddha, Bodhisattva and Dao.

Finally, before we begin our study of Sengzhao and Liu Yimin, I need to say a few things about what a "hermeneutical understanding" entails. A fully hermeneutical understanding, the ideal that theorists such as Gadamer and Ricoeur hold up, is a curious goal. Indeed, it is not so much a "goal" as a dwelling in paradox, an awareness of the limits of one's understanding that is willing to enter into other perspectives while not automatically surrendering itself. Hermeneutical understanding is not cut off from its roots but neither is it forever tethered to one place. Most of all, achieving such an understanding means heeding a call to truth (*alētheia*) that takes us beyond simple, easy formulations. To strive for a hermeneutical understanding is to constantly venture into openness while never forgetting from where one comes.

One of the distinctive marks of hermeneutical understanding is a happy irony. This is not the superficial, smirking irony of popular U.S. culture, which is little more than a "hip" façade betraying a profound lack of appreciation for life and a constricted understanding of what it means to be a human being. Rather, the happy irony that characterizes hermeneutical understanding is based on a deep caring for human life, ideals and institutions that simultaneously knows such things pale in the grand scheme of things. Hermeneutical irony smiles at our own pretensions, secure in its insecurity. Such a stance is undoubtedly quite rare, and may seem impossible for us to reach yet it is a state that humans alone can attain. Gods and angels do not know limits of mortal life and do not need to interpret; animals do not have the capacity for self-consciousness and so cannot recognize the limitations of their own understanding.

Are there models for such ironic understanding? I suggest there are. In the West one thinks of such figures as Socrates, the skeptics of Pyrrho's school, those "fathers" of existentialism Soren Kierkegaard and Friedrich Nietzsche. We find similar figures in "Eastern" traditions among the *jinas* of Jainism, Śākyamuni Buddha, the various Bodhisattvas of the **Mahāyāna**, the laughing Daoist Zhuangzi, or certain *Chan/Zen* masters. I think Sengzhao belongs in these ranks as well. Part of what I argue is that genuine hermeneutic engagement with Sengzhao's writings can actually serve as a way for us to reach such an understanding. In any case, we can only find out by trying. When all is said and done, hermeneutics is a practical matter of turning our attention to a text and opening to its meaning. Such attentive study will not result in a "knowing" that assimilates various facts and information. Instead it will move us into an understanding that is a living process, a deliberate and mindful way of dwelling in the world.

· 1 ·

HERMENEUTICS AND THE QUESTION
OF UNDERSTANDING

What is "Hermeneutics"?

Both Sengzhao's essay "*Prajñā* is Not-knowing" and "The Correspondence" with Liu Yimin center on hermeneutics, but what does this mean? Hermeneutics is an amorphous subject. It often is defined as "the discipline and practice of understanding" but this statement is so broad as to encompass all methods of inquiry. How can we consider something to be a single branch of study when it can cover situations as varied as a novice puzzling over a passage of scripture, an art historian analyzing Michelangelo's "David," or a Zulu hunter making sense of a tangled confusion of animal tracks? Gerald Bruns puts it well when he describes hermeneutics as "a loose and baggy monster ... a less than fully disciplined body of thinking whose inventory of topics spreads out over many different historical, cultural, and intellectual contexts."[1] Bruns' metaphor is wonderfully apt, as monsters are unexpected apparitions, huge and unsettling. The word "monster" stems from the Latin *monstrum* ("omen," "sign"), something that confounds our thinking. Monsters dwell at the edge of reason, and tend to be ugly and dangerous. This, too, is true of hermeneutics, which is a multi-headed monster, like the Greek hydra, and has many voices. It cannot be confined to one field but runs through many areas.

The word "hermeneutics" derives from the Greek verb *hermeneneuien* ("to interpret") and the noun *hermenia* ("interpretation"). Both terms appear in

ancient texts including Sophocles' *Oedipus at Colonus*, several Platonic dialogues, and Aristotle's treatise *Peri hermeneias* ("On interpretation"). Scholars
often trace these "herm terms" to Hermes, the herald who mediates between
gods and humans, transforming what is beyond our ken ("godly speech")
into understandable form. Hermes is the inventor of language and writing,
which permit us to understand and convey meaning.[2] Significantly, Hermes
is a joker, a thief and a liar. Thus even hermeneutics' mythological roots are
marked by ambivalence. Hermeneutics deals with understanding and misunderstanding. To this day hermeneutics radiates something of Hermes' divine
aura, as it is particularly associated with rules and methods for interpreting
scripture.

Although we sometimes equate hermeneutics with methods and techniques, in the strictest sense it refers to the *theory* or *methodology* behind these
operations. Moreover, hermeneutics extends beyond concerns with specific
texts to the notion of human understanding itself. These two areas of focus
are related but separable, and can illuminate each other.[3] Indeed, both entail
each other–interpreting a particular text presupposes a background theory of
understanding (if only implicitly) whereas theories of understanding can only
be derived from actual instances of interpretation.

Hermeneutics is closely related to the practices of exegesis, commentary and translation. *Exegesis*, properly speaking, consists of elucidating the
meaning of passages of writings. As such, it is explanatory in nature. This is
certainly a way of interpreting, and in fact is one of the meanings of *hermeneuein*,[4] but such explanation does not usually involve critical reflection
on the process of exegesis itself. *Commentary* is akin to exegesis but most
commonly denotes the practice of *written* exegesis or the actual explanatory
treatises themselves. Although commentary is a complex intellectual practice, like exegesis, it tends not to be concerned with reflexive considerations.
Translation is the re-wording of something said or written in one language
into another. This also is one of the meanings of *hermeneuein*, and it comes
very close to capturing the structure of hermeneutics itself. In translating
we become aware of the gap (even clash) between languages and worlds,
and of our attempts to bridge this chasm. Translation confronts us with all
the issues of understanding and misunderstanding with which hermeneutic
theory deals, for in translation there are always two worlds, that of the text
and that of the reader, and hence we must assume the role of Hermes in
moving between them.[5]

Hermeneutics in the West

Most scholars agree that Martin Heidegger, Hans-Georg Gadamer and Paul Ricoeur have been the most influential figures in contemporary hermeneutics but their work has deep historical roots. Formal hermeneutic reflection began in ancient Greece but became a major task with the rise of Christianity. Early theologians were particularly concerned with understanding the Hebrew scriptures in light of Christ's life and teachings, and understanding the gospel with respect to pagan writings. In the third century C.E. Origen (184–254) devised a three-tiered scheme of interpreting scripture (literal, moral, mystical) which became the basis for the medieval four-tiered scheme (literal, allegorical, moral, analogical) formulated by Johannes Cassianus (360–435).[6] In addition, Augustine (354–450) developed a more existential hermeneutics that distinguished between the "outer" and "inner" word, an idea that had decisive impact on Heidegger and Gadamer.

For the most part these theories of scriptural interpretation held sway until the sixteenth century when Martin Luther (1483–1546) broke ranks with a more radical hermeneutics centered on the interpreter and scripture alone (*sola scriptura*). Matthias Flacius Illyricus (1520–1575) carried Luther's efforts further by combining long-standing practices of Biblical exegesis with Aristotelian rhetoric in his *Clavis Scripturae Sacrae* (1567). The next few centuries also saw the rise of humanist hermeneutics sparked by renewed interest in Classical Greece and Rome during the Renaissance, and important developments in the hermeneutics of jurisprudence. These movements influenced such philosophers as Christian Wolff (1679–1754) and Johann Martin Chladenius (1710–1759), through whose work hermeneutics as a discipline of interpretation founded on general rules and principles came into being.[7]

The philosophical hermeneutics of Heidegger, Gadamer and Ricoeur, however, was most heavily influenced by the figures of German Romanticism. Of these, Friedrich Schleiermacher (1768–1834) was perhaps the most significant. Schleiermacher realized that hermeneutics required explicit theoretical foundations because understanding could not be taken for granted. He saw hermeneutics as an "art of understanding" (*verstehen*) relying on firm linguistic and grammatical analysis but moving on to empathy with the author(s). One needed to be in immediate relationship with the subject. Thus Schleiermacher in *Hermeneutik und Kritik* gives what is widely considered the motto of Romantic hermeneutics: "To understand the text at first as well as and then even better than its author."[8] Scheiermacher makes plain, moreover, that since we cannot directly know the contents of an author's, a thorough understanding requires that we make ourselves aware of various factors influencing the text, many of which the author himself may have been unaware.

Wilhelm Dilthey (1833–1911) built upon Schleiermacher's work, attempting to make hermeneutics the theoretical foundation for the *Geisteswissenschaften* ("human sciences"). Dilthey made two particularly important contributions to the field. First, he explicitly made the goal of hermeneutics an "empathetic understanding" in which one makes a vital connection to a work or text by transposing oneself into the mind of its author. As Dilthey says, "On the basis of this empathy or transposition there arises the highest form of understanding in which the totality of mental life is active–re-creating or re-living."[9] This empathetic understanding serves as the counterpart to the certainty of the natural sciences which is derived from experiments. Second, Dilthey also grounded such higher, conscious attempts at interpretation on prior elementary forms of understanding derived from our native cultural context.[10] This latter idea exerted great influence on Heidegger, Gadamer and Ricoeur.

Heidegger: Hermeneutics of Facticity

Contemporary philosophical hermeneutics begins with Martin Heidegger (1889–1976), for it is through his work that hermeneutics takes on a fully ontological dimension. Heidegger begins where Dilthey left off by marrying the former's work with the phenomenology of Edmund Husserl (1859–1938). Heidegger redefines the hermeneutic project in his book *Being and Time* as a "hermeneutics of facticity." In *Being and Time* Heidegger breaks with the prevailing subject-object metaphysics of Western philosophy and instead analyzes human being (*Dasein*, "there being") in terms of its involvement in the world. According to Heidegger, *Dasein* is fundamentally hermeneutical. That is, in ordinary activities *Dasein* reveals a basic understanding of Being which constitutes our form of life. This understanding can be likened to the set of coping skills (both manual and cognitive) by which we inhabit our world and which we learn by being raised within a particular society. In Heidegger's view, all of *Dasein*'s actions are hermeneutic. Linguistic statements, the traditional focus of hermeneutics, are a derivative mode of interpretation since *Dasein* is always revealing its basic understanding in its dealings with things. *Being and Time* is an extended explication of this fundamental pre-verbal hermeneutics.

Heidegger holds that *Dasein*'s understanding of Being is *pre-theoretical*. Borrowing from Schleiermacher, Heidegger describes this idea through the notion of the "hermeneutic circle," the interactive domain of observer and work, thinker and text, and human beings in general and their "life-world" (*lebenvelt*). In *Being and Time* Heidegger says *Dasein* is characterized by an understanding of Being which determines its own projected possibilities to be. This understanding manifests as a circular *fore-structure—a fore-having, fore-sight, and fore-conception.*[11] Such understanding forms the basis for all our knowing. He writes:

> What is decisive is not to get out of the circle but to come into it in the right way. This circle of understanding is not an orbit in which any random kind of knowledge may move; it is the expression of the existential *fore-structure* of Dasein itself. It is not to be reduced to the level of a vicious circle, or even a circle which is merely to be tolerated. In the circle is hidden a positive possibility of the most primordial kind of knowing.[12]

For Heidegger, we are already within the circle; the idea is to bring this whole structure to light as fully as possible.

Heidegger stresses that we are "thrown" into the circle and this is part of our own historicity as *Dasein*. Yet we are not at its mercy for we can (and should) elucidate the pre-given structures of our understanding. Thus, Heidegger advocates a *critical* awareness of our hermeneutic situation. As he says, "This development of understanding we call 'interpretation'. In it the understanding appropriates understandingly that which is understood by it. In interpretation, understanding does not become something different. It becomes itself."[13] By making our situation as transparent as possible we appreciate the "otherness" of specific things which we encounter and so can consciously enter into a hermeneutical relationship with them.

In Heidegger's view, interpretation is not a set of specialized techniques or methods but is the central philosophic task. Ultimately, this philosophical hermeneutics can reveal *Dasein* itself. "Hermeneutics has the task of informing; of making each Dasein, in its being, accessible to this Dasein itself; of going back to the self-alienation with which Dasein is oppressed. In hermeneutics the possibility is of Dasein's becoming and being for itself *understandingly*."[14] The goal here is a type of freedom in which *Dasein* is aware of its own situated-ness and on this basis can truly appropriate its tradition. This is "authenticity," the self-reflectively aware being of *Dasein* as finite, informed by a particular history and projecting towards its own future.

Heidegger's insistence on the derivative nature of statements has particular significance for hermeneutics. As he writes, "From the fact that words are absent, it may not be concluded that interpretation is absent."[15]

The archetypal example of the relation between unspoken and spoken interpretation is Heidegger's discussion of a hammer, in which Heidegger shows how *Dasein's* original understanding revealed in ordinary activity (setting the hammer aside) changes to a logical statement of predication ("this hammer is heavy").[16] Note that Heidegger is not denigrating language so much as pointing out that statements are based on a more primordial hermeneutic level of *Dasein's* being, and that good interpretations of what is said should be informed by this basic level of understanding. "Whoever wants to understand something verbal in a hermeneutical manner must constantly attend to what is tacitly meant, though not openly expressed ... and avoid the potentially objectivizing view of language that confines it to the purely logical content of what is stated."[17]

Heidegger's work in hermeneutics does not end with *Being and Time* but continues to develop in a series of essays in which he concentrates on the "history of Being" (Being as understood and articulated through history). Significantly, these essays are themselves hermeneutic exegeses of fragments from early Greek thinkers or poems.[18] A major focus in the later essays is language itself, yet this concern is still hermeneutic. As Heidegger says, "language defines the hermeneutic relation."[19] For Heidegger, language (*logos*) becomes the fundamental structure of human being, that by which Being becomes known yet also remains largely unknown. Much of Heidegger's later work is cryptic, requiring its own careful hermeneutic approach but this underscores his point that language both reveals and conceals. By heightening our awareness of the ambiguous "Hermes quality" of language, Heidegger opens us to possibilities of meaning that a straightforward reading would miss. Thus despite its elusive nature, Heidegger's later work has greatly enriched our resources for hermeneutic thinking.

Gadamer: Hermeneutics within Tradition

Gadamer (1900–2002), one of Heidegger's students, has had even greater influence on hermeneutics. Gadamer provides his fullest account of hermeneutics in his book *Truth and Method*. In this and later works Gadamer lays out his critique of traditional hermeneutics as a "method" while presenting his own analysis of understanding. Understanding, for Gadamer, is the creative, historically situated human consciousness coming to know itself and its world.[20]

Gadamer's work in many ways combines Romantic hermeneutics, Husserlian phenomenology, and Heidegger's ontology.[21] Like Dilthey, Gadamer begins with the problem of foundation of the human sciences. However, Gadamer avoids the impasse of the "subjectivity versus objectivity" debate by means of the hermeneutic circle (cf. Schleiermacher and Heidegger) which he re-defines through the concept of "play," the give and take that marks all creative activity. In play we are caught up in a process which carries us along, and which transforms us. Play usually occurs within the context of a game, a defined set of rules and procedures, but no two engagements are ever the same and the rules do not determine the game's outcome.[22] The same is true for the understanding achieved through the hermeneutic circle–it is creative, open-ended, and emerges from the back-and-forth between interpreter and text.

> A person who is trying to understand a text is always projecting. He projects meaning for the text as a whole as soon as some initial meaning emerges in the text. Again, the initial meaning emerges only because he is reading the text with particular expec-tations in regard to a certain meaning. Working out this fore-projection, which is constantly revised in terms of what emerges as he penetrates into the meaning, is understanding what is there.[23]

Going back-and-forth from text to previously established meaning is, Gadamer maintains, how we play in the circle. This play is not arbitrary or rote but immensely creative.

Gadamer often uses the models of translating a text from one language to another or of an ordinary conversation to illustrate the understanding process. In both examples we are bringing together separate elements (language A and language B, speaker 1 and speaker 2) and deliberately striving to become as familiar with them as possible. This meeting can only take place, though, in light of what we bring to the meeting. From such initial limits our understand-ing then extends itself by our participation in the interpretive encounter.[24]

There are several important things to bear in mind about what Gadamer is saying. First, Gadamer is *not* seeking to devise a new method to guide aesthetic, literary, or philosophical judgment. He is instead providing a phenomenologi-cal account of the understanding process. This has distinct Kantian overtones in that Gadamer is describing a transcendental structure that makes knowledge possible. For Gadamer all human knowing is a dialogical interplay.

Second, Gadamer is striving to rehabilitate the notions of *prejudice* and *authority*. Gadamer writes

> It is not so much our judgments as it is our prejudices that constitute our being. This is a provocative formulation, for I am using it to restore to its rightful place a posi-tive concept of prejudice that was driven out of our linguistic usage by the French

and English Enlightenment. It can be shown that the concept of prejudice did not originally have the meaning we have attached to it. Prejudices are not necessarily unjustified and erroneous. ... They are simply conditions whereby we experience something—whereby what we encounter says something to us.[25]

Part of what Gadamer seeks is recognition that our *prejudice against prejudice* and our suspicion of *all* authority are the products of the European Enlightenment. Prejudice does not necessarily mean "subjective" (in the colloquial sense) and not all authority is arbitrary—authority is also earned through merit and knowledge, and bestowed by a community steeped in a tradition.[26] Those granted authority "implant" prejudices through the tradition in which we are situated. Neither prejudice nor authority, then, should be dismissed out of hand. They guide us and enable our understanding to function. Moreover, those prejudices sanctioned by authority and tradition are justified when they are productive of further knowledge.[27]

Furthermore, Gadamer sees understanding as a practical process, epitomized by juridical and theological interpretations. This is an important albeit subtle point for Gadamer, since he maintains that in interpreting we are not *forcing* what is before us but are engaging with it and submitting to its claims. Like a judge or theologian, we are responding to something greater than us, placing ourselves in its service.[28] To perform such service well, in turn, requires that we develop practical interpretive skill, a sort of jurisprudence or *phronesis* (an ancient Greek term referring to an "ethical know-how" and recognition of the situational good) to achieve success.

Gadamer, as I have indicated, is not proposing mere recapitulation or blind obedience to authority. His ideal is a "hermeneutical understanding" which seeks to be transparent to its own basis and procedures. Following Husserl, Gadamer considers our understanding to be like a delimited area of vision, a "horizon" or openness to the world.[29] Tradition provides us access to the world and this includes the many other horizons available through other traditions; tradition allows "us" to interact with "others." Through such interactions we strive for a "fusion of horizons" in which our understanding joins with the other's and thus is transformed and expanded. This "fusion" can come about only through critical interplay in which we come to understand the "other" and achieve new awareness of our own prejudices.[30] Hermeneutical understanding is therapeutic in that it helps us see our limits and go beyond them.

Distance has a crucial function in the fusion of horizons, for it is only through the distance between a text and ourselves that the initial differences assert themselves. Only by carefully facing difference can we check our own pre-set conceptions. "The important thing is to be aware of one's own bias, so that the text can present itself in all its otherness and thus assert its own truth against one's own fore-meanings."[31] By being aware of the text's initial "otherness" we can then approach it and engage with it. Note that this distance can be temporal, cultural or both, but it is always the starting point of any hermeneutic encounter. A distance must be bridged if understanding is to occur, for one cannot understand from afar. The text, after all, "calls to us" across the distance and it is this call to which our understanding responds.[32] On the other hand, though, Gadamer seems to deny that we must bridge over an "abyss," for we are connected to the text through tradition.[33] For Gadamer, to encounter a text is to already be in a relationship of understanding with it. Hermeneutic interpretation is a matter of deepening that relationship. We must come close yet allow the "other" to be itself, reminding ourselves constantly that it is always distant in some respects.

An important implication of Gadamer's theory is that all texts are semantically inexhaustible. A text can never have just one meaning, but is a series of meanings. Through a hermeneutical understanding we only attain "deeper" readings, a richer awareness and appreciation of what we face. Meaning is never final but an on-going process in which we individually and collectively are engaged. Through continuing hermeneutic engagement, we challenge earlier interpretations, correcting previous errors and bringing to light aspects of meaning that were heretofore obscured or even ignored.[34] By placing hermeneutic practice within such a temporal framework, Gadamer allows us to see how we are all shaped by the traditions of living and thinking which make us up. We are historical beings coming to know ourselves, each other, and the universe, within the present as we are moving into the future. Getting to know ourselves as interpreters allows us to accept our finitude even as we acknowledge our belongingness to tradition which is itself on-going. Tradition is never simple; it does not speak with a single voice, nor is it set in stone. Even within a tradition there are differences of perspective and interpretations, and their multiplicity cannot exclude the possibility that some may overshadow each other.[35]

Ricoeur: Post-Structural Hermeneutics

Along with Heidegger and Gadamer, Paul Ricoeur (1913–2005) has also made important contributions to contemporary hermeneutic theory. Ricoeur differs from the other two, however, in that his work and has been profoundly shaped by structuralism and psychoanalysis. Yet like Gadamer, Ricoeur began his work as attempt to marry hermeneutics with phenomenology. Ricoeur develops many of his ideas on interpretation through analyses of figures such as Freud but he spells out his own theory most clearly in his works *Interpretation Theory* and *Hermeneutics and the Human Sciences.*[36]

Ricoeur's hermeneutics begins with his studies of semiotics. For Ricoeur, semioticians such as Saussure have enabled us to comprehend language as a coherent system of signs. However, such study only deals with language as a closed system, never reaching the level of semantics, the level of meaning in which discourse communicates between speaker and listener. The latter is our shared arena of sense and reference and our lived condition as human beings:

> Language is not a world of its own. It is not even a world. But because we are in the world, because we are affected by situations, and because we orient ourselves comprehensively in those situations, we have something to say, we have experience to bring to language. This notion of bringing experience to language is the ontological condition of reference, an ontological condition reflected within language as a postulate which has not immanent justification; the postulate according to which we presuppose the existence of singular things which we identify.[37]

As with Heidegger and Gadamer, so Ricoeur's theory is ontological. He begins with humans existing within a world. Language arises out of this context of shared meaning and serves as the fundamental aspect of our being.

An important part of Ricoeur's theory concerns the difference between written and spoken language. As Ricoeur sees it, the written text is detached from the actual speech act and becomes fixed in a way that the spoken word never can be. Writing has a life beyond its original author and so always means more than what the author meant.[38] As a semantically autonomous entity, a written text can no longer be circumscribed by authorial intentions. In fact, the presence of an author is not necessary. The written text is thus free to be refigured by the reader.

Refiguration has great significance in Ricoeur's view for it marks the heart of interpretation. In Ricoeur's words, interpretation is a dialectic between the "distanciation of the text" (its semantic autonomy) and its "appropriation" (making one's own what originally was "other") by the reader in which the meaning of the text becomes evident. "Reading is the *pharmakon*, the remedy, by which the meaning of the text is rescued from the estrangement of distanciation and put in a new proximity, a proximity which suppresses and preserves the cultural distance and includes the otherness within the ownness."[39] This relationship between the "distant other" and "proximal same" is the functional equivalent of Gadamer's dialogic encounter between text and interpreter.

For Ricoeur, the interpretive process itself is rooted in ordinary human life, just as it is for Heidegger and Gadamer. However, Ricoeur models his view of interpretation on reading a text, an activity that is always communal (as is all discourse) and hence operates under certain constraints.[40] Ricoeur begins with Dilthey's notions of explanation and understanding, processes that Dilthey considered separate and distinct. Ricoeur, though, places explanation and understanding in a mutual relationship, and extends the meaning of interpretation to include both in a dialectic process such as we find in conversation or reading. Both are dynamic, communal enterprises although Ricoeur generally employs the model of reading rather than interpersonal conversation. Interpretation is this back and forth between text and reader, and those who share in the textual community.[41] As with Gadamer's notion of "play," there is no completion here, for that would treat the text as something that can be used up. The text's historical context must certainly be inserted into this dialectic as part of its explanation but it cannot determine our understanding. Meaning is not the author's intention or a text's historical context, but "the direction of thought opened up by the text."[42]

Ultimately for Ricoeur, interpretation is a way of making *our* world over through the appropriation of meaning, making our "own" that which was initially alien. The text, which was originally dependent on an author but has now achieved its own being, confronts us as an "other" which is distant and so disturbing. Engaging with the text enters us into a tug of war between appropriation and distanciation. We work through explanation, seeking greater understanding. The result is a redescription of our world in terms of what the text opens up. The text discloses new ways of being for a reader to take on. Ricoeur writes, "The reader is rather enlarged in his capacity of self-projection by receiving a new mode of being from the text itself."[43] Far from being the co-optation of an "object" by a "subject," interpretation is the transformation of the interpreter under a text's tutelage.

Like Heidegger and Gadamer, Ricoeur also describes interpretation via the notion of the hermeneutic circle. However, for him the circle encompasses the relation between explanation and understanding. Since interpretation is achieved by the reader's appropriation of meaning, it presupposes objective analysis and subjective evaluation. Such a relation, however, is not psychological but ontological, for it includes the interpreter's mode of being and the mode of being opened up by the text.[44]

Ricoeur's theory of hermeneutics owes much to Gadamer. Both thinkers have engaged in dialogue and neither seems to fundamentally disagree with the other.[45] However, Ricoeur and Gadamer do differ in a few areas. Ricoeur stresses that interpretation must includes *some* method (Ricoeur has said that the title of Gadamer's work might be better as *Truth or Method*). This is because meaning, according to Ricoeur, is "objective" (it is a function of the text's intentionality and can be identified) since every text comes to us from a distance as a result of the inevitable distanciation of writing. For Ricoeur method is a necessary stage of appropriation, if only to unmask the naive presuppositions we bring to our initial reading. The ideal for Ricoeur, thus, is to maintain a sort of critical openness, one marked by a tension between the "hermeneutics of suspicion" and the "hermeneutics of retrieval."

This tension between suspicion and retrieval is a central theme in Ricoeur's work, and seems to be his response to certain criticisms of Gadamer raised by Jurgen Habermas (1929), a critical theorist of the Frankfurt school, who takes Gadamer to task for justifying prejudice. According to Habermas, Gadamer overlooks how tradition functions as a dominating power and cannot account for how one can critique or rebel against it.[46] For Ricoeur, however, interpretation always has a radical element that works to unveil previous illusions and resists ego-centric control. "Reading introduces me to imaginative variations of the *ego* ... In the idea of the 'imaginative variation of the *ego*' I see the most fundamental possibility for a critique of the illusions of the subject."[47] This critical view of our previous "false consciousness" helps us to understand how tradition reinforces such falsehood. Yet for Ricoeur this does not constitute a rejection of tradition. Critique and tradition are not antithetical because hermeneutics entails a critical stage while the critical sciences (Marxist analysis, psychoanalysis) are themselves hermeneutical.[48] In fact, the opposition between tradition and critique is itself a product of a false consciousness that buys into the Enlightenment ideal of Absolute Knowledge. In the end Ricoeur's Post-Structural Hermeneutics relies more on method than either Gadamer or Heidegger's theories, suggesting that Ricoeur seeks to make hermeneutics more consciously objective and critical. To the extent that he does, his project may owe more to Enlightenment ideals than either Heidegger or Gadamer.

Common Features of Philosophical Hermeneutics

Despite their differences, the hermeneutic theories of Heidegger, Gadamer, and Ricoeur have much in common. All three thinkers focus on the existential nature of interpretive encounters. Interpretation occurs among living people enmeshed in contexts of meaning, not free floating rational subjects who have (or will attain) Absolute Knowledge. Heidegger, Gadamer and Ricoeur also view interpretation as culture-based. That is, it begins with humans living within certain traditions that orient their being-in-the-world. These provide initial orientation to the world but do not close us off from the world or other traditions, and furthermore are flexible and changeable. Moreover, Heidegger, Gadamer and Ricoeur see interpretation as discovering meaning in a practical, dialogical encounter which, like any conversation, is not finalizable.

Although their work has sometimes opened Heidegger, Gadamer and Ricoeur to accusations of relativism and subjectivism, such accusations are misplaced. For all three thinkers interpretation is never arbitrary. There are always constraints provided by both the traditions of the interpreter and the text, although there remains a great deal of "play" within these constraints. Multiple interpretations are always present, if only in potential. Furthermore all three stress that interpretation involves transformation. Through a genuinely interpretive encounter, one is always changed. This is more than a matter of accumulating "knowledge;" it is a matter of expanding one's world. A truly deep interpretation brings a new perspective and opens one to a new way of being.

In addition, Heidegger, Gadamer and Ricoeur encourage us to assume certain attitudes in dealing with texts. Among these are care and circumspection in our thinking and a willingness to question previous assumptions. Philosophical hermeneutics does not seek closure but ever-deeper meaning, thus promoting an awareness of the provisional nature of our conclusions. Most of all, philosophical hermeneutics urges us to attend to what the text says rather than what we might like it to say. Philosophical hermeneutics is perhaps unique in working to instill an open yet critical stance that is sensitive to the ever-present danger of misunderstanding.

Hermeneutics as a Pan-Cultural Enterprise

Up to this point we have focused on hermeneutics as it has developed into an academic discipline in the modern West. What relevance does such a method of inquiry have for a study of Chinese Buddhist texts? Even if Gadamer is right about hermeneutic activity being part of what it means to be human, is hermeneutics as a scholarly field merely a Western academic enterprise? Such methodological questions are important to ponder in a study such as this, which strives to be as self-reflexive as possible. After all, I write as a scholar in the "West" who is himself a product of modernity, yet my subject of study is early Chinese Buddhism.

There are several reasons why philosophical hermeneutics is an appropriate guide for studying Sengzhao. To begin with, hermeneutics involves the study of the past and so always crosses temporal boundaries. Archaeologists, Biblical scholars, and classicists are all hermeneuts trying to make sense of things by crossing over to "alien" cultures. This crossing of boundaries is true of all understanding, including (or most especially) understanding ourselves.[49] The key is to cross such boundaries openly, with the idea that we are trying to learn. In doing so we focus on the text as teacher of different meanings, an "other" who may become our most intimate friend. Philosophical hermeneutics thus holds great promise for cross-cultural studies.

Ricoeur echoes such sentiments in an interview in which he discusses the plurality of discourses and the conflicts that inevitably arise. For Ricoeur this is a mark of the creativity of language. In interpreting we join this on-going discussion in a continuously de-centering process that, while bounded initially by the limits of tradition, always pushes beyond them. While elaborating on these themes Ricoeur also addresses the broader issue of philosophical hermeneutics as a discourse founded upon Western notions. He says:

> At the broader cultural level, we must also be wary of attending exclusively to Western traditions of thought, of becoming Europocentric. In emphasizing the importance of the Greek or Judeo-Christian traditions, we often overlook the radically heterogeneous discourses of the Far East for example ... I think there is a certain "degree zero" or emptiness which we may have to traverse in order to abandon our pretension to be the centre, our tendency to reduce all other discourses to our own totalizing schemas of thought.[50]

Here Ricoeur explicitly warns Europeans against attending only to their own heritage. Cultural boundaries need to be transgressed in hermeneutic conversation.

Heidegger, too, expressed great interest in Eastern traditions as a way of moving beyond Western thinking even though he insisted on the European roots of his own work.[51] Gadamer shares this same interest yet he expresses ambivalence as well. In one of the most revealing passages concerning this matter, Gadamer writes:

> Although in the meantime the research in Eastern Philosophy has made further advances, we believe today that we are further removed from its philosophical understanding. The sharpening of our historical awareness has rendered the translations or adaptations of the texts ... fundamentally problematic ... We cannot speak of an appropriation of these things by the Occidental philosophy. What can be considered established is only the negative insight that our own basic concepts, which were coined by the Greeks, alter the essence of what is foreign.[52]

Here Gadamer expresses grave doubts at the prospect of attempting to understand texts from another ("Eastern") culture. Without a doubt this passage
betrays strong assumptions of cultural homogeneity and isolationism, and
scholars such as Wilhelm Halbfass have criticized Gadamer for overlooking the
multicultural roots of *European* tradition.[53] However, the reasons for Gadamer's
hesitation lie in the fact that he, too, insists on the European roots of his own
work. From this basis he actually forms a deep appreciation for the *differences*
between "East" and "West."[54] His point, then, is well taken in light of the
fact that cross-cultural philosophical investigation is still at a very early stage.
Genuine hermeneutic encounters must begin from the recognition of distance
before moving into the greater closeness of deepening understanding.

Several scholars have used hermeneutic approaches in East-West studies
and their work demonstrates the promise that such an approach holds.[55] One
instructive example can be found in the work of Mary Ann Stenger, who
has focused on Gadamer's hermeneutics in particular.[56] Stenger argues that
Gadamer makes valuable contributions to cross-cultural understanding on
several levels: by showing the inherent dynamism in such notions as "reality,"
"knowledge," and "truth"; by opening us to truths present in many traditions;
and by demonstrating the importance persons, ideas, and practices within
such understanding. Moreover, Stenger notes that Gadamer encourages us to
understand the processes involved in cross-cultural knowing (and conflicts
which often arise), helps us avoid both subjectivism and relativism, and provides a way of understanding the diversity of religious truth which may (or may
not) lead us to ultimate unity.[57] Although Stenger speaks only of Gadamer,
much of what she says applies to the work of Heidegger and Ricoeur as well.

Can philosophical hermeneutics aid in the creative encounter with non-
Western traditions as Ricoeur and Stenger suggest? It would seem so, for hermeneutics calls us to careful, honest engagement that is open to genuine change.
Such a course begins by noting that we always start from ways of thinking that
may need revising through conversation. Risking our understanding is crucial
in hermeneutics and this works against the tendency to assimilate an "other"
(text or person) as a mere data.

Gerald Larson and Eliot Deutsch's landmark book *Interpreting Across
Boundaries* brings together essays by various scholars concerning problems and
issues that arise in cross-cultural work. Several contributors make points that
are worth considering when pondering the appropriateness of philosophical
hermeneutics as a means of understanding Chinese and Buddhist traditions.
Karl Potter, for example, in discussing metaphor as a way of understanding
other communities, points out that although there are great differences in

alternative conceptual systems, these are not so firm as to be unbroachable. To a certain extent boundaries are functions of our own beliefs and do not cut us off from one another.[58] Raimundo Panikkar also maintains that cross-cultural interpretation is possible. Drawing heavily on Gadamer, Panikkar proposes a "diatopical hermeneutics" which makes no prior universal claims but proceeds through dialogue in specific cross-cultural encounters.[59] Both Potter and Panikkar argue that we can cross cultural and temporal boundaries (the two often are together) when interpreting but we must do so openly within a dialogue between ourselves and the "other."

Although philosophical hermeneutics holds much promise as a guide to cross-cultural work, we should not be too hasty in claiming it is *the* best way. Taking a hermeneutic approach to our own processes of understanding requires us to resist the urge towards finality, to question our desire to "get it right once and for all," and to constantly work to recognize how our prejudices influence our understanding. Philosophical hermeneutics, even if it is not a rigidly defined field and even if it resists some of the more stringent characteristics of "method," still is a disciplined procedure and it bears the biases inherent in any type of inquiry. There have been challenges to hermeneutics as formulated by Heidegger, Gadamer and Ricoeur and we need to examine these. Some of them, as we shall see, pose serious problems for using philosophical hermeneutics as a way towards cross-cultural understanding.

Before we attend to them, however, we have a more pressing matter. We still have confined ourselves to Western theory and practices. Although this has been useful in clarifying what philosophical hermeneutics involves and the promise it holds for cross-cultural investigation, this is only half the battle. We need to examine the place of hermeneutic concerns and practices in "Eastern" traditions of Chinese thought and Buddhism. This will prove challenging and may force us to revise our questions and our views of hermeneutics. Henry Rosemont makes this point with particular force:

> The methodological question needs to be reformulated, both to reduce the investigator's temptation to read into the texts those issues by which he or she is already seized, and also, thereby, perhaps to generate some answers to the methodological question that are not altogether dependent for their plausibility on the investigator's cultural determinants. Reformulated, then: to what extent do these texts suggest that we should be asking very different philosophical questions?[60]

In turning to Chinese and Buddhist traditions we need to ask how they have wrestled with continuity and change. What are their hermeneutic concerns?

Have Chinese or Buddhist thinkers formulated theories of interpretation? If so, what can we learn from them? Asking such questions will not only open our own horizons and thus help to demonstrate the aptness of using philosophical hermeneutics in our study of Sengzhao, it will provide further insight into the universal nature of all hermeneutic endeavors.

"Eastern" Hermeneutics—Interpretation in Chinese and Buddhist Traditions

I begin my investigation of hermeneutics in Chinese and Buddhist traditions with a few statements of clarification. In this section I treat Chinese "Daoist" traditions (Confucianism, Daoism), Buddhism, and Chinese Buddhism as distinct even though they are actually intertwined. Chinese Buddhism is, after all, a large part of Buddhist tradition and is a vital part of the Chinese "Daoist" heritage, spawning many later developments in Confucianism and Daoism. While treating them as separate traditions may seem somewhat forced, doing so highlights their distinctive characters while showing how they all share basic hermeneutic concerns. My account is necessarily over-simplified and is certainly not the only way to understand these traditions. If Heidegger, Gadamer, and Ricoeur have taught us anything it is that we cannot forge ahead without being aware of our location vis-à-vis traditions to which we do not belong. However, the distance between "our" heritage and that of "another culture" are not different in kind, for in both cases we face something initially "alien" that we *can* come to know. Distance can open us to new ways of knowing. In highlighting the hermeneutic nature of Chinese and Buddhist traditions I show how their interpretive practices and concerns resemble yet differ from those in the West. This, in turn, expands our understanding of interpretation and so better prepares us to engage with Sengzhao.

Chinese Hermeneutics: the "Way of Inner Sageliness and Outer Kingliness"

"Many are the men in the world who apply themselves to doctrines and policies, and each believes he has something that cannot be improved upon. What in ancient times was called the "art of the Way"—where does it exist?"[61]

A major theme in Chinese culture is the concept of Dao. Dao is notoriously difficult to translate. It can mean "path" but also "speech" or "discourse." All of these meanings, though, derive from water, the vital, nourishing element crucial for all existence.[62] Water is a central image in Chinese thought, and its importance is attested by the fact that it is counted among the *wu xing* (lit. "five phases": water, wood, fire, metal, earth), the basic components of Chinese cosmology. Perhaps it is best to translate Dao as "way," as this captures its inherent ambiguity. The English "way" connotes a tendency, a guiding impulse or flow and can thus include physical ways (streams, rivers, paths and roads) as well as ethical or social practices and habits (e.g. the "way of the Master").

Dao is a highly contested idea in Chinese history but what exactly is it? Dao cannot be a specific "thing" but is vague and all-pervasive, having both cosmic and social-ethical aspects. According to the opening lines of the *Daode jing*, Dao cannot even be spoken and so may be beyond our comprehension.[63] Nonetheless most thinkers agree that Dao can be discerned and transmitted from teacher to disciple and this requires the use of words, no matter how clumsy they may be. Throughout Chinese history various interpretations were proposed and argued over. Numerous schools of thought arose, perhaps as many as a hundred during the Warring States era (~480–222 B.C.E.) alone. A. C. Graham approaches Chinese thought in the Classical period as a con-tinuous dispute over Dao, the "way" of humanity and/or the cosmos.[64] Feng Youlan makes a similar point, arguing that we can discern a shared concern within all of Chinese thought for the way of "sageliness within and kingliness without."[65] As a group, Chinese philosophers seek the Way of humanity in the cosmos. Chinese philosophy and religion are a series of attempts to embody or (re)capture Dao.

Despite a variety of interpretations of Dao, two main perspectives stand out: Confucianism and Daoism. These traditions have often opposed each other and to this day scholars typically describe them in such fashion. Thus, for instance, Confucianism is "strict, rational, scholarly, male, social, ritualis-tic" while Daoism is "free, mystical, anti-intellectual, female, individualistic, spontaneous." This oppositional model is based on the ideas of *yin* and *yang*, the two cosmic principles that together form the basis for all existence. In actuality, of course, things are not so simple and boundaries between them tend to blur, particularly at the village level. Moreover, the terms "Confucian-ism" and "Daoism" are themselves constructs of Western thinkers searching for analogues to Christianity and Judaism. Yet Westerners are not alone in using "Confucianism" and "Daoism" as labels for distinct traditions. By the time of the Han dynasty (206 B.C.E.–220 C.E.) Chinese writers were already singling out the followers of Confucius (*rujia*, "Confucians") and the adherents of Daoism (*daojia*, "Daoists") as belonging to distinct traditions.[66] The matter becomes still more complicated when we consider the fact that neither "Confucianism" nor "Daoism" is a singular, static entity but are living traditions with long histories.[67] Nonetheless speaking of Chinese thought as 'Confucian-Daoist' is valid in that there really are self-acknowledged "Confucians" and "Daoists" who often define themselves over and against each other.

David Hall and Roger Ames note that this dialectical analysis of Chinese thought as a contrast of Confucianism (*yang*) and Daoism (*yin*) is common among both Western and Chinese scholars. However, Hall and Ames stress that *yin* and *yang* do not radically oppose each other but are complementary, like "this" and "that." *Yinyang* is a correlative distinction denoting a shared continuum, not two separate "things." Ignoring this fact obscures the *yin* aspects of Confucianism and the *yang* aspects of Daoism.[68] Instead, Hall and Ames suggest we view both aspects together as part of the common Chinese commitment, a continuous process of deepening the relationships that constitute a person in her environment. According to Hall and Ames, this is "the *way* one becomes an elegant human being."[69] Both Confucians and Daoists are seeking Dao. For simplicity's sake, then, I will often speak of both traditions together as "Daoist."

Seeking Dao is an existential quest in China, comparable to the Western search for Truth. A distinctive feature of this search for Dao is that it often has a retrospective quality. That is, Chinese civilization looks backward to a "golden age"—be it the Zhou dynasty (1040–770 B.C.E.) or the times of the legendary Sage-emperors Yao and Shun (~third millennium B.C.E.)—as the ideal society. The present age, by contrast, marks a falling away from the ideal. Perhaps nowhere are such sentiments better expressed than in the thirty-third chapter of the *Zhuangzi*:

> But the world is in great disorder, the worthies and the sages lack clarity of vision, and the Way and its Virtue are no longer One. So the world too often seizes upon one of its aspects, examines it, and pronounces it good. ... Therefore the Way that is sagely within and kingly without has fallen into darkness and is no longer clearly perceived, has become shrouded and no longer shines forth. The men of the world all follow their own desires and make these their "doctrine." How sad!—the hundred schools going on and on instead of turning back, fated never to join again. The scholars of later ages have unfortunately never perceived the purity of Heaven and earth, the great body of the ancients, and "the art of the Way" in time comes to be rent and torn apart by the world.[70]

Hope still exists within this despair, however, for if Dao has been lost, it can be recovered. Most philosophical disputes in China have been about returning to and preserving this long-lost Dao.

The primary way of recovering and preserving Dao has been by transmitting sagely teachings. The teachings were originally spoken and transmitted orally, although eventually written texts become the standard mode. Even here, though, the "oral text" retains a certain priority. The term *sheng* ("Sage"), after all, designates one who hears and says.[71] Writing in China (as in the West) has a divine quality because it is associated with communication of wisdom.[72] Yet there is a basic orality behind the written marks–the true meaning if you will–which is the living presence of the "authors" themselves. Their presence is the authority of the Dao and it is *this* that makes the texts "holy works" or *jing* ("classics").[73]

The *jing* are "binding texts," preserving the wisdom of the Sages and passing it on to future ages. They are the threads that bind generations. Confucius in many respects stands as the paradigmatic figure for all of Chinese when it comes to tracing the thread of sageliness, the path of Dao. Although Confucius denies being a Sage, he certainly becomes revered as such after his passing. Thus when Confucius says, "I was not born with knowledge but, being fond of antiquity, I am quick to seek it,"[74] he articulates one the great ideals of Chinese culture. It is this notion of text as source of wisdom that gives Chinese civilization its concern for learning and study. Learning for the Chinese is *wenhua*, literally "transformation through literature," a broad training that typically included the study of poetry, history, the *jing*, and their various commentaries. Such learning entails constantly renewing the teachings of the Sages, those who could apprehend and embody Dao, and who set it down for posterity. It is also this focus on text as source of wisdom that gives Chinese civilization its hermeneutic orientation, for if texts house wisdom, it is imperative that we strive to understand them.

Many sayings attributed to Confucius reveal the centrality of hermeneutics in Chinese traditions. One of the most significant concerns the process of learning and understanding: "If one reveres the old and so learns the new, one can serve as a teacher."[75] This saying anticipates the work of Heidegger, Gadamer and Ricoeur, and their view of understanding as being pre-conditioned by previous knowledge and understanding. Confucius also says, "I transmit but do not innovate; I am truthful in what I say and devoted to antiquity."[76] On the face of it, this statement sounds like a denial of innovation yet in fact one who transmits is interpreting by applying the old to the new. Furthermore, knowing

Dao is not mastery of "facts" but more of a flexible "know-how" which must be put into practice. This is one reason why Confucius says, "Humanity is able to enlargen Dao, it is not that Dao enlargens humanity."[77]

Chinese wisdom is carried on through those who, like Confucius, comment on the *jing*. In this process wisdom is transformed to apply to the situation at hand. The practice of looking to texts means that commentators assume the power of the Sages, taking on the "magical power" of Hermes. Julia Ching writes:

> The classics are the custodians of the authority coming from the ancient sages. And their interpreters, the exegetes, have become the mediators of this authority. At a time when the sages are no longer among ordinary human beings, their recorded words have taken their places and filled their presence. And the textual scholar, the exegete, has assumed a kind of priestly power, serving as the mouth-piece of the sages whose inspiration is recorded in the classics.[78]

The quest for Dao via commentary (*zhuan*) marks these "Daoist" traditions as hermeneutic. Commentary became the heart of tradition, with some commentaries becoming so revered that commentators themselves were often considered Sages.

The history of Chinese civilization is a veritable history of interpretation, marked by both continuity and radical changes. This quest for Dao is a perennial aspiration to an ethical and aesthetic ideal of social and cosmic harmony. Interpreting the *jing* within such a framework is to look for guidance in the teachings of the Sages. This ethical-aesthetic concern informing Chinese hermeneutics gives Chinese thought a distinct unity amidst its diversity. Regardless of whether one is "Confucian" or "Daoist," one strives to understand the *jing* to live elegantly and harmoniously.[79] Achieving harmony calls for (re)turning to Dao as transmitted through sacred texts. Chinese "Daoist" tradition is a vast hermeneutic endeavor.

Hermeneutics in Buddhism

> "It may be, Ananda, that some of you will think, 'The word of the Teacher is a thing of the past; we have now no Teacher'. But that, Ananda, is not the correct view. The Doctrine and the Discipline, Ananda, which I have taught and enjoined upon you is to be your teacher when I am gone."[80]

Buddhism stretches across a vast cultural and geographic range, thus containing even more variety than Chinese "Daoist" traditions. Nonetheless there are certain things that all forms of Buddhism share, among them the practice of "taking refuge." The ritual of "taking refuge" can be part of a grand ceremony marking the coronation of a ruler or a modest celebration of a young boy joining a monastic order, but in essence it comes down to reciting three simple lines: "I take refuge in the Buddha, I take refuge in the Dharma, I take refuge in the *Saṅgha*." These refuges (the "three jewels," *triratna*) form the center of Buddhist devotion and are the ultimate focus of allegiance and gratitude for all Buddhists.

The Three Jewels, like actual gems, are multi-faceted. The first and third jewels are relatively simple. They designate the Buddha himself, the one who awoke to the true nature of reality and established the path, and the great company of his followers (nuns, monks, laity). The second jewel, though, is more problematic. "Dharma" is an elusive word which depending on the situation can mean "duty," "phenomenon," "truth," etc. In this context, though, it means "teachings," the teachings of the Buddha that unite the *saṅgha* by explaining the truth of suffering and how it can be overcome. The history of Buddhism is the story of the Dharma from the time of the historical Buddha, Śākyamuni (Siddhārtha Gautama) in the sixth century B.C.E., down to today. It is an epic hermeneutic enterprise that spans centuries and continents.

The Dharma has been in a continuous state of diffusion and transformation since Śākyamuni's day. Most scholars have given up the pursuit of the "original message" of the Buddha in favor of the more modest search for the earliest Buddhist doctrines.[81] By all accounts, Siddhārtha was a skilled teacher with an uncanny ability to gauge his students' levels of awareness and teach his message accordingly. Such flexibility made the Dharma wonderfully useful in helping his followers attain enlightenment but it also meant that the actual teachings would vary from one situation to another. Certain basic themes remained constant—*pratītya-samutpāda* ("dependent origination"), *anitya*, *duḥkha*, and *anātma* ("ignorance," "suffering," "no-self"—the "three marks of existence"), the inexorability of karma, the danger of desire, etc.–but the Buddha explained these ideas differently depending on his audience. Moreover, traditional accounts of the Buddha's life also portray him as encouraging his followers to examine his teachings for themselves, rather than blindly accepting them. Thus from the very beginning to be a follower of the Tathāgata required *critical* appropriation of the Dharma.

The fact that the Buddha varied his teachings most likely did not lead to major misunderstandings while Śākyamuni was alive. Problems, however, arose soon after his passing. Early Buddhist records speak of a series of councils held to determine what the Buddha taught, beginning with one at Rājagṛha immediately after his decease.[82] Accounts of the first council state that one monk, Purāṇa, did not accept the council's version of the Dharma, preferring to follow the teaching as he remembered it. This incident suggests that at this point there already were different versions of the Dharma. This variety eventually led to various schisms but it also enabled Buddhism to adapt to new cultures.[83]

Over time the problems presented by the Dharma's multivocal nature became increasingly acute, for the tradition(s) had become the only means of access to the Buddha. The situation was further complicated by the fact that Śākyamuni's enlightenment, the event that transformed him into the "awakened one," was held to be open to all via the Dharma. The teaching thus quickly assumed a variety of forms, but all were attributed to the same figure and aimed at the same goal. To awaken meant one had to encounter the Dharma, hear, and understand it. So it was that compiling and preserving texts became the means of passing on the Dharma and understanding the Dharma became a matter of textual understanding. Moreover, as with Chinese traditions so Buddhist texts were at first oral. One *heard* the Dharma, hence the designation of early disciples as *śrāvakas* ("hearers"). Only later were the texts written down.

Typically the Buddha's words were recorded in the form of *sūtras* ("sermons"). The *sūtras* as "Buddha word" (*Buddha vacana*) were authoritative but their numbers continued to increase after the Buddha's death, especially with the rise of the Mahāyāna ("Great Vehicle"). Moreover, these *sūtras* were alleged to have been preached at various times during the Buddha's career in diverse, even magical locations, and say many different things. Numerous *śāstras* (commentaries) were composed to sort the teachings out, and these became the basis of the many traditions of Buddhism, each of which seeks to interpret the Dharma in a coherent fashion. The three major traditions of Buddhism still extent (Theravāda, Mahāyāna, Vajrayāna) have resulted from centuries of commentary and illustrate how the Dharma has changed through time.

A further complication in this proliferation of teachings concerns the fact that Buddhist texts often contain guidelines for understanding the Dharma, some of which are put in the mouth of the Buddha himself. Most scholars agree that while we can trace the core of these discourses to Śākyamuni, these guidelines are the result of early Buddhist thinkers attempting to formulate basic rules of interpretation. A good example comes from a passage in the *Catuḥpratisaraṇa sūtra* ("Sūtra of the Four Reliances"):

> Rely on the teaching, not the teacher.
> Rely on the meaning, not the letter.
> Rely on the definitive meaning (*nītārtha*), not the interpretable meaning (*neyārtha*).
> Rely on wisdom (*jñāna*), not on [ordinary] consciousness (*vijñāna*).[84]

These reliances comprise specific rules for interpreting texts. Among other things, they ensure that the interpreter works towards an understanding based not merely on personal authority but on the true meaning of the Buddha's words with the aid of direct, experiential knowledge.[85]

The distinction between *nītārtha* ("definitive") and *neyārtha* ("preliminary") spoken of in the above passage warrants special attention. It is one of the oldest hermeneutic devices with Buddhism, dating back perhaps to before the earliest schisms.[86] The distinction looms large role in Mahāyāna texts such as Candrakīrti's *Prasannapadā*, a commentary on Nāgārjuna's *Mūlamadhyamakakārikāḥ* ("Chapters on the Middle Way"), and certainly qualifies as a hermeneutic theory. The practice of distinguishing between *nītārtha* and *neyārtha* is often closely allied with the doctrine of the Two Truths, *saṃvṛti-satya* ("conventional truth") and *paramārtha-satya* ("ultimate truth"). Nāgārjuna makes perhaps the definitive statement of the relationship between *saṃvṛti* and *paramārtha* in the *Kārikās*, 24: 10:

> Without a foundation in the conventional truth,
> The significance of the ultimate cannot be taught.
> Without understanding the significance of the ultimate,
> Liberation is not achieved.[87]

The Dharma can be communicated through everyday language but understanding it requires that we read between the lines. Sometimes, as in the case of the *Akṣayamatinirdeśa sūtra*, Buddhist texts equate *neyārtha* with *saṃvṛti* and *nītārtha* with *paramārtha*. The designation of what teachings count as "conventional" and which are "ultimate," of course, can vary tremendously depending on the subject matter, texts involved, and biases of the interpreter. For instance, according to the *Akṣayamatinirdeśa* statements that speak of *śūnyatā* ("emptiness") are *paramārtha* while others that speak of "self" or "person" are *saṃvṛti*.[88] The doctrine of the Two Truths has had lasting repercussions in Buddhism, and plays a major role in Sengzhao's work.

Another Buddhist hermeneutic theory is the " Three Turnings of the Wheel of Dharma." This theory originates in chapter seven of the *Saṃdhinirmocana sūtra*, wherein the Buddha declares that his teachings can be divided into three separate periods, or "turnings" of the wheel of Dharma. The first two turnings (the Buddha's first sermon, the teachings of *śūnyatā*) are merely provisional whereas the third (the "mind only" teachings of Yogācāra) is definitive. Unlike the *neyārtha/saṃvṛti–nītārtha/paramārtha* theory, this theory of "turnings" claims to be historically based.

All of these Buddhist hermeneutic theories presuppose the idea of *upāya* ("skillful means"), the term for the Buddha's ability to teach the doctrine that best suits his audience. Invoking *upāya* allows Buddhists to harmonize seemingly contradictory teachings and even relegate certain teachings to inferior levels.[89] Perhaps the best illustration of *upāya* is the "parable of the burning house" in the third chapter of the *Lotus Sūtra*. Here the Buddha compares his teaching of the three vehicles (*śrāvaka, pratyekabuddha, Bodhisattva*) to a father luring his children out of burning house by promising them a goat cart, deer cart, and an ox cart.[90] The principle of *upāya* is intriguing and controversial in that it is based upon the Buddha's intention (thus resembling Romantic hermeneutics) and can even serve as a license to "lie" in order to lead one to truth.[91] Once again, Hermes' ambivalent nature shows itself.

For Buddhists, understanding the Dharma is crucial but with such an array of interpretations, what *is* a correct understanding? This remains a major hermeneutic problem. Robert Thurman describes these difficulties in very dramatic terms:

> Imagine for a moment that Jesus taught for about fifty years, to close disciples numbered in the thousands; that his pedagogical aim and skill were such that he formulated his doctrines to resonate precisely with the abilities and inclinations of each disciple; that, while recommending devotionalism to many, he taught others to rely on the intellect, and still others to rely on works motivated by love and compassion; that he constantly demanded critical reflection on the deeper meaning of his teachings; that he sometimes even provided conceptual schemes with which to interpret his own doctrines, which schemes sometimes included dismissal of the ultimate validity of a teaching he had previously set forth unequivocally; that it sometimes happened that two such schemes referred each to the other as merely conditional, valid only in that other context; and that in spite of these apparent contradictions he had to be accepted as a supreme authority, incapable of self-contradiction; and finally that different groups of his disciples preserved traditional records of his promulgations in different places, some not even knowing of the existence of the others during certain periods during and after the Teacher's lifetime. It is easy to see that

all this would result in the situation for later generations in which a bewildering profusion of doctrines, all embedded in hallowed scriptural traditions, is presented as uniformly authentic.[92]

Clearly hermeneutic concerns lie at the heart of Buddhism. Understanding and interpreting the Dharma are the way each succeeding generation receives the Buddha's teachings. This quest for understanding the Dharma forms the thread connecting the *saṅgha* to the Buddha, and remains so even after thousands of years.

Chinese Buddhism: An Uneasy Adoption/Adaptation

"Still, Confucius, Laozi, and Śākyamuni were consummate sages who, in accord with the times and in response to beings, made different paths in setting up their teachings. The inner and the outer [teachings] complement one another, together benefiting the people. As for promoting the myriad [moral and religious] practices, clarifying cause and effect from beginning to end, exhaustively investigating the myriad phenomena, and elucidating the full scope of birth and arising–even though these are all the intention of the sages, there are still provisional and ultimate [explanations]. The two teachings are just provisional, whereas Buddhism includes both provisional and ultimate."[93]

Since Chinese and Buddhist traditions center on hermeneutic concerns, it comes as no surprise that Chinese Buddhism should as well. With Chinese Buddhism we have two complex "Ways" which clash at first but gradually begin flowing together until their currents merge. The result is a new tradition that differs from either of the two sources yet bears the marks of both. Chinese Buddhism is "Daoist" in that it seeks the Way and it is Buddhist in that it adheres to Dharma, but it understands and articulates Dao and Dharma in new ways.

The combining of "Daoist" and Buddhist traditions poses immense difficulties. As Arthur Link notes, "To comprehend Chinese Buddhism we must understand it not just as Indian Buddhism in China but rather as a cultural amalgam, a synthesis of Indian thought and Sinic concepts and ideals."[94] It may make the most the sense to speak of this confluence of Buddhism and Chinese thought as the Chinese adoption/adaptation of Buddhism. Chinese civilization met and absorbed aspects of Buddhism that seemed to have affinity with Chinese heritage, thus transforming Buddhism into its "own" system and finding itself changed by the process. Generally speaking, it was the Chinese who asked the questions, listened to the often conflicting answers which the

Dharma provided, and then sought to harmonize these answers with their own heritage. In other words, Dharma became Dao.

Buddhism entered China in the Latter Han but did not truly establish itself until the dynasty's collapse. In the religious/philosophical vacuum left after the discrediting of Han "orthodoxy" (a synthesis of Confucian, Daoist and Legalist ideas) numerous popular cults sprang up, Daoism sparked increasing interest at all levels of society, and new religions such as Buddhism attracted many new followers. Yet Buddhism in China was part of a much different context than in India. Its "alien" origins always presented a handy target for critics. Buddhism came with certain Indian cultural trappings, among them the notion of celibacy and a tradition of itinerant saints and ascetics (*sadhus* and *sannyāsis*) that clashed with the predominantly this-worldly orientation of China. This meant that Chinese Buddhists approached Buddhism from very different perspectives than their Indian counterparts.

Another factor contributing to the difficulties of Chinese Buddhists was the piecemeal manner in which the Dharma was transmitted. Versions of the Dharma entered China in a very different order from their original Indian chronology. As a result the Chinese received confused and conflicting messages. In part this was due to the fact that Buddhist missionaries were often of different lineages and so presented varying interpretations. It was not until the fifth century that the Chinese even had the opportunity to hear a systematic presentation of the teachings.

Despite these problems of cultural conflict and confused transmission, Buddhism did become integrated into Chinese religious and philosophical culture. Although practices and rituals played a large role here, the Chinese adaptation of the Dharma was from the start heavily textually based. In fitting with the Chinese veneration of learning as *wenhua*, so the teachings of the Buddha came via *wen*. Overwhelmingly, then, understanding and passing on the Dharma was a matter of understanding and passing on texts. Initially the texts came into China through translator-missionaries who would translate and expound their favorite texts to a Chinese audience. The texts selected were often pitched to Chinese tastes or because particular patrons were inclined towards certain ideas or practices. Nonetheless, these texts quickly spread well beyond the circles of their translators and immediate followers. In some cases (e.g. the *Lotus* and *Vimalakīrtinirdeśa sūtras*) the same texts were translated several times, resulting in even more confusion. By the fourth century we already see scholar-monks compiling critical editions of these texts, a strong indication of their growing hermeneutic awareness.

So it was that the Dharma spread in China by texts which were themselves de-contextualized, a fact that made it extremely difficult for the Chinese to understand them. The more learned among the Chinese *saṅgha* could not help being aware of the urgent nature of their hermeneutic struggles. As Gregory observes, "Chinese Buddhists were, as their Indian counterparts were not, called on to make sense out of Buddhism as a totality."[95] On the whole the Chinese followed their "Daoist" inclinations by seeking to harmonize Dharma with itself and their own inherited tradition(s).

Chinese Buddhists, thus, were constantly confronted with difficulties when dealing with texts. Not surprisingly, Gadamer's analysis of the herme-neutic encounter throws new light on how the Chinese interpreted Buddhism through their "Daoist" traditions, a process exemplifying on a massive scale how pre-understanding (with its "enabling prejudices") informs the appropria-tion of new phenomena. The more Chinese Buddhists worked with Buddhist texts the more they came to realize they were dealing with teachings that dif-fered from those of Confucius or Laozi. Even so, Chinese Buddhism remained "Daoist." For the Chinese, the Buddha was a great Sage or immortal and his Dharma always was the Buddha Dao.

As with the indigenous "Daoist" traditions, so too, we can also view the history of Chinese Buddhism as a history of interpretations, with certain peri-ods marked by distinct hermeneutic shifts. During the Latter Han dynasty (second century C.E.), for instance, the Chinese understood Buddhism as a form of Daoism especially concerned with meditation and self-cultivation. With the fall of the Han (third century onwards), Chinese thinkers began to grapple with Buddhism as a tradition of wisdom complementing and challeng-ing their own heritage. This more dialogic way of understanding continued into the Sui and Tang eras (sixth through tenth centuries), during which time Buddhism dominated religious and philosophical thought. With the rise of Neo-Confucianism in the Song (tenth through thirteenth centuries), we see a conscious turning away from Buddhism and returning to the Han heritage, a trend that continued for the next nine centuries. Ironically, though, this Con-fucian renewal was deeply shaped by Chinese understandings of Buddhism.[96]

David Chappell speaks of Chinese Buddhism as a similar series of herme-neutical stages.[97] Chappell distinguishes a normative "Canonical Buddhism" tied to the translation and study of major texts and the three subtraditions of Tiantai, Chan and Pure Land. Each of these subtraditions encompasses three hermeneutic phases: 1.) a phase in which individuals seek new interpreta-tions to satisfy their personal crises; 2.) a phase in which the new tradition is integrated within previously established tradition and so becomes legitimate; 3.) a phase in which the integrated tradition is propagated and simplified to achieve a large popular base.[98]

Chappell's scheme is useful when looking at specific schools or figures within Chinese Buddhism. To begin with, he clearly demonstrates that there is a unity within Chinese Buddhism but one that encompasses numerous differences. Chappell also allows us to see the differences between lineages and even within the lives of specific individuals. Perhaps most of all, Chappell cautions against looking for any single hermeneutic method in Chinese Buddhism. As he says, "it is not legitimate to argue that any particular Chinese Buddhist tradition had a single hermeneutical method or only one underlying hermeneutical concern. There is no 'Buddhist hermeneutic' or even a 'Ch'an hermeneutic.' Instead we find a variety of approaches at different levels."[99] This variety is crucial to bear in mind in order to avoid simplistic views of Chinese Buddhism as univocal or monolithic. There are various Chinese "Buddhisms," each focused on particular texts and practices and tracing themselves back to Śākyamuni Buddha through different lineages. Nonetheless, we can discern a loose unity: the continuous shared hermeneutic endeavor to understand Dharma in the Chinese context.

So it is that Chinese Buddhism is of a piece with the other Chinese "Daoist" traditions and Indian Buddhist traditions in being marked by hermeneutic concerns. This is perhaps inevitable since Chinese Buddhism arises from traditions whose histories involve a great deal of accommodation and reshaping. We should note that these transformations of Buddhism in China have been controversial. In fact, a recent movement known as "Critical Buddhism" has questioned much of this sinification, bluntly arguing that much of Chinese Buddhism is not, in fact, "true Buddhism."[100] Regardless, though, Chinese Buddhism is thoroughly hermeneutic and provides numerous examples of creative re-interpretation, including the writings of Sengzhao.

Clearly Buddhist and Chinese "Daoist" traditions center on hermeneutics. They wrestle with problems of understanding and advocate a transformational mode of interpretation. For Buddhists and "Daoists" of every stripe, to truly understand sacred teachings is to be fundamentally changed. This fact becomes even clearer when we examine studies of specific Buddhist and Chinese thinkers who espouse hermeneutic theories in their writings.[101] In light of such studies we cannot ignore the hermeneutic practices and concerns of Non-Western traditions. They offer perspectives that should be brought into conversation with Western views and we can feel confident that hermeneutical engagement with these traditions can lead to new insight. Hermeneutics, the reasoned discussion of problems surrounding understanding and interpretation, is a universal concern, one that is part and parcel of the human condition.

We need to use caution when making such statements, however. Although Western, Buddhist and "Daoist" traditions resemble each other in their hermeneutic concerns, their actual theories and practices, and the philosophical assumptions behind them, may vary tremendously. We must avoid drawing easy parallels that ignore possible differences. Thus, for example, while Jonathan Herman argues that the Neo-Confucian thinker Zhu Xi (1130–1200) advocates a type of Romantic hermeneutics similar to Schleiermacher and Dilthey, On-cho Ng maintains that Confucianism involves assumptions of meaning that differ strongly from views espoused by many contemporary Western thinkers.[102]

Moreover, we should keep in mind that my discussion is marked by its own biases. This study is itself an interpretation made from my perspective as a scholar interested in hermeneutics across cultures. Other scholars similarly admonish us to be aware of such factors. Donald Lopez, for instance, reminds scholars of Buddhism to keep in mind the specific biases that inform their work as they search for "objective" truths acceptable in an academic context–biases no doubt very different from those of many practicing Buddhists, both past and present.[103] John Maraldo spells this sentiment out even more clearly, arguing that we must not only present the hermeneutics of various Buddhist thinkers and traditions but also critically reflect our own methods and perspectives in the process. He adds, "Until we do so, I believe that our search for hermeneutics within the Buddhist tradition will remain limited and immature.[104] A truly *hermeneutical* understanding of Buddhist interpretation practices requires both knowledge and circumspection. While Lopez and Maraldo are addressing the study of Buddhist hermeneutics their points apply to Chinese "Daoist" hermeneutics as well. Our work here will call for careful reflection as we strive to achieve a deep understanding of Sengzhao's writings on *prajñā*. Before turning to Sengzhao, however, we must consider some criticisms that have been raised against philosophical hermeneutics as they present difficulties we shall also have to face.

Challenges to Philosophical Hermeneutics

One of the duties of hermeneutics is to take seriously Gadamer's statement that, "Openness to the other ... involves recognizing that I myself must accept some things that are against me, even though no one else forces me to do so."[105]

Being careful hermeneuts requires facing challenges that have been made to philosophical hermeneutics, especially those that pose problems for cross-cultural work. Three in particular require our attention:

Objective Hermeneutics—Hirsch and Betti

One major challenge to philosophical hermeneutics has come from theorists such as Emilio Betti and E. D. Hirsch, both of whom reassert the need to have objectively valid textual meaning. Betti, a historian of law, takes Gadamer to task on a number of counts, chiefly for not providing an adequate methodology for the human sciences and for confusing interpretation (*Auslengung*) with the interpreter's practice of conferring meaning (*Sinngebung*). In Betti's eyes, Gadamer (and others like him) have become mired in existential "subjectivity."[106] In a similar vein, Hirsch argues that a proper interpretation of a text must be guided by the author's intentions. This is an objective process for Hirsch, and the problem with Gadamer et al is that they confuse a text's meaning (*Bedeutung*) with the significance (*Bedeutsamkeit*) it has for us.[107]

Betti and Hirsch raise serious objections to philosophical hermeneutics. For both theorists, interpretation must be based on normative principles in order to be valid. They both agree that interpretation requires deep historical and philological investigation. Moreover, a valid interpretation, at least in Hirsch's view, is founded on what the author has in mind, a view similar to the Romantic hermeneutics of Schleiermacher and Dilthey. For many people this view may seem self-evident. However, such an intentionalist theory of interpretation is fraught with philosophical problems. To begin with, this theory assumes the existence of separate and distinct "minds" that lies at the heart of modern Western skepticism and requires the hermeneut to essentially be a "mind-reader" in addition to a text reader. It also runs up against difficulties of verification, the very thing Hirsch seeks to find. Furthermore, both Betti and Hirsch insist that we can distinguish between "objective meaning" and "meaning as we see it," yet neither makes clear what this distinction entails.

Ultimately, though, the hermeneutics advocated by Betti and Hirsch, focusing as it does on deriving a simple method for interpretation, appears to be too narrow and specialized. It shies away from real inquiry into human understanding itself, a chief feature of hermeneutic theory. It tends to ignore or even dismiss actual changes in interpretation of texts that we see over time, and wants to draw hermeneutic conversation to a close. Perhaps most seriously, it overlooks the situation of the interpreter and so fails to take up the task of interpreting as it concerns *us* here and now. Betti and Hirsch, thus, pass over the very issues that most concern Heidegger, Gadamer and Ricoeur. This does not mean that we can discount their criticisms. Their insistence on historical and philological work is to the point and their call for "objectivity" reminds us to stick with careful scholarship. Moreover, they signal the ever-present temptation of intentionalist theories of meaning. We need to bear this in mind when working with texts, if only to prevent ourselves from claiming to have discovered what the author *really* meant.

Postmodern Critiques

Other challenges to philosophical hermeneutics come from thinkers within the postmodern movement, although to even speak of this as a unified "movement" is questionable. Postmodernism challenges long-standing assumptions in Western culture, particularly the modern pretense at knowledge that is absolute and objective, and the modern rationalist claim that we can understand everything. Indeed, some postmodern scholars argue that the belief in our ability to understand everything from human culture and history (a defining belief of modernity) actually results in profound *misunderstanding*.[108] Although it is diverse and eclectic, postmodernism shares two basic tenets: 1.) there can be no single common denominator (e.g. "nature", "God", "Truth"); and 2.) all human systems such as language or politics are self-referential. That is, they do not describe but construct and maintain meaning and value. As such, although these systems are powerful networks of ideas and practices, they are finite and surprisingly fragile.

Jean-Francois Lyotard, a leading postmodern theorist, sharply criticizes the modern view of reason as a liberating faculty that can unite all knowledge. For Lyotard such beliefs are myths, "metanarratives" that legitimate an insatiable quest to encompass all "facts." However, with recent developments in science and technology, and the spread of an economy based on consumption and radical individualism, such grand narratives are no longer tenable. We have, instead, various "little narratives," localized language games that defy reconciliation.[109] In such a situation there is no final truth and attempts to reach such are futile exercises of force. There may seem to be no problem for hermeneutics here but, according to Lyotard, hermeneutics remains modern in that it appeals to the grand narrative of meaning–meaning that can be known and learned.[110]

Michel Foucault, another postmodernist, offers a similar critique. Although Foucault does not have a single method *per se*, we can view him as a "discourse analyst." "Discourse" in the Foucaultian sense is an assumed framework that determines the concepts and methods used, "facts" discovered, and the range of theories that can be formulated. Note that a discourse's exercise of power is both positive (it constructs "knowledge") and negative (it differentiates "truth" from "falsehood"). So, for example, in the discourse of modern physics, Heisenberg's "uncertainty principle" and the behavior of quarks are legitimate whereas "ether" and "phlogiston" are not.

Although much ink has been spilled analyzing Foucault's notion of "discourse," what is most important about it is that it underscores the alliance between knowledge and power. A discourse, ultimately, is political in that it determines what counts as legitimate knowledge. Foucault derives his notion of discourse through the "archaeology of knowledge," which entails conceiving systems of thought as discursive formations, and carries it further through "genealogy," in which we can explain changes in discourses by connecting them to social power structures.

Foucault's immense body of work amounts to a sustained critique of modernity, stressing the connection of knowledge to power and social control. Within such an analysis, interpretation of texts is of little value. Such endeavors will merely exemplify the discursive networks of control. Hermeneutics' search for hidden meanings actually masks the truly hidden, the fundamental structures of power.[111]

Jacques Derrida, however, may be the postmodern thinker whose work proves to be the most challenging. Deeply influenced by Heidegger and sharing most of the same concerns as Gadamer and Ricoeur, Derrida attacks modernity's Enlightenment complacency by deconstructing its foundational claims. For Derrida, all of Western thought is guilty of logocentrism, the illusion that language can convey full "presence" of meaning as something final, clear and distinct. In fact, this is never the case. Language is not an orderly system of referential relations between "words" and "things" but is shot-through by heterogeneity, by differences that defer (*difference*) *ad nauseum*.[112] In Derrida's eyes, hermeneutics is as logocentric as any other discourse. Within all texts we run into unresolved tensions and irreducible differences in meaning. In effect Derrida rules out the possibility of genuine conversation or argument; hermeneutic understanding can never really be achieved.

The challenges postmodernism presents call into question assumptions about meaning and what lies behind it, and even the very notion of a text. Such criticisms are difficult to answer as they undercut so many fundamental beliefs that inform contemporary scholarship. Even if we accept the force of

Lyotard, Foucault and Derrida's arguments, however, it is not clear to what extent they apply to philosophical hermeneutics. We can, for instance, argue that Foucault's discourse analysis is nothing less than an interpretation of how "knowledge" works. Then, too, hermeneutical theorists do not close down meaning but see it as amorphous and ever changing. Texts have multiple meanings and when attending to them we always enter into what Ricoeur rightly calls a "conflict of interpretations."

Postmodern criticisms compel us, though, to re-think the role of modernity within hermeneutics. This is a complex matter, for hermeneutic thinkers do speak of a singular "text." Gadamer's work has a Kantian air about it, as if he is describing a transcendental structure of understanding, and Ricoeur does employ "scientific" methods like structuralism. Yet although the work of Heidegger, Gadamer and Ricoeur bears the influence of modernity, all three oppose modernity's view of reason as an ahistorical, objective capacity and decry its dismissal of tradition. There is little trace of grand narrative here. If anything, these thinkers encourage the exploration of "little narratives." Hermeneutical understanding is not free-floating and all-encompassing but remains within a tradition, even if it views its location critically.

David Tracy has carefully thought through such matters and discusses his ideas for a "postmodern hermeneutics" in his aptly titled book *Plurality and Ambiguity*. Tracy urges us to face squarely the inherent plurality within our various discourses and the messiness we find in the contemporary world. As he says, "Postmodern coherence, at best, will be a rough coherence: interrupted, obscure, often confused, self-conscious of its own language use and, above all, aware of the ambiguities of all histories and traditions."[113] Entering into hermeneutic conversation requires that we take seriously the many narratives encircling us and recognize that any interpretation will be situated within a network of social and political forces, many of which we barely perceive. Hermeneutics, thus, calls for a constant dialectics of retrieval and suspicion that resists finalization. For Tracy religious traditions offer the best hope for such a hermeneutics since they continually challenge what we consider possible even as they call for us to challenge their tendencies to dominance and complacency. Perhaps Sengzhao and Liu Yimin's work with *prajñā* provides us one way for taking up this task.

Orientalism—Speaking for and Constructing the "Other"

Another challenge closely related to those posed by postmodern thinkers comes from an even more explicitly political quarter. In recent decades several thinkers have drawn attention to the tendency for Western scholars to be guilty of Orientalism. Although I have alluded to the notion of Orientalism already, it is a serious problem for those of us who study "other" cultures and warrants a fuller discussion.

Contemporary discussion of Orientalism takes its cue from Edward Said's landmark *Orientalism: Western Conceptions of the Orient*. In this book Said argues that Orientalism is a type of discourse which the West uses to control the East, the alluring yet dangerous "other." Such discourse has deep historical roots but rises to special prominence with Western military and economic dominance, amounting to a means of control by representing and speaking for the East.[114] In its very essence Orientalism is dehumanizing for the Orientalist "expert" alone claims the power to interpret the East, often telling the East itself what it is. Said's views have had great impact, forcing many scholars to re-think assumptions and procedures in their fields.

Despite its criticisms of the West, however, *Orientalism* relies heavily upon certain strains of Western thought, particularly the postmodernism of Foucault and Lyotard in which "grand narrative" is no longer possible. Said says:

> The methodological failures of Orientalism cannot be accounted for by saying that the *real* Orient is different from Orientalist portraits of it. ... It is not the thesis of this book to suggest that there is such a thing as a Real or true Orient. ... I have been arguing that "the Orient" itself is a constituted entity, and that the notion that there are geographical spaces with indigenous, radically "different" inhabitants who can be defined on the basis of some religion, culture, or racial essence proper to that geographical space is equally a highly debatable idea.[115]

For Said, all efforts to construct (true) narratives about "others" should be abandoned. Ironically, this poses problems for Said's own work—is it "true" or just another interpretation, another discourse that assumes the power of representation? Although Said has come under fire for overemphasizing the one-way relationship in Orientalist discourses (ignoring how "Orientals" actively participate in such work) and for seeming to assume that there is only one single true narrative of Orientalism, his work continues to be highly influential.[116]

Said's influence has been deeply felt in Buddhist studies. The Modern Western academic has continually posed as an "expert" on Buddhism, defining what it is and how it should be understood. This assumption of the power of representation has been severely critiqued in *Curators of the Buddha*, a collection of essays which unmasks the implicit Orientalism in the work of Aurel Stein, Giuseppi Tucci and Carl Jung among others.[117] Interestingly, this recent self-critical trend extends to *Japanese* scholarship on Buddhism, not just that of

Western scholars. Japanese scholars have made enormous contributions to the study of Buddhism. Nonetheless, self-critical examinations by some Japanese scholars have brought to light problematic issues and assumptions similar to those found in Western scholarship. In fact, in some cases (notably Nishida Kitaro, Keiji Nishitani and other members of the "Kyoto School") it seems that Japanese scholarship is informed by *European* Orientalist agendas.

We find similar Orientalist tendencies in the study of Chinese "Daoist" traditions. Early European scholars such as James Legge, influenced by their Christian backgrounds or missionary agendas, presented Chinese traditions in monotheistic terms based upon their readings of Chinese texts and work with Chinese converts.[118] Even influential *Chinese* scholars such as Feng Youlan or Wing-tsit Chan who argue against such readings still define Chinese thought in terms derived from Western traditions. This approach may in part be the result of translating texts and writing about them in English, but it can actually limit the scope of inquiry by making "China" and the "West" seem too compatible. In such a situation it is difficult for new insights to arise because potential areas of discord tend to be passed over. Just as with Buddhist studies, so recent scholars of Chinese traditions have critically addressed the work of their forbears, aided by more careful attention to texts as well as the living practices in Chinese culture.[119]

Can philosophical hermeneutics help us deal with the problems of Orientalism without recapitulating the same power structures? Will my discussion of Sengzhao be Orientalist as well? Whatever we may think of Said's claims, these are important questions. As numerous recent studies make clear, too much of the scholarship on Asia is part of the colonialist legacy for us to pretend otherwise. We cannot deny or disown the effects of history. Moreover, we must also beware of the "reverse Orientalism" ("Occidentalism") assumed by European-trained thinkers such as Sarvepalli Radhakrishnan and D. T. Suzuki, who represent the West as *spiritually* inferior to the East and who remain influential at both popular and scholarly levels.[120]

Hermeneutics, though, by encouraging a cautious and reflexive approach to "foreign" texts and cultures, may help us overcome some of the problems associated with Orientalism. Arran Gare, for example, has argued that it may be possible through insights derived from hermeneutics to avoid Orientalism, at least in the strong sense.[121] Gare maintains that Said's approach is problematic because its basic starting point (that all statements are products of a particular discursive formation) itself has no justification and it disallows even the possibility of understanding other cultures.[122] Gadamer, by contrast, shows how such understanding is possible through a process that begins by working through one's initial biases towards a fuller understanding found in the fusion of horizons. Gare adds that MacIntyre and other figures have built on these hermeneutic notions in arguing for a tradition-based rationality that is critical of itself and its past, and which can be transformed through contact with other traditions.[123]

Gare's points are well-taken. Certainly scholars' growing recognition of the problems of Orientalism indicates that more self-reflexive and open approaches are possible. In addition, both Ricoeur and Gadamer's analyses of understanding as an open-ended conversation moving beyond initial limits requires that "Western" thinkers move to engage constructively with all the world's cultures. This process entails acknowledging the problem, critically engaging with previous scholarship founded on Orientalist assumptions, and making an honest effort to *listen* to what the "other" traditions and texts are saying. We begin from difference–a very real difference–and move from there into the closeness of genuine conversation. This engagement will likely prove to be a lengthy, on-going venture but that is precisely what philosophical hermeneutics is about and what this study attempts to do.

We need to especially be aware that in any encounter with others, power always plays a role. Since the time of Francis Bacon, Western thinkers have proclaimed that "knowledge is power" but few have asked *what* this phrase actually means. "Power" is a vague term, connoting force, control and influence. It thus raises ethical concerns of violence and subjugation. The role of power lies at the heart of the problems of totalization and Orientalism. Can there be a hermeneutic encounter if the parties involved are not on equal footing? Does achieving understanding require asserting power by "gaining mastery" of the material or the meanings involved? These are serious philosophical questions for all of us to consider.

In this regard it may prove helpful to view hermeneutics as encouraging us to approach understanding as a "standing under," that is, an approach in which we conscientiously struggle to let the text tell us its meaning, not the other way around. At the very least we should not assume that the self-reflexive approach of philosophical hermeneutics is a means to domination. In fact, philosophical hermeneutics can undermine manipulative power structures and the institutionalized violence that have so often characterized Modern encounters with other cultures. As Tracy and Ricoeur both say, we need a hermeneutics that includes both retrieval of the past and suspicion of its prejudices and practices, as well as our own. This more careful hermeneutics would thus be informed by strong ethical considerations.

A crucial thing to bear in mind here is that a genuinely hermeneutic encounter occurs within a shared sphere of meaning. The appropriation of meaning that both Gadamer and Ricoeur describe does not entail violating the "other" for our own ends. This "appropriation" is not *assimilation* since understanding moves beyond its initial grounding in a particular subjectivity. Rather, philosophical hermeneutics attends to the voice of the "other" as it continually confronts us. In one of his later essays Gadamer writes, "Where one is not concerned with learning how to control something, we will always and again learn through experiencing our own biases, the otherness of the other in its other-being. To participate with the other and to be part of the other is the most and the best that we can strive for and accomplish.[124] Gadamer offers a profound hope here, one that is echoed by Richard King. King notes that the aim of hermeneutics is an on-going self-critical engagement that we share with others. He writes, "In confronting other cultures, other prejudices and, indeed, the implications that others draw from our own traditions we learn to reflect on both our assumptions and our ideas of reason and to amend them in the direction of *better* interpretation."[125]

We need to take seriously these challenges and the problems that they raise even if we cannot resolve them. Philosophical hermeneutics requires that we continually question ourselves along with a text. We must accept the contextuality of interpretation while aiming at a fully hermeneutical understanding. This is a delicate process, and calls for great care and circumspection. I will return to these challenges in Chapter Five as part of the self-critical understanding towards which this study aims.

Hermeneutics, as we have seen, is not a specific method or an easily delineated field. It is certainly not a technique for obtaining verification but is about how we make sense and find meaning. It is so basic to our lives that we hardly notice it except when faced with obstacles to our understanding. Such was the case with Sengzhao, who was struggling with the notion of *prajñā* just as Chinese Buddhism was emerging from its "Daoist" and Indian roots. Sengzhao was simultaneously negotiating conflicting interpretations and differing worldviews while seeking the ultimate meaning and goal of human life. Philosophical hermeneutics can provide valuable insight into his work for it truly offers "a bridge and a ford for ages to come."

· 2 ·

PRAJÑĀ BEFORE SENGZHAO

Buddhism and Chinese "Daoist" traditions center around hermeneutic issues
of continuity and discontinuity, understanding and misunderstanding. These
issues gained particular prominence with the integration of Buddhism into
Chinese culture, a process that took place over the course of several centuries
and in which Sengzhao himself had a hand. However, Sengzhao's struggles
with *prajñā* were merely part of a long history of attempts by Buddhists to
understand the Dharma. We thus need to look at some of this history to see
what is at stake in *"Prajñā* is Not-knowing" and "The Correspondence."
Before we begin, though, we must deal with some preliminary hermeneutic
matters concerning the notion of "context" and our preconceived notions of
prajñā.

Reflections on Sengzhao's "Context" and Our Preconceptions of *Prajñā*

What do We Mean by Sengzhao's "Context"?

"Context" is a controversial topic in hermeneutic study. Generally speaking,
context is the larger frame of reference within which we understand a "text"

and usually includes extra-textual factors that help illuminate a text's meaning. Context forms a background network of relationships from which we infer meaning. There are problems, though, surrounding the notion of context and its relationship to the text, including the fact that context itself is constructed within a particular perspective (that of the interpreter) and is by its nature indeterminate.

These considerations have immediate bearing on our present study, as context will vary depending upon the questions an interpreter asks of a text and his/her point of view. An interpretation of Sengzhao's work within a political and economic history of early Chinese Buddhism will have a different context than one focusing on more philosophical matters. The former would probably include an economic and social profile of Chang'an and an analysis of the reign of Yao Xing, the ruler who brought **Kumārajīva** and Sengzhao to Chang'an to serve in his translation bureau. Although such factors do hold interest, they figure only peripherally in our perspective, as we will focus on issues of understanding and misunderstanding.

Some scholars have also identified a problem dubbed the "contextual fallacy" in which over-emphasis on context actually impedes understanding by putting constraints on the hermeneutic encounter.[1] There is a real sense in which understanding requires decontextualizing; we must center our attention upon our subject and hence have to relegate other factors to the periphery. Too much attention on context, though, distances us from the claims of a text so that we refuse to engage with it. In such cases, the text becomes an "object" to be studied and not a partner in conversation. This runs counter to the aim of a truly *hermeneutic* study such as the one we are engaged in, for it would prematurely close off potential meanings that could emerge. Distance is productive of meaning but it must not supersede our conversation with the text.

There is no *a priori* way to resolve the problems of context. As Heidegger, Gadamer and Ricoeur remind us, we must accept the inevitable contextuality of interpretation while aiming at a hermeneutical understanding. When we turn to context of a specific text, we also face the difficulty of indeterminacy for there is usually little in the text itself that explicitly delineates what counts as context. Coming to terms with the contextuality of one's own perspective and deciding the parameters of a particular text's context are matters of judgment, the *phronesis* of interpretation. Context will always be somewhat cloudy; only careful attention in each case can determine the relevant context and even then such judgments will be provisional.

What is "Prajñā"?

If Sengzhao's context is initially unclear then the same is also true of his theme, *prajñā*. With any study we always begin with preconceptions. From a herme-neutic standpoint, it is helpful to examine these to the extent we can. What exactly *is prajñā*? Buddhists both before and after Sengzhao have asked this question and they have proposed many answers. This makes *prajñā* difficult to study. Ironically, scholars have only added to the difficulty. Some scholars associate *prajñā* exclusively with Buddhism. Tadeusz Skorupski is a good case in point. In his entry in the *Encyclopedia of Religion* Skorupski declares that *prajñā* is central to all Buddhist traditions, uniting them and distinguishing them from other religious and philosophical systems.[2] Skorupski bases his view of *prajñā* on solid textual and historical evidence, and most scholars probably agree with him. Unfortunately he is only partly correct; *prajñā* is *not* strictly Buddhist and actually figures prominently in various Indian traditions. There are references to *prajñā* in the *Upaniṣads* and Patañjali's *Yoga sūtras* as well as the works of the Sāṁkhya and Advaita Vedānta schools. A common synonym for *prajñā* is *buddhi*, a term whose meanings range from the discriminative faculty, to the transpersonal consciousness of an individual, to the first phase in the evolution of *prakṛti*.[3]

In addition to regarding *prajñā* as exclusively Buddhist, scholars create problems with how they translate *prajñā* into English. *Prajñā* can be translated as "wisdom," "insight," or "intuitive knowledge." It is often considered to be an abbreviation of *prajñāpāramitā* which scholars frequently regard as a "mystical vision" beyond the reach of ordinary thought. Yet do the terms "wisdom" and "insight" mean the same thing? How do they relate to "mystical vision"? Paul Williams, a scholar of Buddhism, furnishes an important clue for us when he observes, "Wisdom is, alas, all-too rare; *prajñā* is not."[4]

Prajñā is closely related to the word *jñāna* ("knowledge"), another San-skrit term that may even be synonymous with *prajñā* in some instances, although the relationship between them is knotty. Christian Lindtner and Ian Charles Harris both maintain that *prajñā* and *jñāna* form a nexus in which *prajñā* develops into specific intuitive insights (*jñāna*).[5] In contrast, Skorupski views *prajñā* as beyond concepts while *jñāna* can be graded from the empirical up to the transcendent level.[6] Such scholarly disagreement indicates that both terms defy easy definition. The late scholar of Buddhism David Snellgrove notes, "to fix the meanings rigidly of the Sanskrit terms *jñāna*, knowledge or wisdom, and *prajñā*, wisdom or insight or knowledge, is in practice impossible, as the meaning varies in both cases depending upon the context in which these terms are used. One can argue endlessly about which suits where."[7]

Etymologically, *prajñā* stems from the Sanskrit root *jñā* ("to know"). The prefix *pra* functions as an intensifier. Thus *prajñā* would be "*intense* awareness or knowing." The roots of *pāramitā*, however, are more ambiguous. One possibility is that it derives from *parama* ("highest," "most distant"). Another possibility is that it is a combination of two words–*pāra* ("beyond," "the further bank or shore") and *mita* ("that which has arrived"). In this case, *pāramitā* would be "that which goes beyond" or "transcendent."[8] *Prajñāpāramitā*, then, could be defined as "intense understanding going beyond (the ordinary)" or "transcendent knowing." Note that there is no indication here that *prajñā* is necessarily "mystical" or even "religious."

It appears, then, that we should question common assumptions about *prajñā*. Such considerations underscore the fact that we cannot presume to know what *prajñā* is at the outset. Our initial ideas will prove useful in our investigation, serving as our "enabling prejudices" which allow us to project meaning and so enter the hermeneutic circle. However, they are not the final outcome and will have to be modified as our understanding progresses. The hermeneutic circle is not "vicious" provided we heed Heidegger's admonition that we enter the circle in the right way. By becoming critically aware of these factors (vagueness of context, common assumptions, problems in translation) we are in a better position to begin our study of Sengzhao's discussion of *prajñā* and its relationship to Buddhist and "Daoist" traditions.

Indian Views of *Prajñā*

Historically, Sengzhao's efforts to understand *prajñā* took place during what Erik Zurcher calls the "formative stage" of Buddhism in China (300–589 C.E.), an era when Buddhism began to make serious in-roads at both the popular and elite levels. In the fourth century many Chinese scholars were struggling with *prajñā* teachings found in the texts that missionaries had brought with them. However, these texts were the products of a long history of opinion about *prajñā* within Indian culture. Examining Indian ideas of *prajñā* allows us to see the roots of the Chinese debates and so more fully appreciate the enormity of Sengzhao's efforts.

Indian notions of *prajñā* are complex and manifold. Although it has Vedic roots, Buddhists have always endowed "*prajñā*" with special significance. From the time of Śākyamuni, *prajñā*, along with *śīla* ("morality") and *samādhi* ("meditative absorption"), comprised the "Threefold Training," a shorter formulation of the Eightfold Path. This notion of *prajñā* as a basic component of the Path fits with the pragmatic character of early Buddhism, wherein teachings focused on overcoming *duḥkha*. Essentially *prajñā* was a faculty of clear understanding. *Prajñā* guided life, leading one along to the attainment of *nirvāṇa*. *Prajñā* entailed specific knowledges such as the "three-fold knowledge" of one's previous lives, past and future lives of others, and the destruction of impurities (*kleśas* and *āsravas*).[9] *Prajñā* even included magical powers such as the "divine ear" or clairvoyance.[10]

Prajñā's various shades of meaning are apparent when we look at some early discourses. In a passage from the *Mahāttipādopamasūtta* concerning material existence, the Buddha says, "By means of perfect intuitive wisdom (*prajñā*) it should be seen of this as it really is, thus: this is not mine, this am I not, this is not my self."[11] Note that although the Buddha speaks of *prajñā* here as "intuitive" it is an *analytic* understanding. In the *Culadukkhakhandasūtta*, the Buddha describes *prajñā* in the context of his own cultivation, observing that it leads to rapture far beyond the pleasures of those with "unskilled minds."[12] In these discourses, *prajñā* is both analytic and ethical and, ultimately, is the only means of ending ignorance (*avidyā*).[13] *Prajñā* essentially is the clear perception of the basic *dharmas* (mental phenomena) of human existence. Elsewhere we find three forms of *prajñā* recognized: *prajñā* arising from teaching (*śrutamayi*), *prajñā* based upon reflection (*cintamayi*), and *prajñā* born out of meditation (*bhāvanāmayi*). Only the last of these, however, results in *nirvāṇa*.[14]

During the Abhidharma period (third century BCE–second century CE) *prajñā* became the subject of systematic elaboration by different schools and an even greater array of meanings emerged. These interpretations have their roots in the early discourses but they all show the marks of the more theoretical, "scholastic" orientation of the Abhidharma thinkers. Of the two surviving Abhidharma collections (Theravāda and Sarvāstivāda), the Sarvāstavāda has the more detailed discussion of *prajñā*. *Prajñā* in the Sarvāstivāda Abhidharma is a generic category of insight, of which there are several species. It also is a moral faculty developed gradually through a process of purifying the *impure prajñās* of ordinary human existence.

In the opening verses of the *Abhidharmakośa* Vasubandhu defines the whole of Sarvāstivādin Abhidharma as *amala prajñā* ("immaculate *prajñā*"), explaining what this statement entails in his own commentary (*bhāsya*):

> 2a. The Abhidharma is the immaculate *prajñā* with its retinue.
> The *prajñā* that will be defined below is the discernment of *dharmas*. The immaculate (*amala*) *prajñā* is the pure *prajñā* (*anuśrava*). That which is called "retinue" (*anucara*) of *prajñā* is its escort (*parivara*), namely the five pure *skandhas* that co-exist with *prajñā*. This is the proper meaning of "Abhidharma."

> 2b. It is also entirely *prajñā* and the treatise that helps obtain immaculate *prajñā*.
> In common usage, the word "Abhidharma" also designates all *prajñā* that makes one obtain the Abhidharma in its proper sense: impure (*saśrava*) *prajñā* whether inborn or natural (*upapattipratilambhīka*) or the result of effort, listening, reflection, or concentration (*śrutacintabhāvanā-mayi*) receives by convention along with its retinue the name "Abhidharma." The treatise is also named "Abhidharma" because the treatise makes one obtain pure *prajñā*: it is then a creator of "Abhidharma" in the proper sense.[15]

For the Sarvāstivādins mental purification and *prajñā* work together. In addition to the forms of *prajñā* listed above, there is also *kuprajñā*, an understanding involving judgment and sometimes equated with *dṛṣṭi* ("view"). In the latter sense, one can have a "view" arising from rigorous albeit defective analysis (*mithadṛṣṭi*, a view based on unreal objects such as the *ātman* and often held by non-Buddhists) or a "correct view" (*samyakadṛṣṭi*, focused on the *dharmas* hence in accord with Buddhist teaching).[16] Thus *prajñā* for Sarvāstivādins has multiple senses. It is an ethical guide as well as a skillful discernment developed through mental discipline. *Prajñā*, above all, is *practical*, a part of a series of acts by which we attain enlightenment (*bodhi*).[17]

The Sarvāstivādins, moreover, often extol *prajñā*'s abilities beyond the mundane level; attaining the *amala prajñā* of which Vasubandhu speaks requires overcoming lower forms of *prajñā* marked by emotional attachment. *Prajñā* develops as we refine our "knowing," in some circumstances taking on extraordinary power. Specific acts of *prajñā* lead to states of mental "cessation" (*pratisaṃkhya-nirodha*), a pure direct awareness. High levels of *prajñā* bring deep insight into Buddhist teachings such as *pratītya-samutpāda*, although in these cases the mind transcends all concepts.[18] Such pure *prajñā*, although transient, has lasting effect.[19] For Sarvāstivādins, highest *prajñā* marks the climax of the Path, wherein the mind cuts through the ignorance at the root of *saṃsāra* and attains *nirvāna*.

Prajñā in early Mahāyāna Buddhism:
The Prajñāpāramitā sūtras

Around the beginning of the Common Era a new form of Buddhism arose, combining popular ideas and practices with critical responses to Abhidharma stress on analysis.[20] This movement became known as Mahāyāna, "The Great Vehicle." The Mahāyāna shows the classic tension between continuity and discontinuity characteristic of hermeneutic traditions. The very name "Mahāyāna" highlights this tension, for it indicates an expansion beyond earlier Hīnayāna ("Small vehicle") while remaining true to the spirit of Śākyamuni's teachings. "Hīnayāna" is, of course, a pejorative term employed by Mahāyāna followers and most likely refers to certain strains of Sarvāstivāda (not Theravāda as some textbooks mistakenly say). Moreover, it is important to emphasize that followers of Mahāyāna do not consider "Hīnayānists" to be "heretics" (tīrthikas) but view their understanding and practice of Dharma as too rigid.

One effect of the Mahāyāna expansion and reinterpretation of Buddhism was a tremendous expansion in the scope and meaning of prajñā. This expansion of meaning stems from the teaching that the dharmas themselves are śūnya ("empty"). Dharmas are empty because they arise from the combination of various causes and conditions; they lack any permanent "own-being" (svabhāva). This teaching lies at the heart of the first Mahāyāna scriptures, the Prajñāpāramitā sūtras, an enormous body of texts ranking among the most famous in all of Buddhist literature. Although their time and place of origin are uncertain, they are presented as dialogues between Śākyamuni Buddha and his foremost disciples, especially the venerable Subhuti.[21]

The Prajñāpāramitās extol prajñā as a power defying rational analysis that allows us to overcome barriers between "self" and "other." As with earlier Buddhism so in these texts (and the entire Mahāyāna), prajñā leads to freedom from suffering but this freedom includes everyone. Prajñā is the compassionate knowing and being embodied in the Bodhisattva, one who vows to attain enlightenment for all beings.

The Prajñāpāramitā sūtras overwhelmingly concentrate on prajñā as perfected, i.e. in its complete attainment.[22] They offer little step-by-step instruction on how to perfect prajñā or overcome lower forms of prajñā. This lends the texts a transcendent tone that makes it difficult to apprehend what prajñā is. It also means that comparisons with Abhidharma discussions must be carried out carefully. There may, for instance, be little difference between Sarvāstivādin notions of amala prajñā, the seemingly pure awareness attained in moments of *nirodha*, and various ideas of *prajñā* spoken of in the *Prajñāpāramitās*.[23]

Perhaps the most common description of *prajñā* in the *Prajñāpāramitās* is non-attachment to objects and ideas. Śākyamuni considered attachment to be the root of suffering and taught its elimination by following the Eightfold Path. In the Abhidharma schools attachment is eliminated by *dharmic* analysis, what we might call the application of "Abhidharmic *prajñā*." In the *Prajñāpāramitā sūtras*, however, *prajñā* extends to non-attachment to the *dharmas*. Thus the *Aṣṭasāhasrika prajñāpāramitā* ("Perfection of *Prajñā* in 8,000 Lines") proclaims that one approaches *prajñā* through non-attachment to or non-differentiation of all *dharmas*.[24] The *Pañcavimśatisāhasrika prajñāpāramitā* ("Perfection of *Prajña* in 25,000 Lines") describes *prajñā* as "marked by non-attachment" while the Bodhisattva who attains it takes no *dharma* as her basis.[25]

The *Prajñāpāramitās* extend non-attachment beyond *dharmas* to all of Buddhism.[26] A Bodhisattva should not be attached to practices, the path or states of attainment. Such a being "remains unattached even to his thought of enlightenment, the thought which equals the unequalled."[27] This radical non-attachment even includes *prajñāpāramitā* itself:

> But if it occurs to the Bodhisattva, the great being, that "he who courses thus, who develops thus, he courses in perfect wisdom, he develops perfect wisdom; I course in perfect wisdom, I develop perfect wisdom", if he perceives thus, then he moves away from perfect wisdom, he gets far away from the perfection of wisdom … the perfection of wisdom does not settle down in any dharma, nor is it capable of doing so.[28]

The idea here is that *prajñā* transcends nominal (i.e. verbalized) teachings to reality itself, the constant flow of things and events. Hence "a non-coursing is the Bodhisattva's coursing in perfect wisdom."[29]

The *Prajñāpāramitās* often speak of *prajñā* as non-discrimination, a seemingly direct denial of interpretations of *prajñā* as discriminative analysis. In *prajñā* no discriminations exist. "Just as the Tathāgata is one who has forsaken all constructions and discriminations, even so perfect wisdom has forsaken all constructions and discriminations."[30] This non-discrimination is the absence of dualistic thinking and opinions. A passage in the *Pañca* reads, "The nonduality of existence and nonexistence, as well as the absence of intellectual multiplicity with regard to dharmas, such as form, etc. and also with regard to the emptiness of form, etc. that should be viewed as the inherent mark of nondiscrimination."[31] Such nonduality, however, is not necessarily non-conceptual so much as a perception of the complete equality or sameness (*samatā*) of all beings. One who sees this truth realizes "the dharmic sameness of the common people, and that of Streamwinners ... and in this sameness there is not any difference."[32]

Ultimately this non-attached, non-discriminative *prajñā* results from realizing *śūnyatā*, "emptiness." As Subhūti says, "I will teach you how a Bodhisattva should stand in perfect wisdom. Through standing in emptiness should he stand in perfect wisdom."[33] The *Prajñā-pāramitās* emphatically proclaim this emptiness. Everything—ordinary things, fellow sentient beings, thoughts, *dharmas*, Buddhist teachings, even Bodhisattvas and Buddhas—are "like a magical illusion, like a dream."[34] A Bodhisattva does not attach any weight to what she meets but courses in the freedom of *prajñā*:

> The Bodhisattva's development of perfect wisdom reaches its fulfillment, if, when he courses in perfect wisdom, he does not review 'dharma' or 'nondharma', 'past', 'future', or 'present', 'wholesome, unwholesome, or indeterminate', 'conditioned' or 'unconditioned', the world of sense desire the world of form, the formless world, the perfection of giving, etc. *to*: the knowledge of all modes. And why? Because this is on account of the essential marks of Dharma, on account of irreversibility, of nullity, vanity, unsubstantiality, and voidness.[35]

So hard do the *Prajñāpāramitās* strive to avoid making their teachings dogma that they even say a Bodhisattva must not settle down on *śūnyatā* itself. With the realization of *śūnyatā*, all divisions cease. "Knowing" and "being" are one. *Prajñā* becomes *śūnyatā*.

The association with meditation and states of absorption that we see in early Buddhism and the Abhidharmas becomes very strong in the *Prajñā pāramitās*, where *prajñā* can lead to states of non-conceptual awareness (*nirvakalpakaprajñā*). Moreover, by means of *prajñā* a Bodhisattva gains mastery of all levels of *samādhi*, attaining such skill that she develops *simha-vijrmbhīta-samādhi* ("concentration like a lion's yawn"), the ability to rapidly enter into and emerge from highest concentration.[36] *Prajñā* here arises from an *intense* analysis in which the mind transcends itself and attains a nondual "knowledge" (*advayajñāna*) enabling the Bodhisattva to travel easily through all states of awareness to reach the sameness of all *dharmas*.

The relationship of *prajñā* and meditation within the *Prajñāpāramitās* underscores the fact that discussion of *prajñā* always takes place in a practical context. *Prajñā* develops through intentional cultivation in the *Prajñā pāramitā sūtras*, something especially evident in their lengthy descriptions of the teachings and behavior of Bodhisattvas. The Bodhisattva path is an arduous journey said to involve eons (*kalpas*) of learning and practice. Later texts such as the *Daśabhūmika sūtra* and the *Bodhisattvabhūmi* lay out the *Prajñāpāramitās'* Bodhisattva teachings in a systematic fashion. Although these texts present the Bodhisattva path according to differing schemes, in broad outline they agree. They divide the Bodhisattva path into a series of stages (*bhūmis*) through which an aspirant moves on her development towards Buddhahood. A Bodhisattva-in-training ascends through the *bhūmis* gradually by perfecting the skills of *dāna* ("generosity"), *śīla* ("morality"), *kṣānti* ("patience"), *vīrya* ("vigor"), *samādhi* and *prajñā*.[37] In all cases, though, *prajñā* is the ruling perfection, the impetus and guide in perfecting of each skill. As the *Aṣṭa* puts it, "Wisdom controls him who gives gifts, And also morality, patience, vigour [sic] and concentration."[38]

Prajñā's perfection is a Bodhisattva's crowning achievement, when all divisions between "self" and "other" fall away. *Prajñā* at this point *is* compassion (*karuṇā*), and the *Prajñāpāramitās* describe it in fittingly paradoxical yet superlative terms:

> Perfect wisdom is great, unlimited, measureless and infinite because form, feelings, etc., are so. Hence one does not settle down in the conviction that this is a "great perfection," an "unlimited perfection," a "measureless perfection," an "infinite perfection." That is why perfect wisdom is a great perfection, unlimited, measureless and infinite. Perfect wisdom is an infinite perfection because objects as well as [individual] beings are infinite. Perfect wisdom is an infinite perfection because one cannot get at the beginning, middle, or end of any objective fact [since as a dharma it has no own-being].[39]

Such wisdom goes far beyond ordinary "wisdom," even the wisdom of the Abhidharmas. It is a transcendent power surpassing our rational (dividing, limiting, defining) faculties.

The *Prajñāpāramitās* are difficult texts, spilling forth passage upon passage of soaring rhetoric. Rather than systematically argue, they boldly assert the true way of things and exhort us on how to behave in light of this knowledge. Many statements made by the Buddha and his interlocutors in the *Prajñāpāramitās* are uttered from the perspective of *prajñā*, the level of Ultimate Truth in which nothing is truly real. Yet this enlightened perspective includes ordinary knowing in which everyday "things" exist, the level of conventional truth. Those beings who course in *prajñāpāramitā* reside at the intersection of both levels of truth, cognizing the "marks" (conventional) yet surrendered to the "markless" (ultimate).[40] By jumping back and forth between these levels, the *Prajñāpāramitās* generate numerous contradictions and paradoxes, speaking what we might call a special "*prajñic*" language.[41]

Not surprisingly then, it is impossible to get a clear fix on what perfected *prajñā* entails. To cite just one example, in a passage in the *Aṣṭa* Subhūti says:

> It (*prajñāpāramitā*) does not make form, etc., greater or smaller, and it does not assemble nor disperse form, etc. It also does not strengthen or weaken the powers of a Tathāgata, nor does it assemble or disperse them. It does not even make that all-knowledge greater or smaller, nor does it assemble or disperse it. For all-knowledge is unassembled [uncollected] and undispersed [undisturbed]. If a Bodhisattva perceives even this, then he courses not in the perfection of wisdom ... the absence of own-being in beings should be known as belonging to the very essence of the perfection of wisdom. One should know that the perfection of wisdom is without own-being because [or: in the same way in which] beings are without own-being; that the perfection of wisdom is isolated because beings are isolated; that the perfection of wisdom is unthinkable because beings are; that the perfection of wisdom has an indestructible nature because beings have; that the perfection of wisdom does not actually undergo the process which leads to enlightenment because beings do not; that the perfection of wisdom taken as it really is does not undergo the process which leads to enlightenment because beings, as they really are, do not undergo that process; that the way in which the Tathāgata arrives at the full possession of his powers should be understood after the way in which beings arrive at the full possession of their power. It is in this manner that the perfection of wisdom is a great perfection.[42]

Although Subhūti waxes on at great length about *prajñā* in this passage, he actually gives neither a precise description nor a step-by-step account of how one attains it. Such passages are so common in the *Prajñāpāramitās* that, as Jaini puts it, "one sometimes feels that nothing definite can be said beyond the statement that *prajñā* is something which was attained by the Buddha and is attainable by the Bodhisattvas."[43]

The Rise of Mahāyāna Scholasticism—Prajñā in the Mādhyamika School

The *Prajñāpāramitās* are rooted in earlier Buddhist views but increasingly lift *prajñā* up as a grand, transformative power. At times the texts speak of *prajñā* as analytic discrimination but then portray *prajñā* as non-conceptual knowing, a mysterious nondual awareness that eludes our grasp. In the end *prajñā* is skillful analysis, a miraculous "salvific" *gnosis* that is the very essence of Buddhahood and true nature of reality, *śūnyatā* itself. The slippery nature of *prajñā* in these *sūtras* as well as their confusing mix of superlative and paradoxical language prompted Mahāyāna thinkers to write various treatises in the attempt to systematically explain their teachings. The earliest such treatises were composed by Nāgārjuna (150–250) and his disciple Āryadeva (200–300), whose work formed the basis for the Mādhyamika ("Middle Way") school. My discussion will focus on Nāgārjuna as he is usually regarded most representative of Mādhyamika thought and had the most direct influence on Chinese notions of *prajñā*.

Although he draws upon earlier Buddhist tradition, Nāgārjuna's treatises rely heavily on the *Prajñāpāramitās*. The major themes in the *Prajñā pāramitās* form the background for the Mādhyamikas' distinctive style, a negative dialectic (*prasaṅga*) emphasizing logic and polemics over the *sūtras'* more constructive and effusive discourse. This difference in style reflects Nāgārjuna's approach as an exegete, an interpreter of scripture seeking to articulate Buddhist teachings in a reasoned, scholastic fashion. Scholars generally agree that in much of his work Nāgārjuna argues against Sarvāstivāda and other Abhidharma schools. However, his Mādhyamika stress on negation is also an extension of the *Prajñāpāramitās'* negative descriptions of *prajñā* as non-attachment, non-discrimination, nondual etc.

Nāgārjuna and later Mādhyamikas agree with the *Prajñāpāramitās* that the purpose the Dharma is nonattachment. Indeed, the relentless negative dialectics to which Nāgārjuna subjects all aspects of Buddhism in the *Kārikās* parallels the *Prajñāpāramitās'* insistence that a Bodhisattva coursing in *prajñā* must be completely unattached and must not settle down in any *dharma* whatsoever. Nāgārjuna drives this logic of nonattachment home most forcefully when he says "No Dharma was taught by the Buddha at any time, in any place, to any person."[44]

The *Prajñāpāramitās* speak of the nonattached "knowing" of *prajñā* as "non-discrimination," an awareness transcending the distinctions habitually made by ignorant consciousness. The Mādhyamika school picks up on this theme as well. In one a famous passage in the *Kārikās*, Nāgārjuna describes non-discrimination as the essence of the Dharma:

> By the buddhas, patrons of the world,
> This immortal truth is taught:
> Without identity, without distinction;
> Not nonexistent in time, not permanent.[45]

For Nāgārjuna, the truth taught by the awakened ones is free from the distinctions projected by the mind trapped within *saṃsāra*. It is "not thought, without distinctions."[46]

At times the *Prajñāpāramitās* speak of *prajñā* as a nondual perception of the sameness of all things. Nāgārjuna echoes such sentiments in the opening verses of the *Kārikās*:

> I prostrate to the Perfect Buddha,
> The best of teachers, who taught that
> Whatever is dependently arisen is
> Unceasing, unborn,
> Unannihilated, not permanent,
> Not coming, not going,
> Without distinction, without identity,
> And free from conceptual construction.[47]

Nāgārjuna sums up this nondual view of reality best in chapter twenty-five, where he declares there is no difference ultimately between *nirvāṇa* and *saṃsāra*:

> There is not the slightest difference
> Between cyclic existence (*saṃsāra*) and *nirvāṇa*.
> There is not the slightest difference
> Between *nirvāṇa* and cyclic existence.

> Whatever is the limit of *nirvāṇa*,
> That is the limit of cyclic existence.

> There is not even the slightest difference between them,
> Or even the subtlest thing.[48]

Awakening leads beyond even the "fundamental truths" preached by Śākyamuni himself.

The *Prajñāpāramitās* speak at length of emptiness, another major theme for Nāgārjuna. As in the *Prajñāpāramitās*, so for Nāgārjuna insight into emptiness marks the attaining of nonattached, non-discriminative awareness. In his *Dvādaśamukha śāstra* ("Twelve-Topic Treatise"), Nāgārjuna declares that understanding emptiness is understanding Mahāyāna.[49] In the *Kārikās* Nāgārjuna explains that since all *dharmas* arise from the combination of causal conditions (*pratītya-samutpāda*), there is nothing that is not empty (of own-being). As he incisively writes

> For to him whom emptiness is clear,
> Everything becomes clear.
> For to him whom emptiness is not clear,
> Nothing becomes clear.[50]

Emptiness is *the* central insight taught by the Buddha. As such, emptiness is not a "view" but refutes all views to which one could cling, even that of emptiness itself.

Yet despite the evidence that Nāgārjuna's work builds upon the *Prajñā pāramitās* he actually says surprisingly little about *prajñā*.[51] He never mentions *prajñā* in the *Kārikās*, although he does use the related term *jñāna* in a way reminiscent of descriptions of *prajñā* in the *Prajñāpāramitā sūtras*.[52] Where he does mention *prajñā* his usage fully accords with the *Prajñāpāramitās*. In the *Bodhisambhāraka*, for instance, Nāgārjuna describes *prajñā* as the main preparation for enlightenment, based upon the attaining of the other perfections. *Prajñā* is not an immediate experience but must be ripened gradually.[53] In his *Acintyastava*, one of four devotional hymns to the Buddha, Nāgārjuna says that by means of *prajñā* one eventually becomes a Buddha.[54]

Later Mādhyamikas such as Bhāvaviveka (500–570) and Candrakīrti (600–650) speak of *prajñā* more explicitly than does Nāgārjuna. While they clearly rely on his work they present somewhat different interpretations. Candrakīrti in particular emphasizes *prajñā*'s non-conceptual nature, marking a definite break with earlier views. He also says a Bodhisattva abides in *prajñā* by perceiving the conditioned nature of existence, thereby attaining *nirodha*.[55] The most detailed Mādhyamika discussion of *prajñā* is in the *Bodhicaryāvatāra* of Śāntideva (650–750), wherein we find all the previous associations of *prajñā* with analysis, meditation, ethics and even a state of non-conceptuality.[56] Other Mahāyāna movements discuss *prajñā* as well but they had little influence on early Chinese notions of *prajñā* and their interpretations sometimes contradict Mādhyamika views. Nonetheless they attest to how a fundamental concept within a religious tradition gets articulated differently from various perspectives.[57]

As we can see, *prajñā* is a complex concept in Indian Buddhism. At the most basic level, *prajñā* is knowledge or insight but over time it takes on religious, even salvific connotations. Systematic presentations of the Buddhist path describe *prajñā* as a skill of discernment cultivated gradually through discipline. *Prajñā* is also associated with states of meditation, which is always an integral part of Buddhist practice. In the Mahāyāna *prajñā* is elevated to a transcendent level of experience where "subject" and "object" collapse into each other, and thus is beyond discursive thinking. *Prajñā* overcomes barriers between our notions of "self" and "other," and manifests as compassionate living. In this sense *prajñā* is the essence of Buddhahood, reality itself.

Prajñā, thus, has a host of definitions and connotations. It defies precise articulation. Examining various traditions within Indian Buddhism shows that *prajñā* was subject to many interpretations. We find a similar proliferation of interpretations in China, although there the situation is marked by even more contention and confusion.

Chinese Views of *Prajñā*

Background: Chinese Thought in the Wei-Jin era (Third-Fourth Centuries)

Chinese notions of *prajñā* are bound up with developments in early Chinese Buddhism. During the Latter Han there were several trends in Buddhism, with the most prominent centering on *dhyāna* and *prajñā*. Both the *dhyāna* and *prajñā* movements had strong appeal to the literati. *Dhyāna* focused on meditation practices laid out in the Hīnayāna translations of An Shigao and his disciples, and its main centers were north, in Loyang and Chang'an. *Prajñā* studies, on the other hand, concentrated on the Mahāyāna teachings found in the texts translated by Lokakṣema and Zhi Qian, and its main centers were in the south.[58] Yet even though they differed, these movements were not mutually exclusive. The Chinese did not distinguish between Hīnayāna and Mahāyāna, and many pursued both *dhyāna* and *prajñā* studies. *Dhyāna* practices aimed at clear, calm "knowing" which practitioners may have considered a mark of *prajñā* but generally speaking, *prajñā* scholars were more philosophically inclined.

Chinese fascination with *prajñā* owed much to historical circumstances. When the Latter Han dynasty ended China entered the "period of disunity," a time of great discord. During this time the Han Empire broke up into several small states, each with its own territory. Often these states were at war with each other or subject to invasion by non-Chinese ("barbarian") peoples.[59] The collapse of centralized authority led many to question Han socio-political philosophy, an amalgam of Confucian, Daoist and Legalist teachings based on a correlative cosmology involving *yin* and *yang* and the *wuxing*.

Many scholars were distrustful of official service in such circumstances, opting instead to "retire" to private life. These thinkers gravitated to Daoist texts such as the *Laozi* and the *Zhuangzi*, and the *Yijing* ("Book of Changes"), since these works seemed to offer an escape from the trials of the world.[60] This cultural movement has been dubbed "Neo-Daoism," a broad term that actually covers several trends of thought. Generally speaking, Neo-Daoism was a Confucianized reinterpretation of early Daoist ideas and texts but, contrary to many accounts, it was not purely escapist. Neo-Daoism was also a protest movement to the political and social conditions of the time. As Julia Ching notes, Many Neo-Daoists were bureaucrats disillusioned with mainstream Han interpretations of the *jing* who turned to Daoist texts to find the true basis of reality in an uncertain era.[61] Others were persons with artistic leanings who retired from politics to indulge in wine and *qingtan* ("pure conversation," philosophical and poetic exchanges emphasizing clever turns of phrase).[62] Both of these currents had a distinctly religious flavor. Among the Neo-Daoists seeking transcendence through "retirement," the most famous were the "Seven Worthies of the Bamboo Grove," an illustrious group of friends who lived during the 250's and whose unconventional exploits are widely celebrated to this day.[63] Others sometimes labeled "Neo-Daoists" were practitioners of "religious Daoism" (*Daojiao*) such as Ge Hong (253–333), who drew on Confucian and Daoist ideas in discussing immortality and alchemy.[64]

Within Neo-Daoism there was a strong tendency towards speculative philosophy, a trend usually called *xuanxue* ("dark/profound learning"). Philosophically, *xuanxue* was a "gnostic" movement drawing on Confucian and Daoist teachings to explore questions of an ontological rather than practical nature.[65] Taking their cue from the *Laozi* and the *Zhuangzi*, followers of *xuanxue* stressed the "dark mystery" (*xuanming*), the source transcending words which they equated with Daoist notions of *xu* ("void") and *wu* ("non-being," "non-existence").[66] Fang Xuanling (578–648), author of the *Jinshu* ("History of the *Jin* Dynasty") says of these thinkers:

> They established the theory that Heaven and Earth and the ten-thousand things have non-being as their root. As for "non-being," it is that which opens up all beings and completes the task, and which is present everywhere. *Yin* and *yang* rely on it in transforming and producing and the ten-thousand things rely on it to realize their forms.[67]

Xuanxue also had a strong mystical aspect, and many *xuanxue* discussions concern ways of realizing the essence of reality and the nature of the Sage. Such themes resonate strongly with the *Prajñāpāramitās* so it is little wonder that *xuanxue* adherents were also drawn to Buddhism.

One of the first *xuanxue* masters was He Yan (190–249), who composed several treatises on the *Laozi*, but the most influential *xuanxue* thinkers were Wang Bi (226–249) and Guo Xiang (252–312). Although they lived in different decades, both Wang and Guo became famous for their philosophical interpretations of Daoist texts and their respective commentaries on the *Laozi* and *Zhuangzi* influenced how those texts would be read for centuries. Their work helped establish the basic metaphysical vocabulary with which later Chinese thinkers understood and articulated Dharma.

Wang Bi may be the first Chinese thinker to really focus on ontology. Although he died at the age of twenty-four, his commentaries on the *Yijing* and the *Laozi* have earned him high honor in Chinese history.[68] The main theme of Wang's philosophy is *wu*, the mysterious "oneness" underlying all phenomena. Rather than mere "nothingness," *wu* is the source of all concrete things.[69] For Wang, *wu* is the constant, nameless beginning, the creative sustaining power upon which all things depend but which has no positive identity in itself.[70]

Although we find this emphasis on *wu* in various early Daoist texts, Wang truly makes it the heart of his ontological vision. Wang conceives of the entire cosmos in terms of a dynamic pattern of emerging from and returning to *wu*, yet this is not necessarily a temporal process. It is rather a dialectic of ontological creativity which Wang speaks of through a number of different terms. *Wu*, the mysterious source, manifests in *you* ("being," "existence") as *li* ("principle," "order"), the intelligible structure of existence. *Wu* and *li* are "one" yet not identical "things," for each is truly nothing ("no-thing"). *Li* is *wu* as we can apprehend it within *you*, neither different nor the same. It is the ontological principle of unity and causation.[71]

Wang's ontological scheme has had lasting repercussions in Chinese thought, much of which lies beyond the scope of our present study. At present it is enough for us to note two important correlated ideas. First, for Wang it is difficult, indeed impossible to truly speak of Dao as *wu* (cf. *Laozi* 1), but we can speak of it metaphorically, through such terms as *ben* ("root"), *mu* ("mother"), or even *pu* ("the uncarved block"). Second, Wang speaks of the Sage as one who apprehends *wu* as *li*, this underlying structure but not necessarily the trivial details of existence. Moreover, the Sage embodies (*ti*) this principle of Dao in everyday life. Another way of getting at this is to say that the Sage puts Dao into practice, taking Dao as his "function" or "use" (*yong*) in the world of things.[72] In doing so, the Sage acts naturally, spontaneously (*ziran*), and so responds effortlessly to the world. This decidedly Daoist view of the Sage prompted accusations that Wang had abandoned Confucius for Laozi, or had even lost the Way by becoming "excessively abstruse and wild."[73]

Guo Xiang, like Wang Bi, was renowned for his skill in debate and also served as an official.[74] He, too, was enthralled with Daoist texts and his commentary on the *Zhuangzi* is often regarded as the definitive text of *xuanxue*'s second phase.[75] Guo builds upon Wang's notion of *wu* but emphasizes its vacuity. True to its grammatical meaning of "lack," Guo views *wu* as the ultimate *lack* of substantive ground. According to Guo Xiang *wu* is not a "creator," not a "thing" that produces other things. Guo writes, "Not only that non-being cannot transform into being, being cannot transform into non-being. Therefore, existing things, although constantly changing through ten-thousand transformations, cannot unite in non-being. Thus there is no time when there is no being; being always exists."[76] Unlike Wang Bi, then, Guo Xiang conceives *wu* nominally rather than ontologically. *Wu* is merely a designation for the "bottomless nature" of reality. The world depends on "nothing" but it perpetually exists as the multitudes of things.

Guo Xiang is not an ontological nihilist, however. The key concept in his philosophy is *ziran*, the spontaneous self-transforming nature of things and the principle (*li*) that governs the universe. Wang Bi had also discussed *ziran* but Guo took such discussion to new depths. For Guo, *ziran* is the ever-changing transformation of all phenomena. In actuality Dao is merely a name for this principle of spontaneous, natural change that all things follow. Each thing is its own self-transforming nature (it has its own *fen* or "portion") yet this individualized transformation is the True Way of the Universe. According to Guo Xiang, the principle of the myriad transformations is expressed in all things, hence acting "naturally" is the way to become a Sage (or *zhiren*, "perfected person"). Thus despite their differences both Wang Bi and Guo Xiang focus on how to realize the nature of things and live accordingly. In other words, both speak of "the Way of sageliness within and kingliness without."

Perhaps it was inevitable that *xuanxue* thinkers would be drawn to Buddhist teachings in addition to Confucianism and Daoism. We find no specifically Buddhist terms in the works of either Wang Bi or Guo Xiang, but by the latter part of the Western Jin (265–316) *xuanxue* thinkers began looking to Buddhism as another source of wisdom.[77] This rapprochement of Buddhism and *xuanxue* is not surprising given the fact that both traditions deal with problems of ontology and the limitations of language, seek to find the true nature of human existence, and espouse non-attachment.

One result of the interplay of Buddhism and *xuanxue* was that monks and scholars borrowed terms from one another, thus further blurring the differences between the traditions. In Sengyou's *Chu sanzang jiji* ("Excepts from the Tripiṭaka"), for example, we find Liu Qiu (438–495), a prominent thinker of the time, saying,

> Of themselves Ultimate teachings respond to the world [and it is only when] joining
> with the worldly that they diverge. The Spiritual Dao saves creatures [but only in our]

declarations of their influences do they attain differences. From Xuan Pu eastward the term 'Great Oneness' is used. From Kashmir westward the term 'sambodhi' (enlightenment) is used. Whether one looks longingly toward 'non-being' or cultivates 'emptiness', the principle involved is the same.[78]

Clearly Liu regarded Buddhism and Daoism as essentially teaching the same thing, and in this he was not alone. Many Chinese regarded Buddhism and Daoism as similar variations of a basic Dao; to be "Buddhist" was to be "Daoist" and vice versa. We see further evidence of this melding of traditions in essays such as the Daoxian lun ("Treatise on Buddhist Monks and Daoist Worthies") of Sun Cho (301–380), in which the author compares seven Buddhist monks to the Seven Worthies.[79] Daoan explicitly remarks in his Binaiye xu ("Preface to the Vinaya") on the similarity between the teachings of his Neo-Daoist contemporaries and ideas found in the Prajñāpāramitā sūtras.[80] There is also the famous incident (ca. 357) in which Huiyuan (334–416) clarified a point in Daoan's sermons by drawing on ideas from the Zhuangzi, and thus was able to win an opponent over.[81] Such free and easy doctrinal mixing became a main way for the Dharma to spread and for the Chinese to understand it.

It is important that we differentiate this common way of interpreting Buddhism through xuanxue concepts from the practice of geyi ("matching meanings"). Geyi has often been confused with Chinese "Daoist" interpretation of Buddhism yet it actually appears to have been a distinct, rather specialized hermeneutic method seemingly devised by a small group of fourth century Chinese Buddhists to compare lists of categories from Abhidharma texts with similar numerical lists in Chinese texts.[82] Although guided by the implicit theory that the Dharma could only be true if it elaborated upon the wisdom of the Sages, geyi marks a significant departure in that it was consciously devised as a method of explanation and had limited application. Geyi also sought correspondence with numerical lists in Confucian as well as Daoist texts.

Buddhist xuanxue scholars gained a wide audience among the literati, initiating what is often called "gentry Buddhism," which was confined to the literate classes and probably had little to do with popular worship and devotion. With the rise of gentry Buddhism we also see the creation of a new social class, the scholar-monk who lived a religious life yet followed typical xuanxue and qingtan pursuits. The scholar-monk was a variation of the Neo-Daoist "retired gentleman," the learned person who declined office to live a secluded, "natural" life. As Buddhism grew, scholar-monks gained prominence in intellectual circles, becoming some of the leading thinkers of their day. By the fourth century Buddhist xuanxue ("Buddho-Daoism") was a major intellectual movement and it had a lasting impact on Chinese Buddhism. Chinese thinkers used *xuanxue* concepts and terms such as *wu* and *wuwei* in interpreting Buddhist ideas and continued to rely on the basic Buddho-Daoist ontological scheme for centuries.

Perhaps the best examples of Buddho-Daoist mixing were the so-called "*prajñā* schools." These "schools" were part of the *prajñā* movement in China and were all based on earlier translations of the *Prajñāpāramitā sūtras*. The first of these translations, a version of the Asta by Lokakṣema (fl. 168–188) known as the *Daoxing poruo jing*, proved so popular it was re-translated by Zhi Qian (fl. 220–252) and given the new title the *Daming tu jing*.[83] *Prajñā* study increased during the third century as Central Asia missionaries such as Mokṣala (fl. 291) and Dharmarakṣa (266–308) brought new Mahāyāna texts to China, chief among them the *Pañca*.[84] In addition, other Mahāyāna *sūtras* were translated into Chinese during this time and they strongly influenced the formation of the *prajñā* schools. Among the foremost of these texts was the *Vimalakīrti nirdeśa sūtra*.[85] This text, with its depiction of the layman Vimalakīrti vanquishing various monks (including expert Abhidharmist Śāriputra) in debate and receiving lavish praise from the Buddha, was a favorite among the gentry. Many saw in the figure of Vimalakīrti an attainable ideal, even a projection of their own lives of *xuanxue* and *qingtan* as truly religious. The *Vimalakīrti* also centers on the paradoxes of *prajñā* and the Two Truths, and thus shares the same features of the *Prajñāpāramitās* that so fascinated medieval literati.

Traditionally the *prajñā* schools are numbered at six or seven.[86] Jizang (549–623), our best source, claims there were seven although he describes the views of eight teachers. Anchō (763–814), a later commentator, follows Jizang.[87] These schools are:

1. *Benwu* ("School of Original Non-being")
2. *Benwu yi* ("Variant School of Original Non-being")
3. *Jise* ("School of Form/Matter as such")
4. *Xinwu* ("School of Non-existence of Mind")
5. *Shihan* ("School of Stored Impressions")
6. *Huahu* ("School of Illusory Transformations")
7. *Yuanhui* ("School of Causal Combinations")

Reconstructing the schools' tenets is difficult, as surviving sources are fragmentary. Jizang and Anchō give the most details but even their discussions are cryptic.[88] Nonetheless we need to study them as they indicate the variety of interpretations of *prajñā* circulating in China.

1. Benwu ("*Original/Fundamental Non-being*")

This school strongly resembles the views of Wang Bi and may have been the "orthodox" position of Buddhist *xuanxue* thinkers.[89] Jizang says that it was led by Daoan, who taught that emptiness was the "original non-being" that existed before the myriad things evolved. When we realize the truth of this teaching, our ignorance comes to an end. As Jizang says, "What obstructs humanity are derived beings (*moyou*). If the mind abides in *benwu*, erroneous thoughts will cease ... If we examine this idea, we see that according to Daoan's explanation of original non-being, all *dharmas* are in their original nature void and empty, hence the term '*benwu*.'"[90] Anchō essentially says the same thing:

> The monk Daoan says in his *Benwu lun*: when the Tathāgata arose in the world, he proclaimed the teaching of *benwu*. That is why all the *vaipulya* (Mahāyāna) *sūtras* make clear that the five *skandhas* are originally non-existent. The *benwu* doctrine has a long history. Its meaning is that non-being is prior to the first evolution, and emptiness is the beginning of the many forms. Humanity is obstructed by being confined to secondary beings. If mind abides in *benwu*, erroneous thoughts will cease.[91]

The *Benwu lun* has been lost but several of Daoan's prefaces and introductions to *sūtras* survive. Interestingly, he never once uses the term *benwu* in them.[92] The idea of *benwu* as the source of all things owes much to Daoist creation myths but it also shows the influence of Wang Bi's ontological scheme. No doubt as well, Daoan was encouraged in his reading by the sinified translations of the *sūtras*.[93]

There is an intriguing ambiguity in Daoan's view, for it could be that he regards *benwu* in cosmological or ontological terms, or perhaps both. One clue may be that Daoan says that humanity can realize *benwu*, thus eliminating erroneous thoughts—an impossibility if *benwu* were merely cosmological (i.e. if it were the original *temporal* source). Daoan's *benwu* school, then, seems to be based on understanding emptiness in *xuanxue* metaphysical terms. Other teachers associated with the *benwu* school include Zhu Fatai (320–387), a colleague of Daoan's, as well as Huiyuan (334–416) and Zhi Dun (Zhi Daolin, 314–366), although neither Jizang nor Anchō mention them in this regard.[94]

2. Benwu yi ("*Variant School of Original Non-Being*")

Neither Jizang nor Anchō give this school a separate title but they attribute it to Dharma master Fashen (286-374).[95] Jizang writes that Fashen "said that by *benwu* is meant that before there was any *dharma* of form, there was first of all non-being. Therefore being came out of non-being. Since non-being is prior to being, and being exists after non-being, it is called 'original non-being'."[96] Anchō includes more details:

> In the treatise composed by him, he [Shen] says: "*Benwu*, what is it? A void without shapes, yet out of which the ten-thousand things are produced. Though the existent is productive, the non-existent has power to produce things. That is why the Buddha told the Brahmacarin that the four *mahābhūtas* (great elements earth, water, fire, air) arise from emptiness (*kong*)." And in the second part of the chapter on the Two Truths in the fifth book of the *Shanmen xuanyi* it is said "Again there is Chu Fashen who said that all *dharmas* are originally non-existent. The emptiness that is without shapes represents the highest truth; the myriad things produced out of it constitute worldly truth.[97]

Fashen's *benwu* doctrine differs from Daoan's, and appears to rely even more heavily on Daoist creation myths. Fashen equates emptiness with the primal void that first "exists" and then produces the various things; thus he views *śūnyatā* in *cosmological* rather than *ontological* terms. The difference here, though slight, is significant.

3. Jise *("Form/Matter as Such")*

The tenets of this school concern the relationship of *rūpa* and *śūnyatā*.[98] According to Jizang and Anchō, there were two schools by this name. The first was proclaimed by an anonymous teacher in the *guannei* area (lit. "inside the passes"–the environs of Chang'an). This teacher held that *rūpa* as such is empty because it has no self-nature yet *rūpa* is not empty in its original nature.[99] Anchō clarifies this somewhat:

> The theory of this teacher is: Through the conglomeration of fine matter coarse matter is formed. As regards emptiness, it is only coarse matter which is empty and not fine matter. From the point of view of fine matter, coarse matter is not matter itself. Thus in the same way, from the point of view of black color, when there is white color, this white is not color itself. That is why, when it is said that *rūpa* as such is empty, this does not mean that all *rūpa* is entirely non-existent.[100]

This view is that "*rūpa* as such" is empty, lacking a permanent nature while its original underlying nature is not empty. This is because "*rūpa* as such" is coarse, resulting from the conglomeration of finer stuff. It thus, is "empty" whereas the fine is not.[101]

Both Jizang and Anchō agree that there was another *jise* school, that of Zhi Dun, who wrote *Jise yuxuan lun* ("Treatise on Wandering in the Mystery As

Such") to explain that *rūpa* as such is empty. Jizang says that Zhi Dun "speaks of the true state without rejecting temporary names. This is no different form Master Daoan's theory of the emptiness of original nature."[102] Anchō is more descriptive:

> The fifth book of the *Shanmen* says that the eighth was Zhi Daolin, who wrote the *Jise yuxuan lun* in which he says, "As to the nature of *rūpa*, it is not *rūpa* itself. Not being so in itself, though *rūpa*, it is [really] empty. [Similarly] knowing does not know of itself. Though it knows, it remains ever tranquil." His idea here is this: *rūpa* and mind are both empty as to their natures–this is the highest truth. Yet this empty *rūpa* and mind are nowhere non-existent–this is worldly truth. The commentary says that he wrote the *Jise lun* ("Treatise on *rūpa* as such") in which he says, "I maintain that *rūpa* as such is empty and does not need to be destroyed to be so. What does this mean? As for the nature of *rūpa*, it does not exist as *rūpa* of itself. *Rūpa* does not exist of itself, [thus] though *rūpa*, it is [really] empty. [Similarly] knowing does not know of itself, [thus] although it knows, it remains constantly tranquil.[103]

Unfortunately the works these sources quote are now lost but there is enough overlap between these accounts to reconstruct Zhi Dun's view. He says that the nature of *rūpa* as such does not exist of itself, hence it is empty. Nonetheless, *rūpa* still is *rūpa* even though empty. In other words nothing is (ultimately) real yet everything (phenomenally) exists. Awakening to this truth is the key to tranquility. For Zhi Dun, emptiness is the true state of conventionally separate things, a view that may very well be a variation of *benwu* teachings as Jizang notes.

4. Xinwu ("Non-existence of Mind")

Jizang attributes this school to Dharma master Zhu Fawen (fl. ~374), a disciple of Fashen. According to Jizang:

> "Non-existence of mind" is lacking a [deliberate] mind (*wuxin*) towards the ten-thousand things. The ten-thousand things themselves, however, are never non-being. The explanation of this idea is: within the scriptures [it] says that all *dharmas* are empty. The desire [here] is to lead our minds to the substance of reality (*ti*), to be void, "forget" and not grasp [anything]. Thus it speaks of "nothingness." The non-emptiness of external things just is the non-emptiness of the objective sphere of the ten-thousand things.[104]

Anchō, quoting several texts that are now lost, adds:

> Now then, being is what has shape; non-being is what lacks form. Thus "what has shape" cannot mean non-being, and "what lacks form" cannot mean being. Therefore

being is "real being" and *rūpa* "true *rūpa*." As for what the *sūtras* mean by "*rūpa* is empty," it is only to stop the mind within and does not obstruct external *rūpa*. External *rūpa* are [just] no longer preserved by the resultant internal feelings. It is not the case that they are non-being–how could they be? How could this [teaching] really mean all is void, lacking shapes and *rūpa*?[105]

This school seems to teach that emptiness is a "subjective" (epistemic) experience. One should have a non-deliberative (*wu*) mind towards things. Things themselves are not non-existent, and scriptural claims of such are meant to encourage detachment. It is not the case that external things are empty. This is very close to Guo Xiang's view of the Sage as "void" (detached) while in contact with the world.[106] Other figures associated with this school were Zhi Mindu (fl. 326–342) and a monk named Daoheng (d. 417).[107]

5. Shihan ("*Stored Impressions*")

Of this school, Jizang writes:

> The fifth is the theory of *Shihan* founded by Yu Fakai. Its tenets are: the Triple World (*triloka*) is the abode of the long night, and the mind is the basis of a great dream. All that we see is seen in this dream. When we awaken from the great dream, and the long night gets to be dawn, then the consciousness that produces illusions will be extinguished and the Triple World will be seen to be empty. At this time nothing is produced and yet nothing is not produced from it.[108]

Anchō agrees, adding that for Fakai worldly truth is what is seen through illusion while Ultimate truth is the "emptiness" of all things which we realize upon our awakening.[109]

Yu Fakai was a disciple of Yu Falan but there is some confusion regarding his dates.[110] Questions of dates aside, however, his teachings are rather cryptic. Fakai seems to say that the reality we ordinarily experience is illusory, like a dream. Our awakening (it seems to be inevitable) will consist in realizing that our world is a dream, and that what we thought was real will be "empty" (i.e. not real). Even more intriguing, Fakai says that the consciousness that produces our illusory life will be extinguished upon our awakening. None of the other *prajñā* schools speaks of anything comparable. Wing-tsit Chan translates this school as "consciousness contained in spirit," basing this on Tang's contention that Fakai distinguished "consciousness" (*shi*) from spirit (*shen*), with the former serving as the function of the latter. Thus it would be spirit that awakens.[111] This is a plausible interpretation since most Chinese Buddhists of the time believed in an immortal *shen* and much of Daoist cultivation centered on purifying one's *shen* so that it could rise up and meld with the cosmic *shen* of the universe.

6. Huahu ("*Phenomenal Illusion*")

The leader of this school was Daoyi (d. 401), a disciple of Zhu Fatai.[112] The tenets of his school are sketchy but according to Jizang, Daoyi taught that *dharmas* of worldly truth are like illusory transformations, hence the *sūtras* say that from the very beginning they have never existed.[113] Ancho is more informative, quoting Daoyi as saying that "All *dharmas* are equally illusory and so constitute worldly truth. But the Spiritual Mind is true and not empty, and so is ultimate truth. For if Spirit were also empty, to whom could the Dharma be taught, and who would cultivate the path, renounce the world and become a sage? Thus we know that Spirit is not empty."[114]

Daoyi states that everyday phenomena are like illusions and have never really existed. That is worldly truth. However, beneath this level is an immortal (hence real) *shen*. Spirit constitutes the "substance" of humanity and persists through time. It is not empty, and so Daoyi considers it to be the realm of Ultimate truth.

7. Yuanhui ("*Combining of Conditions*")

Jizang says this school was led by Yu Daosui (fl. 360), a disciple of Yu Falan.[115] Daosui held that existence is due to combining of conditions (*yuanhui*) and this is worldly truth. When these conditions disperse, there is non-being, which is the "Truth of One Meaning" (Ultimate Truth).[116] Anchō explains this view through the analogy of a house made of clay and wood. The clay and wood combine to make the house, hence it exists. Before then the house was only a name. After the clay and wood disintegrate the house will once again exist in name only.[117]

Daosui's theory is based on *pratītya-samutpāda* but his interpretation seems more Hīnayāna than Mahāyāna. The everyday "things" of conventional reality are the result of various causes and conditions and these "things" will no longer exist when the conditions that produced them disperse. Daosui seems to have only partially understood emptiness, seeing it as the basic impermanence of things realized when they no longer exist.

Interpreting the Prajñā Schools

The *prajñā* schools, as we can see, are puzzling and difficult to sort out. Clearly they are all attempts to understand the teachings of the *Prajñāpāramitās* but there are problems with our accounts of them. Our sources are fragmentary and show much confusion over the schools' tenets, teachers and their dates. Over the past few decades scholars have differed considerably in their assessments of them, particularly the *xinwu* school. Paul Demieville considers Mindu's version of the *xinwu* theory to be "hardly Buddhistic" and merely part of the *xuanxue* debates on *you* and *wu*. Leon Hurvitz, by contrast, says "the proponents of this view came remarkably close to a proper understanding of *śūnyatā* only to wreck it with their conclusions. That the concept of "emptiness" is an epistemic one they understood perfectly, but then went on to say that beyond the senses is a world of objective reality."[118] Whalen Lai alone takes the view that *xinwu* marks an improvement over the other schools, being an attempt to get at the teaching of *anattā*.[119] At least a few of the schools were contemporaneous since their proponents debated one another but it is likely that some schools arose later than others.[120]

Although each school presents a different interpretation, they all share the basic characteristics of *xuanxue* Buddhism and, like their Indian counterparts, were striving to grasp the essence of *prajñā*. At first blush, though, the Chinese *prajñā* schools seem not to be about *prajñā* but rather the nature of reality. That is, they tend to focus on ontology rather than epistemology, although they do not wholly neglect the latter since they all maintain that insight into the nature of reality is a mark of spiritual development. We see this clearly, for instance, in Daoan's insistence that insight into *benwu* allows humanity to become "unobstructed" and Zhi Dun's statements that knowing *rūpa* is empty leads to "tranquility." This is a main characteristic of *prajñā* in Indian Buddhism as well. However, the *prajñā* schools arose in China and as such, they have to be understood in an intellectual context dominated by *xuanxue* arguments about the nature of the Sage, what the Sage knows and how to attain such knowledge.

We can easily see how the *prajñā* thinkers were guided by Chinese concepts in their interpretations of *prajñā* teachings when we examine their views. *Ben wu* may be the most obvious example. This phrase *"benwu"* clearly points to the basic *xuanxue* ontological scheme first articulated by Wang Bi in which one realizes the "non-being" at the very heart of "being." While some thinkers conceived this as a temporal process (e.g. Fashen's *benwu yi* school) others such as Daoan seem to have realized that the two aspects are always together, much like the Two Truths. Zhi Dun's *jise* school seems to be another way of getting at this same notion through the concepts of *rūpa* and *śūnyatā*.

The *xinwu* school is another good example. According to *xinwu* theorists, we realize emptiness by "emptying our minds." This seems to be a detachment similar to that advocated in the *Prajñāpāramitās* but it is also very Daoist. Most likely the idea of *xinwu* is based on the notion of *wuxin* ("no mind"), one of what David Hall and Roger Ames call the "*wu* forms"–words expressing a typically Daoist form of deference that involves putting oneself in another's place. Thus *wuxin* marks a way of comportment perhaps best described as "non-deliberative."[121] We have no indication, though, that *xinwu* thinkers grasped the emptiness of ordinary "things" or *dharmas* however. Thus they miss the full ontological import of the *Prajñāpāramitās*.

In addition, the traditional Chinese notion of *shen* figures prominently in some *prajñā* schools, specifically *shihan* and *huahu*. *Shen* is deeply rooted in Chinese religion and is considered to be the "spiritual" aspect of a person that can be cultivated to join with the cosmos at the time of death. Such release is how one attains immortality.

It is important to note that from an Indian Buddhist perspective the *prajñā* schools make numerous mistakes. Most commonly, they collapse the Two Truths to the level of conventional truth and view *śūnyatā* cosmologically, as a moment in creation rather than the true nature of all things. Several schools also hold fast to the notion of an eternal "soul" (*shen*), seemingly in direct opposition to the Buddha's teaching of *anattā*. Although on this basis some might wish to dismiss these schools as "un-Buddhist," we should beware of doing so. At the very least such a stance assumes a single perspective ("Indian Buddhism") as the only legitimate one when even in India there were numerous "Buddhisms." In China Buddhism and Daoism were often conflated at first, and many if not most literati were ignorant of their own naivete. Even educated scholar-monks continued to cling to the notion of an immortal *shen* for decades despite **Kumārajīva**'s consistent explanations of *anattā*.[122] A key factor here seems to be that several of the *prajñā* teachers interpreted the strange language of the *sūtras* literally, taking claims about the illusory nature of everyday perception and the "nothingness" of *śūnyatā* at their word. One of Sengzhao's strengths is that he does not fall prey to such an error.

When all is said and done, the Chinese *prajñā* schools do not fit easily with Indian notions of *prajñā*. This is not surprising since their proponents only had access to Buddhist teachings by way of Chinese translations. Until the fifth century only two *Prajñāpāramitā sūtras* had been translated into Chinese (the *Aṣṭa* and the *Pañca*). Yet despite this paucity of original texts a range of interpretations emerged. Not only were there the several schools, but some (e.g. *benwu, jise, xinwu*) included various subschools and these sometimes differed widely.[123] Such a variety of interpretations indicates that there were many "Buddhisms" in China at this time, just as there were in India. This plurality of competing Buddhisms has been a prominent feature of Chinese history down to the present, and parallels the various Dao's of the Warring States era. The *prajñā* schools thus are far more important than generally recognized, for even if they were rather short-lived, they set the stage for future developments.

Moreover, philosophical hermeneutics can provide further insight into the *prajñā* schools and challenge previous scholarly interpretations of them. As Heidegger, Gadamer, and Ricoeur argue, our ways of understanding are rooted in our own socio-cultural situation. We are informed by our cultural conditioning and it is only with much effort and risk that we are ever able to move beyond our original horizons. Buddhism's entry into China provides a large-scale illustration of this process. Despite problems with the historical records, the *prajñā* schools give us our most detailed view of an early moment in the sinification of Dharma when Chinese thinkers were pushing against the confines of their conceptual categories. The Chinese were reaching towards the meaning of the Dharma as proclaimed by missionaries and in translated texts. They did so on the basis of their Confucian-Daoist heritage, and continued to work towards further understanding through more study and their own writings.

Shifting our perspective slightly reveals another aspect of the *prajñā* schools that has been all-but ignored until now, the political rather than strictly philosophical nature of their conflicts. This subject warrants our close attention, as contemporary hermeneutics makes such unmasking of power relations part of achieving a fully hermeneutical understanding. We cannot forget that the *prajñā* schools arose in the midst of great political instability. "China" at the time was a patchwork of small states, each riven by internal conflicts and often at war with its neighbors. The monks of the *prajñā* schools were caught up in these same conflicts since they derived support directly from state governments and wealthy aristocrats. The rivalries between the *prajñā* schools thus have a highly political sub-text, and undoubtedly mirror the oppositions among the powerful clans and the beleaguered imperial courts of both north and south.

Clearly Wing-tsit Chan's characterization of the *prajñā* schools as being based on "individual philosophers and isolated theories without any systematic philosophy,"[124] needs revision. Not only were these schools *not* the products of isolated thinkers pondering the mysteries of *prajñā* behind cloistered walls, they were part of a lively cultural conversation, a true conflict of interpretations that had lasting repercussions. Moreover, this conflict appears to have had a decidedly political subtext. Certainly several figures associated with the *prajñā* schools (e.g. Zhidun) rubbed elbows with the more cultured aristocrats of their day, with many monks coming from the gentry classes. As a result, they were often caught up in the rivalries between warring families, and undoubtedly the conflicts between the *prajñā* schools were influenced by these "secular" rivalries. All in all, we still have much to learn about the "politics of *prajñā*" in early medieval China.

The differing views of the *prajñā* schools highlight the heterogeneity of early Chinese Buddhism and point to important political influences behind the intellectual scene. *Prajñā* was the subject of varied interpretations. Sengzhao was certainly well aware of these and his essays were important responses to this situation. However Sengzhao's work was also heavily influenced by Kumārajīva, the Mādhyamika master whose arrival in Chang'an marks a major turn in Chinese understanding of the Dharma.

Kumārajīva and a New Hermeneutic Turn

Kumārajīva's Life

Kumārajīva was probably the most important foreign monk in the history of Chinese Buddhism. An unparalleled translator and exegete, his work propagating Mahāyāna in China ushered in a more mature understanding of the Dharma. The accounts of his life have all the trappings of a grand epic and betray the exaggeration typical of haggiography.[125] He was born in the mid-fourth century (there is confusion over the exact year) into an illustrious family in Kuchā, a powerful kingdom along the Silk Road. He entered monastic life at the age of six and proved so precocious he was sent to India where he rapidly mastered all Buddhist and non-Buddhist teachings. At twelve Kumārajīva went to Kashgar to study the Sarvāstivādin Abhidharma and there he encountered the Mahāyāna for the first time. Allegedly he was so astonished by the notion of *śūnyatā* that his struggles led to a deep awakening. Afterwards he immersed himself in Mahāyāna studies, especially the writings of Nāgārjuna and Āryadeva. Eventually Kumārajīva returned to Kuchā and took full ordination. His reputation for wisdom spread throughout Asia and monks flocked to Kuchā to be in his presence.

By 379 **Kumārajīva**'s fame had reached Chang'an, then under the rule of Fu Jian (338–385), one of the "barbarian" rulers of the North. Although a despot, Fu Jian was a devout Buddhist who was anxious to help the Dharma spread. Earlier he had brought Daoan to Chang'an to be *guoshi* ("national preceptor") and oversee the propagation of Buddhist texts. It was Daoan who established the official translation bureau in Chang'an that marked a fundamental change in Chinese translation practices, and it was Daoan who urged the Emperor to send for **Kumārajīva**. **Kumārajīva** was equally impressed with Daoan's reputation and at times would "worship him and pay him homage from afar."[126] Fu Jian sent general Lu Guang to conquer **Kuchā** in 382–383 and take **Kumārajīva** prisoner. En route back to Chang'an Lu learned of Fu Jian's overthrow and changed his plans. Lu set up a new state, the Latter Liang, where he ruled for seventeen years, keeping **Kumārajīva** prisoner as his "advisor." During this period the Yao clan, the new rulers of Chang'an, repeatedly made offers for **Kumārajīva** but Lu refused. Finally in 401 Emperor Yao Xing overthrew the Liang state and brought **Kumārajīva** and his entourage back to Chang'an as spoils of war. There **Kumārajīva** was installed as *guoshi* and placed in charge of the translation bureau that Daoan had set up.

Kumārajīva's Translation Activities

Kumārajīva was a great translator of Buddhist texts. At present there are fifty-two translations in the *Taishō* under his name and their authenticity is fairly well accepted. These are mainly "*Prajñā* Buddhist" works (the *Aṣṭa*, *Pañca*, "Heart" and "Diamond" *sūtras*, treatises by **Nāgārjuna** and **Āryadeva**) but also include works from the **Sarvāstivāda** Abhidharma along with devotional and meditation texts. This wide assortment indicates that **Kumārajīva**'s view of "Mahāyāna" embraced all existing sects and practices although he stressed *prajñā* teachings and the Bodhisattva path. **Kumārajīva** retranslated many previously translated texts in addition to translating new texts from Kucha and those stockpiled in Chang'an. His translations were often done at the request of donors or his disciples but also according to his own tastes.[127]

As we have seen, *prajñā* was very perplexing to the Chinese and **Kumārajīva** set out to correct their views through his translations. His translations, thus, were explicitly hermeneutic in that they were attempts to deepen understanding of the Dharma and correct previous misunderstandings. In so doing he faced several difficulties, most notably the language barrier. The majority of Chinese at this time could only approach Buddhism through translations employing *xuanxue* terms and concepts.[128] Before the fifth century few Chinese had even a rudimentary knowledge of Sanskrit or other Indic languages and the scholar-monks of the fourth century seem to have ignored Sanskrit entirely.[129] To a great extent this encouraged the Chinese in their "Daoist" readings since for them the Dharma came already clothed in Daoist and Confucian terminology through early translations.[130] Kumārajīva challenged the "Daoist" interpretations of Buddhism with his knowledge of Indic languages although it is unclear how well he knew Chinese. He most certainly did not have command of the literary Chinese prized by *xuanxue* scholars and so he relied heavily on his senior disciples as editors and translators.

Kumārajīva took great pains in his translations. He began with the structure and methods that Daoan had established, and employed many of the same people. There is evidence that some of Daoan's followers disagreed with these methods, even considering them "sacrilegious" and leading to the distortion of the Buddha's message.[131] Others however accepted and tried to follow Daoan's principles while translating with Kumārajīva. Sengrui, one of the chief scribes, writes, "[When I] held the brush, I thought three times about my former master's (Daoan) instructions about the five deviations and three difficulties."[132] Kumārajīva tried to adhere to Daoan's principles, revising earlier translations mainly when it came to technical terms. However, his revisions were often extensive. In Sengrui's biography we read:

> Sengrui edited the *sūtras* that Kumārajīva translated. Previously Dharmarakṣa had issued the *Saddharma-puṇḍarīka sūtra*. The chapter on "Prediction" says, "The gods see humans and humans see the gods." [When] Kumārajīva was translating the *sūtra* and reached this passage he said, "These words and the western text have the same meaning but [the Chinese] adheres to the words yet goes beyond the substance. Sengrui said, "Should it not be 'Humans and gods are in contact and so both see each other'?" Kumārajīva said, "It is truly so."[133]

Although this is a minor change it shows how Kumārajīva relied on his disciples to make his translations conform to Chinese tastes while struggling to capture the Sanskrit. At times Kumārajīva seems to have abridged some texts (mainly *śāstras* rather than *sūtras*) to a great extent due to pressures from his audience. Huiyuan, for instance, writes in a preface to a condensed version of the *Dazhi du lun* that Kumārajīva's abridgement left out more than three times the amount translated yet was still considered too verbose by Chinese scholars.[134]

The actual translation process included several stages with much discussion and explanation of the texts' meaning. Typically Kumārajīva held the text and explained its meaning twice in Chinese. When passages were missing he tried to obtain another copy. Yao Xing himself was often present during these sessions, examining the texts and the Sanskrit originals. The Chinese monks would mull over the texts, trying to grasp the details of their teachings while also passing judgment on their literary style. Kumārajīva consistently worked to clarify points in the Chinese by checking with the original. Only after long study and discussion by all parties did the monks actually commit the text to writing.[135] No doubt it was a complicated situation in which Kumārajīva was teaching his aides the very ideas they were supposed to be translating.

Furthermore these oral translations were public events. Indeed, they were sacred ceremonies attended with religious devotion by hundreds of people. Thus Kumārajīva was performing as well as teaching and translating. Once the text (often with the accompanying explanations) was written down, it was repeatedly revised and polished.[136] Differences and deviations from the Sanskrit and the oral explanation were inevitable.

Kumārajīva's translation work was an intensely hermeneutic undertaking. It seems to have been very self-conscious in some respects but not so in others. Certainly Kumārajīva guided the translations but other perspectives were brought to bear on them. The transmission of Kumārajīva's version of Mahāyāna was thus not a simple, straight-forward process and was conditioned by a multitude of factors including the biases of Kumārajīva, his disciples and scribes, and the very structure of the Chang'an translation bureau. We cannot expect the result to be the same as Indian Mahāyāna, something we need to bear in mind when examining his view of *prajñā* and when we turn to Seng-zhao, who had an intimate role in this transmission.

Kumārajīva's View of Prajñā

Despite his vast body of translation work, evidence for Kumārajīva's *own* view of *prajñā* is difficult to come by. He composed only one original treatise, the *Shixiang lun* ("Treatise on the Real Mark of Things") but this is now lost.[137] Kumārajīva was a translator and exegete, not a Buddhist philosopher such as Nāgārjuna or a *xuanxue* essayist like Sengzhao. What's more, the translations bearing Kumārajīva's name are the products of the official translation bureau and thus are "team efforts" that passed through many hands. Although scholars agree that they bear the imprint of Kumārajīva's personality, it would be wrong to regard him as their sole author. We must therefore treat Kumārajīva's translations cautiously as sources for his personal views.

Fortunately there are other sources that provide more direct evidence of Kumārajīva's notion of *prajñā*, but the references in them are scattered. One of the best sources is his correspondence with Huiyuan regarding Mahāyāna doctrine.[138] This exchange took place in the early fifth century and was instigated by Huiyuan to clarify points for his own understanding. At this time Kumārajīva was fully immersed in his translation activity and he quotes liberally from various *sūtras* and *śāstras* to get his points across. Not surprisingly, he proves himself an orthodox Mādhyamika, although he claims he is merely proclaiming Mahāyāna doctrine.[139]

Kumārajīva's explanations are virtually identical to the views of Nāgārjuna and other Mādhyamikas, stressing the emptiness of all *dharmas* (even the "emptiness of emptiness") and the Bodhisattva's non-attachment to all things and teachings.[140] Like both the *Prajñāpāramitā sūtras* and Mādhyamika commentaries Kumārajīva says that the Buddha's teachings ultimately come from and lead us to a level beyond words and thought.[141] Because the Buddha and Bodhisattvas reside in this transcendent realm (which is none other than our present world) their wisdom enables them to use various *upāya* to lead suffering beings to enlightenment. Apparent contradictions and confusions in Buddhist texts are due to their *upāya*, which accommodate to the audience's level and lead them to truth.[142] Kumārajīva even suggests that the teachings in the *sūtras* may delude those who are unprepared, i.e. at a lower level of understanding.[143]

According to Kumārajīva, we truly understand the Dharma only when we attain complete and pure *prajñā*. *Prajñā* is the means of removing all obstacles and hindrances, all attachments–even attachments to itself. As Kumārajīva says, "In the Buddha-Dharma, the medicine of *prajñā* is just like this. By this medicine one demolishes the objects of addictions. If within *prajñā* beings then conceive addiction, [then] one must practice a method of treatment. If within *prajñā* there are no addictions to *prajñā*, then further treatment is not applied."[144]

Most of these ideas concerning *prajñā* are echoed in the *Dazhidu lun*, the great treatise attributed to Nāgārjuna but which in its present form is actually a transcript of Kumārajīva's explanations during translation sessions.[145] In this treatise the author-translator emphasizes "great wisdom" (*dazhi, mahāprajñā*) as abandoning and separating from all things.[146] Indeed, *prajñāpāramitā* is not coursing in or acquiring *any dharma whatsoever*.[147] Kumārajīva describes such practice as "right thought" in which one cuts off all discriminations.[148] By practicing "right thought" etc. one attains *prajñā* that transcends all dualities such as "defilement and purification" and "wisdom and non-wisdom".[149] *Prajñā* even transcends the duality of *samsāra* and *nirvāṇa*.[150] According to Kumārajīva as well, *prajñā* reveals the emptiness of all things and the "emptiness of emptiness" itself.[151] Although he speaks more explicitly about *prajñā* than Nāgārjuna does in most of his writings, Kumārajīva clearly is in line with him on these points.

Moreover, Kumārajīva goes on at even greater length about *prajñā* in many passages, extolling its virtues in the same fashion as the *Prajñāpāramitā sūtras* until it becomes impossible to define. At points, *prajñā* is the act of knowing and the eternal ultimate principle of knowledge. *Prajñā* has various levels and names, includes all types of "knowing" but ultimately is one, the all-knowing (*sarvākarajñāta*) of the Buddhas which inspires the Bodhisattvas in their striving.[152] Yet since *prajñā* transcends all distinctions it is not just "knowing" but also the real of nature of things, the undeniable indestructible *dharma* which is constant and eternal.[153]

For Kumārajīva, *prajñā* is all encompassing, beyond distinctions between "subject" and "object," "self" and "other." It embraces epistemology and ontology. It is little wonder, then, that he declares we cannot grasp *prajñā* with our ignorant minds:

> The *dharma* that is called *prajñapāramitā* is most profound, difficult to apprehend. [In their real nature which is the same as *prajñāpāramitā*] all *dharmas* are entirely devoid of all determinate natures, thus *prajñāpāramitā* [the real nature of things] is truly profound. In it all thoughts and all activities of mind come to an end, thus it is difficult to see. Moreover, in it there is no clinging even to *prajñāpāramitā* and thus it is said to be difficult to comprehend. In it the three poisons (delusion, hatred, desire) and all kinds of *prapañca* (conceptual elaboration) come to an end and thus it is called peace. Attaining the wondrous taste of *prajñā*, one realizes a permanent fulfillment and there is nothing more sought. All other kinds of *prajñā* are coarse, rough, devoid of joy, thus this *prajñā* is called most wondrous.[154]

Kumārajīva proclaims that *prajñā* eludes our attempts at conceptualizing it because all concepts are marks of attachment. Ultimately *prajñā* has little to do with arguing and wrangling and everything to do with moral/spiritual cultivation. It could be that such passages are direct responses to the debates among the Chinese *prajñā* schools although we cannot be certain.

From all of these passages we can see that Kumārajīva espoused an all-inclusive "Mahāyāna" at the center of which was a complex, multi-faceted notion of *prajñā* derived from Mādhyamika works and the *Prajñāpāramitā sūtras*. Clearly he was an "orthodox" Mādhyamika, although his views betray a more positive approach than the typical negative dialectics of Nāgārjuna. This difference probably stems from their different roles rather than any philosophical disagreement; Nāgārjuna was writing to other Buddhists and arguing over technical aspects of the Dharma whereas Kumārajīva was a missionary-translator devoted to expounding Mahāyāna to the Chinese.

Kumārajīva was a true follower of Nāgārjuna and Āryadeva quite dedicated to proclaiming their message. He was a man of immense learning with a distinct air of authority (no doubt bolstered by his official status in Kucha and Chang'an) yet had a kindly nature. He was well suited to bring order to *prajñā* studies and he attracted scholars from all over Asia. One of these was Sengzhao, a young monk eager to learn who needed a master to lead him through the convoluted notions of *prajñā* in his day.

Sengzhao's Life and Training

Sengzhao's Biography

Sengzhao came of age amidst the currents of *xuanxue* speculation and *prajñā* studies. We are fortunate in that several sources discussing his life still exist, the most important being Sengzhao's biography in the *Gaosengzhuan*. In addition, there are brief accounts of Sengzhao's life in other works including commentaries on his essays,[155] and we can adduce some things from his own writings. Sengzhao seems to have lived from 374–414[156] and spent most of his life in the Chang'an area. His family was poor so he worked as a copyist. Through his work he became especially fond of the *Laozi* and the *Zhuangzi* but upon reading the *Vimalakīrti* he converted to Buddhism and became a monk. Learning of Kumārajīva's captivity, Sengzhao journeyed west to join him in Liang, returning to Chang'an in 401 when Kumārajīva was brought back by Yao Xing. Yao Xing appointed Sengzhao to the Changan translation bureau where he served as an assistant while attending expositions of Buddhist texts. He wrote various essays, prefaces and commentaries and was commissioned by Yao Xing to write Kumārajīva's obituary after his master's death in 413. Sengzhao himself died of unknown causes a year later.

None of the surviving accounts of Sengzhao's life, of course, can be accepted as the full truth, as they are all mediated by authorial bias, in some cases were written long after his death and probably draw on sources that are not mentioned. Thus we must rely on them with caution. Moreover, as with my reconstruction of the *prajñā* schools, so I must remain aware that here I am also taking fragmentary evidence from previous accounts and producing my own interpretation of Sengzhao's life.

Several aspects of Sengzhao's life warrant special attention, for they mark him as different from his contemporaries and may provide clues for interpreting his writings. From an early age he was drawn to Daoist texts, especially the *Laozi* and the *Zhuangzi*. We know nothing about his family of origin or even his given name, and the biographical silence around this is curious. Unlike the typical scholar-monk, Sengzhao was not from the gentry class but had to support himself by working as a copyist. It is unclear what this position entailed, but it obviously was not an official post, as his biographers would certainly have noted this. Most likely he was a low-level scribe who had neither the opportunity nor the resources to pursue a life akin to the "Seven Worthies."

We also know little about Sengzhao's education. Despite his humble origins he earned a reputation as one of the foremost *xuanxue* thinkers in the Chang'an area.[157] Huijiao says he attained his learning through his profession, reading the *jing* as well as the *Histories*, but such informal schooling seems insufficient for a literatus. A true *xuanxue* scholar needed to be versed in a wide range of literature as well as the *li*, the rituals of etiquette and social grace, and, as several sources make clear, had to conduct themselves according to meticulous rituals.[158] A minor scribe would not be in a position to acquire such learning so Sengzhao must have received more formal training. We know from his writings that he read the *Analects* and the *Yijing* in addition to the *Laozi* and *Zhuangzi* and most certainly knew the commentaries on them.[159] It seems likely, then, that he was educated through monastic schools, advancing into learned circles only after becoming a monk.

Yet Sengzhao was not merely one of the many *xuanxue* scholars in the Chang'an area. He was reputed to be brilliant. Some of his contemporaries were quite jealous yet they held him in awe. Wei Shou gives us a hint of his abilities:

> Daorung (a fellow disciple) and the others were all knowledgeable and [their] learning was penetrating [but] no one was Sengzhao's superior. When Kumārajīva was translating Sengzhao always 'held the brush' and defined the meaning of terms. He commented on the *Vimalakīrti* and also published several treatises. They all have wondrous meaning and scholars venerate them.[160]

Sengzhao invariably refers to his own talents with modesty but Kumārajīva held him in high regard. Undoubtedly it was Sengzhao's reputation and close association with Kumārajīva that led Yao Xing to appoint him a member of the translation bureau.

A notable aspect of Sengzhao's biography concerns his conversion to Buddhism upon reading the *Vimalakīrti*. This text, as we have noted, was immensely popular in Buddho-Daoist circles and the figure of Vimalakīrti was often upheld as an ideal. For Sengzhao to be convinced to "convert" by this text, then, entailed no great leap of faith on his part. Yet this text must have had an incredibly powerful effect on Sengzhao, for it prompted him to venture west to study with Kumārajīva. To undertake such an arduous journey and even to share in the captivity of the Kuchean Master indicates Sengzhao's deep commitment to explore the mysteries of the Dharma.

Curiously, in Sengzhao's biography we find no mention of any master before he went to study with Kumārajīva. This would technically be impossible since all monks had a master overseeing their novitiates. In all probability the biographical silence means his master was not a monk of great repute ("eminent" in Huijiao's sense) although we cannot be sure. Nonetheless, this absence of a master during his formative period is rare in biographies of eminent monks. We also have no idea when Sengzhao went to Liang although it was obviously well after 383.

Like many scholar-monks, Sengzhao attained a highly privileged position during his prime. When Yao Xing brought Kumārajīva to Chang'an, Sengzhao accompanied him as one of the revered "inner circle" of disciples. Sengzhao was part of the translation bureau and played a key role in the translation process. Although we cannot tell which translations he took part in, he very likely had a hand in producing many texts that bear Kumārajīva's name since unlike other disciples (e.g. Daosheng) Sengzhao never seems to have left the Chang'an area after his appointment. He remained with his master, participating in translations and attending expositions of Buddhist texts until Kumārajīva's death in 412. Sengzhao thus was an "imperial monk" and would have commanded a great authority in the *saṅgha*, just as Daoan and Zhi Dun did before him. This aura of authority extended to Sengzhao's treatises and lent them further weight, as we can see in Yimin's correspondence and remarks by Sengzhao's commentators.[161]

Sengzhao's reputation has led to numerous works being attributed to him over the years although only a few (approximately fourteen) survive.[162] While this may seem a paltry number, it amounts to the largest body of work by a monk of the Wei-Jin era. On this basis alone Sengzhao would be a significant figure. Furthermore, his writings also show remarkable literary skill, subtlety, and rhetorical flourish ... qualities that mark him as a creative spirit open to depths of experience and capable of great flights of imagination.

The Role of Hermeneutics in Reconstructing Sengzhao

We need to be careful with the account of Sengzhao's life I have given for it is by no means a straight reading of "the facts." To begin with, Sengzhao's biography reads like the life of a stereotypical "eminent scholar-monk," someone too good to be true. John Kieschnick has noted several defining characteristics of the scholar-monk: the ability to memorize texts quickly, deep understanding of their teachings, artistic leanings, eloquence in exposition, and skill in debate.[163] The aspects of Sengzhao that I have emphasized (scholarly but of humble origins, brilliant yet modest, loyal to his master, devoted to the Dharma study but with the heart of a poet) coincide with Kieschnick's list to an uncanny degree. Thus our sources have predisposed us to view Sengzhao as a "genius" and to regard his writings as masterly works of philosophical literature. We approach them as sources of deep insight into the Buddha Dao and so it should be no surprise that we, like Sengzhao's contemporaries, find them full of profound meanings.

Moreover, if the "scholar-monk" was something of a stock character in Chinese literature of the fifth and sixth centuries, Sengzhao's biographers also employ other literary devices and embellishments. We see indications of this in some of the details of his life. For instance, Sengzhao's humble origins recall passages in the *Laozi* (chapter 70) and the *Analects* (7.15). His fondness for Daoist texts may be a veiled reference to the Daoist notion of *ziran*, and his natural brilliance is echoed in biographies of other eminent monks. Furthermore, it is no coincidence that he allegedly converted to Buddhism from reading the *Vimalakīrti*, a perennial favorite of Chinese intellectuals. To a large extent, then, "Sengzhao" comes to us as a literary figure, a character created by his biographers whom I also create in reading and writing about him.

Note that these reflections do not mean that I believe Sengzhao never existed or that his biographies are works of fiction. I am only pointing out factors that have influenced my own interpretation of Sengzhao. Biography, like any history, is a hermeneutic enterprise always open to question. We cannot obtain an uninterpreted account of Sengzhao's life, only interpretations of his life based on the traces found in the *Gaosengzhuan* and other sources. We must use them carefully. The interpretive portrait I have sketched takes into account the available evidence and helps further our work in at least two ways. First, it keeps us mindful of the hermeneutic character of the present study. In so doing we remain conscious of the open-ended and dialogic nature of interpretation and so continue striving for a fully *hermeneutical* understanding. Second, my interpretive portrait sheds light on Sengzhao's writings as part of his own textual struggles with Buddhist teachings and Confucian-Daoist traditions. In this portrait we see a man well-suited to enter into the contested arena of *prajñā* studies during his time.

Sengzhao faced a situation in which *prajñā* had multiple meanings and associations. As he observes, "discussions of different teachings [of *prajñā*] have caused confusion for a long time."[164] There was no uniform conception of *prajñā* but many different interpretations. Through his studies Sengzhao reached a deep but critical understanding and on this basis composed "*Prajñā* is Not-knowing." It is to this essay that we turn in the next chapter.ways. First, it keeps us mindful of the hermeneutic character of the present study. In so doing we remain conscious of the open-ended and dialogic nature of interpretation and so continue striving for a fully *hermeneutical* understanding. Second, my interpretive portrait sheds light on Sengzhao's writings as part of his own textual struggles with Buddhist teachings and Confucian-Daoist traditions. In this portrait we see a man well-suited to enter into the contested arena of *prajñā* studies during his time.

Sengzhao faced a situation in which *prajñā* had multiple meanings and associations. As he observes, "discussions of different teachings [of *prajñā*] have caused confusion for a long time."[164] There was no uniform conception of *prajñā* but many different interpretations. Through his studies Sengzhao reached a deep but critical understanding and on this basis composed "*Prajñā* is Not-knowing." It is to this essay that we turn in the next chapter.

· 3 ·

"PRAJÑĀ IS NOT-KNOWING"
AND SENGZHAO'S "WILD WORDS"

As we have seen, China was in great intellectual ferment after the fall of the Han dynasty. With the official "Confucian" orthodoxy discredited as the empire disintegrated into separate territories, other schools of thought rose to the fore. In many respects the era resembled the Warring States era with its competing views of Dao. Buddhism, which had entered China in the Latter Han, was having increasing influence throughout Chinese society, especially among those drawn to Daoism, since its teachings seemed to echo themes in texts such as the *Daode jing*. Thus it was only natural that Chinese thinkers interpreted Buddhism along Daoist lines. The Buddho-Daoism that developed out of these early interpretations came to dominate intellectual circles but led to much confusion. Some of this confusion was due to the nature of the Buddhist *sūtras*, which had been sources of conflicting interpretation even in India. Such conflicts only increased when Buddhist texts were translated into Chinese. Early translations were clumsy and relied on Chinese scholars who knew little of Indian culture or languages. This situation prevailed until **Kumārajīva** came to Chang'an and presented Buddhism in a systematic fashion.

It is at this point that Sengzhao entered the picture—truly the right man in the right place at the right time. His native intelligence, *xuanxue* training, and strong desire to learn carried him to the forefront of **Kumārajīva**'s disciples. As an integral part of the Chang'an translation bureau, Sengzhao attended lectures and eagerly sought out his master for further explanations. It was only a matter of time before he took up his own brush in the service of the Dharma.

"Prajñā is Not-Knowing"—A Brief History and Overview

"*Prajñā* is Not-knowing" draws on earlier Chinese ideas of Buddhism and Kumārajīva's more orthodox views, but the essay is not a mere synthesis. According to the *Gaosengzhuan*:

> Sengzhao realized that the former Sages had long since departed and that the meaning of their words had become confused. Previous translations sometimes had strayed into error. When he saw Kumārajīva, he would consult with him and ask questions, and so increased his comprehension still more. Thus it was that after the translation of the *Pañca* (~403–404) Sengzhao wrote the essay "*Prajñā* is Not-knowing," totaling a little over two thousand words. Upon finishing, he presented [the essay] to Kumārajīva, who studied it and praised its skill. He then said to Sengzhao, "My explanations do not yield to yours but in [their] appropriate expression [we might] benefit each other."[1]

Clearly Sengzhao was able to articulate the mysterious subject of *prajñā*, so long a source of bewilderment, in an especially incisive fashion. Kumārajīva's praise for "*Prajñā* is Not-knowing" probably lent it additional authority. The essay circulated among literati and by 408 had reached Lu Shan, where both Huiyuan and Liu Yimin received it with enthusiasm.[2] Thus "*Prajñā* is Not-knowing" achieved wide-recognition in the early fifth century. What was it about the essay that made it so highly esteemed?

The thesis of "*Prajñā* is Not-knowing" is not difficult to comprehend. From the title we can infer that for Sengzhao, *prajñā* is "not-knowing." By this he does not mean that *prajñā* has no cognitive power, only that it differs from the ordinary knowing which demarcates "objects" and which operates on the basis of preconceived ideas (i.e. the basic *avidyā* underlying human existence). Such knowing is "selfish," influenced by the desires and attachments of *saṃsāric* existence. *Prajñā* is free from such, hence one who has *prajñā* responds appropriately to all situations. *Prajñā*, then, is not so much "not-knowing" as "all-knowing" (*sarvājñā*), for it calmly "mirrors" the True Nature of things.

"*Prajñā* is Not-knowing" fits well with the Buddhist and *xuanxue* discussions of the day. Indeed, much in the treatise is not particularly original. The essay's theme (the nature of the Sage/Bodhisattva) is a tried and true one for

Buddhist and Chinese thinkers, and Sengzhao borrows many ideas and expressions from previous sources.[3] Nonetheless, "*Prajñā* is Not-knowing" has several distinguishing characteristics.

To begin with, "*Prajñā* is Not-knowing" arises out of an *explicit* recognition of hermeneutic difficulty. The *Gaosengzhuan* says that Sengzhao was aware of the distance between his time and that of the Sages, that meanings had changed and that some translations were mistaken. Sengzhao even states that different interpretations of *prajñā* have been rampant for some time, implying that he will rectify the situation.[4]

"*Prajñā* is Not-knowing" also stands out for its **Mādhyamika** influences.[5] By the time Sengzhao wrote the essay, **Kumārajīva** had translated Āryadeva's *Hundred Treatise*,[6] and begun work on the *Dazhi du lun*, so Sengzhao was familiar with **Mādhyamika** texts and reasoning.[7] Sengzhao was aware of the disjunction between language and reality (a major **Mādhyamika** theme) and at one point even borrows a style of inference **Nāgārjuna** uses in the *Kārikās*.[8] These, along with Sengzhao's clear understanding of the "middle way" between grasping and non-grasping, rejection and affirmation, mark a great departure from his predecessors.

Ultimately, though, what sets "*Prajñā* is Not-knowing" apart is Sengzhao's language. Most of Sengzhao's phrasing comes from earlier Buddhist and Chinese writings yet at points he makes some puzzling moves, such as declaring that *prajñā* is too mysterious to be expressed while proceeding to write an entire essay on the subject.[9] Many passages are filled with superlatives, syntactical twists, and rhetorical flourishes that make no sense. It is as if Sengzhao devises a code in which to speak of *prajñā,* one that resembles the literary Chinese of his day yet departs from it in significant ways. It seems *prajñā* requires a special language to convey its insights. Before turning to this special language, however, we should discuss the basic ideal in "*Prajñā* is Not-knowing" (the Sage/Bodhisattva) and the sources Sengzhao draws upon. This will allow us to become familiar with the essay and get a feel for what Sengzhao is doing.

Sengzhao's Model of *Prajñā*: The Sage/Bodhisattva

The Neo-Daoist Sage—A Cultural Paradigm

The Sage, the paradigmatic figure in Confucian-Daoist tradition, was a perennial concern of *xuanxue* thinkers. Originally a quasi-divine ruler such as Yao or Shun, the Sage became increasingly important after the fall of the Han. This period was marked by a yearning for personal transcendence as well as tremendous growth in "religious Daoism." It was truly an "Age of the Holy Man," and this cultural ideal had great importance.[10]

The religious dimension of *xuanxue* centered on attaining sageliness, and retired gentlemen strove for it. Many saw such a life as a way to express their true nature and hence superior to the artificial lives of most people. In his *Shisi lun* ("Essay on Dispelling Self-interest"), Xi Kang, one of the "Seven Worthies," writes,

> The Gentleman, in doing the worthy, does not first examine to see if this will bring him good fortune and only then act. He follows his heart without exhausting it; he does not first debate the good and only then decide what is proper. He manifests his feelings with no concern [with what others might think]; he does not first discuss whether something is right and only then do it. For this reason, unrestrained he forgets about the worthy, and the worthy and good fortune coincide. Indifferent to all else, he follows his heart, and his heart and the good come together. Forgetting himself, he has no concerns, and his actions are one with the right.[11]

For Xi Kang, the ideal person was *fangwai* (lit. "outside the square," one who lives outside the bounds of social convention)[12] but such a person was not self-indulgent. There is a strong anti-Confucian strain here but the stress is not on moral laxity so much as moving beyond artificial (and harmful) rules and regulations.

This same concern with sageliness runs through much of Wang Bi and Guo Xiang's thought, as we have seen in the previous chapter. For Wang Bi, the ultimate essence of reality is *wu* (non-being). *Wu*, however, is merely the beginning in Wang's thought, for it is always connected with *you* (being). *Wu* is the root (*ben*) while individual things are the branches (*mo*). The Sage is a person who realizes and fully embodies (*ti*) this nondual ontological relationship and so attains true virtue (*de*). We can see this idea informing Wang Bi when he writes, "How is virtue to be attained? It is to be attained through Dao. How is virtue to be completely exhausted? It is by considering non-being as its function. If non-being is its function, then nothing will not be embraced. Thus in regard to things, if [we perceive] non-being 'in them,' then there is nothing not regulated."[13] The influence of Wang's ontology also shows when he discusses how the Sage is simultaneously both at rest and in motion. Dao as *wu* is rest and constancy, whereas Dao expressed in *you* is motion and change. The two aspects of reality are neither different nor the same, but interpenetrate and express each other. The Sage reflects and embodies this paradox. Wang writes in his commentary on the *Yijing*:

> The ceasing of activity always means quiescence but quiescence does not oppose activity. The ceasing of speech means silence, but silence does not oppose speech. ... through the revolving changes the myriad transformations come [yet] through silence [we] reach non-being. This is their origin. Thus by ceasing activity within Earth, the mind of Heaven and Earth becomes visible.[14]

Quiescence underlies all the myriad changes but both stem from the same root.

For Wang Bi the Sage embodies *wu* and so remains "still" even while acting in the world. Wang clearly derives his understanding from the *Daode jing* yet he follows Han thinkers by making Confucius the paradigm of such attainment rather than Laozi.[15] This "Daoisized" Confucian Sage realizes the identity of quiescence and movement, and so attains freedom. By reaching inner stillness and achieving "spiritual understanding" (*shenming*), the Sage differs from ordinary people. Unlike other *xuanxue* thinkers (e.g. Xi Kang and He Yan), Wang regarded the Sage as having "feelings" (*qing*) yet not being ensnared by them. The Sage responds to events but is in essence untouched. Acting by "not acting" (*wuwei*), the Sage skillfully flows with Dao while remaining empty and tranquil within its movement.

This same idea informs Guo Xiang's writings. Guo explains the relation of motion and stillness, action and non-action, as a trust in the natural flow through which one finds "freedom" within the determined order. As he explains when commenting on *Zhuangzi*, chapter thirteen: "The carpenter is in non-action in carving wood, but he is in action in using the ax. The prince is in non-action in managing affairs, but he is in action in the control of ministers. The ministers can manage affairs while the prince can control the ministers. The ax can carve the wood while the carpenter can use the ax."[16]

As with Wang Bi, so for Guo Xiang it is the Sage (or rather the *zhiren*) who conforms to principle and realizes the harmony of Heaven and Earth. In fact, the realization of this cosmic harmony is precisely one's "enlightenment." The *zhiren* acts according to his nature (*ziran*) and joins with the transformations. He "mysteriously identifies 'self' and 'other',"[17] living freely without imposing distinctions yet is fully part of society. At one point Guo compares the *zhiren* to water, which is always tranquil in its natural flow. Just as water remains water even when outwardly disturbed, so the *zhiren* remains tranquil in all circumstances. "Thus the *zhiren* sincerely responds to existing things with no conscious mind yet mysteriously coincides with principle. [The *zhiren*] joins with evolution and regards the world as his measure. So it is that he can lead things yet flow with time forever."[18] Guo Xiang's *zhiren*, like Wang Bi's Sage, understands and embodies movement and quiescence, action and non-action. Such a person is within and without the world, working in all situations while remaining undisturbed.

Chinese Buddhists readily adopted this same ideal as the model for the Buddhas and Bodhisattvas. We can see this in their descriptions of the Buddha's actions and his teachings. For example, in his preface to An Shigao's *Anpan shouyi jing* Daoan writes:

> *Ānāpāna* is out-and-in [breathing]. [The Sage] journeys in the Dao and there is nowhere he does not abide. [His] myriads of virtue (*de*) nowhere lacks lodging. Therefore in [his] *ānāpāna* he guards his mind through perfecting his focus. He passes through the four *dhyāna* and [perceives] the ten thousand forms through his perfect *samādhi*. ... because of his *wuwei* there is no form to which he does not conform. Because of his lack of desire, he has no affairs yet he does not fail [to direct them]. Since there are no forms to which he does not conform, he is able to "open up a way for things." Since he has no affairs yet does not fail [to direct them], he is able to complete his tasks. "Completing his task" is his identifying with the ten thousand beings and taking "the other" as himself.[19]

Another example is Sun Chuo's description in a passage from his *Yudao lun*: "As for the Buddha, he embodies (*ti*) Dao. He passes unhindered, responding to everyone's needs. He is one who [dwells in] non-action yet there is nothing not done."[20]

There is, however, an important difference with the Buddhist Sage/Bodhisattva. Buddhists generally spoke of their ideal within a *moral* view of the cosmos founded on the doctrine of *karma* and so avoided the quietism of Guo Xiang's views. Guo, after all, based his philosophy on a fatalistic idea that things should follow their natures and doing so is "correct."[21] For Buddhists, however, such a view would leave no basis or motive for embarking on the path.

Not surprisingly, the ideal Buddhist Sage was usually a monk. During the fourth century the populace came to see Buddhist clergy as being closer to the Sagely ideal than *xuanxue* gentlemen. Monks, although often from the ranks of the gentry, presented a more humble and disciplined face to the world, moving easily among all classes of people. They appeared both more present yet more removed, more "perfect" yet more approachable, invulnerable despite their vulnerability. A monk also espoused compassion and service, stressing a peaceful way of life. Indeed, the presence of such figures was a sign of Heaven's blessing.[22]

The Buddhist Sage/Bodhisattva transcended the world while remaining within it. This difference is summed up in a famous story found in the *Shishuo xinyu* and the *Gaosengzhuan* about a debate between Zhi Dun and a *xuanxue* scholar on Zhuangzi's tale of the great Peng bird and little quail. The Peng bird ("Great Understanding") flies freely beyond the bounds of earth. The quail ("small understanding"), by contrast, views such flight with disdain, convinced that his small flitting from branch to branch is true freedom. The scholar, following Guo Xiang, argued that both were free since freedom was merely following one's nature. Zhi Dun countered that this was incorrect, for then the earlier evil kings would also have to be counted as men of Dao.[23] For Zhi Dun, following one's nature leaves one enmeshed in *saṃsāra*. The true *zhiren* (the Buddha or Bodhisattva) has severed all attachments and makes no distinction between transcendent and immanent, *saṃsāra* and *nirvāṇa*. This Buddhist interpretation goes beyond the relativism of Guo Xiang and thus prevailed in learned circles from then on.[24]

The Buddhist Sage was a sophisticated version of the *xuanxue* Sage whose mysterious Dao expressed the basic *xuanxue* ontology and the non-abiding and non-discriminating way of the Bodhisattva. Philosophically this was not a synthesis but a "middle way," a dwelling that was neither "nowhere" and "nowhen" nor "everywhere" and "everywhen." Sengzhao's discussion in "*Prajñā* is Not-knowing" follows other Buddhists in his understanding of the Sage. For Sengzhao as well, the problems concerning this ideal—What is the nature of the Sage? How does the Sage differ from ordinary people? How can we attain Sagehood?—were precisely those with which the *prajñā* schools wrestled. Yet unlike his predecessors Sengzhao also had two sagely examples of *prajñā* before him: Kumārajīva and Emperor Yao Xing.

Sengzhao's Living Examples–Kumārajīva and Yao Xing

Kumārajīva had a reputation for wisdom, and this played a decisive role in his coming to China. Wei Shou says the Kuchean master was "deeply perceptive and discerning, and his thought penetrated the writings of East and West."[25] The *Gaosengzhuan* describes Kumārajīva as brilliant and compassionate. "Rarely was there one like him. His nature was humane and his heart was filled with an all-embracing love. Without self-regard, he skillfully led [his students] night and day without tiring."[26] As far as his followers were concerned, Kumārajīva *was* a Sage.

This notion may seem quaint to us in the present day but sageliness was a deeply rooted theme in China that had great social and political consequences. The Sage, the person who knew the *jing* and hence the very secrets of the universe, was an important figure. The fourth and early fifth centuries in China mark a time when charismatic religious figures were eagerly sought out by rulers and took an active role in politics. This was especially true in the North, where Buddhist monks were kept as "court chaplains" and had great reputations for their supernatural abilities.[27] In the southern regions the Sage ideal was also pervasive but the emphasis there was more on scholarship and self-cultivation than occult powers.

Kumārajīva's intelligence and skill in exposition virtually guaranteed that he would attain a reputation for sageliness. We see this even when he was in Kuchā, as his fame drew monks from all over Central Asia. Lu Guang seems to have viewed Kumārajīva in a similar light and sought his advice in various matters, although his reverence was mixed with contempt.[28] Yao Xing, who was more educated than Lu Guang and certainly more devout, considered Kumārajīva a true treasure of his kingdom. Yet, even his reverence was mixed with his desire to further the fortunes of the dynasty and at times he also overrode the bounds of propriety.[29]

For Sengzhao, of course, there was no question of violating propriety. He revered his master and *"Prajñā* is Not-knowing" provides even more evidence:

> There is an Indian *śramaṇa*, Kumārajīva, who when young trod the "Great Square."
> He investigated thoroughly the details of this subject (*prajñā*) and alone rose beyond
> the surface of "words and symbols." He was wondrously conformed to the "region of
> the unseen and unheard." He harmonized the different teachings in Kapilavastu and
> stirred up the Pure Wind from the fans of the east. He was about to bring light to the
> various regions when he was made to hide his glory in the land of Liang. Therefore
> [we know] the Dao does not vainly respond; its responses necessarily have their cause.
> In the third year of *hungshi* under the zodiac sign of *xingji*, the kingdom of Jin took
> advantage of [Liang's] plan to invade the country and mustered an army for the pur-
> pose of bringing him [to Chang'an]. So I think the prophecy concerning the North
> was destined to come true.[30]

This passage, based on events in Kumārajīva's life and replete with references to Daoist and Buddhist texts, depicts the Kuchean master as truly divine. According to Sengzhao Kumārajīva's arrival in Chang'an and proclamation of the Dharma was the fulfillment of destiny.[31] Kumārajīva was cosmically favored, like Śākyamuni himself. In a real sense, *"Prajñā* is Not-knowing" is

Sengzhao's poetic and scholarly portrait of Kumārajīva—a rather poignant foreshadowing of the official obituary he wrote some ten years later.

Yao Xing's status as a Sage is far more ambiguous than Kumārajīva's. "*Prajñā* is Not-knowing" does hold the Jin emperor up as an ideal, however:

> The Divine King of the Great [state of] Jin, whose Way (Dao) rises above the principles of the hundred kings [of the past] and whose virtue (*de*) will pervade a thousand generations to come, effortlessly manages the "ten-thousand details" [of state] and so expands the Dao night and day. I believe him to be like Heaven for the common people of this latter age, and a [strong] support for Śākyamuni's Dharma. At this time he has gathered more than five hundred *śramaṇas* of proper learning in the Xiaoyao monastery. He personally holds the Jin text and along with Kumārajīva takes part in translating the *vaipulya sūtras*. What they have promulgated will not only be a benefit to the present day but will serve as a ford and a bridge for many *kalpas* to come.[32]

As with Sengzhao's description of Kumārajīva so, too, his portrait of Yao Xing is replete with Daoist and Buddhist allusions.[33] By most accounts Yao Xing was devout and had a deep desire to spread the Dharma. He spared no expense in bringing Kumārajīva to Chang'an and establishing him in his translation bureau. He also attended translation sessions although his role during them is uncertain. Sengzhao was indebted to him and it may be, of course, that his praise is mere flattery. In any event, Sengzhao depicts Yao Xing in Sagely terms, although his depiction of Yao Xing differs from that of Kumārajīva. It seems likely that Sengzhao's portrayal of the emperor draws on the more "kingly" side of the Sage, and perhaps was also influenced by the Buddhist ideal of the great *dharmacakravartin* Aśoka.[34]

Sengzhao and Yao Xing appear to have had a close relationship. Yao Xing personally chose him to write Kumārajīva's obituary and Sengzhao presented Yao Xing with a copy of "*Nirvāṇa* is Nameless," the final essay of the *Zhaolun*, which the emperor praised and circulated among his relatives.[35] The parallels between this incident and Sengzhao's presentation of "*Prajñā* is Not-knowing" to Kumārajīva seem more than coincidental. They hint at a filial relationship between Sengzhao and the Jin emperor.[36] It seems, then, that "*Prajñā* is Not-knowing" should be read as a descriptive evocation of an idealized Yao Xing as well as the Sagely Kumārajīva.

Sengzhao interprets both Kumārajīva and Yao Xing through the Chinese Sagely paradigm but having two living examples of Sagehood before his very eyes must have shaped his own understanding of Sagehood in general. Sengzhao would have read previous discussions of the Sage in a new light.

He would have seen their strengths and their weaknesses, how they both succeeded and failed to capture the essence so wonderfully embodied by his master
and patron. Is there a way we can tell which discussions of the Sage were the
most important for him?

Sources

The ideal of the Sage/Bodhisattva was part of Sengzhao's intellectual *milieu*.
However, the significance of "*Prajñā* is Not-knowing" lies not in its content
so much as the manner in which Sengzhao uses common ideas and sources to
convey a deeper understanding of *prajñā*. By tracing Sengzhao's sources we
can cast more light upon his essay and further show how he fit with both the
Buddhist and *xuanxue* traditions. Sengzhao was very much a man of his age,
and examining "*Prajñā* is Not-knowing" in light of his sources reveals much
about his erudition.

Explicitly Cited Sources

Sengzhao quotes a number of Buddhist and Daoist texts in "*Prajñā* is Not-
knowing," especially in the early sections wherein he cites *sūtra* passages as
"proof" for his conception of *prajñā*. The *sūtras* he most commonly cites are
the *Fangguang* (T.221, the version of the *Pañca* translated by Mokṣala) and the
Daoxing (T.224, Lokakṣema's translation of the *Aṣṭa*), the two main scriptures
studied by literati Buddhists of his time.[37] He also quotes the *Vimalakīrti* (both
T.474, the Zhi Qian version, and T.475, Kumārajīva's translation) several
times. In addition he quotes the *Viśeṣacintā Brahma-paripṛcchā* (T.586, the
Kumārajīva translation) and the *Chengju guangming tingyi jing* (T.630, a text
translated in the third century that was quite popular among the literati).
Sengzhao also quotes the *Kārikās* in "*Prajñā* is Not-knowing" and refers to
the *Lalitavistra sūtra* (T.186, translated by Dharmarakṣa in 308) or possibly
the *Vibhāṣā śāstra* (T.1547, an abridged translation by Saṅghabhadra, a late
fourth century Kaśmirian missionary).[38] From these references we can see that
Sengzhao primarily focused on texts from the "*prajñā* tradition" but also knew
the wider range of Buddhist thought.

    In addition to its many Buddhist references, "*Prajñā* is Not-knowing" con-
tains numerous quotations from and allusions to Chinese texts. The majority
of these are to the "three mysteries" (*Laozi, Zhuangzi, Yijing*) but also include

the *Analects*. The exact number of such references is difficult to determine and modern scholars give different counts,[39] but together with the many Buddhist quotations and allusions they constitute clear proof of Sengzhao's great learning as a *xuanxue* scholar-monk. They also attest to his own literary talent, as he often weaves phrases from these texts directly into his writing. Like the Sage who harmonizes both outer and inner worlds with ease, Sengzhao mixes Buddhist and Chinese texts without effort.

"Hidden" Sources

Aside from the sources Sengzhao explicitly quotes, there are a number of unnamed works that he also draws upon in *"Prajñā* is Not-knowing." We are on shaky ground here as the discovery of such "hidden" sources calls for speculation and inference on our part. However we can at least establish a reasonable basis for our conjectures and hazard several educated guesses as to what these sources were.

Sengzhao as a master of *xuanxue* Buddhism was intimately familiar with Buddhist and Chinese writings, and *"Prajñā* is Not-knowing" is replete with direct quotes from various Buddhist and Chinese writings. In addition, Sengzhao would have known commentaries on those works, especially the commentaries of Wang Bi and Guo Xiang, which exerted such strong influence on how later thinkers read the *Laozi*, *Yijing* and *Zhuangzi*. Indeed, some passages in *"Prajñā* is Not-knowing" follow so closely certain passages in earlier *xuanxue* writings that it seems likely Sengzhao used them as models for his own work. For instance, in an early section of the essay Sengzhao describes the Sage as one who courses both within and beyond the world:

> [The Sage's] Spirit has the function of responding to occasions yet there is no deliberation in it, thus it alone can rule beyond the outer world. Wisdom's "not-knowing" is thus able to darkly illuminate external phenomena. Although Wisdom [darkly illuminates] external phenomena, it never lacks these phenomena. Although Spirit [rules beyond] the outer world, day and night it remains within the bounds [of reality]. Therefore, [the Sage] looks up [to Heaven] and down [towards Earth], and so accords with the transformations. His responses endlessly touch [all things].[40]

This passage uncannily echoes a section of Guo Xiang's commentary:

> There has never been one who wanders to the extreme beyond the world and yet does not mysteriously harmonize the inner world. Nor has there ever been one who mysteriously harmonizes the inner world and yet does not wander beyond. Thus the

Sage always wanders beyond the world thereby expanding the inner [world]. Without deliberation he accords with all beings and thus although his body labors night and day his spiritual *qi* remains unchanged. He looks up [to Heaven] and down [to Earth] he deals with the ten thousand details.[41]

Liebenthal suggests Sengzhao is referring to Guo Xiang in other sections of the essay,[42] while Sengzhao's Chinese commentators often point out where he is drawing on other *xuanxue* sources such as Wang Bi. For instance, Yuankang suggests that Sengzhao is following Wang Bi's commentary on the *Yijing* in the early part of his description of Kumārajīva,[43] and Huida says that Sengzhao is referring to Wang Bi's same work when speaking of *prajñā* as "void and yet not failing to illuminate."[44]

Sengzhao's "hidden sources" also include works of earlier *xuanxue* Buddhists such as the proponents of the *prajñā* schools. The best evidence of this comes from one of Sengzhao's other essays, "The Emptiness of the Unreal."[45] In an early section of "Emptiness of the Unreal" Sengzhao addresses the theories of three of the *prajñā* schools—*xinwu*, *jise* and *benwu*.[46] It is unclear if Sengzhao is criticizing specific teachers as he does not mention anyone by name, but later commentators and scholars have taken him as arguing both for and against several of the leading figures.[47] It may be, of course, that Sengzhao studied the *prajñā* schools only after composing "*Prajñā* is Not-knowing" but that seems unlikely. In fact, there are indications that Sengzhao is addressing their views in certain sections of "*Prajñā* is Not-knowing."[48]

Furthermore, passages in the writings of earlier Buddho-Daoists strongly resemble sections in "*Prajñā* is Not-knowing." Daoan's description of "perfect wisdom" in his "Preface to the *Daoxing*" (*Daoxing jing xu*) anticipates much of Sengzhao's thought:

Great indeed is Holy Wisdom! The ten thousand Sages depend on it to penetrate the totality [of Reality], venerate it and so become perfect. Like Earth including [all things] and like the Sun illuminating [all things], there is no *dharma* it does not comprehend. Not relying [on anything] and not abiding [anywhere], it views named things as hindrances. Since it is beyond names, it also disparages the Formless [realm]. It forgets both alternatives (eternalism and nihilism) and is profoundly indifferent, alone, without a master. These are the marks of Wisdom.[49]

Daoan freely mixes both Daoist and Buddhist expressions here to convey the being of *prajñā* ("wisdom") much as Sengzhao does in his essay.

Is Sengzhao drawing upon these texts in "*Prajñā* is Not-knowing"? If so, which ones and to what extent? We cannot provide definitive answers to these questions but Sengzhao surely was familiar with such writings. Together with the works he explicitly quotes they form his own "textual storehouse," the philosophical and literary treasury from which he draws his basic ideas and phrasing. Yet for Sengzhao, none of these sources capture the wondrous being of the Sage. Indeed, language is unable to describe the Sage's being. As Sengzhao himself laments:

> Truly Sagely Wisdom is subtle, deeply obscure, difficult to fathom. It is without marks and, being nameless, [it] cannot be attained with words and symbols. [So it is that I] will use "deceiving symbols" to [grasp] its inner essence by merely entrusting it to "wild words". How dare I say that the Sagely Mind can be analyzed! Yet I will attempt to discuss it.[50]

The Sage is too important a topic to dismiss, even it if is impossible to accurately discuss it. The result of Sengzhao's attempt is *"Prajñā* is Not-knowing."

Structure of *"Prajñā* is Not-Knowing"

In *"Prajñā* is Not-knowing" Sengzhao's debt to Kumārajīva is obvious, as it was the Kuchean master's presentation of Mahāyāna by way of Nāgārjuna and Āryadeva that enabled his disciples to understand the "middle way" at a deeper level.[51] *"Prajñā* is Not-knowing" thus is both a *xuanxue* and Mādhyamika treatise. This combination is evident in the essay's title, which is an allusion to a passage from the fourth chapter of the *Zhuangzi*, where Confucius says to his disciple Yan Hui: "You have heard of the knowledge that knows, but you have never heard of the knowledge that does not know."[52] Sengzhao is drawing on Daoist ideas yet he is using a Buddhist term, *prajñā*. The title, thus, perfectly expresses the point of his entire essay. Examining the essay's structure will show this synthesis even more clearly and help us understand how the essay works.

Like most Chinese treatises, *"Prajñā* is Not-knowing" is brief. All told it amounts to some 2500 characters and takes up less than two pages in the *Taishō*. The essay's brevity marks it as a typically *Chinese* versus (Indian) Buddhist text, since the latter tend to be much longer than the former. The verbosity of Buddhist *sūtras* was a major obstacle in the textual transmission of Buddhism to China, as many literati found Buddhist texts lengthy and "inelegant."[53] This was one reason why even Kumārajīva abbreviated and abridged texts when translating, and why debates between the *prajñā* schools typically centered on short commentarial essays rather than actual *sūtras*.

"*Prajñā* is Not-knowing" has three main parts, each with various sub-divisions:[54]

Part 1 (153a: 8–23)

In this section Sengzhao presents the theme of his essay and provides context for his interest in *prajñā*. His opening line is a great lion's roar announcing the profound and mysterious nature of *prajñā*: "*Prajñā*, void and 'dark,' is perhaps the beginning and end of the Three Vehicles. It is truly One, lacking all duality."[55] The main point of the section is that *prajñā* has not been understood in the past but Sengzhao will endeavor to clarify this important subject. This section includes a brief account of Kumārajīva's life extolling the great Dharma-master's abilities and an encomium praising Yao Xing. It is in this section as well that Sengzhao first explicitly equates *prajñā* with Sagely Wisdom and the Sagely Mind.[56]

Sengzhao concludes this introductory section in rather notable fashion. After spending several lines extolling *prajñā*, Kumārajīva and Yao Xing for their cosmic significance, he speaks of himself as something of a simpleton. In so doing, he sets up a contrast of extremes that echoes the first line of the treatise wherein he speaks of *prajñā* as both the beginning and end of the Three Vehicles. Here Sengzhao is the one at the beginning of the Vehicles whereas Kumārajīva and Yao Xing (true Sages) are at the end. Yet *prajñā* encompasses all of them. Sengzhao then heightens the cognitive dissonance set up in these clashing extremes by declaring that *prajñā* is too abstruse and subtle to be conveyed by language. The introduction thus ends on a dramatic note, leaving the reader in anticipation. It is a masterful piece of rhetoric in its combination of highs and lows, praise for others and deprecation of self, and constant stress of the ultimate mysteries of *prajñā*. Sengzhao pulls us into the text, piquing our interest and drawing us along by his promise to attempt what he says is impossible–to convey the depths of Sagely Wisdom through the inadequate tools of "words and symbols."

Part 2 (153a: 24–b: 18)

Sengzhao presents his actual explication of *prajñā* in this section. He begins by quoting several *sūtras* before launching into his exegesis. Sengzhao offers three arguments that *prajñā* is "not-knowing": one based on the distinction between "all-knowing" and specific acts of knowing,[57] one based on the idea of non-purposive activity,[58] and one based on definitions of certain mutually opposed pairs of terms ("real" vs. "unreal", "existent" vs. "non-existent").[59] Sengzhao then backs up his claims by citing passages in the *sūtras* and the *Laozi*.

This section of "*Prajñā* is Not-knowing" includes some of Sengzhao's most poetic and abstruse writing. It is longer and more complex than Part 1 but is also a rhetorical gem sprinkled with allusions. This portion of the essay provides an excellent sample of the flavor of Buddhist *xuanxue* and, keeping with this metaphor, we can imagine Sengzhao as a literary gourmet, adding just the right amount of classical spice to suit the literati palette. This section also demonstrates what we might call Buddho-Daoist scholasticism, since Sengzhao argues for his points based on scripture.[60] This aspect of the treatise comes even more to the fore in Part 3.

As with Part 1, Sengzhao concludes this section with particular flourish:

> Therefore *Prajñā* can be considered void yet it illuminates. Ultimate Truth (*paramārtha*) can be forgotten yet [still] known. The ten thousand moving [things] can be considered identical in stillness. The Sage's responses can be considered non-existent yet he acts. This then is "not-knowing" [calculatively] but spontaneously knowing, and not acting [deliberately] yet spontaneously acting. What more can it be said to know? What more can it be said to do?[61]

Using only twenty-one characters Sengzhao captures *prajñā*'s paradoxical nature as empty yet illuminating, moving yet still. *Prajñā* neither knows nor acts yet does know and does act. Indeed, unlike ordinary people who are limited in their knowings and doings, those who have *prajñā* know and do everything; they are not separate from Dao. At this point Sengzhao has fully explained what *prajñā* is. The rest of the essay merely addresses potential misunderstandings or further clarifies certain points.

Part 3 (153b: 19–154c: 19)

This part comprises the bulk of the essay and betrays the most influence from Sengzhao's *sūtra* and *qingtan* sources. Basically it is a series of nine questions on Sengzhao's views and his replies. Some questions are highly critical (and thus could be considered "objections") whereas others are more irenic in tone and seem to want clarification. The feeling is of a debate or a dialogue between a master (Kumārajīva?) and his disciples after the master has finished his opening sermon. Since some of the questions are rooted in views held by earlier *xuanxue* and *prajñā* scholars, this section provides a wonderful window on the world of thought during the Eastern Jin.

In this section Sengzhao further explains *prajñā* by either refuting mistaken views or elaborating on particularly abstruse points. It includes some of Sengzhao's most masterful work and amply demonstrates his command of both Buddhist and Daoist terminology. The fact that the whole section is presented as a debate is especially interesting. Although we in the contemporary world usually think of debate as a means of victory over and opponent, that may not accurately reflect debates in Sengzhao's time. In medieval Europe, *disputatio* was a distinct form or teaching and learning, coming after lecture (*lectio*) and the sermon (*praedicatio*).[62] Sengzhao seems to follow this same order in "*Prajñā* is Not-knowing" although he was obviously not following European models. Jose Cabezon notes that the function of debate in the Tibetan dGe lugs pa tradition is for the participants' to embody their tradition, "to become vessels of scripture."[63] While the dGe lugs pa lineage arose much later than Sengzhao's time, it may reflect common *Buddhist* understandings and practices, and it is a reasonable supposition that *xuanxue* as a scholastic tradition would engage in similar pursuits.

As a debate, this section serves several functions. By bringing different perspectives to bear on the subject through questions and objections, Sengzhao further illuminates *prajñā* and presents a fuller picture of it than he could through simple monologue. The debate format is lively and interesting. In reading it we jump back and forth, shifting our focus. Thus Sengzhao forces a certain nimbleness upon the reader's mind, recalling the idea of *prajñā* as "non-abiding" or the *zhiren* "wandering at ease." Finally, engaging in arguments and reasoning lends the essay weight. It is serious (albeit playful) stuff. Sengzhao's discussion of *prajñā* comes off not as mere gibberish or ignorant rambling but as learned philosophic discourse.

Formally speaking, then, "*Prajñā* is Not-knowing" is a wonderful example of Chinese philosophical literature but it does not break new ground. Sengzhao does not create a new genre but traces the familiar patterns found in Buddhist *sūtras*, *xuanxue* essays and debates, and **Kumārajīva's** exegeses. This is most evident in Part 3 of the essay with its dialogic exchanges. Sengzhao's *sūtra* sources (the *Pañca*, *Aṣṭa* and *Vimalakīrti*) are all dialogues and such exchanges were popular among Neo-Daoists. The dialogue is a long-standing tradition in China, going back to the time of the Warring States. Evidence also suggests that the translation sessions presided over by **Kumārajīva** consisted of the master quoting the scriptures, explaining their meaning, and then inviting and answering questions from his disciples. In "*Prajñā* is Not-knowing," thus, Sengzhao models his own discourse on that of his sources.

However, even though Sengzhao derives much of "*Prajñā* is Not-knowing" from authoritative sources, he expands upon them. Sengzhao does not merely rehash the same old ideas on *prajñā* but delves into them more deeply than his predecessors. At the same time he has not produced something entirely new, for he locates himself within a long line of thinkers. In "*Prajñā* is Not-knowing" Sengzhao takes on the mantle of tradition to address his own age regarding the Sage/*prajñā*, an important subject about which there has been much misunderstanding, and one which Sengzhao aims to correct by truly speaking of *prajñā*, or rather, letting *prajñā* truly speak itself.

The Language of *Prajñā*: "Wild Words"

My discussion of "*Prajñā* is Not-knowing" thus far has skirted the issue of Sengzhao's language and focused instead on the essay's theme, sources, and structure. This was necessary to provide a feel for the essay and show how such a short work can be deceptively simple in its appearance. Sengzhao is at once both a good Daoist and good Buddhist in this regard. We now are ready to examine Sengzhao's *prajñic* language.

One of the best examples of the *prajñic* language Sengzhao uses in "*Prajñā* is Not-knowing" occurs in the opening of the fourth section of Part 2. Sengzhao writes, "So as for [the Sage's] existence, it is real (*shi*) and yet he does not exist (*buyou*) [as a 'thing']. It is void (*xu*) and yet he is not [merely] non-being (*buwu*)."[64] In this passage Sengzhao describes *prajñā* (the Sage's essence) using pairs of mutually opposed terms: *shi* ("real") versus *buyou* ("not-existent"), and *xu* ("void") versus *buwu* ("not not-being"). On the face of it, this sentence does not make sense. Ordinarily these terms Sengzhao is using mark off separate spheres or realms of being and knowing: one cannot be both "real" and "not-existent" at the same time, nor does it make sense to speak of something as "void" yet "not not-being." Ordinary discourse rationalizes (*ratio*–to divide and apportion) by separating and fixing reality into various, sometimes opposed categories. It is the manner in which most of us think and live, and the basis upon which Sengzhao's opponents in "*Prajñā* is Not-knowing" operate. According to "*Prajñā* is Not-knowing," however, these categories are not separate for the Sage/Bodhisattva, whose mind embraces all things. *Prajñā* resides between being and non-being yet encompasses them both, just as the

Bodhisattva dwells neither in *samsāra* nor in *nirvāṇa* but both and neither.
A good description of such "non-abiding abiding" comes from chapter two of
the *Zhuangzi*, in which the Sage's Way is contrasted to the way of ordinary folk
caught up in a view of reality that divides and discriminates:

> Therefore the Sage does not proceed [in such a way], but illuminates all in the light of
> Heaven. He too recognizes a "this," but a "this' which is also a "that," a "that" which
> is also a "this." His "that" has both a right and wrong in it; his "this" too has both a
> right and wrong in it. So, in the end, does he still have a "this" and "that'? Does he in
> the end no longer have a "this" and "that"? When "this" and "that" no longer attain
> their opposites we call it the "hinge of the Way." When the hinge is fitted into the
> socket, it can respond endlessly. Its right then is a single endlessness and its wrong too
> is a single endlessness. Thus I say the best thing to use is Understanding (*ming*).[65]

For Sengzhao, *prajñā* is this Understanding, a "knowing" embracing all of reality
rather than the "small knowing" that is confined within a selfish perspective.

In *xuanxue* Buddhist terms, *prajñā*, or rather the Sage/Bodhisattva whose
being is *prajñā*, fully embodies the structure of reality. Such a person is united
with all things while yet remaining truly himself. This wondrous unity amidst
difference is impossible to describe. *Prajñā* is not rational—it does not divide
reality into separate portions; it is *a-rational*. *Prajñā* is the being-knowing of
the Sage, where there are no separate and distinct things, no separate and
distinct spheres of being, and no separate and distinct "us." Instead, we are
simultaneously inside and outside, void and full, still and moving, illuminating
everything "darkly" in an "all-knowing" which is "not-knowing."

This scheme of two views or spheres of reality and the idea that "wisdom"
can embrace both sides has ample precedent in the Mahāyāna teaching of
the Two Truths and Neo-Daoist discussions of "being" and "non-being." Where
Sengzhao distinguishes himself is in his way of bringing together the separate
spheres. Indeed, such conjoining is the true "work" of the essay.[66] "*Prajñā*
is Not-knowing" accomplishes its work through what Sengzhao terms "wild
words" (*kuangyan*), a special language that coveys the *prajñic* perspective.
"Wild words" form a complex, slippery mode of discourse in which no single
perspective can be maintained and clear distinctions cannot be made.

What are "Wild Words"?

The phrase *kuangyan* (*kyōgen* in Japanese) has a host of meanings. According
to *Matthews Chinese-English Dictionary*, it means "nonsense, lies."[67] The entry in

Herbert Giles' *Chinese-English Dictionary* gives a similar definition, "incoherent talk."[68] The *Encyclopedic Dictionary of the Chinese Language* (*Zhongwen da cidian*) lists three definitions for *kuangyan*: exaggerated or inappropriate speech, boastful and robust discourse, and a genre of Japanese literature.[69] The phrase has gained currency in Japan, where it connotes trickiness or make-believe, and mainly refers to the short comedies performed along with *Noh* dramas.[70]

The phrase "*kuangyan*" appears several times in Chinese literature, most notably in chapter twenty-two of the *Zhuangzi*, where Ah Hokan, Shen Nung and Yan Gantiao discuss Master Lao Long and his mysterious "wild words."[71] We should note as well that this particular chapter of the *Zhuangzi* bears the title "Knowledge wandered North," which would seem once again to point to associations with *prajñāpāramitā* and the prophecies concerning the north to which Sengzhao alludes in the early sections of his essay.[72] It seems likely, then, that Sengzhao gets the phrase "*kuangyan*" from this passage of the *Zhuangzi*. There are, though, other possible sources. For example, **Kumārajīva** uses a similar form of the phrase "*kuangyan*" when writing to Huiyuan: "The *sūtras* delude (*kuang*) the eyes of worldly people."[73]

Perhaps not surprisingly, the expression *kuangyan* has been translated in variety of ways, each of which has different shades of meaning. I borrow my translation ("wild words") from Burton Watson but Martin Palmer translates it the same way.[74] This translation is extremely close to Robinson's translation ("crazy words")[75] and Victor Mair's ("mad words.").[76] These renderings of *kuangyan* all indicate an exuberant or "zany" quality. This aspect of *kuangyan* is underscored by James Legge's rendering of the expression as "heedless words,"[77] and Liu's translation as "irrelevant words."[78] Clearly *kuangyan* involve transgressing established rules and procedures, or bending these rules to show how artificial and confining they are. However, both Liebenthal and Fangcheng Hsu give a markedly different translation of *kuangyan*—"inadequate language."[79] At first glance this seems an inadequate translation yet it points to another aspect of *kuangyan*. The fact that Sengzhao turns to *kuangyan* at the very point when he concludes that language cannot convey *prajñā* indicates that for him language *is* inadequate to his task. Nonetheless he proceeds to use *kuangyan*. *Kuangyan* seem, then, to be the only recourse when one is compelled to speak of that which cannot be spoken.[80]

All of the uses and associations with *kuangyan* and its English translations point to a general notion of trickiness, humor, something of a "put on." One using "wild words" is "playing around" with us, trying to confuse or even delight us. Perhaps significantly, the radical for the word "wild" (*kuang*) in the phrase "wild words" is also the term for "dog" (*quan*). Dogs are "insiders" and "outsiders," domesticated animals who still retain their savage nature. In China, dogs have often been associated with the uncivilized peoples of the "barbarian" south, an area of mystery and darkness which in early times was a center of ecstatic religious practices and shamanism. Much of the roots of "religious Daoism" can be traced to this area.[81] Finally, the south has strong associations with *prajñāpāramitā* in Buddhism, as it is alleged that the teachings originated there before moving east and then north.

Girardot notes that in ancient times *kuang* or *kuangfu* referred to clowns or fools who were "shamanically possessed." These *kuang* figures participated in agricultural festivals by impersonating demons. They wore masks and had a distinctive motley dress symbolic of their "uncivilized wisdom." *Kuangfu* were weird beings but seem to have had an almost sagely reputation.[82]

For Chinese Buddhists like Sengzhao and his audience, *kuangyan* had deep-seated associations with powerful ideas. To speak in *kuangyan* would be to speak boastfully to be sure, but also barbarically, exotically, mysteriously. *Kuangyan* are, indeed, "wild words"–the language of "dogs," wizards, shamans, those who are "unconfined" and know "perfect wisdom." Such words are "antinomic" in that they run counter to the accepted rules of language.[83] *Kuangyan* are "Hermes speak." *Kuangyan* are amusing and unsettling, bouncing between "sense" and "nonsense." In "*Prajñā* is Not-knowing," Sengzhao uses *kuangyan* to let *prajñā* speak itself as "wildly" as it will.

Sengzhao's use of "wild words" to convey *prajñā* has roots in both Buddhism and *xuanxue* as both traditions tend to stress language's limitations when it comes to reality. In Buddhist *prajñā* texts, a common theme is the struggle to find an adequate language. Words seem destined to fail, and even to attempt to speak of *prajñā* is to court disaster, for it is beyond the reach of concepts. Thus scriptures and treatises resort to all manner of linguistic tricks to speak of *prajñā* even while claiming that it is inexpressible. The *Prajñāpāramitā sūtras* engage in paradox and contradiction, often launching into exuberant superlatives when discussing the miraculous qualities of the Bodhisattva. Vimalakīrti, when asked about the highest truth of nonduality maintains his infamous "wise silence." Nāgārjuna and his followers speak in a constant stream of denials and negations, claiming that language is an inadequate means of articulating Ultimate Truth even though it is the only way we have.

Similarly the limitations of language when dealing with the mysteries of Dao are a constant theme in *xuanxue* discourse. Time and again *xuanxue* thinkers emphasize that no words or symbols can reach ultimate non-being or the Mind of the Sage. Terms "fix" (*ding*) or "tie" (*xi*) the mind to specific things but the "mystery of mysteries" is all-embracing and undefinable. It can only be named provisionally by words such as "Dao" or "great."[84] Yet despite its inadequacy, we are trapped in language and must use it.

It is important to note, though, that not all thinkers of the era shared this "free and easy" view of language. Some of the more "Confucian-minded" figures held that words had (or needed to have) a strict one-to-one correspondence to reality. These were the adherents of the *mingjiao* ("school of names"), those who concerned themselves with *mingli* ("name and principles").[85] *Mingjiao* theories were heavily influenced by the Pre-Han "nominalists" such as Huizi (380–305 B.C.E.) and Gongsun Long (b. 380 B.C.E.), as well as the Confucian doctrine of the "recitification of names." However, their views seem most in concert with the views of language in the Moist canon. According to Mozi (fl. 479–438 B.C.E.), "There must be a standard erected, using language without a standard is like trying to establish the direction of sunrise and sunset with a revolving potter's wheel."[86]

For the followers of the *mingjiao*, language was vital in understanding and dealing with reality. Moreover, just like the Moists, they defended a common sense view of language that was in accord with ordinary language use but their overriding concern was how language functions to guide behavior.[87] These concerns were intimately bound up with issues of knowledge. "Knowing," for them, was a skill, especially a skill in applying names properly and acting accordingly. To be learned, to be skilled in *wen*, had real social, political and cosmic consequences since language in their view determined in large part how people approached, responded to and even "created" reality. There was, furthermore, ample support for such views even in the so-called "mystical" texts the *xuanxue* thinkers loved. For instance, in the *Yijing* there are passages describing the Sages as inventing the "words and symbols" to divine the secrets of the cosmos.[88] The *mingjiao* was an important school of thought in the Post-Han era, and it exerted tremendous influence among *xuanxue* thinkers. Buddhists certainly were familiar with *mingjiao* teachings. Indeed, Sengzhao argues against adherents of the *mingjiao* at several places in "*Prajñā* is Not-knowing."[89]

In this heady mix of opposing views of language, Sengzhao generally followed the conventionalism of the most Daoist among the *xuanxue* and the most **Mādhyamika** among the Buddhists. Just like many of his predecessors and contemporaries, Sengzhao held that words, even of the words of the *sūtras* and the *jing*, were expedient devices (cf. *upāya*) used to convey the teachings.[90]

Language is a tool that must be handled skillfully to get one's point across, especially when one is speaking of Ultimate Truth. Sengzhao's willingness to manipulate language in the "wild words" of "*Prajñā* is Not-knowing" is a double-edged sword. It permits great freedom and creativity yet the resulting discourse may be disjointed and hence prone to great misunderstanding.

Five Ways "Wild Words" Work

At first glance, it appears that in "*Prajñā* is Not-knowing" Sengzhao uses "wild words" only at certain points.[91] However, when we read carefully we see that "wild words" wander freely and easily throughout the essay. "Wild words" are a manifold manner of speaking, for their saying mirrors the play of Dao itself. Although "wild words" are not exactly amenable to rational examination, I have picked out several aspects of this textually Daoist play: literary allusion, "chain arguments," paradox, playing with metaphors and puns. These are not so much separate ways of writing (Sengzhao often uses them within the same passage) as moves within Sengzhao's rhetorical repertoire. In "*Prajñā* is Not-knowing," "wild words" shift across the divisions we impose upon reality (our rational "grids"), forcing us to think across them as well.

1. Literary Allusion

Sengzhao was a master of literary allusion, a common practice among Chinese literati and in literate cultures worldwide. The fact that allusion is so common may blind us to its complexity and rhetorical power. In essence, allusion is an *implicit* reference to something—a person, event, or another work of literature or art—that serves as an appeal to the reader to share an experience with the author. Allusion assumes an established literary tradition, a body of common knowledge, and an audience sharp enough to pick up a reference.[92] Allusion is sly and its force is akin to that of an "inside joke."

From this description we see that allusions have the character and function of "wild words." Allusions are one of the best-known instances of verbal play (the root of "allusion" is the Latin *ludens*—"to play") and do not work if read in a straightforward manner. Allusions also have a weird textual location, being simultaneously within the text as well as the text alluded to, or perhaps residing in neither so much as flitting between them. Allusions can have surprising effect, for by lending a work unexpected depth they often provoke deep insight. Perhaps most of all, allusions cannot be explained so much as "gotten."

Allusions work by direct recognition. All of these factors make them truly "wild," and it is little wonder that Sengzhao makes many allusions, often to multiple texts at the same time.

Although "*Prajñā* is Not-knowing" is replete with allusions, some in particular stand out. In an early section where Sengzhao is explaining what *prajñā* is, we read, "Although Spirit [rules beyond] the outer world, day and night it remains within the bounds [of reality]. Therefore, [the Sage] looks up [to Heaven] and down [towards Earth], and so accords with the transformations. His responses endlessly touch [all things]."[93] This is a remarkable passage. Not only does Sengzhao allude to *Laozi* twenty-five ("day and night it remains within the bounds")[94] and the operations of the Sagely ruler of the *Yijing* ("[the Sage] looks up [to Heaven] and down [towards Earth]"),[95] he also is referring to the Bodhisattva, who appears where needed to preach Dharma.[96] Moreover, it is hard not to catch echoes here of a passage from Guo Xiang which we cited earlier. Thus Sengzhao makes three, possibly four allusions in one line. The brevity and conciseness with which he does so belies the mental expansion he induces in the reader.

Later, when replying to the proponent of *mingjiao* (question #2), Sengzhao performs yet another sly, multiple allusion: "It is a nameless *dharma*, thus we are not dealing with speech and what can be spoken. Although it cannot be spoken of through words, yet it is not the case that words lack the means of conveying it. Therefore the Sage 'speaks night and day yet never speaks.'"[97] In this passage Sengzhao alludes to Nāgārjuna's remarks that although *paramārtha* is beyond the reach of *saṃvṛti* we still must get at it through *saṃvṛti*.[98] He concludes the passage, though, with a phrase directly out of the *Zhuangzi* ("the Sage 'speaks night and day yet never speaks'").[99] Moreover, as Robinson points out, the same phrase is also an allusion to the *Tathātagataguyha sūtra*.[100] All told, this passage constitutes a most tricky yet literate way of putting the advocate of *mingjiao* in his place while underscoring *prajñā*'s wondrous abilities. These are, indeed, "wild words," a fact Sengzhao emphasizes in the next line of his treatise.[101]

One of Sengzhao's most "wildly worded" allusions, though, comes in his reply to question #6. Sengzhao's opponent argues that *prajñā* can be considered to have an object (i.e. to be an ordinary knowing) even though its object (Ultimate Truth) is without marks (distinct features). This very lack of marks *is* the mark of Ultimate Truth, hence it can serve as *prajñā's* object. Not surprisingly, Sengzhao will not accept this line of reasoning; Ultimate Truth is *never* an object, for it cannot be comprehended through dualistic knowing.

He then launches into a "description" of *prajñic* knowing and being that plays through several texts at once:

> Therefore the *zhiren* abides in being yet does not exist and dwells in non-being yet does not "not-exist." Although [the *zhiren*] does not grasp at being or non-being, so he also does not reject either being or non-being. For this reason he blends his brilliance into the "dust and toil," and makes the circuit through the Five Destinies. Silently he departs, shyly he comes. Serenely not-acting (*wuwei*) yet there is nothing he does not do.[102]

These lines constitute a veritable *tour de force* of allusion. Sengzhao begins by repeating one of the most popular lines among the literati ("he blends his brilliance with the dust and toil") found in both the fourth and fifty-sixth chapters of the *Laozi*.[103] He then goes on to make another double allusion to two different chapters from the same book ("non-acting yet there is nothing he does not do").[104] Sengzhao thus performs a "double double-allusion." What's more, the opening lines on the *zhiren* derive from the *Zhuangzi* (especially chapter 6).[105] It may even be that Sengzhao is echoing the *prajñā* schools here, especially *xinwu* with its stress on attaining a "non-deliberative" mind.

From these examples it is obvious that allusion is a strong component of "wild words." Sengzhao draws his reader into his textual universe and permits us to experience his own textual play. We are simultaneously present in various places but constantly shifting through them. Sengzhao is "wild" here, even somewhat sloppy (his phrasing is often inexact) but his "wild words" help engender a wide, all-embracing mind that mimics the Sage's mind of *prajñā*.

2. "Chain Arguments"

"Wild words" are also characterized by a peculiar rhetorical style sometimes known as "chain argument," a term Arthur Waley coined to refer to the style of certain passages in the *Laozi*.[106] In "chain arguments" pairs of sentences are turned back upon each other. The latter half of each pair of sentences is repeated at the beginning of the next pair, thus forming an interlocking chain. This is a common rhetorical form in ancient and medieval Chinese writings. Although "chain arguments" resemble formal arguments in Western (or Indian) logic, they do not represent a form of progressive reasoning (deductive or inductive) leading towards a definite conclusion. They are mainly a means of exposition rather than "proof."

Sengzhao uses "chain arguments" at several places in "*Prajñā* is Not-knowing." The first is in his exposition of *prajñā* in Part 2 of the essay:

[We may] desire to speak of its existence but it lacks name and form.
[We may also] desire to speak of its non-existence but the Sage becomes Divine through it.
Since the Sage becomes Divine through it, it thus is void but does not fail to illuminate.
Lacking name and form, it thus illuminates but does not fail to be void. It illuminates while not failing to be void, thus it mixes [with the ten thousand things] yet does not change.
It is void while not failing to illuminate, thus it moves and thereby contacts ordinary [things].
Therefore the function of Sagely Wisdom never begins or ceases even for a moment. We seek it in form and marks but it never for a moment can be attained.[107]

The logical structure of this argument runs thus:

~A, because B.   ~C, because D.
D so E.   B so F.
F so G.   E so H.
Therefore I and J.[108]

Although this argument appears to reach some sort of conclusion (I and J), it does not do so through logical inference. Instead, Sengzhao presents a series of interlocking statements that force us to move back and forth through the passage.

Another "chain argument" comes only a few lines further on in the treatise. Interestingly, Sengzhao's first opponent voices this argument, perhaps indicating that "wild words" are not confined even to the "correct" perspective:

The True Mind of the Sage is unique in its brightness, illuminating thing after thing.
Its responses effortlessly touch [all things] and its movements meet all phenomena.
Since it illuminates thing after thing, in its "knowing" there is nothing neglected.
Since its movements meet all phenomena, its meetings do not miss the cosmic workings.
Because its meetings does not miss the cosmic workings, there necessarily is a "meeting" and "what can be met."
Because in its "knowing" there is nothing neglected, there necessarily is a "knowing" and "what can be known."
Since there necessarily is a "knowing" and "what can be known," the Sage does *not* vainly know.

Since there necessarily is a "meeting" and "what can be met," the Sage does *not* vainly meet.

So [the Sage] both knows and meets and yet you say "he is one who has no knowing and no meeting." How can this be?[109]

This passage is longer and more complex than the first. Logically, its structure runs thus:

A and B.   A so C.
B so D.   D so E.
C so F.   F so G.
E so H.
G and H, so not ~G and not ~H.[110]

Once again we see the same cross-order of propositions. In this case, the "conclusion" is a doubly negated conjunction that repeats an immediately prior positive conjunction as a sort of "mirror reflection". Note that this argument is not illogical but its reasoning bounces back and forth within the passage in a "wild" manner.

Sengzhao also engages in "chain argument" when replying to his opponents' questions. For instance, in his reply to question 3 he writes:

Knowing and what-is-known combine and so mutually come into existence, and mutually go out of existence.

Because they mutually go out of existence, things do not [really] exist.

Because they mutually come into existence, things [at the same time] do not "not-exist."

Since things do not "not-exist," that which arises (knowing) is conditioned by its object.

However, since things do not [really] exist, the object [of knowing] cannot itself be produced.

As the object [of knowing] cannot itself be produced, [knowing] illuminates its objects yet is not a "knowing."

Since what arises (knowing) is conditioned by its object, knowing and its object are produced in mutual dependence.

Therefore knowing and "not-knowing" truly are produced from what-is-known.[111]

The logical structure of this argument is almost identical to the previous one:

A and B.   B so C.
A so D.   D so E.
C so F.   F so G.
E so H.
Therefore G (?) and H (?)[112]

The same crossed reasoning runs through this passage but the "conclusion" is different. It is the conjunction of two propositions that do not actually appear in the argument proper but are more or less semantic equivalents of propositions that do. Technically, to be logically valid the argument needs an extra step to convert the propositions into those in the conclusion. This is a strong indication that such "chain arguments" are not exercises in formal logic. They are exercises in mental agility that train the mind to move freely across ideas rather than confine thinking to a strictly linear path.

"Chain arguments" are a distinct feature of Sengzhao's writing and are one of the most obvious indications of his debt to earlier forms of Chinese prose, although other Buddho-Daoists use this form as well. Sengzhao may be one of the last Chinese writers to use this old form but it does not mark his only style of argument, as he also borrows certain forms from Nāgārjuna. However, the important thing to remember about "chain arguments" is that they are *not* instances of logical inference. "Chain arguments" require one to jump back and forth within the text; the reasoning they employ is neither progressive (deductive or inductive) nor logical in the formal sense. In "chain arguments" we find no instances of terms being converted and no application of the laws of contradiction or the excluded middle.[113] "Chain arguments" do not operate according to rules of inference. Instead, they engender an awareness that moves between different perspectives and ideas. Their "logic" slides into and around various positions within the treatise. All views are accepted here but none are clung to.

3. Paradox

The "wild words" of "*Prajñā* is Not-knowing" also work by means of paradox. Paradoxes are among the most common rhetorical devices in religious texts. The term comes from the Greek phrase *para doxan*, "violation of opinion." Originally a paradox merely contradicted accepted views but paradox has now come to mean a figure of speech involving an apparently contradictory or absurd statement that harbors a deeper truth, one that reconciles conflicting opposites.[114] Like Hamlet's line, "I must be cruel only to be kind,"[115] paradoxes arrest our attention and disturb ordinary reasoning. Paradoxes provoke thought. They are also inherently unstable, seeming to encompass both truth and error simultaneously.[116]

Sengzhao's "wild words" include a bewildering array of paradoxes.[117] A few examples, though, can give us a taste for how they work in his essay. Towards the beginning of Part 2 after he cites the *Fangguang* and the *Daoxing*,

Sengzhao uses a paradox to "explain" the Sage's "knowing": "If there is that which is known, then there must be that which is not known. [However] since the Sagely Mind is "not-knowing," there is thus nothing that it does not know. This 'not-knowing knowing' we call 'all-knowing'."[118] *Prajñā* knows but does not know "things," thus there is nothing that it knows. Yet since it knows nothing (no thing) it nonetheless knows "everything." Here Sengzhao speaks of *prajñā*'s relationship to ordinary knowing. *Prajñā* is a "not-knowing knowing" but we can only "know" it through this paradox. As if that were not enough, Sengzhao underscores this fact two lines later with another paradoxical description of the Sage as "knowing day and night yet never knowing."[119]

Sengzhao uses another paradox in Part 3 of "*Prajñā* is Not-knowing" in his reply to his second opponent: "The Sagely Mind is subtle and marvelous, lacking all marks [hence] it cannot be considered to exist. Its function is to be extremely active, thus it cannot be considered to not exist."[120] Unlike ordinary "things," the Sage is not confined to the extremes of existence and non-existence but spans both "being" and "nothingness." There can be no doubt that these are "wild words," for Sengzhao clearly tells us they are in the sentence immediately preceding the passage quoted.

Towards the end of the same passage Sengzhao presents one of the most paradoxical statement in the entire essay. It resembles the first paradox we discussed concerning the Sage's "not-knowing knowing." Sengzhao writes, "Therefore, its (*prajñā*'s) knowing is identical to its not-knowing and its not-knowing is identical to its knowing."[121] This powerful declaration of identity echoes the famous line from the "Heart *sūtra*": "Emptiness is form, Form is emptiness." Sengzhao is not contradicting himself here but "wildly" speaking the truth of Sagely Wisdom.

These few examples scarcely do justice to Sengzhao's talents but they do illustrate the role of paradox in "wild words." However, some scholars maintain that there are problems with his paradoxes. Richard Robinson, for one, argues that Sengzhao's paradoxes are only apparent and can be easily resolved when we realize that Sengzhao is equivocating in his use of terms such as "knowing" and "speaking."[122] Robinson is certainly correct yet he misses the point: equivocation is precisely the function of "wild words." "Wild words" have several meanings and are capable of more than one interpretation. This does not mean, though, that we should take their equivocation in a pejorative sense. "Wild words" do not lie but speak of the Sage who *consciously* inhabits both the substance and function of the universe. The Sage has attained *prajñā* and so notes no difference between *saṃsāra* and *nivāṇa*. "Wild words" are the only way of getting this across.

4. The Play of Metaphors

Another way "wild words" work is by playing off metaphors of space and light. Metaphors are among the most common of rhetorical devices. The term "metaphor" comes from the Greek *metapherein*, "carrying from one place to another," and this is an apt description. Essentially, metaphors function on the basis of resemblance—in a metaphor a term that resembles another is substituted for that term, as in the phrase "marble brow." Unlike similes, however, metaphors work *implicitly*, presenting their substitution directly to the reader.[123] Sengzhao uses metaphors to great effect in "*Prajñā* is Not-knowing." "Wild words" speak of *prajñā* as "dark light," "empty fullness," a knowing which simultaneously looks up and down, a way of being which abides both inside and outside. By mixing these metaphors Sengzhao upsets our expectations and usual thought patterns, helping induce a non-grasping awareness, the "not-knowing knowing" of *prajñā* itself.

The controlling metaphors in the essay's discussion of the Sage's knowing and being mainly concern space and light. This should not be too surprising since space and light are the means by which we normally orient ourselves, and are necessary conditions for most everyday experiences. It is just this primal sensory and perceptive level which founds our other more abstract modes of thinking and being. This, in turn, raises intriguing questions. In the absence of both light and space, do we have experience? Do "we" even exist? Opinions have varied over the ages but it seems clear that space and light are basic to our being-in-the-world.

George Lakoff and Mark Johnson have argued that metaphors are what allow us to engage with the world and in so doing structure our way of thinking. So basic is this "metaphoric shaping" that we often do not notice it, yet this shaping effectively defines our modes of rationality.[124] Two particularly common metaphors concern human knowing—"knowing is light" and "knowing is nearness, proximity." These spatial and light metaphors pervade Western discussions of human knowing as well as such discussion in Indian and Chinese cultures,[125] and are particularly prevalent in Buddhism.[126] They are of utmost importance in "*Prajñā* is Not-knowing" as they define the field within which "wild words" operate. Sengzhao's "wild words" play off these basic spatial and light metaphors of knowing and being. Typically, "wild words" begin with the accepted metaphors only to mix them up. They pull the reader around between extremes, plunging one into an enlightening darkness.

One of the boldest examples of the play of spatial and light metaphors in "*Prajñā* is Not-knowing" comes in the essay's opening line: "*Prajñā*, void and 'dark,' is perhaps the beginning and end of the Three Vehicles."[127] *Prajñā*, the "enlightened" knowing of the Sage is *dark*. It is "nothing," a void. This is, to say the least, counterintuitive. We would expect *prajñā* to be a wondrous light, a miraculous something. Sengzhao unsettles us from the very beginning of the essay. He then plays around with notions of space. *Prajñā* is both the beginning, the start (near) of all Buddhism and its end (far). The same line can also be read as "*Prajñā* is the originary axis (*taiji*) of the Three Vehicles." In this reading, *prajñā* is the central pole around which the Buddhist paths spin. Now we are in the center of everything and the paths do not lead anywhere other than where we are. Once again, this upsets pre-conceived ideas that the Buddhist path (the Sagely Way) is a step-by-step progression from "here" (*saṃsāra*) to "there" (*nirvāṇa*).

Sengzhao also speaks of *prajñā* by playing off the opposition between "empty" and "full." At one point he says, "Therefore the Sage empties his mind yet 'fills' his illumination."[128] Immediately on the heels of this line Sengzhao throws up the analogous contrast of "dark" and "light": "Thus he can darken his brightness and hide his brilliance."[129] The Sage knows and operates through contrasting extremes that defy our expectations. Normally we would assume the Sage shines for all to see, having everything in his mind. Instead Sengzhao speaks of the Sage as darkening his brilliance, emptying his mind, and, curiously, filling his illuminating.

Although most of these examples occur in the essay's opening sections where Sengzhao presents *prajñā* in all its wondrous weirdness, Sengzhao continues to play off spatial and light metaphors when answering his opponents. For instance, in his reply to his first opponent who claims to know what *prajñā* really is, Sengzhao says, "The Sage's merit surmounts the Two Principles, and yet he is not humane. His brightness exceeds the sun and moon, yet he is all the darker."[130] The Sage is a cosmic being here, illuminating the entire world and beyond yet he is "dark." Once again, the accepted metaphor is turned on its head.

One of the most dramatic examples of metaphoric play of space and light comes near the end of the essay, in Sengzhao's reply to the eighth objection:

> Inside, there is the clarity of [the Sage's] solitary mirroring; outside, there is the reality of the ten thousand *dharmas*. Although the ten thousand *dharmas* are real, it is not that illumination does not attain them. [Rather], inside and outside join together and so perfect [*prajñā's*] power of illumination ... Although the inside illuminates, yet it is "not-knowing." Although the outside is real, yet it has no marks. [Since] inside

and outside are still, they both together are "non-being." This is the stillness in which [even] the Sage cannot differentiate [them].[131]

We are presented with a portrait of the Sage's life that pulls our perspective around. We go from inside to outside, and these "spheres" are conjoined in an unfathomable manner of illuminating that is "not-knowing." The Sage resides in non-being yet is fully involved with all of reality. By playing with these metaphors of light and space, Sengzhao overturns set structures (strictures?) of thinking. We are incapable of understanding them if we cling to our old conceptual grids.

5. Puns

Puns are yet another way in which "wild words" work to suggest the "not-knowing" knowing of *prajñā*. Puns are figures of speech that involve "plays on words," as in Scrooge's dismissive remark to Marley's ghost: "There's more of gravy than of grave about you."[132] Puns work through apparent similarities between words (either of sound or sight) and suggest different meanings by juxtaposing words that ordinarily appear in different contexts. There are various types of puns but like many rhetorical devices they occur in every culture. Although they generally are considered humorous, puns can be serious as well.[133]

There are several instances in "*Prajñā* is Not-knowing" where Sengzhao makes puns with his "wild words." The very first of these is in the essay's title. In Chinese, the title is *Panruo Wuzhi*, literally "*prajñā* lacks knowing." *Wuzhi* is one of the many "*wu*-forms" of words that Daoists employ to convey the open participation in the flow of Dao but there is more than that here for Sengzhao and his audience. For the Neo-Daoists *wu* was "non-being" and had a deeply creative and ontological sense. *Xuanxue* Buddhists maintained the same association, especially in the *benwu prajñā* school. Sengzhao is punning on this in his title, saying not only "*prajñā* is not-knowing" but also that "*prajñā* is non-being knowing." This becomes more obvious when we reflect on the fact that the Sage, whose knowing is *prajñā*, is (as Wang Bi maintained) also *wu*. Non-being thus "knows" as the Sage knows, and this is *prajñā*. This philosophical pun works by bringing together *xuanxue* and Buddhist ideas in a clever, somewhat "wild" way.

A more obvious example of Sengzhao's puns comes in his reply to his opponent who asks what the difference is between the "not" (*wu*) of Sagely

Wisdom and deluded "wisdom." Sengzhao answers, "The 'not' of Sagely Wisdom is 'not-knowing' while the 'not' of deluded 'wisdom' is 'knowing nothing.' Although their 'nots' [seem] the same, what is 'notted' differs."[134] This is one of Sengzhao's funniest lines and it is humor with a point. The Sage and the deluded are exact opposites of each other: the Sage knows without knowing, the deluded person, even if considered "wise," knows nothing. The implication is that the ignorant have it backwards and that becoming wise requires a turning around or conversion to a new way.[135]

One of Sengzhao's best puns involves playing off two closely related words that are pronounced nearly the same and have nearly the same meaning: *zhi* ("knowing") and *zhi* ("Wisdom"). In general, Sengzhao uses the second *zhi* to speak of *prajñā* and the first *zhi* to speak of ordinary knowing.[136] This is a very interesting rhetorical move on Sengzhao's part. Orally, the two words are indistinguishable but the difference is clear when we look at their written forms. The second *zhi* contains all of the first *zhi* but places it over top of the radical for "sun." Visually, this *zhi* is something akin to "sun-like knowing," recalling those passages in the *Lotus Sūtra* comparing the Buddha to the sun and moon in illuminating all things equally.[137] Just as the sun's light illuminates all things more fully than smaller lights, so the "knowing" of *prajñā* encompasses the more confined "knowing" of ordinary people. This is a wonderful pun Sengzhao is making, as it forces us to think on the difference between mere "knowing" and Wisdom. Note as well that Sengzhao does *not* use the second *zhi* for *prajñā* all the time. That would be too easy, making the distinction between them far too neat. This pun is truly "wild" because it refuses to be pinned down once and for all.

There are other puns in "*Prajñā* is Not-knowing" but they are all similar to the ones I have cited. Not all of them are necessarily funny (although they are clever) but puns need not be funny. Puns are "plays on words" that work by twisting our thoughts away from their usual discursive processes. In so doing they draw our attention to the disjunction between language and reality, for words are not stable and do not always have the same meaning. This is why Sengzhao can use them to speak of *prajñā*, although he must use them in an extraordinary, "wild" manner. *Prajñā* is not "knowing" but a "not-knowing" that we can come to know through "wild words."

An Image of Prajñā: The Mirror

One of the most intriguing dimensions of this "wildly worded" play in "*Prajñā* is Not-knowing" concerns Sengzhao's use of the mirror as an image of the enlightened mind. Mirror imagery occurs in many religious traditions, often in their more mystical writings. The Sufis of Islam, for example, use mirror imagery when speaking of attaining a "knowing" that transcends distinctions.[138] The image of the mirror appears in many traditions of Buddhism, perhaps most famously in the poems of the Chan patriarchs Shenxiu and Huineng.[139] And of course, Zhuangzi explicitly says, "The zhiren uses his mind like a mirror–going after nothing, welcoming nothing, responding but not storing. Thus he can bear all things yet not be distressed."[140]

Sengzhao uses the image of the mirror several times in "Prajñā is Not-knowing." The first instance occurs early on, when he says of the Sage, "His empty mind darkly mirrors [Heaven and Earth]. Closing up his Wisdom and blocking his hearing, [the Sage] thus alone awakens to the deep and profound."[141] In the next line he continues, "So it is that Wisdom is a mirroring that probes all secrets yet it has 'not-knowing' in it."[142] Towards the end of the treatise, Sengzhao describes prajñā as the "clarity of [the Sages's] solitary mirroring" which exists "inside."[143]

The mirror image calls for some reflection. Why is the mirror such a common symbol for wisdom? Mirrors are peculiar objects. They are invisible in total darkness but even in partial light they exhibit a distinctive shine. Mirrors also play with our notions of space, opening up the world in ways ordinary vision does not. Mirrors expand our vistas and allow us to see more than we normally would. Moreover, mirrors present the world as it is without interference. But it is when we gaze into a mirror that its true magic reveals itself. If the mirror is well polished, it all but disappears, leaving only our reflection. As Michael Sells says, "vision has become self-vision,"[144] but this vision is turned around, the opposite of our usual perspective.

In China mirrors have long had strong supernatural associations. Ge Hong writes that adepts venturing into the mountains always carried mirrors to ward off evil spirits, for mirrors reflected their true appearance.[145] Mirrors were often used in Daoist meditation to "return to the origin" and archaeologists have found many bronze mirrors dating back to the Han dynasty which are decorated with miraculous landscapes, wild animals, and immortals. Such mirrors seem to have been a means to perceive the fundamental image of the universe.[146] The Zhouli and the Huainanzi also speak of mirrors that could generate fire and others that could produce water.[147] Clearly mirrors were wondrous things with divine powers.

It would thus appear that Sengzhao is using an image with rich associations to speak of the Sage's prajñā. The mirror image is "wild" just like "wild words" in that it not only crosses boundaries of culture and religious tradition, but the power of a mirror plays with our normal perceptions and presents us the world directly opposite to the way we experience it. The mirror is the perfect image of the Sage, whose Wisdom (*prajñā*) is calm and luminous, accepting all things but showing them in a different perspective.

How to read "Wild Words"— A Transformative Interpretation

What are we to do, then, with these "wild words"? Can we make sense of them? What options do we have for scholarly discussion of them? On one level we cannot discuss them, for Sengzhao's "wild words" contradict ordinary usage. "Wild words" speak non-rationally and non-analytically, whereas scholarship is preeminently rational and analytic. "Wild words" are "nonsense" and always will be. Modern scholars who have tried their hand at "wild words" provide many insights into early Chinese Buddhism yet they get us no closer to understanding "*Prajñā* is Not-knowing." Ironically, despite their different methods and conclusions, previous studies of Sengzhao's work share a common perspective: they treat "*Prajñā* is Not-knowing" in an "objective" manner.[148] The treatise becomes an object to be studied, analyzed into its constituent parts, and manipulated to certain ends. A good example is Richard Robinson's discussion in *Early Mādhyamika in India and China*. Robinson treats "*Prajñā* is Not-knowing" just as he would a work of contemporary Western philosophy. That is, he makes the essay over into a series of propositions about "reality." While his approach has advantages it misses the essay's poetry, how it resonates with other texts and its overall rhetorical flourish.

One would think that dealing with *prajñā* calls for a different sort of engagement. Sengzhao, after all, is not a logical positivist but a *śramaṇa* seeking the Buddha Dao. "*Prajñā* is Not-knowing" was written from a follower of a tradition to other followers. We probably should view Sengzhao as a Buddho-Daoist scholastic struggling to clarify the "truth" of his tradition along the lines suggested by St. Anselm's motto *fides quarens intellectum* ("Faith seeking understanding"). Sengzhao does not question the possibility of enlightenment or the "truth" of the Sages and Bodhisattvas, nor are the trappings of formal logic his primary consideration. In "*Prajñā* is Not-knowing" Sengzhao is seeking the depths of Sagely Wisdom, a Way that unites Heaven and Earth and overcomes the ignorance and suffering that underlies *saṃsāra*.

This religious and salvific aspect of the text becomes clear when we reflect on the essay's concluding sentences:

Thus the *Chengju* says, "[The Sage] does not act yet surpasses acting." Ratnakuta says, "[The Buddha] lacks mind and consciousness but has no unawakened knowing." These [lines] probe Spirit and exhaust Wisdom; they discuss the Ultimate that is beyond symbols. [If you] go through and understand my words, the Sagely Mind can, indeed, be known.[149]

Sengzhao tells us explicitly that "*Prajñā* is Not-knowing" is a means of truly knowing the Sagely Mind, but few scholars have commented on Sengzhao's meaning. Instead, they follow the objective approach such as Robinson employs when paraphrasing Sengzhao's arguments. This method may actually block the text's truth. Certainly it would prevent a more dialogical exchange with the text such as Gadamer counsels. It may be no coincidence that these same scholars pass over "wild words" in silence.[150] In so doing, though, they miss Sengzhao's point. Like Sengzhao's opponents in "*Prajñā* is Not-knowing," most scholars confine themselves within ordinary discourse, the realm of *ratio* and the *mingjiao*, yet this runs directly counter to Sengzhao's warning that the Sagely Mind cannot be analyzed.[151] These scholars thus invariably never "get" *prajñā*.

But what if we approach the essay differently? What if we actually listen to what Sengzhao says? Then "*Prajñā* is Not-knowing" will not be a treatise *about prajñā* but a textual way *to prajñā*. Through "wild words" Sengzhao brings us into *prajñā*'s unconfined, all-embracing mind. We can truly understand "*Prajñā* is Not-knowing" only by playing along, letting "wild words" play on us. As Zhuangzi says, "Just go along with things and let your mind move freely."[152]

"*Prajñā* is Not-knowing" is not a rational work. It messes up ordinary categories of understanding in order to provoke realization. Buddhist scholar Roger Corless has observed that "Buddhist teaching is transformation mani-festing as information."[153] Sengzhao certainly is a good Buddhist (and a good Daoist), and "*Prajñā* is Not-knowing" is his invitation to transform. "*Prajñā* is Not-knowing," really is a "*prajñā* workbook" and to understand it means entering into a transformative hermeneutic relationship with the text and opening ourselves to a different understanding of the world. One requirement for entering this new understanding is approaching language differently than we have before. We must accept a freer view of language in which words flow and move in multiple ways as Buddhist and Daoist texts demonstrate—a language of "wild words." Sengzhao's *kuangyan* are amusing and unsettling, and call for a willingness to follow their lead. A linguistic orientation that separates, defines and demarcates things breaks down when "wild words" enter the picture. "Wild words" romp through neatly defined categories, upsetting our properly proportioned take on reality. They are not "civilized" and therein lies their power. "Wild words" require a transformative reading.

Steven Katz, a scholar of mysticism, argues that language in religious texts does not just have denotative or referential meaning. "Mystical" language in particular often performs various tricks that defy normal meaning.[154] As Katz writes, "Such linguistic ploys exist in many places throughout the world, usually connected with the conscious construction of paradoxes whose necessary violation of the laws of logic are intended to shock, even shatter, the standard epistemic security of 'disciples,' thereby allowing them to move to new and higher forms of insight/ knowledge."[155] Mystical texts, then, are not descriptions of reality so much as linguistic paths leading to greater realization. This is exactly what Sengzhao is doing in "*Prajñā* is Not-knowing." His essay is a mystical text and its "wild words" call for a transformative reading.

Other scholars have noted the need for transformative readings of texts from various religious traditions. In *Theology After Vedānta*, Francis Clooney describes Advaita Vedānta as a *textual* tradition wherein realization occurs as an event in a practiced, educated reader. "Truth" emerges from engagement with the text even though this "truth" is beyond language. One works through the text to attain the realization of the tradition, not really to get information about the tradition. As Clooney states, "Though the liberated state is beyond words it occurs, like Advaita's truth, after the Text, after its words and procedures of reading and arguing, its intellectual and social practices, and not apart from it. One reaches wordlessness through words, after them, according to them."[156] The engagement called for by the "wild words" of "*Prajñā* is Not-knowing" is analogous to that of Advaita Vedānta. In both cases, the text accomplishes its work only if the reader follows the text's lead. The texts work by playing with the ordinary rational mode of thought we bring to the text in order to lead us beyond discriminations and divisions. In the case of Sengzhao, such play through rationality leads to *prajñā*.

Kuang-ming Wu makes a similar point concerning the Daoist "philosophy" of the *Zhuangzi*. As Wu notes, Zhuangzi describes his own discourse as comprised of "goblet words" (*zhiyan*)–words that, like a goblet, tip when full but right themselves when empty. Thus, Wu says, "goblet words adapt to and follow along with the fluctuations of the world. They do so in order to arouse an appropriate discernment and response."[157] According to Wu, such words form an *evocative discourse*, an indirect means in which words, reader, and message are redefined; the medium itself is the message that "carries over" the reader into a fresh understanding and authentic living.[158] This is the life of the Sage who conforms to Dao, who wanders freely and happily throughout Heaven and Earth, naturally and without self-interest. Similarly, Sengzhao's "wild words" also comprise an evocative discourse. By evoking a "Daoist" understanding, "wild words" transform the reader's ordinary mind into the Mind of *Prajñā*.

Questions about "Wild Words," Irony, and the Problem of Misunderstanding

Needless to say, there are numerous questions provoked by the "wild words" of "*Prajñā* is Not-knowing." My interpretation of the essay is the result of my on-going engagement with the text and has been shaped by repeated questions I have posed. Such questioning is the very heart of interpretation and can continue indefinitely. It may be helpful, then, to briefly examine three questions that have arisen during my reading that I believe are important for understanding the essay and Sengzhao's other works:

1. Does Sengzhao use "Wild Words" in His Later Essays?

This is an interesting question, for the term "wild words" (*kuangyan*) does not occur in the other essays in the *Zhaolun*. We might conclude from this that Sengzhao dispensed with "wild words" as his thinking matured. However this conclusion is not born out when we examine his other works. Although Sengzhao does not use the phrase "wild words" in them, he maintains the same view of language as he does in "*Prajñā* is Not-knowing," and employs the same rhetorical tricks.[159] Moreover, he designates the language he uses to discuss such abstruse subjects (the same language used by the *sūtras* and other texts he cites) with special terms. In "Things Do Not Shift" he speaks of "true words," whereas in "Emptiness of the Unreal" he describes it as "deep and far-reaching words."[160] Most likely these are different designations for the same tricky language,[161] a "wild" language that "unsays" by turning back on its underlying presuppositions and pushing us towards direct realization.

2. Do "Wild Words" Anticipate Later Developments in Chan and Zen?

Chan Buddhism ("Zen" in Japan) is famous for its paradoxical view of language as unnecessary for awakening while using language in the form of koans (*gongan*) to provoke such awakenings. Koans constitute a special type of discourse used extensively in various Chan and Zen schools (e.g. Rinzai) as an integral part of training.[162] Their main purpose is to lead students to progressively greater awakenings (*satori*) and so transform their minds. In fact, Katz uses koans as his primary example of transformative language in religious traditions.[163] Sengzhao's "wild words" are also instances of transformative language, so is it possible that they influenced Chan and Zen tradition? Based upon the evidence, the answer is a definite but qualified yes.

Sengzhao had a reputation in later centuries as a Chan patriarch (although he was not part of any Chan lineage),[164] and his writings were commented upon by Huideng (ca. 839) of the Ox-head school and by Deqing (1546-1623), who reports that reading the *Zhaolun* spurred his own awakening.[165] Sengzhao's writings were incorporated into koan collections such as the *Biyan lu*, and may even be alluded to in the *Mumonkan*.[166] Heinrich Dumoulin observes "It is hard to exaggerate the influence of Seng-chao on Chinese Buddhism. In particular, his spirit has left its stamp on Zen, mainly through his description and praise of prajna as wisdom in all its clarity, 'unnameable, undefinable, existent and nonexistent, not real not unreal,' making its home in the realm of the Absolute."[167] By quoting Sengzhao's discussion of *prajñā* here, Dumoulin emphasizes that Sengzhao's influence on Chan and Zen revolves around his "wild words." Apparently later masters continued to find "wild words" effective long after Sengzhao's time. I will return to the relationship between "wild words" and koans in Chapter Five.

3. What is the Relationship between "Wild Words" and Claims of Ineffability?

Michael Sells in his *Mystical Languages of Unsaying* explores the theme of language's basic inadequacy to express ultimate matters, a problem that he calls the "aporia (unresolvable dilemma) of transcendence."[168] This aporia is not confined to any particular culture or religious tradition. Texts dealing with this aporia typically employ a special type of discourse, *apophasis* (lit. "speaking away") in order to speak of that which cannot be spoken. Sells' discussion of the aporia of transcendence and the cross-cultural nature of apophasis point towards one of the fundamental problems of religion and philosophy, the mystery at the heart of existence. The Ultimate Truth has attracted and evaded humanity's comprehension since earliest times and it is often claimed that it cannot be fully known or spoken of. Thus, it is said, Truth is ineffable. The mystery lies beyond the reach of words and concepts.[169]

Is Sengzhao claiming in "Prajñā is Not-knowing" that prajñā is ineffable? At first blush this does indeed appear to be what he says, for he writes in the Part 1, "It (prajñā) is without marks and, being nameless, [it] cannot be attained with words and symbols."[170] Yet in the very next line he says that he will attempt to speak of prajñā using "wild words" and does so for the rest of the essay. There would be no reason for this if Truth were completely ineffable. Sengzhao, then, is not making a claim of radical ineffability, only that language must work differently when it comes to such questions as the nature of the Sage/prajñā. "Wild words" in their weird way affirm language as a means to truth. The key is understanding language and knowing how to use (and interpret) it skillfully.

In the end, "Prajñā is Not-knowing" speaks of a different way of knowing and being-in-the-world. This "Sagely way" freely conforms to reality and so transcends ordinary distinctions. Such a life cannot be attained by following the clean crisp road map of rational analysis. Perhaps we can describe Sengzhao's "wild words" as "religious" in the sense of the Latin religio, a joining of what is separate, or "mystical" in that such words speak of a mysterious, direct engagement with Truth. This is subject to which I will return in Chapter Five. I prefer to use the term "holy," for Sengzhao's "wild words" speak of prajñā as a way of recognizing the fundamental wholeness of reality. More than this, though, they "hallow" the holy and call us to participate in its play.

There is a great irony in my discussion of "wild words," for despite my urgings to go with their free and easy romping, my own words remain rather tame. Irony is a chief mode of evocative discourse. Masters of irony such as Zhuangzi, or Nāgārjuna put forth no thesis but speak (or write) by saying what they do not mean. Theirs is an agile word play, a flitting between "being" and "nothingness" that perpetually calls into question our ideas and our "selves." Sengzhao, too, is a master of irony, for his "wild words" work by saying one thing while meaning various other things. We can even regard Sages and Bodhisattvas as ironic, for they engage in serious work that is effortless and playful; their concern for others is married forever to the knowledge that those "others" and their sufferings are not truly real. My own discourse, however, is not ironic in the same measure. Although it may be playful at times, on the whole it is descriptive rather than evocative. By addressing Sengzhao's "wild words" in a scholarly fashion, I am confined by academic rules, bound by the strictures of my discipline. My words do not embrace all of reality but "seek him through intellectual investigation and inquire after him with arguments." Thus I say, "This is what Sengzhao is doing." But is he *really*? I am striving to make "Sengzhao" settle down in *this dharma*. Can anything but *duḥkha* come of this? Is it possible to engage in scholarship that does not grasp? Interpretation is never final, and perhaps ultimately all interpretations must be surrendered.

Questions abound and proliferate within interpretation. In the perspective I present, the "wild words" of "*Prajñā* is Not-knowing" are not propositions about reality nor a systematic analysis of superior intelligence but are a means of inscribing the *prajñic* perspective. Sengzhao's "wild words" comprise a Dao, a linguistic path or way of speaking about and orienting ourselves within the world. "*Prajñā* is Not-knowing" marks out such a path and invites us to travel along. It is a strange path that twists and turns through dark and light and calls for extraordinary mental agility. Perhaps only one who has attained "perfect wisdom" can follow it. The way is (t)here but, as Zhuangzi reminds us, ultimately such a way is made by people walking.[171]

Kumārajīva seems to have gotten Sengzhao's "wild words" as did later Chan and Zen thinkers but others were perplexed. According to sources, the members of Huiyuan's community at Lu Shan did not understand Sengzhao. One of them, the lay recluse Liu Yimin, wrote to Sengzhao asking for clarification. In the next chapter we will see how he mistakes Sengzhao's meaning and how Sengzhao once again uses "wild words" to make his points. Liu misunderstands Sengzhao and, sadly, Sengzhao also misunderstands Liu. Their correspondence is, thus, a failure. But I believe it is a "Daoist" failure that can help us understand other aspects of "wild words" and perhaps the process of understanding itself.[172]

· 4 ·

LIU YIMIN'S FAILURE TO UNDERSTAND SENGZHAO'S "WILD WORDS"

"*Prajñā* is Not-knowing" was born of Sengzhao's hermeneutic concerns. By his day the Dharma had become a source of conflict and discord. The Buddha Dao was in danger of being lost. Fortunately, **Kumārajīva's** appearance along with Yao Xing's rise to power and dedicated support signaled an important change. The time was now ripe for recovering the true message of the Dharma and spreading it through the world. So it was that Sengzhao turned to *prajñā*, a highly controversial but crucial subject in Buddhism. Inspired by his master's exegeses and his own studies, Sengzhao endeavored to explain *prajñā* even though *prajñā* defies articulation.

"*Prajñā* is Not-knowing" centers on the figure of the Sage/Bodhisattva. The essay follows Sengzhao's predecessors in identifying these ideals as one and the same yet differs on several points. First, it critically engages previous notions of *prajñā*, arguing where they are mistaken. Second, the essay draws upon **Mādhyamika** thought and texts. Third, the essay confronts the aporia of transcendence and overcomes it through "wild words," a confused and confusing rhetorical style that leads to the all-embracing mind of Sagely Wisdom. "*Prajñā* is Not-knowing" does not *describe prajñā* so much as seek to *inscribe* it in the mind of his reader.

"Wild words" are the special language Sengzhao uses to convey the Sage's *prajñic* perspective. They cannot be read *informatively* but require a *transformative* reading. Although **Kumārajīva** and some of Sengzhao's commentators got this point, not everyone did. Many of Sengzhao's contemporaries were bewildered by his work and one, Liu Yimin, wrote Sengzhao a letter asking him to clarify certain points. Sengzhao replied to this letter, and their exchange, appended to "*Prajñā* is Not-knowing,"[1] is a fascinating text for hermeneutic investigation. "The Correspondence" illustrates one of the great ironies of creative hermeneutics—that *misunderstanding* often results when traditions are brought together in new ways. It thus seems to confirm Schleiermacher's view that misunderstanding "occurs as a matter of course."[2]

How to Approach "The Correspondence"—Some Preliminary Considerations

Regarding the exchange between Liu Yimin and Sengzhao Liebenthal observes, "Though a basic difference is revealed which cannot be overcome because both have learnt to interpret the world on other analogies, the sincerity with which they confess to that fact and nevertheless remain friends is noteworthy."[3] The friendship between Liu and Sengzhao was based in part on how much they had in common. Both were literati and so shared a similar intellectual formation. Liu and Sengzhao dedicated their lives to religious pursuits, having both "left the world" albeit in different fashions (Liu was a hermit but remained a layman while Zhao was a monk but not a hermit).[4] Both men were devoted to their respective masters and were singled out by them as "special." Furthermore, their careers mirrored each other, but in opposite ways. Liu was born into wealth and fame but retired to spend his days in solitude. Sengzhao was poor but achieved fame as a monk, eventually holding a post in Yao Xing's translation bureau.

In light of such considerations, we should view Liu and Sengzhao as "fellow seekers in Dao" similar to the "Seven Worthies" or Masters Si, Yu, Li and Lai from chapter six of the *Zhuangzi*, who had "no disagreement in their hearts."[5] "The Correspondence" resembles the *qingtan* discussions that were in vogue in *xuanxue* circles except that as a *written* exchange, it differs from an oral dialogue. Written exchanges tend to be more literate and philosophical, as the medium allows for the correspondents to more finely craft their responses.

Written correspondence flourished among Buddhists in Sengzhao's day. During the early middle ages, monks and laity often used letters as a medium for explaining and propagating teachings. Although some letters were personal, they also provided a forum for discussing doctrinal matters.[6] The most famous of these exchanges took place between **Kumārajīva** and Huiyuan.[7] Begun after the completion of the *Dazhi du lun* (~405) their correspondence marks a milestone in Chinese Buddhism. Not only did **Kumārajīva** and Huiyuan's exchange help differentiate Buddhism from Daoism, it opened up lines of communication between Chang'an and Lushan. In so doing they paved the way for Liu and Sengzhao to begin their correspondence.

Before examining "The Correspondence," however, we need to reflect on what our task requires. We are switching from one text ("*Prajñā* is Not-knowing") to another ("The Correspondence"), and so must also shift our focus to another context as well. Moreover, this new text is comprised of two separate letters,[8] so when we deal with it we, in a sense, have two contexts—the translation center in Chang'an and the community at Lushan. Nonetheless both letters share with "*Prajñā* is Not-knowing" the same larger context of early fifth century China. This "scene switching" is important to keep in mind, for it affects how we understand both "*Prajñā* is Not-knowing" and "The Correspondence." We cannot treat the letters and Sengzhao's essay as the same sort of texts, despite their similarities and the fact that they share the same cultural context. This changing of texts and contexts puts us in mind again of the hermeneutic difficulties that arise from distance, be it geographic, cultural, or temporal. As both Ricoeur and Gadamer note, distance *is* productive in interpretation but it must be crossed. Liu and Sengzhao tried to close the distance between themselves some 1500 years ago, meeting with only limited success. Our task is more difficult, for we must cross a greater distance without the benefit of mutual friends or a shared heritage.

Through the rest of this chapter I will examine "The Correspondence" as a text about problems of understanding that also poses difficulties for our understanding. In the next section I reconstruct Liu's life and situation on Lushan and the circumstances surrounding the reception of "*Prajñā* is Not-knowing," all of which form the context for Liu's letter. I then turn to Liu's letter, specifically his questions. This section involves not only translating Liu's questions but hearing what lies *behind* them so that we can see where he differs from Sengzhao. Such activity is the very heart of interpretation.[9] After examining Liu's letter and his questions, I then shift to Sengzhao's reply, focusing on what Sengzhao does and role of "wild words" in his letter. In the final section I step back and examine my findings in order to pinpoint some of the sources of the misunderstanding between Liu and Sengzhao.

Each step I take in this chapter is part of my attempt to make sense of the exchange between Sengzhao and Liu Yimin, just as both Liu and Sengzhao try to make sense of what each other says. My interpretation is based upon judgments and speculations informed by my concerns as a scholar and my historical and cultural situation just as their interpretations are based on judgments and speculations informed by their own concerns and situations. This raises an intriguing question: would either Sengzhao or Liu Yimin understand my take on their exchange? This seems unlikely, for we come from vastly different worlds and the cultural and linguistic barriers between us are formidable. Perhaps, though, we should not ask *if* Liu or Sengzhao would understand my account but to what extent and in what manner they would, for as Gadamer says, we understand differently if we understand at all.

Lushan, Liu Yimin, and the Reception of *"Prajñā* is Not-Knowing"

The History of Lushan

It may prove helpful to look at the history of Lushan to get a sense of the factors influencing Liu's perspective. Lushan, located near the city of Xunyang, was one of China's many holy mountains. Long associated with Daoist hermits, it had been a Buddhist center since the late Han. To the Chinese Lushan exuded an aura of magic with its wondrous scenery and mysterious grottoes, and many legends were told of the immortals and spirits dwelling on its slopes. Sometime around 385 it became the home of Huiyuan, the intellectual leader of the Chinese *saṅgha* before Kumārajīva's arrival. Huiyuan had been involved in the debates between the *prajñā* schools but was particularly devoted to worship and meditation. He came to Lushan at the invitation of a fellow monk, and local authorities were so honored they constructed a monastery for him, the Donglin si ("Monastery of the Eastern Grove").[10]

Under Huiyuan, the Donglin si became a thriving center, known for the purity and austerity of its inhabitants and their intense *dhyāna* practice and worship. Huiyuan's reputation as a holy man was so great that he was the *de facto* head of the southern clergy even though he held no official post. Like Kumārajīva, he was something of a living Sage to his followers. He lived on Lushan for thirty years and according to the *Gaosengzhuan*, in all that time he never left the mountain.[11] His life of withdrawal seems to have been his way of demonstrating that a *śramaṇa* must be pure and avoid contact with the "dust and toil" of worldly affairs. Huiyuan strove to keep his retreat above the political intrigues of his day, and by and large he was successful, for Lushan was spared the purges various rulers imposed on southern monasteries.

Yet though Huiyuan tried to flee the world, the world would not let him go. He was repeatedly sought out for advice, had audiences with many rulers and even used his holy charisma to protect his community and southern monasteries from state regulation.[12] Huiyuan cultivated contacts at the southern court of Jiankang and among the rulers of Chang'an, who held him in high esteem. Yao Xing and his brother Yao Song sent him numerous letters and religious artifacts from Central Asia. They informed him of Kumārajīva's arrival and Yao Xing even requested that Huiyuan write an introduction to the *Dazhi du lun* after Kumārajīva had translated it.[13] Through such contacts Huiyuan established Lushan as a bridge between north and south, and the mountain became an important stopping place for monks travelling between Chang'an and the southern cities. These circumstances allowed Lushan's inhabitants to stay in contact with the outside world without leaving their retreat.[14]

Several characteristics of Lushan have direct bearing on "The Correspondence." It was a community based on the ideal of withdrawal from the world, although in reality Lushan had an ambiguous status as both central and peripheral to the affairs of state and *saṅgha*. From 391 to 397 Lushan was home to Gautama Saṅghadeva, a Sarvāstivāda Abhidharma master who had lasting influence there despite Huiyuan's interest in *prajñā* studies and attraction to Kumārajīva's Mādhyamika teachings.[15] Lushan was also dominated by Huiyuan's charismatic presence and its inhabitants were inspired by his views on purity and detachment. In addition, the community was *not* focused on translation and did not struggle with hermeneutic difficulties like the translation bureau in Chang'an. Lushan was a place of worship and meditation. The cult of Amitābha, the Buddha of the "Pure Land" (Sukhāvat, Qingtu) was strong there and Huiyuan encouraged *dhyāna* practice among his followers and throughout the south.

Lushan, then, was a retreat modeled on the Neo-Daoist qingtan ideal but run under strict Buddhist discipline. It was something of a "hide-out," and as a result, the mountain attracted many people—monks, nuns and various cultured laity. Several of the latter were quite famous, among them a retired official known as Liu Yimin.

Liu Yimin—"Gentry Recluse"

Liu Yimin[16] (354–410) is an intriguing figure. He has no official biography but we can glean some information on him from a document written by Huiyuan now preserved in the *Guang hongming ji*.[17] Liu was originally Liu Chengzhi and hailed from Pengcheng. His family claimed descent from the Han ruling house, and Liu served as a prefect in Hubei for a time but "retired" due to social and political unrest.[18] Eventually he came to the Western slopes Lushan where he built a meditation cell. The date of his retirement is uncertain but he was one of the first gentry recluses to arrive and he remained on Lushan for the last fifteen years of his life.[19]

Liu was a man of intense religious devotion so it is little wonder he got along well with Huiyuan. In his letter to Sengzhao he speaks of his life on Lushan with deep reverence and gratitude,[20] and he dedicated himself to a *dhyāna* practice of visualizing the Western Paradise of Amitābha. This practice, a form of *buddhānusmṛti* ("recollection of the Buddha"), entailed prolonged concentration on a Buddha image in order to attain a vision of Amitābha in his Paradise.[21] Huiyuan extolled the practice and many of his lay followers engaged in it. Although not particularly complex, this practice was very difficult easy, requiring strict moral purity and strong devotion. After three months the devotee withdrew to a secluded spot to concentrate on Amitābha night and day for a week. Afterwards, Amitābha would appear and preach the Dharma directly to the practitioner.[22] This form of meditation was extremely powerful; some accounts state that Liu's visions were so vivid that they enabled him to foresee his own death.[23]

Several texts are attributed to Liu, including a song in a collection of hymns by the Lushan community ("Collected Odes on *Buddhānusmṛti-samādhi*") which Sengzhao praises.[24] Liu's most famous work, though, is the Lushan community's collective vow to be reborn in *Sukhāvatī*, composed and first recited in 402.[25] Liu died in 410, most likely from the illness to which he alludes in his letter to Sengzhao.[26]

This brief sketch does not do Liu's life justice but it provides information that will help us understand his letter to Sengzhao. Liu was very much a gentry recluse, albeit one of deep faith and strict discipline whose life centered on religious practice. We have no evidence of him sharing Sengzhao's hermeneutic concerns about spreading Dharma,[27] nor was Liu involved in the critical "cutting edge" work of the Chang'an community. In addition, Liu seems to have been very much under Huiyuan's sway as his chief lay disciple.[28] This latter point is significant, for it means that Liu probably shared Huiyuan's deference to Kumārajīva's circle in doctrinal matters. All of these factors influenced Liu in his reading of "*Prajñā* is Not-knowing."

The Reception of "*Prajñā* is Not-Knowing" at Lushan

Our best sources of information on the arrival of Sengzhao's essay are Liu and Sengzhao's letters. In his letter Liu writes, "At the end of last summer the venerable Daosheng first showed me a copy of your treatise '[*Prajñā*] is Not-knowing'."[29] Sengzhao writes of the same person in his letter to Liu: "The venerable Daosheng was here a short time ago, having stayed with us for several years. [Whenever] we had occasion for words, [he] always sang your praises. [I understand that] during his journey south you saw each other."[30] The person to whom they refer was Zhu Daosheng (360–434), the eminent monk whose work on the *Nirvāṇa sūtra* had great consequences for the development of Chinese Buddhism.[31] Daosheng had been a disciple of Zhu Fatai (one of the figures associated with the *benwu* school) and came from Pengcheng, Yimin's homeland. He arrived at Lushan in 397 where he studied **Sarvāstivāda** Abhidharma under **Saṅghadeva** before venturing to Chang'an in 405 or 406 at Huiyuan's prompting. There he participated in various translations. In 408 Daosheng returned to Lushan, carrying with him a copy of "*Prajñā* is Not-knowing." [32]

Sengzhao's treatise was received enthusiastically on Lushan. Liu was one of the first to see it and was among the foremost in his praises. According to the *Gaosengzhuan*,

> When the Lushan "retired scholar" Liu Yimin saw Zhao's essay he emphatically said, "I did not think that there was a Pingshu (He Yan) among the Buddhist clergy." Thereupon he passed it on to Huiyuan, who was also enthusiastic. Yuan exclaimed "Never has there been [anything like it.]" As a result all [in the community] read and savored [it], and each wanted to keep it longer.[33]

The overwhelmingly positive nature of Liu's response is even more clear in Liu's letter:

> It is written in a pure and refined style, and the meaning of its contents are deep and convincing. Your exposition of the words of the Sages is pleasant and it returns [the reader to the True meaning]. I savored your flourishing [prose] and could not put it down. Truly we can say you are one who has bathed your mind in the depths of the *vaipulya* [*sūtras*] and attained knowledge of the profound that is beyond [common] understanding. When this essay is published, then *prajñā*'s various currents will probably no longer be debated, for [it] will be [fully] under-stood. How could this not bring such joy and happiness?[34]

Liu adds that both he and Huiyuan studied the treatise thoroughly and that many in the Lushan community cherished it.[35]

Although the popularity of "*Prajñā* is Not-knowing" owes much to the influence of Liu and Huiyuan, credit must also go to Sengzhao's literary talents. Sengzhao was a master of allusion and clever turns of phrase. Liu's praise of the essay's style and his comparison of Sengzhao to He Yan as well as Huiyuan's comment on its uniqueness show that Lushan was an appreciative audience. We also should not discount the aura of authority surrounding the text. Sengzhao, after all, was a scholar of some renown. He was one of Kumārajīva's chief disciples and his essay carried the Kuchean master's blessings as well as the air of his association with Yao Xing, the Heavenly King of Jin.

Sengzhao's elegant style and air of authority gave "*Prajñā* is Not-knowing" great weight and importance, and predisposed those on Lushan to read it as a definitive declaration of Sagely truths. But there is more to the essay than fine style and presentation. The main reason "*Prajñā* is Not-knowing" created such a stir was because of its discussion of *prajñā*. *Prajñā*, the wisdom of the Sage/Bodhisattva, was a great concern on Lushan. To varying degrees all of the inhabitants were striving towards it and they had a living model of this ideal before them in the person of Huiyuan. Thus they would have deemed *any* discussion of Sageliness quite relevant to their situation, particularly one that was beautifully written by a scholar who also dwelt in the presence of two other Sagely figures, Kumārajīva and Yao Xing.

Problems, however, soon arose. Although those who read "*Prajñā* is Not-knowing" praised the essay, they were also perplexed by it. Liu says several times in his letter that he does not follow Sengzhao and that many of his colleagues wrestled with the essay's lines.[36] In his conclusion he writes that Huiyuan understood the essay thoroughly but if so, the venerable monk did not enlighten his charges. It seems that on a fundamental level, the Lushan community could not make sense of this work.

Thus we find the readers of "*Prajñā* is Not-knowing" lost in a cloud of unknowing. Sengzhao, long concerned that Sagely Wisdom be properly understood and convinced that the prophecies concerning the new age of Wisdom were coming true, wrote his essay to clarify what *prajñā* was. The catch is that his "clarification" works via obfuscation. From the perspective of ordinary knowing (the "small understanding" of the quail, the mind enmeshed in *saṃsāra*), *prajñā* is a "dark light," a "not-knowing." Yet this "not-knowing" is really an all-knowing (the "great understanding" of the Peng bird, the Mind of the Sage/Bodhisattva) that embraces everything without distinction. Language cannot describe such knowing because language functions by making distinctions. *Prajñā* slips through the net of words and symbols. However, words and symbols *can* help us if we are mindful of how to use them. Sengzhao understood this fact and wrote "*Prajñā* is Not-knowing" to show how *through* words we can attain the Wisdom *beyond* words. He does so through "wild words" but these make his Dao (discourse) a dark and twisted path. The essay calls for dedication and nimbleness of intellect, so it is no wonder many of his readers did not understand.

"*Prajñā* is Not-knowing" clearly baffled those on Lushan and it was because of this that Liu Yimin wrote to Sengzhao. The date of his letter is uncertain, although Liu most likely wrote Sengzhao in the last month of 409.[37] "*Prajñā* is Not-knowing" had arrived at Lushan over a year before and had been discussed for several months, perhaps even becoming a source of conflict between various parties. The evidence from Liu and Sengzhao's letters, though, is meager at best. At this point we will turn our attention to Liu's letter and examine it in detail before going on to Sengzhao's replies.

Liu's Letter to Sengzhao

Overview

Liebenthal says that the exchange between Liu and Sengzhao evinces the "high cultural level on which the literate Chinese society at that time stood."[38] If by this Liebenthal means that both men demonstrate grace, learning and elegance of style then he is right. Both letters follow certain formalities: they each are prefaced by a covser letter, speak of the weather, make inquiries concerning the recipient's health, and are sprinkled liberally with polite praises. Obviously both Liu Yimin and Sengzhao are at home in the *li* (rituals of etiquette and social intercourse) and irrespective of their religious vocations, they were true "Confucian" gentlemen and scholars.

Liu's retirement on Lushan fits the *qingtan* ideal of the early medieval literati. It should be no surprise, then, that his letter bears the trappings of a *xuanxue* Buddhist treatise. The *xuanxue* character of Liu's letter shows in his florid prose style. His introduction[39] is especially precious, and its nuanced lines make for difficult reading. The letter is also filled with allusions to the *Laozi*, *Zhuangzi* and *Yijing*, and Liu uses common *xuanxue* phrases such as "beyond words and symbols,"[40] and "the Nameless."[41] Throughout his letter Liu demonstrates an abiding concern for Sageliness similar to Sengzhao's and he appears to be familiar with the positions of Sengzhao's "opponents."[42] Furthermore, Liu also refers to "*prajñā*'s many currents,"[43] an indication that he knew of the debates between the *prajñā* schools.

Nonetheless Liu's letter shows greater concern with Buddhist practice than we usually find in the writings of other *xuanxue* thinkers. We see this, for instance, in Liu's emphasis on the purity and discipline of Huiyuan and the Lushan community,[44] and in his mention of *samatha-vipassanā*.[45] Moreover, it appears that Liu's ideal Sage was influenced by the image of Amitābha in Sukhāvatī.[46] None of these subjects are mentioned in debates between the *prajñā* schools or in Sengzhao's essay but probably reflect Liu's life on Lushan.

Overall, Liu's letter is an interesting piece of writing. Rather ornate in style, it demonstrates Liu's familiarity with Buddhist and *xuanxue* terms and his deftness in handling them. Liu also shows great skill in posing his questions to Sengzhao, a fact that will become clearer when we examine the letter in detail in the following pages.

Structure of the Letter

Liu's letter has a deceptively simple structure masking a surprising rhetorical complexity. It is rather short (less than one thousand characters) and has three main parts: cover letter, main letter, and closing. The main letter includes an introduction and three smaller sections in which Liu poses his questions.

Cover Letter (154c: 25–27)

The cover letter is the shortest portion. Liu opens by greeting Sengzhao and expressing delight in hearing from his friend. He then assumes a rather "chatty" tone as he discusses the weather, inquires about Sengzhao's health and mentions his own illness. Liu closes this section by explaining that he now has the opportunity to communicate with Sengzhao through Huiming, an otherwise unknown monk who will act as courier.

Although this is the shortest part of Liu's letter it is very significant. In this section Liu introduces the recurring theme of reaching across distance, of trying to become close despite separation. Even in its formal tone, we find intimations of genuine friendship between Liu and Zhao in Liu's concerns for his health, his longing for the company of his fellow "seeker," and his desire to make his feelings known. Interestingly, Liu refers to himself as Sengzhao's "disciple," thus rhetorically placing himself in Sengzhao's lineage and establishing a closeness between them. The letter thus becomes the means for Liu to have an audience with his "master."

Main Letter, Section 1 (154c: 28–155a: 20)

This first section is the longest and most complex part of Liu's letter. Liu opens by referring to the people of antiquity (distant in time) who were also distant in space, just as he and Sengzhao are. Yet he longs to close this distance and in a sense he does by turning his attention to the Chang'an community. Liu gives his best to **Kumārajīva** and praises Sengzhao before once again lamenting being so far away. He then shifts his focus to Lushan and Huiyuan, praising his master and expressing his joy at being in such noble company. Liu then shifts back to Sengzhao and speaks of "*Prajñā* is Not-knowing." He praises the essay lavishly, stating his belief that it will finally resolve all debates on this abstruse subject although he adds that few will be able to appreciate it due to *prajñā*'s difficult nature. As if to demonstrate this, Liu makes a few comments on one section of the essay before expressing his uncertainty on a few points and inviting Sengzhao to explain them to him again.

This section is quite clever, marked by a constant back and forth movement between closeness and distance that mirrors our own interpretive interplay with the text. Liu continually emphasizes his desire to overcome the distance between Sengzhao and himself yet just as often reminds us of their separation. In the lines of his letter he tries repeatedly to bring the two of them together before finally doing so through their shared interest in *prajñā*. Liu then turns to Sengzhao's essay, which now becomes their common ground. At this point Liu then addresses explicitly hermeneutic matters, closing with just the right amount of praise and insight so as to make Sengzhao *want* to answer:

> The obscurity of Principle is difficult to state. The lone singer [of such songs] has few respondents. Truly, unless there is one who [can] make manifest what is beyond words and symbols, [those who] are led in accordance with symbols will end in error. I think the section of your reply on using the "object" (*ālambana*) to seek out Wisdom is convincing and quite conclusive. Indeed, it is extremely clever and cannot be faulted. Nonetheless, one [such as myself] who is dull has difficulty understanding it all at once. I still have one or two doubts remaining. When you have time to study the subject [again] I hope that at your leisure you can once more give me a rough explanation.[47]

Here Liu not only asks the "master" for guidance but entices him to provide such.

Main Letter, Section 2 (155a: 20-27)

Liu poses his first question in this section. He tries to establish Sengzhao's thesis that *prajñā* is neither existent nor non-existent, void but illuminating, by quoting two passages from Sengzhao's essay[48] and a *Fangguang* passage that Sengzhao also cites.[49] Liu goes on to quote two other passages from "*Prajñā* is Not-knowing" which support the same thesis. Finally he tries to restate Sengzhao's meaning in more familiar *xuanxue* terms only to confess that he does not understand this theory.

This is a fascinating section, for Liu does not actually pose any specific questions here nor does he systematically present his own views. Instead, he quotes various parts of Sengzhao's treatise. It seems that Liu is testing his interpretation of "*Prajñā* is Not-knowing" and asking the monk for further guidance. This would explain why Liu is so inexact in his quotations (he is struggling to understand, not arguing) and why he tries to paraphrase the essay in different words–words he has probably borrowed from more familiar texts. It seems likely as well that we are dealing with Liu's own attempt at understanding Sengzhao here.[50] Finally, this section shows Liu's honesty in his admission of failure. Liu may be "far" from Sengzhao both geographically and intellectually but by admitting his limitations the "disciple" is perhaps never closer to his "master" and invariably we are also drawn closer despite our even greater distance.

Main Letter, Section 3 (155a: 28–b: 5)

In this section Liu becomes a mouthpiece for the entire Lushan community. As he says, "Yet now [let us] discuss what [we on Lushan] doubt with respect to the meaning of your most excellent treatise. We wish to seek out the differences within the Sagely Mind."[51] It appears that Liu and his colleagues are confused over Sengzhao's portrayal of the Sagely Mind (*prajñā*) as a "not-knowing knowing." Liu examines both knowing and not-knowing separately, framing them as mutually exclusive alternatives. In the first case, he compares the Sage's "knowing" to the insights arising out of *samatha-vipassanā*. In the second case, Liu speaks of the Sage's "not-knowing" as a natural process in which his Spirit remains outside the transformations, leaving only his "wise understanding" (*huiming*). At this point Liu asks for proof of Sengzhao's theory so that he and his colleagues can examine it.

This section is more complex than the preceding one. Liu makes little attempt to quote Sengzhao's essay (although he does misquote Sengzhao in one place) but he still is trying to interpret Sengzhao's ideas in more familiar terms. More importantly, Liu proposes two alternative ways of understanding what Sengzhao is getting at, both of which seem to end in absurdity. We see a distinctly critical edge here,[52] and this tone is underscored by Liu's asking Sengzhao for additional proof. It may be that Liu is veiling his personal criticisms of Sengzhao behind the mantle of the entire Lushan community or he may be reporting others' views. Nonetheless he still indicates that he will defer to Sengzhao by phrasing his alternative proposals as questions and requesting proof not to challenge Sengzhao but so that he and his colleagues can get clearer on this matter.

Main Letter, Section 4 (155b: 5–18)

This section is longer than either Section 2 or 3, in part because Liu's question here is actually two-fold. As with the previous section, Liu is communicating the difficulties his colleagues have in understanding Sengzhao's middle way. The first part of Liu's question concerns Sengzhao's depiction of the Sage as existing yet not existing. Liu declares that those on Lushan[53] think that a Sage who responds to the details and observes the transformations cannot be said to "not exist" (buyou). Liu quotes a passage from Sengzhao's essay in which the monk says the Sagely Mind is free from ignorant perception,[54] pointing out that Sengzhao never fully explains this idea. Liu then offers two possible alternatives, neither of which make sense, and asks Sengzhao to explain his point again.

In the second part of Liu's question he focuses on the Sage's "matching" and "affirming." Liu and his colleagues do not see how the Sage can be said to not "match" things with names yet leave nothing not "matched" and to not "affirm" the truth of statements yet have nothing not "affirmed." Liu quotes several lines from Sengzhao on these points,[55] and then tries to reason out what Sengzhao means by proposing three alternatives, two of which end in absurdity and one of which merely distinguishes between ignorance and understanding. As with the first part of this question, Liu concludes by once again asking for Sengzhao's instruction.

This is the most challenging of Liu's questions and marks the climax of his letter. Once more Liu is voicing the views of others in the Lushan community and is trying to put Sengzhao's ideas in more familiar terms. The critical edge of the previous section dominates here, as we can see in the alternative explanations that Liu proposes. He makes these proposals based on Sengzhao's own statements yet all of them end in absurdity. In several instances Liu asks for more proof and explanation, even saying at one point that he does not understand Sengzhao's meaning.[56] In the very last line, however, Liu reverts to a more deferential tone, saying, "I really desire that you instruct [me] once more and so disperse my ignorance."[57] The combination of deference and criticism throughout this section gives it great rhetorical power. It evinces independent thinking on Liu's part and challenges Sengzhao's statements while still inviting further guidance. By this section, "The Correspondence" has taken on the air of a debate between equals rather than a question and answer session between master and student.

Closing (155b: 18–21)

In the final section of his letter Liu shifts to a more general discussion of Sengzhao's treatise such as we saw in his introduction. Liu relates how when the essay arrived he studied it along with Huiyuan whom, he says, fully understood it. Liu then insightfully observes the differences between his and Sengzhao's views seem to be rooted in their own presuppositions, a point he emphasizes by adding that many on Lushan struggled to understand Sengzhao's essay. Liu closes by expressing his regrets that he and Sengzhao cannot be together.

The closing section resembles the cover letter in brevity and formality and, like the cover letter, is highly significant. Here Liu assesses the situation and evinces remarkable hermeneutical awareness: "Yet it appears as if each [of us] has his own base [of understanding] and so perhaps our principles are not necessarily entirely the same."[58] Although Liu addresses this line to Sengzhao it may also apply to his colleagues since he may not share all the opinions he voices.[59] Is Liu saying that such differences, rooted as they are in previous understandings, are irreconcilable? Perhaps by relating how he and Huiyuan studied Sengzhao's essay and how others on Lu Shan eagerly poured over it Liu is reassuring Sengzhao that they are a willing audience *despite* their differences.

Be that as it may, Liu's final line is most intriguing. He writes, "We regret not being with your honored self at this time."[60] In these words Liu is not just saying that he regrets their geographical separation but also their *philosophical* separation.[61] Moreover, he is also hearkening back to the opening lines of his letter where he speaks of those in antiquity who were separated from each other. Such people did not share the same place in space/time with each other (or with Liu and Sengzhao for that matter) yet they were close despite the distance between them. Similarly, Liu suggests that although he and Sengzhao are distant—geographically and philosophically—such distance can be overcome. The concluding phrase "at this time" leaves open the possibility that they will close this distance through continued correspondence.

Liu Yimin's Questions and his Presuppositions

All in all, Liu's letter to Sengzhao is quite sophisticated. It is concise yet erudite, and shows Liu really struggling to understand Sengzhao's points. The letter challenges Sengzhao's statements, seeks guidance and further explanation, yet conveys an air of authentic friendship and sincerity. A more detailed examination of Liu's questions will reveal what exactly he is asking Sengzhao and what lies behind his letter.

As we have seen, Liu asks a total of three questions in his letter, although to call them "questions" may technically be incorrect since the term "question" generally refers to a simple, explicit interrogative. None of Liu's "questions" is simple or explicit. Indeed, Liu's first question is *implicit* and is signified only by his confession that he does not understand Sengzhao's thesis. Liu's second question contains two proposed answers, both of which seem to lead to absurdity. Liu's third question actually comprises two questions. In each of these "sub-questions" Liu also proposes two alternative answers that both seem to end up in absurdity.

The fact that Liu argues by pointing out the absurd implications of Sengzhao's statements raises the possibility of Liu being familiar with Mādhyamika thought. Such *reductio ad absurdum* arguments (*prasaṅga*) are a hallmark of Mādhyamika reasoning and Sengzhao uses them in "*Prajñā* is Not-knowing."[62] Did Liu pick up this technique from Sengzhao and use it against him? Perhaps. Could Liu have become familiar with Mādhyamika *before* reading Sengzhao? This scenario is unlikely. We have no evidence for Mādhyamika texts entering China prior to Kumārajīva and Liu had retired to Lushan years before then. Furthermore, Chinese intellectuals used of the laws of contradiction and the principle of the excluded middle (both of which are integral to *prasaṅga* arguments) as far back as the Warring States era.[63] Liu more than likely learned to argue from native Chinese texts although he may have studied Buddhist argument as well.

Throughout his letter Liu constantly asks for Sengzhao's guidance to help him understand his meaning. In his second and third questions, though, Liu increasingly challenges the implications of Sengzhao's statements. His letter, then, is really a critical response to "*Prajñā* is Not-knowing" and reveals a lot about his own understanding and the differences that separate him from Sengzhao. As we shall see, these differences have great hermeneutic implications.

Question 1

This is the least critical of Liu's questions. It not only contains the most quotations from Sengzhao's essay (five), it also is our best evidence of Liu attempting to retranslate Sengzhao in terms that are more familiar to him. As Liu says:

> Now then, the Sagely Mind is wondrously still. [It is] Principle, ultimately identical with non-being. [Truly, we can speak of it as] "hurrying without haste" [and] "sitting still yet racing around." Therefore, in knowing it does not dispense with stillness and in stillness it does not dispense with knowing. Never is it *not* still; never is it *not* knowing. Thus His Way of moving things to their perfection and transforming the world, although it abides in the midst of the Named yet is remote, [ultimately] identical with the Nameless. The obscurity of such Principle defies comprehension! I remain obstinate in my perpetual dim-wittedness [regarding this theory].[64]

This is a fine example of *xuanxue* writing, with its allusions to Daoist texts and nods to He Yan's *Wuming lun*. More to the point, we can see in this question Liu admitting his failure to follow Sengzhao and implicitly asking for more clarification. Between the lines he is saying, "tell me how I can understand this theory."

There are several striking things about this passage. To begin with, Liu misses Sengzhao's point. Liu says that the Sagely Mind never is not-knowing when Sengzhao clearly says in the very title of his treatise that *prajñā* is (always) not-knowing. Even more telling, though, is how Liu frames his question on the assumption that the Sage is an individual in meditation. This betrays his own orientation towards the *dhyāna* practice of "recollection" so popular on Lushan.[65] Liu speaks of the Sage in terms of knowing (*zhi*) and stillness (*ji*), yet in the passages from "*Prajñā* is Not-knowing" that Liu quotes Sengzhao does not use these terms. Rather, Sengzhao speaks of the Sage as beyond the difference between existence and non-existence, combining stillness (*ji*) and function (*yong*) and so calmly responding to all things. Sengzhao does *not* mean a person who attains insight in meditation. His Sage, like Guo Xiang's *zhiren*, does not sit quietly in the forests[66] but has awakened to the principles of reality and embodies them here and now. Sengzhao's Sage is a Bodhisattva who realizes the essential sameness (*samatā*) of all *dharmas* and knows no difference between *saṃsāra* and *nirvāṇa*.

Question 2

Liu's second question is more serious, for it concerns the difference between the Sage's knowing and not-knowing. For our purposes it makes little difference whether this question is Liu's own or that of his colleagues on Lushan. What is important is what Liu says and how he says it:

> Can we say that the probing of [the Sagely Mind] supernaturally reaches the end of all items [in the cosmos], all the way to the "hidden tallies" [of our lives]? Or is it that the Sage's Mind is essentially spontaneous, supernatural and perhaps alone in influencing [all things]? If the probing of [the Sagely Mind] supernaturally reaches to the end of all items [in the cosmos], all the way to the "hidden tallies" [of our lives], then what you call "still illumination" is essentially *samatha-vipassanā*. If the Sage's Mind is essentially spontaneous, supernatural and alone in influencing [all things], then his responses to the multitudes of things will certainly thereby cease. [The Sage's] mindfulness of the cosmic items is "dark," yet he alone illuminates the revolving [of all things]. His Spirit is pure and outside of the transformations, yet the brightness of his wisdom remains [within]. We should have some profound proof [of this theory] that we can examine in order to distinguish them.[67]

This passage is pure Buddho-Daoism yet its significance lies in how Liu both strives to get Sengzhao's meaning and actively challenges him, asking for more proof. Despite his deference, Liu is an independent thinker.

What is even more striking in this passage, though, is Liu's focus on the Sage in relation to individual religious practice. This seems to be Liu's overriding concern, as evinced by his mention of *samatha-vipassanā* and of Sagely Wisdom as extending to the very mysteries of our fates.[68] As such, this passage resembles Question 1, which shows the same concern for meditation. In "*Prajñā* is Not-knowing," though, Sengzhao does not discuss such matters but focuses on the Sage's nature. This confusion between the practical and the ontological seems to lie behind Liu's misquoting of Sengzhao as saying "still illumination" (*jizhao*) when Sengzhao actually speaks of "stillness and function" (*jiyong*).[69] Perhaps most telling of all, in seeking to understand *prajñā* as knowing and not-knowing Liu proposes two mutually exclusive alternatives. Liu sees the Sage as a meditator attaining cosmic insight or a personification of natural laws (responding to and directing all things) but not both. He separates the Sage's knowing from his being-in-the-world, which runs directly counter to Sengzhao's treatise. It is as if Liu were trying to separate a Bodhisattva's *prajñā* and *karuṇā* when these, although distinguishable in thought, are always together.

Question 3

This question comprises two separate but related questions and allegedly expresses the views of Liu's colleagues on Lushan. It is also the most critical section of Liu's letter, taking Sengzhao to task on several points. In order to make clear what lies behind this question, I will deal with each part separately.

The first part of this question focuses on the Sage as existing yet not-existing. Specifically, Liu is trying to reconcile Sengzhao's paradoxical declarations of the Sage's manner of knowing and being and the *xuanxue* ideal of the Sage as a compassionate cosmic personage. Liu writes:

> Those who doubt [your treatise] think that a knowing that carefully meets and responds to the cosmic changes and that observes the transformations cannot really be said to be "not-existing." Yet your treatise says, "it (*prajñā*) fundamentally lacks the knowing [characterized by] deluded grasping." But you never explain the principle of not-grasping on which [the Sage] relies. We think you ought to first determine the Way (Dao) of responding that the Sagely Mind relies upon. Is it that he matches [names with things] by only illuminating the markless (i.e. Ultimate Truth)? Or is it that he matches by fully observing the changes? If [he matches] by observing the changes, then this differs from [illuminating] the markless. If he only illuminates the markless, then he does not meet the cherished [things]. Since [you seem to say that the Sage] does not meet the cherished [things] yet has the power of cherishing and meeting, we do not apprehend your meaning. Please do us the favor of instructing us again.[70]

As we can see, Liu's difficulty centers on the Sage's knowing and acting. The Sage acts by meeting (and guiding) the ten thousand things and establishing names for them, thus he must know existing things. Sengzhao, however, says the Sage's knowing is *not* a knowing but an "illuminating" of the Ultimate. How are these ideas to be reconciled?

This is a revealing passage. To begin with, although Liu is critical, he offers Sengzhao a way to "save face" by explaining his meaning in greater detail. Liu has also put his finger on a real difficulty in how Sengzhao speaks of the Sage. Does the Sage passively illuminate the Ultimate or observe the cosmic workings and actively guide existing things? In Liu's view, the Sage must exist in order to guide things and to establish their proper names since names only concern things that exist. But if the Sage merely illuminates the Ultimate, then how can he be said to be compassionate or involved with existence? Liu seems to conceive of the Ultimate as a separate realm from worldly existence. This passage also shows that Liu views the Sage as someone who orders the cosmos, much like the mythic Fu Xi in the *Yijing*. In addition, we should not forget Liu's concern for religious practice and his devotion to Amitābha. Liu knew the Sage was real because he and his fellow devotees contacted him in their *samādhi*. For Liu, the Sage is a cosmic person like Fu Xi and a compassionate savior like Amitābha. In neither aspect can the Sage be impersonal or uninvolved with the realm of names and things. Logically speaking, then, the Sage *must* exist.

The second part of Liu's question finds him once again grappling with the Sage as existing yet not-existing, although here he focuses on the Sage's "matching" and "affirming." After quoting a passage from "*Prajñā* is Not-knowing" Liu writes:

> Now then, if [the Sage] has no matching and yet among things there is nothing not matched, then why [even] consider this as perfectly matching [all things with their proper names]? If [the Sage] has no affirming [of statements as Ultimately True] and yet among things there is nothing not affirmed, then why [even] regard this as truly affirming? How can it be that [the Sage] truly affirms [statements] while yet not affirming [them as Ultimately True] or perfectly matches [all things with their proper names] while yet not matching? And still you say, "[the Sage] matches yet has no matching" and "affirms yet there is nothing affirmed"? If you mean that perfectly matching [all things with their proper names] is not constantly matching [them up] and truly affirming is not constantly affirming [statements as true], this [your statement] simply speaks surreptitiously of the basic difference between understanding and ignorance. In my stupidity I do not understand the meaning of what you say. I really desire that you instruct [me] once more and so disperse my ignorance.[71]

Liu is concerned here about the Sage's matching things with names and affirming statements as true. They thus have to do not only with how Sengzhao speaks of the Sage but also how the Sage understands and uses language. Theses matters are directly related to Sengzhao's depiction of the Sage as existing yet not-existing because language deals only with existing things.

This is one of the most philosophically interesting passages in Liu's letter, for it shows the strong *mingjiao* influence on his thought. As we saw in Chapter Three, among the cardinal tenets of the adherents of *mingjiao* are the ideas that things have a one-to-one relationship with their names and that these names are clear and distinct. The Sages of antiquity established these names and ensconced them in their writings (the *jing*). Those who attain Sagehood comprehend the relationship of names and things, and their words and teachings continue the proper use of names. Sengzhao, though, speaks of a Sage who does not obey such rules and seems to use names in an almost careless fashion. Sengzhao's "Sage" matches names with things but does not regard this as a binding relationship and affirms the pragmatic truth of statements without considering such statements as really true. This notion strikes Liu as incredible, for he takes Sengzhao to mean that the Sage is ignorant of the proper use of language.

Such concern with the proper use of language may seem trivial to us but for Liu and his colleagues it was a serious matter. If the Sage were ignorant of how language works, it would be disastrous. Not only would the "wise" be unable to apply the wisdom of the past to the present, the words enshrining that "wisdom" would be untrustworthy guides. The entire heritage—the *jing* (both Confucian-Daoist Classics and the Buddhist *sūtras*) and the *zhuan* (commentaries)—would be called into question. Dao could be lost and perhaps never recovered. Even worse, Dao might never have been attained in the first place, since the original Sage rulers might have been ignorant. Religious life would have no basis. Hymns, instructions for meditation and *mantras* might prove ineffective in leading the worshipper to insight or bliss. The very way of life on Lushan would be undermined, for the power of the community's vow to be reborn in Sukhāvatī and perhaps even Amitābha's vow to save the faithful would be in doubt.

Both parts of Question 3 reveal basic differences between Liu and Sengzhao concerning the Sage. In the first part, Liu focuses on the Sage's relationship with existing things. For Liu, the Sage must exist to know things and guide them, especially the individual religious practitioner. In the second part, Liu zeroes in on the Sage's use of language. In Liu's view, the Sage must know how to match language properly with reality and do so once and for all, otherwise all Sagely discourse is in doubt. Liu argues similarly in both parts of this question, referring to Sengzhao's words from "*Prajñā* is Not-knowing" and proposing possible alternative answers that are mutually exclusive. Both parts point to a fundamental assumption Liu makes. For Liu, the Sage's knowing is separate from his being-in-the-world. The Sage either knows the Ultimate or engages with the ten thousand things. The Sage either matches things with their proper names and affirms their truth, or has no knowledge of language and its relation to the world. Liu divorces *prajñā* from *karuṇā*, wisdom from acting. This assumption is a far cry from Sengzhao's non-dualistic vision of *prajñā*, and the hermeneutic gulf separating Liu and himself becomes even more apparent when we look at Sengzhao's answering letter.

Sengzhao's Reply Liu Yimin

Overview

Although overlooked by some scholars, Sengzhao's reply to Liu Yimin is a significant piece of writing. Totaling over two-thousand words, it is longer than either "Things Do Not Shift" or "Emptiness of the Unreal," rivaling "*Prajñā* is Not-knowing" in length. By the time Sengzhao wrote his reply, Kumārajīva had finished translating the *Kārikās* as well as the *Dvādaśamukha śāstra* ("Twelve Topic Treatise," T.1568), thus completing all of the "Four Treatises,"[72] and Sengzhao had written "Emptiness of the Unreal" and "Things Do Not Shift." During this period Sengzhao had learned a great deal more about Mādhyamika thought than he had when he wrote his first essay. His reply to Liu may be his most mature work and can be considered his revised take on *prajñā* after several additional years of Mādhyamika study.

One of the most important features of Sengzhao's letter is the portrait of the Chang'an community that he provides.[73] Sengzhao speaks not only of Kumārajīva's translation activities and the vast treasury of texts still to be translated, but also of teachers of meditation, *Vinaya* and Abhidharma whom Yao Xing had invited to Chang'an. From such details it is apparent that in Chang'an both the intellectual and practical aspects of Buddhist life (discipline, meditation and worship) flourished. Under Yao Xing Chang'an was the greatest Dharma center China had yet seen. It is little wonder that monks from Lushan would travel there and that they would look to someone like Sengzhao for guidance.

Sengzhao's reply to Liu is a prime example of *xuanxue* Buddhism even while showing great Mādhyamika influence. Sengzhao liberally alludes to and quotes from Daoist and Buddhist texts as he further elucidates the mysterious character of the Sage. Sengzhao's reply also evinces the friendliness and admiration that we see in Liu's letter. Zhao praises Liu for his questions and speaks admiringly of a collection of songs from Lushan that he received earlier. He also mentions that he is including a copy of his commentary on the *Vimalakīrti* along with his replies to Liu's questions. Such remarks are more evidence of the on-going exchanges between Chang'an and Lushan and further indicate how important these exchanges were to the members of those communities.

There is some confusion concerning the date of Sengzhao's letter. Sengzhao writes that he received Liu's letter in the twelfth month of the previous year and dates his own cover letter the 15th day of the 8th month.[74] He refers to events (the arrival of certain Central Asian teachers, translation activities in progress, the presence of Daosheng) that indicate his letter was written after 407 or 408. According to Mano Senryū, Sengzhao received Liu's letter in 409 and replied in 410.[75] However, Seiichi Kiriya maintains that Zhao received Liu's letter in 410 and replied in 411.[76] All questions of dates aside, Sengzhao's letter is an important philosophical and literary work. The sophistication of this text becomes quite apparent when we look at its rhetorical structure.

Structure of Sengzhao's Letter

Like Liu's letter, Sengzhao's has three parts: cover letter, main letter, closing. The main letter includes several sub-sections in which Sengzhao praises Liu and his colleagues on Lushan and relates the activities of the Chang'an community, but he dedicates most of the letter to answering Liu's questions. Although Sengzhao's letter merits serious attention for its skillful composition, due to constraints of space we will only briefly examine its sections before turning our attention to its most important feature: Sengzhao's use of "wild words" to once again convey the *prajñic* perspective.

Cover Letter (155b: 23–26)

The cover letter is quite brief. In it Sengzhao expresses his longing to meet Liu and frustration at their separation but his distress is assuaged to an extent by the arrival of Liu's letter. He relates that it filled him with joy, as if meeting Liu in person. He then engages in basic formalities regarding the weather, his health etc., closing with a statement that he will be brief since a messenger is leaving soon.

   Despite its brevity, this cover letter is notable for several reasons. It is dated (the 15th day of the 8th month), and this along with Sengzhao's references to various events enables us to be reasonably sure of its time of composition (~410). The cover letter also picks up and echoes Liu's desire to meet and indicates Sengzhao's joy at receiving Liu's questions. Sengzhao shows concern for Liu by asking after his health (recall Liu's mention of his illness) and informs his friend that he, too, is sick. Interestingly, by speaking of his health Sengzhao provides a subtle clue for interpreting his letter and his relationship to Liu. The character Zhao uses to refer to his illness, *bing*, is the same character Zhuangzi uses when speaking of Master Yu falling ill,[77] and the same character that denotes the feigned illness of Vimalakīrti.[78] In the latter two cases neither "illness" is cause for alarm or a source of suffering. Master Yu's illness is an example of the wondrous workings of Dao while **Vimalakīrti's** illness is illusory. Similarly, Sengzhao's "illness" may be a literary device—a hint that what follows will reveal the truth of Dao.

Main Letter, Section I (155b: 26–156a: 4)

The first section of Sengzhao's main letter has three parts: an introduction, a section praising Lushan and Huiyuan, and Sengzhao's discussion of the Chang'an community. Throughout this section Sengzhao echoes Liu's refrain of longing to close the distance between them but Sengzhao emphasizes their closeness over their separation. Sengzhao praises Liu and his colleagues for their pure and secluded lives but reserves special praise for Huiyuan. As he tells Liu, "Being in the presence of a gentleman of such purity everyday, [you should] rejoice and take pleasure in [his vast] understanding."[79] Sengzhao switches to a more "newsy" tone when detailing the activities of his colleagues in Chang'an, saying how fortunate he is to be present in such august company and expressing his wish that Liu could join him. It is as if Sengzhao were saying, "I am fine. Wish you were here." Sengzhao concludes by complimenting Liu on his song "Meditation on the Buddha"[80] and relating how he is enclosing his commentary on the *Vimalakīrti* for Liu to review. He then praises Liu for his insightful questions and announces that he will do his best to answer them.

Overall Section I of Sengzhao's letter closely mirrors Section I of Liu's letter. We see in Sengzhao's lines the same reaching across the distance and rhetorical effort to bring the correspondents closer. Like Liu, Sengzhao expresses regret at their separation and veneration for his friend's companions and master. He also refers to himself with humility and expresses gratitude for his holy community. Sengzhao also politely flatters Liu and his writings much like Liu flatters Sengzhao. Finally, Sengzhao is able to convey his concern for Liu in this section through rather poetic yet formal language. We see here Sengzhao's Confucian side, his ease and skill with *li*. This raises an interesting question—is Sengzhao modeling his letter on Liu's? If so, then the "master" truly is learning from his "disciple." The similarities between the letters may point to a standard model for such correspondence that each is following but it is difficult to be sure. On the other hand, the similarities may reflect a *qingtan* literary game of "call and response." In any event, the letter's parallel structures provide a fascinating glimpse of *xuanxue* Buddhist rhetoric. Both correspondents are skilled literati.

There are, however, some important differences between this section of Sengzhao's letter and the corresponding section in Liu's. Sengzhao tends to stress the closeness between he and Liu rather than the distance, as if set-ting Liu's mind at ease. His allusions are also more explicit than Liu's as, for instance, in his comparing the Lushan community to the Seven Worthies.[81] The most striking difference, though, is that Sengzhao gives far more details about Chang'an than Liu gives about Lushan. There are probably several rea-sons for this, including Sengzhao's conviction that the growth of Buddhism at Chang'an proves that the prophecies he alludes to in "*Prajñā* is Not-knowing" are coming true.[82] Nonetheless, politics plays a role here as well. Chang'an was a cosmopolitan city, the site of Yao Xing's throne and the translation bureau headed by Kumārajīva. By detailing the various activities in Chang'an Sengzhao both communicates the richness of his situation and gently puts Liu in his place by asserting his superior prestige. Sengzhao would also have been encouraged to do so by the deferent tone Liu assumes in his letter.[83]

Main Letter, Section II (156a: 4–157a: 6)

Section II is where Sengzhao addresses Liu's questions. It comprises two main parts, the first of which is very short while the second is quite long and com-plex, having seven sub-sections. Sengzhao does not proceed in a straightforward manner in this section but jumps forward and backward through all three of Liu's questions. In the first part Sengzhao briefly addresses Question 1, becom-ing more critical in the second part. There, he begins by addressing Question 2, explaining how both alternatives that Liu proposes are incorrect. He then returns to Question 1 and combines it with Question 2 to demonstrate that both have absurd implications. Sengzhao then turns to Question 3, countering each set of alternatives that Liu proposes. At this point he then turns back to Question 2 and argues that the presuppositions behind it are wrong. Sengzhao then argues in the same way against the presuppositions behind Question 3. He ends this section by addressing Question 3 again, explaining that since ultimately the Sage eludes definitions, all words prove inadequate.

One of the exciting things about this section is what it reveals of Sengzhao's debating skills. Sengzhao had a reputation as a debater and in this part of his letter we can see why. He is very exact in his approach, quoting Liu's words precisely at various points and addressing each of Liu's questions twice. He also cites scripture several times to back up his claims, much as he does in "*Prajñā* is Not-knowing." Overall, his replies are strong and convincing. Sengzhao comes off as authoritative but not harsh, further indication that in this relationship he is indeed the "master" albeit a gentle one.

In addition to demonstrating Sengzhao's skill in debate, this section also shows his growing familiarity with Mādhyamika dialectics. For example, when countering Questions 1 and 2, Sengzhao uses a *prasaṅga* argument to show the absurd implications of Liu's statements.[84] Later he uses yet another *prasaṅga* argument to counter Liu's views in Question 3.[85] Although Sengzhao uses a *prasaṅga* argument once in "*Prajñā* is Not-knowing,"[86] the fact that he uses the style *twice* in his reply indicates that he was more comfortable with it by this time. Sengzhao also tells Liu several times in this section that to understand the Sage we must take a middle way between assertion and negation.[87] Nāgārjuna, of course, insists that this is the way of the Buddha, who taught the way between *all* extremes. The clearest evidence that Sengzhao has studied Mādhyamika, though, is his use of the *catuṣkoṭi* (four-cornered negation or "tetralemma") when he argues against the presuppositions behind Question 2:

> [When I] speak of it (*prajñā*) as "not an existing [thing]," [my] words do not affirm it as "existing." [However], I do not mean to affirm it as "*not* existing [as a thing]." When I speak of it as "not a nothing," [my] words do not affirm it as "nothing," [yet] I do not mean to affirm it as "not a nothing." [*Prajñā*] is neither an existing [thing] nor is it not an existing [thing]. Neither is it nothing nor is *not* a nothing.[88]

The *catuṣkoṭi* is an invention of Indian logic. Nāgārjuna uses it repeatedly in the *Kārikās* and it is one of the hallmarks of Mādhyamika reasoning. Sengzhao's use of the *catuṣkoṭi* in the above passage is not quite Nāgārjunian[89] but it does show that he had studied the Mādhyamika master and had developed a real understanding of his arguments.

Although Sengzhao has several criticisms of Liu and his colleagues in this section his strongest critique concerns their focus on words as the way to arrive at truth. Sengzhao implicitly criticizes this view of language when first addressing Liu's difficulty in Question 1[90] but he is more explicit later when he says, "Those [of you] who discuss [my essay] lay too much emphasis on words to fix my meaning."[91] Liu and his friends view language as having a clear and precise relationship to reality whereas Sengzhao knows this is not the case. Sengzhao drives this point home in the very last lines of the main body of his letter where he tells Liu, "I am afraid that [all this] producing of matching [things with names] and affirming [them as true] is just our calling things 'so'. [In reality] those things in themselves are not 'so'."[92] This undue reliance on the power of words to describe reality is the root of Liu and his colleague's difficulties with "*Prajñā* is Not-knowing" and, as we shall see, is a major reason for their misunderstanding.

Section III, Closing (157a: 6–11)

The final section of Sengzhao's letter is the most clever. After arguing against Liu's statements at some length, Sengzhao proceeds to call into question the very basis of such discussion. Like Zhuangzi, Sengzhao puns his way along in order to point beyond all words. In the end, he even admits that he has been too prolix and so leaves it to his audience to go outside of language.

This section is one of Sengzhao's true masterpieces. Replete with wonderful word-play, it amounts to a stinging critique of those who are fixated on language as well as an ironic commentary on Sengzhao's own wordiness:

> So then, our words are an abundance of traces, the product of [many] different paths. And yet with words there is what is not worded, just as with traces there is what is not traced. Therefore those skilled in wording words seek to word what they cannot word; those skilled in tracing traces seek to trace what they cannot trace. The Ultimate Principle (*prajñā*) is "void" and "dark." To [attempt to] determine it by thinking is already to go astray. How much more [do we stray] by using words? I fear what I have transmitted is far from [your understanding]. [Perhaps] all you keen-minded gentlemen will, by using my words, anticipate [what lies] outside speech.[93]

Here Sengzhao provides yet another clue to help us wind our way through the labyrinth of his essay and his answers to Liu Yimin. Ultimately, his lines lead to *prajñā*.

The Role of "Wild Words" in Sengzhao's Replies to Liu's Questions

Sengzhao's letter is complex. Masterfully written and incisive in its criticisms, it patiently instructs us how to apprehend Dharma. In his text, Sengzhao seeks to lead his readers to understand *prajñā*. Yet these features do not distinguish it from Liu's letter, which is also a complex and critical piece that shows a similar concern for understanding. What sets Sengzhao's letter apart is that in answering Liu, he again uses the *prajñic* language of "wild words," just as he does in "*Prajñā* is Not-knowing."

Sengzhao clearly states that ordinary language will not lead to *prajñā*. He writes, "Moreover, to reach our destination there are no words. Words will only divert [us] from our destination. [We] make statement after statement [yet it] does not end. And after all, what can be distinguished? So I will address your points with 'wild words' instead."[94] This is an extremely important passage, for Sengzhao signals here that he will shift away from the ordinary discourse he has been using to the extraordinary discourse of *prajñā*. At this point he begins another effort to induce *prajñā* using the same rhetorical moves as he does in "*Prajñā* is Not-knowing": literary allusion, "chain arguments," paradox, playing with metaphors and puns.

1. Literary Allusion

Literary allusions are one of the most common rhetorical devices Sengzhao uses in "*Prajñā* is Not-knowing" so it is no surprise he uses them again in his reply to Liu. As I have noted, allusions are ways of playing in and with other texts and they can be found in the writings from cultures the world over. Allusions frequently appear in Chinese literature and their function depends upon the common heritage that the literati shared. Allusions function like hints or "inside jokes." In alluding, the writer is subtly playing with texts and the reader in order to provoke greater understanding. Allusions mine the heritage for insight; the old becomes new. This means that allusions are always "wild" in a sense, for they push us beyond our previous notions.

Sengzhao makes many allusions in his letter to Liu. One of the first comes in his first reply to Liu's first question where Sengzhao instructs to Liu on how to open his mind and understand: "[I suggest that you] consider this [idea] as [something] to ponder in your heart of hearts. Attain it inwardly by 'forgetting the words.' Take it up and fix you mind upon it. [Moreover, let me ask you something:] Why should it suffice to use the inconsistency of peoples' feelings to seek for the difference within the Sagely Mind?"[95] This is a double allusion to the *Zhuangzi* and Wang Bi's *Zhouyi lueli*, both of which advocate "forgetting words" to attain true understanding.[96] Another allusion occurs in the next section of the letter where Sengzhao says, "[The Sagely Mind] is the mysterious mechanism secretly revolving [Heaven]. It functions but does not move."[97] This line refers to the opening of chapter fourteen of the *Zhuangzi* in which Zhuangzi speculates on who (if anyone) controls the workings of the universe.[98] With both allusions Sengzhao expands our perspective by bringing in other texts while pushing us to find the meaning of his words for ourselves. He says more by saying less, hence his instruction is that much more effective.

Perhaps the most interesting and playful of Sengzhao's allusions comes in the midst of a section in which he addresses Liu's third question. Right after Sengzhao has told Liu that he puts too much emphasis on words,[99] he says:

> [You] search the Great Square and seek [four] corners. In your inner minds you foresee [events] and regard it as manifesting the Dark [Principles]. [You] hold on to the certain matches that you know. Therefore, when you hear that the Sage has "knowing" you take it to mean that he has a mind [like an ordinary person]. And when you hear that the Sage has "no knowing" you take it to mean that he is like a great void. [However], the ideas of "having" and "not having" are one-sided views that you hold. How can this be dwelling in the Way of Non-duality?![100]

Here Sengzhao alludes to chapters forty-one and thirty-eight of the *Laozi*[101] as well as one of Confucius' statements in the *Analects*,[102] all to point out Liu's shortcomings. In the first case, Sengzhao suggests Liu is so focused on words that he would take a colloquial expression for the whole of reality (the "Great Square") literally and try to find its corners. In the second case, Sengzhao compares Liu to someone who has premonitions and considers them to be deep insights into the nature of Dao. With the third allusion Sengzhao is chiding Liu for not "getting" the various hints he has dropped throughout his writings. All three allusions illustrate the superficiality of Liu's understanding, a fact that Sengzhao elaborates in rest of the passage. The allusions here are also somewhat humorous (particularly the third) and that allows Sengzhao to make his point more easily. Sengzhao not only takes us to Laozi and Confucius' texts, he also shows us where Liu falls short (perhaps bringing us a smile along the way) and encourages us to go deeper. We see for ourselves that we must let go of our literal and superficial views that try to fix words into a single, set definition. By alluding to the *Laozi* and the *Analects*, Sengzhao gets this across far more effectively than if he directly told us that Liu is wrong. Instead, he forces Liu (and us) to think deeper *through* his words. Our awareness must shift beyond mere analysis and risk dwelling in non-duality.

The examples I cite are not the only instances of Sengzhao's use of allusions in his reply to Liu but they demonstrate with good effect how such allusions are "wild." Sengzhao's allusions create an intertextual movement in his work that pushes us to different angles of understanding. They also attest to his skill in composition and serve to quietly complement the more obvious intertextual movement we see in Sengzhao's quotations from *sūtras* as well as Liu's letter and "*Prajñā* is Not-knowing."

We should note that Sengzhao's allusions do not logically counter Liu's views. Allusions are not rational arguments. From a strictly logical standpoint allusions are extraneous ornamentation, perhaps even veiled appeals to authority and thus, signs of fallacious reasoning. Yet this is not a problem for Sengzhao. Sengzhao certainly does reason with Liu but more importantly, he is trying to lead him to *prajñā*. In light of this it is significant that none of the allusions I cite occur within arguments. The first comes in a passage where Sengzhao is coaching Liu in how to attain insight through his text whereas the last two come after Sengzhao has concluded his arguments. It seems that Sengzhao first counters Liu and only then uses allusions to coax him to fuller understanding. Moreover, although Sengzhao does allude to the *Analects*, most of his allusions in "The Correspondence" are to the *Zhuangzi* and the *Laozi*. These texts were perennial favorites of *xuanxue* thinkers and had reputations for being somewhat "wild," making them fitting source texts for Sengzhao's own "wild words."

2. "Chain Arguments"

Despite having learned a great deal about formal reasoning after writing "*Prajñā* is Not-knowing" and demonstrating a greater command of logical inference than in his earlier essay, Sengzhao still employs "chain arguments" in his reply to Liu. In itself this is a strong indication that *prajñā* cannot to be attained through rational thinking. "Wild words" do not move in a linear fashion towards a set conclusion but move in various directions to open up many different points of view.

One of the first "chain arguments" in Sengzhao's reply comes on the heels of an extensive series of inferences in which Sengzhao is countering Question 3. He writes:

> Now then, [since the Sagely Mind] lacks obstructions, he resides in hidden still-ness. [In] hidden stillness he is cut-off [from our world of multiplicity], thus [we use the term] "void" in order to speak of him. [The Sage] mysteriously exhausts the stores of the cosmic contents. [Since he mysteriously exhausts] the cosmic contents, [he knows] the contents and thereby responds to them. [As he knows] the contents and thereby responds to them, he thus moves along with the events he matches. [Since we must use the term] "void" in order to speak of him, his Way extends outside the names. [The Sage's] Way extends outside the names, hence we speak of his "non-existence." He moves along with the events he matches, thus we speak of his "existence."[103]

This is an interesting passage in that until now Sengzhao has been reasoning progressively. Suddenly he jumps back to an earlier point in the argument, moves forward again, jumps backwards yet again, only to move forward to his "conclusion." Sengzhao is illustrating that *prajñā* is not a linear way of thinking although it can encompass what we normally conceive of as "logic."

Another "chain argument" occurs several lines further on. Here Sengzhao follows the more typical "chain argument" pattern we saw in "*Prajñā* is Not-Knowing":

> Therefore the Sage neither regards them (things) as things among [other] things nor denies that they are things among [other] things. Since he does not regard them as things among [other] things, he denies such "things" [really] exist. Since he does not deny that they are things among [other] things, he denies such "things" [really] do not exist. He denies their existence, hence he does not grasp. He denies their non-existence, hence he does not reject. He does not reject, thus his mysterious awareness is identical to Ultimate Truth. He does not grasp, thus he does not rely on names and marks. Since he does not rely on names and marks, we deny that he has knowing. Since his mysterious awareness is identical to the Ultimate Truth, we deny that he has "not knowing."[104]

In structure the argument runs thus:

~A and ~B	~A so C
~B so D	C so ~E
D so ~F	~F so G
~E so H	H so ~I
G so ~J	(~I and ~J)

This is one of Sengzhao's most intriguing arguments for its use of so many negatives. It begins with the stated conclusion of the previous argument and its conclusion is an unstated conjunction of two negatives (~I and ~J) that resembles its beginning. Furthermore, Sengzhao seems to contradict the thesis of his essay by saying that *prajñā* is *not* not-knowing! Interestingly, Sengzhao makes a similar statement in "*Prajñā* is Not-knowing" when he says, "So it is that Wisdom [in fact] is not 'Not-knowing.'"[105] Perhaps in both instances Sengzhao has made a mistake or is contradicting himself. However, I take these statements as further illustrating his point that no proposition—even a seemingly "correct" one—can define the Sage.

In addition to these examples, there is another "chain argument" in Sengzhao's reply but this one is subtler than the previous two. When we look at the section of Sengzhao's main letter where he addresses Liu's questions,[106] we see that his reasoning mimics the "chain argument" structure. Schematically, the flow of Sengzhao's answers runs like this: Q 1; Q 2; Q 1 and Q 2; Q 3; Q 2; Q 3, Q 3.

Once again, Sengzhao moves backwards and forwards within his arguments. To follow his reasoning our minds must jump back and forth within Liu's questions, not settling anywhere for long. We are not headed towards any particular conclusion but are opening up to the play of *prajñā* across all positions. We do so, of course, by going through "wild words."

3. Paradox

Paradoxes are among the most potent of Sengzhao's "wild words" in "*Prajñā* is Not-knowing." As we have seen, paradoxes are powerful rhetorical devices that seem contradictory while pointing to deeper truths. By juxtaposing apparently contradictory statements within the same sentence at various places in his essay, Sengzhao is able to provoke the sort of deep insights that characterize *prajñā*. We find him doing the same thing in his reply to Liu as well.

One of the first examples of Sengzhao's paradoxes is in his first reply to Question 2. Sengzhao has just quoted the two alternative explanations of the Sage that Liu has made in his letter to show how Liu has misunderstood the nature of the Sage.

> [Yet] the idea spoken of by [the phrase] "all the way to the 'hidden tallies' [of our lives]" cannot be attained by the name "*samatha-vipassanā*," and [the phrase] "supernatural and perhaps alone in influencing [all things]" cannot be expressed [by saying] "[his responses to] the multitudes of things will certainly thereby cease." Although both statements seem contradictory, [in the Sage's] marvelous functioning they are always the same. Traces and the person [who makes them] proliferate but in the case of the Sage they do not differ.[107]

Sengzhao's point here is simple—in seeking to understand the Sage in more familiar terms Liu has tried to fix the Sage's Dao through categories that do not apply. Liu and his colleagues maintain that the Sagely Mind (*prajñā*) must be either the illumination attained in meditation or a natural (unconscious?) cosmic force. Such an approach fails, however, as the Sage cannot be confined in accord with our narrow perspective. Sengzhao emphasizes this by explaining that these apparently contradictory statements are harmonized in the mysterious being of the Sage.

We find another paradox later in the essay when Sengzhao addresses Question 3. Once again Liu has been struggling with two mutually exclusive notions, in this case, that the Sage must either exist or not exist. To shake him out of this trap of rationality Sengzhao draws upon paradox to evoke the freedom of Sagely being:

> Therefore [the Sage] illuminates the markless yet does not fail in his ability to carefully meet [all things]. He observes the transformations and movements but does not stray from his affinity for the markless. From the first his being does not differ from non-being; from the first his non-being does not differ from being. Never once not existing, never once not not-existing. Hence [the *Fangguang*] says, "[The Tathāgata] does not move from Perfect Enlightenment (*sambodhi*) yet establishes all *dharmas*."[108]

Liu seems trapped by "understanding" the Sage through a series of false dichotomies when in actuality the Sage escapes such confines. Sengzhao counters Liu by speaking of the Sage as eluding the extremes of existence and non-existence, making his point with particular flourish by drawing on the authority of scripture.

One of Sengzhao's most startling paradoxes occurs towards the very end of his letter, after he has countered each of Liu's questions and has gone on to warn Liu against making assertions about the nature of the Sage. Sengzhao says, "Therefore the Sage has emptiness as his inner mind. He lacks [normal] consciousness (*vijñāna*) and has 'no knowing.' He dwells in the region of movement and function and yet remains settled in the territory of non-action (*wuwei*). He abides in the named things and yet rests in the district that is cut-off from words."[109] Here Sengzhao cuts to the heart of Liu's attempts to understand the Sage on a rational basis. Liu's approach fails because the Sage lacks the limited perspective of "normal" unenlightened mind. In attaining *prajñā* the Sage is no longer stuck in either movement or stillness, the named or the unnamed but resides between, in the heart of the cosmos but moving freely throughout it.

With all three of these paradoxes Sengzhao shows how Liu is stuck trying to make the Sage conform to his preconceptions rather than opening himself to Sagely Dao. These paradoxes starkly confront Liu (and we who read Sengzhao's reply) with the clash of contradictory ideas. A mind fixated on a rational "understanding" that seeks to define and confine the Sage fails to understand. The Sage is beyond such boundaries. The Sage is "wild" and to truly understand the Sage, we must be "wild" as well.

4. Playing with Metaphors

One of the most intriguing aspects of Sengzhao's "wild words" is how they play with metaphors. Metaphors are so deeply embedded in discourse that we tend to forget their presence, yet they structure our understanding in important ways. When learning a language we naturally pick up its root metaphors and these shape our thinking at a basic, prereflective level. With his "wild words" Sengzhao takes hold of these metaphors and mixes them up, thus confusing our thinking so that we may move beyond rationality.

As with "*Prajñā* is Not-knowing," so too there are many examples of such metaphoric play in Sengzhao's reply. One instance of Sengzhao's playing with basic metaphors comes when he addresses Liu's attempt to understand the Sage as either achieving insight through *samatha-vipassanā* or directing cosmic events:

> The term "*samatha-vipassanā*" is not identical with your declaration [of the Sage] being "outside" [the transformations]. If declaring [the Sage to be "outside" the transformations] is to produce identity [with a declaration about the Sage's] "inner" [illumination], then we have declarations that are not identical. If declaring [the Sage attains insight through meditation] is to produce identity [with your other declaration about the Sage] being "outside," then such declarations do not concern the [Sage's] "self."[110]

Here Sengzhao uses a *prasaṅga* argument to draw out the absurd conclusions of Liu's own statements about the Sage as either an enlightened meditator or a personage who remains outside the bounds of existence. Sengzhao's argument hinges, however, on a basic play between spatial metaphors of "inside" and "outside." The Sage cannot be "inside" or "outside" but must be both and neither. Within the space of a few lines Sengzhao takes us both "inside" and "outside" while negating both locations as final resting places for the Sage. Like the Sage, we cannot settle down in any *dharma*.

Sengzhao continues his "wild" metaphoric play as his reply progresses. In a later passage of his letter Sengzhao once more addresses Liu's confusion over the Sage's "not-knowing knowing": "What [then] does Sagely Wisdom know? When the world speaks of "not knowing" it means the insentience of wood, stone, the void etc. [*Prajñā*, however,] supernaturally mirrors, darkly candles. Even when forms were not yet displayed, Dao had no hidden workings. It is better to speak of this [knowing] as 'not knowing'."[111] In this passage Sengzhao juxtaposes "worldly not knowing" (insentience) to *prajñā*'s "not knowing" (wisdom). The contrast of stupidity and lucidity is jarring but the metaphors for *prajñā*'s "not knowing knowing" are themselves rather tricky. *Prajñā* is a "supernatural mirroring" that "darkly candles." It is a mysterious, even occult illumination. Such phrases run counter to our expectations but point to the cognitive power needed to penetrate the obscure workings of Dao.

Sengzhao plays with these basic metaphors even as he draws his reply to a close. Towards the very end of the concluding section of his letter to Liu, Sengzhao writes, "The Ultimate Principle (*prajñā*) is 'void' and 'dark'. To [attempt to] determine it by thinking is already to go astray. How much more [do we stray] by using words?"[112] Here Sengzhao plays off the usual metaphors in two ways. First and most obviously, by declaring that *prajñā* ("Ultimate Principle"), which we would ordinarily expect to be clearest light, is "void and dark." More interestingly, though, he also counters metaphors that implicitly structure how Liu understands cognition. For Liu, to know is to delimit, define and "fix" something. Sengzhao, however, maintains this "knowing" is not *prajñā*. *Prajñā* is free, unhindered, an open flowing awareness. *Prajñā* is "wild."

We can see, then, that Sengzhao's "wild words" in his reply to Liu Yimin include this playing around with basic metaphors. Sengzhao takes the implicit metaphors of ordinary discourse and mixes them up. In doing so he brings us up short, upsetting our thinking and challenging our expectations. To get his point about *prajñā* we must re-think our usual ways thinking. He makes us aware of how language shapes our experience and highlights its essentially conventional nature. Thus once again, Sengzhao's "wild words" push us towards a different, more enlightened way of being and knowing, the Way of the Sage/Bodhisattva.

5. Puns

Of the various rhetorical moves Sengzhao makes in his "wild words," though, it is probably his use of puns that most excites our interest. A pun, or "play on words," is among the trickiest of linguistic devices. A pun is a dynamic part of speech that evokes two or more meanings of a word simultaneously. Puns hinge on the ineluctably plurivocal nature of language by bringing us to the intersection of different spheres of discourse. A pun enriches our understanding, however briefly, and frees us from the illusion that discourse is fixed and monolithic. Perhaps most of all, a pun often elicits joy and laughter and so allows us to participate in the cosmic exuberance of Dao.

Sengzhao puns repeatedly in *"Prajñā* is Not-knowing" and he continues to do so in his reply to Liu. In fact, Sengzhao begins to make puns in his cover letter, perhaps as a way of foreshadowing what lies in store when he announces his switch to "wild words" in the first section of his main letter.[113] A better example of Sengzhao's punning occurs when he addresses the Liu's difficulties in Question 1 for the second time. In a seemingly off-handed manner,

Sengzhao remarks, "The Sage's 'dark' (*xuan*) Mind darkly (*mo*) illuminates [the universe]."[114] The pun revolves around notions of darkness and light, and their various connotations. *Xuan* can mean "dark" in the literal sense but also "profound" and "mysterious" as in "*xuanxue*." Here Sengzhao uses this double meaning to play off the word *mo*, which also has the sense of being "dark" and "secret" or "silent."[115] Using both words in discussing the illuminating power of the Sagely Mind underscores their double meaning.[116] In this sophisticated pun involving two similar words Sengzhao masterfully leads us to new insights into the workings of the Sagely Mind. This passage is thus a wonderful example of how "wild words" work.

An even more complex example of Sengzhao's use of puns comes further on where he addresses the presuppositions behind Liu's difficulties in Question 2. As Sengzhao says, "So it is that [the *Fangguang* tells us] Subhūti expounded *prajñā* night and day yet said that he spoke of nothing. *This* is [truly] knowing the Dao that is cut-off from words but how can it be transmitted? I only hope that all you gentlemen versed in the mysteries will also meet it."[117] This passage is a punster's *tour de force* beginning from the first line (an allusion to the *prajñā sūtras* to be sure). Subhūti says that in preaching on *prajñā* he has taught nothing–on the surface, merely a monk's polite modesty. Yet his statement also contains a great Buddhist truth: *prajñā* is, after all, nothing (no thing). Indeed, it is insight into the true "nothingness" of *everything*. Sengzhao then affirms that Subhūti's statement on "nothing"[118] demonstrates true knowledge of Dao that cannot be spoken and appears to lament the possibility of transmitting it. However, he is playing on the word *zhuan* here, a word that means "to transmit" but also refers to the commentaries on the *jing*. Sengzhao's lament is actually a rhetorical question: how if the Way is beyond words can we have these commentaries which do lead to the Way? Finally, Sengzhao ends by gently mocking Liu and his colleagues for failing to understand. Sengzhao refers to them as *xuan junzi* ("dark gentlemen"), meaning *xuanxue* intellectuals, but he is also playing on the more literal sense of *xuan*. Liu and his colleagues may be well versed in philosophy but when it comes to *prajñā*, they are truly in the dark! These three puns coming in such quick succession make this one of the "wildest" passages in all of Sengzhao's work. His words confront us with their multiple meanings and call into question our insistence that discourse must be precise and clear-cut. These "wild words" also show us how the Way of the Sage/Bodhisattva spills forth in joy and humor.

Even at the end Sengzhao cannot resist the pun's temptation. In the very last line of his reply after he has addressed Liu's questions and made his point that Sagely Wisdom cannot be fully grasped or clarified through discursive reasoning, Sengzhao writes, "[Perhaps] all you keen-minded gentlemen will, by using my words, anticipate (*qi*) [what lies] outside speech."[119] The pun here is on the word *qi*, "to await," "to hope for" but even more commonly "limit" or "fix." On one level Sengzhao seems to be encouraging Liu and his colleagues to continue in their attempts to "limit" and "fix" what *prajñā* is by carefully analyzing Sengzhao's treatise. Simultaneously, though, he is instructing them to do the opposite, to read his treatise (his "marks") transformatively by letting "wild words" (his Daoist discourse) take them to what is outside of words, *prajñā*. It is a simple pun in which Sengzhao once again pokes fun at those who constantly attempt to reason out what *prajñā* means. This Parthian shot serves as yet another clue to how to read "*Prajñā* is Not-knowing" and Sengzhao's replies to Liu Yimin. We have to allow the "wild words" to work instead trying to force them to make sense.

The puns just cited, along with his playing with basic metaphors, use of paradoxes and "chain arguments" and his many allusions are the same sorts of rhetorical moves that make up Sengzhao's "wild words" in "*Prajñā* is Not-knowing." They demonstrate that Sengzhao retained and even sharpened his rhetorical skills through his continuing efforts to convey the Sagely perspective. Sengzhao's use of "wild words" in his reply not only hearkens back to his use of them in his earlier essay, it also serves to re-emphasize their use there. Although Liu employs some of the same rhetorical moves in his letter (allusions, "chain arguments"), he does not use them as often or to the same effect as Sengzhao; he and his colleagues simply do not get "wild words." There can be no doubt that "wild words" are, for Sengzhao, the key to attaining Wisdom and going beyond the limited "knowing" that characterizes the mind caught in *saṃsāra*.

In addition to the examples of "wild words" we have cited, Sengzhao's use of the *catuṣkoṭi* adds yet another move to his "wild" rhetorical repertoire. Sengzhao employs this device in a passage already cited above when explaining to Liu what he means by speaking of *prajñā* as both "not being" (*feiyou*) and "not non-being" (*feiwu*).[120] The *catuṣkoṭi* exhausts the four possible positions one can take regarding a proposition (affirmation, negation, both affirmation and negation, neither affirmation nor negation) while making no claims for an alternative position. It is part of formal Indian logic but it became a favorite foil of Buddhist thinkers. In the hands of a master such as Nāgārjuna, the *catuṣkoṭi* is devastatingly effective for it demonstrates the futility of definitive predication.[121] The *catuṣkoṭi* is "wild," in that it pushes us beyond rational thought. By adding the *catuṣkoṭi* to his "wild words" Sengzhao increases their power immensely. He also demonstrates that "wild words" are not a fixed set of rhetorical moves but are a way of wording words that allows us to see the "empty nature" of all discourse.

Closely related to Sengzhao's "wild words" are his repeated references to the distinction between what words appear to say and what they really mean. He does so explicitly, for instance, when he explains that when the *Pañca* speaks of *rūpa* and non-*rūpa* (*śūnyatā*), it means to identify them rather than distinguish them.[122] He invokes this same distinction when he further explains that referring to Sageliness as "not being" (*feiyou*) and "not non-being" (*feiwu*) does not mean that the Sage is either a "non-existent thing" or a "not non-existent thing."[123] "*Prajñā* is Not-knowing" and Sengzhao's reply to Liu are both lengthy explanations of what seemingly nonsensical statements about Sagely Wisdom truly mean. We would only expect such from someone like Sengzhao, who was so concerned with hermeneutic issues. Nonetheless, this constant juxtaposition of real versus apparent meaning indicates that Sengzhao is invoking an important hermeneutic theory, the distinction between *neyārtha* and *nītārtha*.

The *neyārtha-nītārtha* distinction is a common hermeneutic strategy in Buddhism, particularly in the Mahāyāna. Nāgārjuna relies on it in the *Kārikās* and the Buddha himself distinguishes between the two types of discourse in several *sūtras*. Moreover, Mahāyāna exegetes often consider the skillful use of these two types of discourse to be part of the Buddhas and Bodhisattvas' wondrous *upāya*. The Buddhas and Bodhisattvas teach what is provisionally true but ultimately false (*neyārtha*) in order to lead all beings to enlightenment. Could Sengzhao be invoking this distinction as justification for his "wild words"? Are "wild words" a form of *upāya*? It is an intriguing possibility and we have indirect evidence of this notion of *upāya* when at one point Sengzhao writes that "People's circumstances are not the same, thus the teachings wander and have their differences."[124] Although this statement would seem to refer to the words of the *sūtras* and *śāstras* (the *jing* and the *zhuan*), in context we see that it also refers to Sengzhao's own puzzling and often contradictory discourse.

Here, however, we must add an important caveat. "Wild words" do not make sense on the surface. Their apparent meaning is confused and contradictory, thus they form an especially playful *neyārthic* discourse. When we go with the flow of "wild words," we find ourselves going beyond rationality to the awakening of Sagely Wisdom. Attaining such Wisdom would be the real meaning (*nītārtha*) of "wild words" but this truth cannot be captured in words hence in the strictest sense, there is no *nītārtha*. The truth of *prajñā* cannot be definitively uttered. For Sengzhao, the *nītārtha* that we can speak, like Dao, is not the *true nītārtha*.[125]

All in all, Sengzhao uses "wild words" to great effect in his reply to Liu Yimin. His "wild words" shake our conventionally fixed categories loose from their moorings. They rhetorically slide us around to show reality from new perspectives and so expand our "small understanding" to the "Great Understanding" of the Sage/Bodhisattva. Our "knowing" is no longer attached to a particular face that things may present to us but accepts them equally in all their facets. "Wild words" also free us from our bondage to the idea that our linguistic constructions capture reality in all of its nuances. Instead, they remind us that language is a construct, a web of words like a rabbit snare or a fish trap. Such a complex device is extremely useful, even a necessity, in making our way in the world but it is not an end in itself. Moreover, "wild words" demonstrate the elasticity of words and allow us to appreciate the playfulness of our language games without taking them seriously. If we can arrive at this understanding in reading Sengzhao, though, it still remains for us to examine some of the reasons why Liu could not apparently reach this point, or why he actually seems to misunderstand.

Why Liu Fails to Understand Sengzhao

We have examined both what Liu asks in his letter to Sengzhao and Sengzhao's detailed replies. We must now turn again to the most crucial matter of their correspondence—the misunderstanding that motivated Liu's letter in the first place. We might be tempted to say that Liu misunderstands Sengzhao because he does not get his "wild words" and leave it at that. In making such an assessment we would certainly be correct, but this explanation is only half the story. We need to uncover what lies behind Liu's failure to understand Sengzhao. To do so it may be helpful to recall that understanding concerns not just individuals but communities.

Stanley Fish and Interpretive Communities

Much of our study in this and the preceding chapters has focused on Sengzhao's and Liu Yimin's understanding of *prajñā* and the competing notions of *prajñā* argued over by their predecessors. While this has brought to light numerous details and prompted me to make several suggestions that previous scholars have either passed over or ignored, it may have left the impression that interpretation is a solitary pursuit which takes place only between the reader and the text. Nothing could be further from the truth. Just as there is no such thing as a private language or culture so there is no such thing as a private understanding. Hermeneutics is always a communal endeavor based on shared ideas and ideally aims at reaching common ground. Although this is a basic tenet of philosophical hermeneutics, few figures have brought out the implications of the communal basis of interpretation as clearly as has Stanley Fish.

In a series of essays from the 1970's, Fish sketches out the role of communities in determining where interpretation begins and how it progresses. According to Fish, interpretive acts are based on strategies for making sense that we constantly employ and which we typically assume unreflectively. They essentially function as "predecisions" that dispose us to look for certain things and configure texts in specific ways. By employing these interpretive strategies we "write" the text that we read.[126] Such interpretive strategies are purely conventional in nature and even change over time.

A crucial thing to bear in mind is that these strategies are communal. Those who share the same strategies make up *interpretive communities* who set the rules for how to proceed and what counts as a viable interpretation. Not surprisingly, interpretive communities often conflict with communities employing different strategies. The communal basis of interpretation accounts for the stability of interpretation among some groups (they belong to the same interpretive community) as well as the variety of interpretations a single person may hold during her life (she belongs to different communities at different times). The stability achieved, though, is only temporary, for interpretive communities continually grow and decline. As Fish puts it,

> The notion of interpretive communities thus stands between an impossible ideal and the fear that leads so many to maintain it. The ideal is of perfect agreement and it would require texts to have a status independent of interpretation. The fear is of interpretive anarchy, but it would only be realized if interpretation (text making) were completely random. It is the fragile but real consolidation of interpretive communities that allows us to talk to one another, but with no hope or fear of ever being able to stop.[127]

The way we make sense of something is always constrained by our communal context.

Fish offers no real explanation of the rise and decline of interpretive communities or how an individual can belong to several interpretive communities at the same time.[128] However, we need not go along with him all the way to appreciate his insights. Fish provides a useful model for understanding what lies behind understanding and misunderstanding. Those who create texts give us the opportunity to make meanings by inviting us to execute certain interpretive strategies. They presume the invitation will be recognized, mainly by projecting the set of moves they would make if encountering the same set of sounds or marks.[129] Someone "understands" if she employs more or less the same strategies. An "outsider," by contrast, would use a different set of strategies and so find different meaning, and hence would "misunderstand." The "outsider" would not so much "misread" (or "mishear") as "mispreread" because she belongs to an interpretive community having different strategies for making meaning.

With Fish's help we can now offer a more substantive account of the misunderstanding between Liu Yimin and Sengzhao, bearing in mind of course that this account is, too, an interpretation. Ultimately their misunderstanding stems from the fact that Liu and Sengzhao are members of different interpretive communities.[130] As members of different interpretive communities they employ different interpretive strategies and so they read texts differently. Furthermore, their interpretive strategies are based on different presuppositions about Sageliness and language, and point to different scholarly and religious concerns.

There is, of course, a strong political subtext in relations between interpretive communities. Sengzhao's community in Chang'an was at the center of Imperial and Dharmic power. His association with both Yao Xing and Kumārajīva and the latter's explicit endorsement lent his words even greater weight than they would have had by virtue of his own reputation and talents. Lushan, while by no means a second rate center, was not the equal of Chang'an and Sengzhao was not above flaunting his mantle of authority in his reply. Liu and his colleagues would have been predisposed to interpret Sengzhao's writings as works of great import that should be carefully poured over. It perhaps would not have occurred to them that Sengzhao might not even address the practical concerns that were uppermost in their minds. For Sengzhao's part, he could basically overlook such "minor" concerns and may not have even been aware that his points were being missed. His writings, after all, were a continuation of his Master's exegeses. He was spreading the True Dharma. If some were baffled now, they would eventually get the message.[131]

So it is that with Liu and Sengzhao we have a case of individuals who never find the common ground they seek. They never reach the mutual understanding shared by members of the same interpretive community, primarily because they begin from different positions and bring different concerns to their exchange. We can see this clearly from our examination of "The Correspondence." All three of Liu's questions point to real differences in how he and Sengzhao understand Sageliness. Liu does not comprehend the non-differentiation of *nirvāṇa* and *saṃsāra*. For him they are distinct realms, like being (*you*) and non-being (*wu*). Liu's understanding is informed by *mingjiao* presuppositions about existence and non-existence and the relationship between language and reality. Ultimately, the Sage must really exist to know and guide things. In addition, Liu's idea of the Sage shows the influence of his community's notions of purity and discipline, and their intense devotion to *buddhānusmṛti*. Lushan, moreover, had long-been associated with Daoist recluses and ascetics, and had been home to the Sarvāstivādin master Saṅghadeva. The Sagely ideal to which the members of the community aspired, thus, was marked by Daoist asceticism and Sarvāstivāda monasticism. Their religious lives centered on withdrawal and detachment from the world, much like the Buddha's disciples in the *Vimalakīrti*.[132] The embodiment of this ideal was most certainly Huiyuan, whose austerity was legendary. When we read Liu's letter to Sengzhao, we are thus confronted with an interpretation of Sageliness that is somewhat at odds with the more liberal and worldly view upheld by Kumārajīva's circle.

Perhaps the greatest differences between Liu and Sengzhao, though, have to do with their respective views of *prajñā* and language. Liu cannot comprehend *prajñā* as an all-embracing, non-dual awareness and for him language must describe reality precisely. Significantly, Liu only mentions *prajñā* by name twice in his letter—once when expressing his hope that "*Prajñā* is Not-knowing" will finally settle the debates over *prajñā* and once when quoting a passage from Sengzhao's essay.[133] It may be that Liu shares Sengzhao's assumption that *prajñā* just is Sagely Wisdom (common among Buddho-Daoists of all stripes) but his silence could indicate a lack of familiarity with *prajñā* texts and their paradoxical proclamation of the Bodhisattva ideal. Liu only refers to Mahāyāna texts two times—once when he uses the generic phrase "*vaipulya* [*sūtras*]" and once when quoting one of Sengzhao's quotes of the *Fangguang*.[134] Together these facts point to an understanding of Sageliness that shows little if any influence of Mahāyāna philosophy. Even Liu's "Pure Land" devotionalism was heavily indebted to Daoism. In all likelihood Liu, like many Buddho-Daoists, probably did not really distinguish between "Hīnayāna" and Mahāyāna.

This is not to say that Liu was not Buddhist, only that his understanding of Buddhism was mixed with popular Daoism and lacked doctrinal nuance.

Moreover, Liu may be philosophically more "Hīnayāna" than Mahāyāna, especially given the fact that Saṅghadeva had taught Sarvāstivāda Abhidharma on Lu Shan while Liu was there. In addition, we have already seen evidence of the influence of the *mingjiao* on his thought. It seems likely that Liu's view of Sagely Wisdom was indebted to Sarvāstivāda and *mingjiao* ideas. Sarvāstivāda notions of *prajñā* as primarily analytic have much in common with *mingjiao* insistence on each thing having one specific name. In both traditions, realization entails clear and distinct knowledge and rational description. Liu, of course, did not devote his life to Sarvāstivāda or the *mingjiao* studies but nonetheless he shared some of their assumptions.

Sengzhao's views stand in marked contrast to Liu's. His understanding of Sageliness was informed by Daoist freedom and skepticism combined with Mahāyāna notions of incomprehensibility and inclusiveness. Sengzhao drew inspiration from the Daoist texts he so loved in his youth, the wily Bodhisattva Vimalakīrti, and Kumārajīva's exegeses of Mahāyāna texts. For him, the Sage's *Prajñā* was a marvelous, all-encompassing vision overflowing the constraints of words and symbols. It could not be confined to a single perspective. In Sengzhao's view, *prajñā* does not divide and discriminate but reveals things in their true empty being. *Prajñā* is one with Dao. Attaining it, one flows effortlessly with the changes, compassionately engaged with things but unaffected by suffering.

Moreover, for Sengzhao language is far more than a means of ordering our world. Language is itself a Dao, a slippery ever-flowing way that when skillfully navigated leads to Wisdom. Unlike Liu, Sengzhao invokes the notions of *upāya* and the distinction between *neyārtha* and *nītārtha* to bring forth the deeper meaning of sacred texts. His "wild words," derived from Daoist and Buddhist sources, become a way of exploiting the plurivocal nature of language to lead his audience to greater realization. Sengzhao evokes and provokes but does not describe or explain. He is not clear because real clarity lies in the darkness of not-knowing.

It is for all of these reasons and perhaps others as well that Liu fails to understand Sengzhao. He does not really hear what Sengzhao's "wild words" say and so cannot find his way through them to Sagely Wisdom, "true *prajñā*," the *Mahāprajñāpāramitā*. But the misunderstanding is mutual. Although his reply shows that he is aware of Liu's difficulties, Sengzhao fails to address Liu's concerns about Buddhist practice or the efficacy of words. Sengzhao does not really hear what Liu is saying *behind* his words. What's more, he does not adequately prepare Liu for his rhetorical gymnastics. His "wild words" fall on deaf ears. The misunderstanding thus involves both parties.

What we have in "The Correspondence," then, is a failure to communicate. There is a deep and strange irony here. Sengzhao and Liu Yimin were educated men with much in common. They had talent, shared a similar formation and were both dedicated to the Buddha Dao. In their letters they profess mutual admiration and affection for each other, and a profound desire to close the distance between them. At the time, written correspondence was a common means of clarifying and instructing in Buddhist circles and in some cases it succeeded. However, in this case it did not. And it is Liu, not Sengzhao, who seems to realize this when he suggests that the distance between he and Sengzhao is doctrinal as well as geographical.

Could Liu and Sengzhao have ever overcome their separation to find common ground? It is impossible for us to say, although both showed a genuine willingness to communicate that might have led them to a mutual understanding. In any case, by the time Sengzhao's reply arrived at Lushan, Liu was dead and within a few years Sengzhao died as well. Perhaps it was then that the two friends finally did meet, joining together in the Great Transformation where ultimately all beings dwell.

· 5 ·

WHAT CAN WE SAY
ABOUT *PRAJÑĀ*?

So far we have concentrated on what Sengzhao and Liu Yimin say about *prajñā* in two texts, "*Prajñā* is Not-knowing" and "The Correspondence." As we have seen, *prajñā* is a complex subject with Sengzhao's essay merely part of a larger cross-cultural conflict of interpretations. The key to Sengzhao's discussion of *prajñā* is his use of "wild words," a dynamic discourse that does not *describe prajñā* so much as *inscribe* it. "Wild words" do not *inform* us of what *prajñā* is but *transform* our minds into the mind of *prajñā*, the Sagely Wisdom of Buddha. This makes "*Prajñā* is Not-knowing" an unstable work, prone to be misunderstood. Such was the case with Liu Yimin, who read the essay but was baffled. He wrote to Sengzhao seeking for clarification and offering criticisms to which Sengzhao replied. By examining their exchange, we have drawn some conclusions regarding their misunderstanding, much of which stems from the varying presuppositions that Liu and Sengzhao held as members of different interpretive communities.

It may be that this is enough. After all, we have shed a great deal of light on the controversies surrounding *prajñā* in early fifth century China. As herme-neuts, though, we must always probe deeper in our interpretations. Moreover, my discussion is somewhat distorted, since Hermes always tells the "truth" with a nod and a wink. My examination of "*Prajñā* is Not-knowing" and "The Correspondence" is itself an interpretation informed by my perspective as a scholar interested in Chinese and Buddhist traditions and hermeneutics.

The perspective-bound nature of my study, however, calls for more extensive reflection.

Interpretation can never end, for a text always generates new meanings as we come to it with our questions. The present case is no exception, for Sengzhao and Liu Yimin still have much more to say and we have not followed many potential threads. Overwhelmingly, however, our inquiry has been focused on the past—on Sengzhao and Liu's texts and world, on the issues influencing their writings. This may leave the impression that hermeneutic study is an investigation of museum pieces, "artifacts" produced from another time and culture which interest only a few specialists. This is at best a half-truth. Hermeneutics does look to texts from the past but it does so to understand the present. In the "fusion of horizons" our perspective shifts and our world is redescribed in light of a text's meaning. This shift, in turn, can provoke new insights into old problems. In this way interpretation becomes a creative renewal that critically retrieves "old meaning" from the past to find new solutions in the present. We must, then, bring our engagement with Sengzhao and Liu to bear on issues *we* face. Both Sengzhao and Liu speak to us here and now. We are compelled to make sense of them, and doing so will change our world and challenge us to revise our ways of thinking.

In this chapter we will focus on what *we* can say about *prajñā* based on our study of Sengzhao and Liu Yimin, although this does not mean neglecting our hermeneutic duty to be self-critical. In that vein I begin by returning to the challenges to philosophical hermeneutics raised in Chapter One. We need to examine our tentative conclusions about Sengzhao and Liu to see how in reaching them we have (or have not) dealt with the problems raised by these challenges. From there I will shift my attention to another area of scholarship where our work with Sengzhao and Liu Yimin has direct relevance: the relationship between *prajñā* and "mysticism." "Mysticism" is an extremely controversial subject in the academy and our discussion can shed additional light on this intriguing but troublesome topic. I will then return to Sengzhao and Liu's views of *prajñā* to see if they need revision in light of our discussion regarding "mysticism," and from there once again reflect on what we can say about *prajñā*.

This chapter thus involves a constant shifting of perspectives as we take another look at earlier parts of our study and challenge them in order to refine our understanding of *prajñā*. Hermeneutics proceeds in a back and forth movement from reader to text in the continual effort to gain greater understanding. The chapter's structure illustrates the dynamics of understanding as it emerges in a hermeneutic encounter.

Issues in Cross-Cultural Hermeneutics

We begin by returning to the challenges to hermeneutics discussed at the end of Chapter One. Such critical challenges call us to think carefully about hermeneutic method and our findings, and have important implications for cross-cultural studies. We need, then, to reexamine our study and reflect on how we may or may not have met these challenges. Such critical reflection may, in turn, point to problems for that require further investigation.

Objectivity and Intention

The first critical challenges to hermeneutics we considered were those offered by proponents of "objective interpretation" such as Emilio Betti and H. D. Hirsch. Both Betti and Hirsch are responding to Gadamer's work but their criticisms apply to philosophical hermeneutics in general. Although they make different points, they both agree that philosophical hermeneutics does not provide a clear principle for deciding meaning and that it confuses a text's meaning with the significance it has for us. For Betti and Hirsch, there is a truly objective and definitive interpretation and it is up to the interpreter to find it. Moreover, this meaning is tied to the meaning intended by author, even though this may not necessarily be "conscious." Betti and Hirsch's views strongly resemble those of Schleiermacher and Dilthey, and both consider an interpreter to be essentially a decoder of verbal meaning.

Betti and Hirsch make strong cases. Their call for objectivity steers us to what the text actually says and away from idiosyncratic impressions. They also voice a necessary counterpoint to the naïve relativism that "my interpretation is as good as yours." The sort of interpretation that Betti and Hirsch advocate requires research guided by careful reasoning and a great deal of philological and historical investigation. All of these points are well taken and even necessary to achieve any solid, scholarly interpretation worthy of consideration.

How do these points affect my interpretation? In my work I have relied on various historical accounts to reconstruct a picture of early medieval China, have explored the roots of Buddhist and Chinese traditions, and have delved into the linguistic and philosophical meaning of Sengzhao and Liu's writings. All of this is common hermeneutic practice. At times my discussion may have tended towards excess but undoubtedly more could be done. I have not examined every primary or secondary document, nor explored all the ramifications of many points. Hermeneutic study reveals the richness of meaning, ever more possibilities of exploration, and asks us to rethink our conclusions. The results are not "objective" in the way that Betti and Hirsch advocate (i.e. absolute and final) yet our findings are not merely "subjective" in the sense of being the product of unreasoned opinion based on our initial biases and experiences. They are the result of careful scholarship but remain open to revision.

The idea that the true meaning of a text is the one the author intends is another matter. Often we speak of this as "what the author had in mind" without examining what this statement means or what it implies about the role of the interpreter. To the best of my knowledge I do not presume to know Sengzhao's "mind" or claim to have reached the final interpretation of his writings but the *mentus auctoris* still hovers in the background of my discussion. In particular it seems to rise to the fore in my discussion of "wild words" as a means of transforming the reader. This rhetorical device implies a mind shaping the text in a decisive fashion. Even so, though, there is no reason to assume that the meaning of the text ultimately lies in this "mind." While texts obviously have authors in the sense of "original creators" these authors do not control the meaning of their creations. I do not doubt that a monk named Sengzhao took brush, ink and paper and produced something that we have come to call "*Prajñā* is Not-knowing" but the text's meaning does not depend solely upon what Sengzhao may have meant. Rather, its meaning(s) emerge in the various engagements between the text and its interpreters.[1] We can even see this when comparing my work with that of Liebenthal and Robinson, whose interpretations differ considerably from mine.

Of course we often find a strong intentionalist tendency in Buddhist and Chinese texts but it is unclear that this requires invoking an author's mind. The Buddha Mind, the Mind of the Sage, is not a private psychological fact "inside" a person nor is it a "state of mind" in the ordinary sense. It is, rather, a realization of our nature, an awakening to Dao that defies attempts to reduce it to mere ideas. This is not an "objective fact" to be studied at arm's length. True Mind is not divorced from our being. My reading of Sengzhao and Liu Yimin makes us aware that *prajñā* is not a thing among other things, nor is it a "knowing" (i.e. a simple cognitive faculty). I suggest that Sengzhao's essay and reply to Liu open us to *prajñā* without explicitly spelling it out. This requires us to participate in finding and fulfilling meaning. Sengzhao's writings are exhortatory, not definitive, and my own reading of them is the same.

Postmodern Criticisms

The challenges of postmodern thinkers contrast strongly with those of Betti and Hirsch. Admittedly it is difficult to characterize postmodernism but those whom we label "postmodern" share strong suspicions and criticisms of modern aims at final, all-encompassing knowledge and objectivity. Thus it is that Lyotard speaks of the collapse of "grand narratives" purporting to explain everything. Foucault's discourse analyses reveal how "knowledge" is based on socially constructed fields of inquiry tied to political power and institutions. Derrida through his playful deconstructions draws our attention to the disruptive aspects of texts and the multivocal character of language. We no longer can use "method" to arrive at final truth, and postmodernism questions the very possibility of understanding. This has great implications for hermeneutics.

Postmodern challenges are compelling and deeply troubling. Modernity's cry for Truth will undoubtedly haunt us like Banquo's ghost for years to come. Postmodern thinkers shine a strange "dark light" on scholarship and force upon us a hard honesty. Postmodern scholarship will be fallible, limited and impenetrable at times. We must consciously face discord and alterity, and cannot ignore inevitable conflicts of interpretation that arise. Claims to objectivity are difficult to accept as anything other than rhetorical grabs at power. Ours is a world, or rather an assortment of worlds, marked by plurality and ambiguity, with no final meanings.

If meaning is never final, though, it still can be found and articulated. "Hermes speak" is not just the twittering of birds; it really says something even if what it says is not fixed. We could even argue that this puts us in a situation rather analogous to Sengzhao and Liu Yimin—an arena of contested meanings and misunderstanding but in which sincere engagement can and does occur, however imperfectly. I have emphasized repeatedly that my account is partial and open to revision. It is *not* a "grand narrative" but a "little narrative," rough around the edges. In constructing it I have challenged myself and my account has altered over time. This is only to be expected, though, since interpretation involves a shifting series of "fusions of horizons."

The role of power is most instructive here. Power was certainly instrumental in forming the discourse of *prajñā* in early China and in the texts we have been studying. The texts themselves, whether *jing* or *zhuan*, look back to the authority of key figures (e.g. Buddha and the Sages) and were produced by editors and translators often working at the behest of wealthy patrons such as

Emperor Yao Xing.[2] **Kumārajīva** and Sengzhao shared in Yao Xing's imperial air of authority, and Sengzhao makes use of it in his essay and his letter to Liu. Similarly, power is also at work in my account: I have followed procedures of various academic disciplines (history, sinology, philosophy) and these shape what I have produced. This means that my account differs considerably from "traditional" Chinese and Buddhist accounts, as the latter are often written from within an explicitly religious perspective.

Even more importantly, my account also differs from earlier studies of Sengzhao's work such as those by Liebenthal and Robinson. Interpretation involves assuming certain powers and privileges that come with making meaning. In scholarly interpretations this means critically analyzing one's predecessors, taking issue with them, pointing out their shortcomings, and arguing for new conclusions that differ in key respects. The result rarely supercedes previous work but it does alter the field by contributing a new perspective. Contemporary scholarship is an on-going discussion or debate. In this respect it *does* resemble "traditional scholarship" albeit the emphasis is on criticism and "new" insights instead of retrieval.

Postmodern attention to the inherent instability of language such as we see in Derrida is always puzzling, and has the potential to stop all inquiry in its tracks. In this case, however, it has actually illuminated Sengzhao's "wild words" in new ways. It has prompted me to take a fresh look at Sengzhao's writing as well as his sources (Zhuangzi, **Nāgārjuna**, Laozi, Guo Xiang). My view of "wild words" stresses their dynamic character; "wild words" are transformative, not informative. This means their saying is not fixed or finalizable. Sengzhao is working with the multivocal nature of language as he articulates *prajñic* discourse. We can understand that Sengzhao is in some sense not trying to be understood in an ordinary way.

Over the past few chapters, then, I have striven for an interpretation mindful of postmodern challenges to hermeneutics. There are other interpretations available and always will be. I do not think, though, that hermeneutics need be abandoned. We have no reason to assume that interpretation requires working out *all* possibilities of meaning, only the meanings that result from our engagement with texts. Any interpretation involves fleshing out available meanings that emerge within a hermeneutic conversation. In such cases we do not require final decisions of "truth" nor must we reduce meaning to forces that shape a text's formation. Understanding is process not product, greatly furthered by drawing on various academic disciplines as I have done.

Orientalism

The problems posed by Orientalism are perhaps the most serious. The creation of Orientalist discourses by "Western" scholars continues to be influential. As Said and others have shown, Orientalism is about power and is intimately related to the modern quest for totalization. The Orientalist assumes the power to define the "Orient" and to explain in detail what the "Orient" includes, both to a "Western" and "Oriental" audience. Overwhelmingly Orientalist discourses have developed in tandem with European exploration and colonization. Orientalism may not necessarily be "evil" but it hinges on subjugating "others" in the name of "objectivity."

Orientalism is a many-sided phenomenon that pervades much of religious and philosophical work, often with the aid of Western-trained "Orientals." In the postcolonial era such practices have come under increasingly critical scrutiny, resulting in the rise of new academic fields such as Subaltern Studies.[3] Contemporary hermeneutics must take account of these developments. For a true hermeneutic encounter to take place, the Orientalist tendency towards domination and totalization must stop, perhaps especially on the part of we who remain Modernity's heirs. These are pressing concerns that bear directly on Buddhist and Chinese studies and our present investigation of Sengzhao.

Although there are vestiges of Orientalism in the work of Heidegger, Gadamer and Ricoeur,[4] none of them discusses "Eastern" cultures at any length. Neither does philosophical hermeneutics as a "method" seem Orientalist. As we have seen, hermeneutics is self-critical, always pushing us beyond our initial prejudices. However, the academy has a long Orientalist history of defining "Buddhism" and "Chinese religion/philosophy" in Western terms, and this matter warrants serious attention.

In light of recent criticisms of Orientalist strains in scholarly circles, I find myself in a peculiar position. My own interest in Sengzhao was born in part from the work of Wing-tsit Chan and Feng Youlan, and in my studies of Buddhism and Chinese philosophy and religion I am certainly heir to many Orientalist influences. Both Liebenthal and Robinson, whom I have often consulted, are also informed by Orientalist assumptions.[5] Am I, then, also guilty of Orientalism in my study of Sengzhao and Liu Yimin? To an extent, the answer must be "yes." Clearly I have been marked by Eurocentric agendas and as someone striving for a hermeneutical understanding I acknowledge that the prejudices of the past have shaped my own understanding. In some ways, I am an Orientalist, even though I recognize the dangers and limitations of such a perspective. Leaving this matter in such terms, however, is overly simplistic and even hermeneutically naïve; my own Orientalism calls for careful philosophical examination.

One thing to notice about the question "Am I guilty of Orientalism?" is that it is premised on the same essentialist assumptions as Orientalism. That is, the question tacitly assumes the existence of an ahistorical essential "Orientalism" and "Modernity" defined over and against some real "East" when such essentialism is precisely one of Said's main criticisms. The question, thus, relies upon the same power dynamics of Orientalism–that there is a single "Truth" known by scholar-experts by which they judge all accounts. The question also implies that we can create "true" (objective) representations of this real Orient, when this myth of "true representation" is one of the main assumptions of Orientalist discourses. Even more seriously, though, the question implies that "culture" is the ultimate social reality. This is, at best, dubious since it is premised on assumptions that a "culture" is homogeneous (admitting to no variation among the individuals who collectively make it up) and exists in isolation from other "cultures." Finally, the question all but rules out in advance the possibility of genuine cross-cultural exchange. Perhaps, then, the question "Am I guilty of Orientalism?" is the wrong question. A more hermeneutically sensitive and fruitful question would be, "How have I been influenced by Orientalism and how can I move away from Orientalism's destructive effects?"

Orientalism is a throny topic, a collection of discourses that differ greatly in terms of content and conclusions. All of them, though, share the same functions of defining and controlling their subjects. I have consistently endeavored *not* to do this, even while employing the rigors of academic disciplines. I avoid putting Sengzhao and Liu Yimin's views and positions in Western terms. I cite Chinese and Buddhist sources and precedents for their work. I also am cautious in drawing parallels to Western ideas and practices. I do not, for instance, equate Sengzhao's use of **Mādhyamika** with Deconstruction, although I do point out similarities between his work and that of other apophatic writers. Similarly, I never equate Liu's Pure Land devotionalism with Christianity but do draw attention to analogies between his practices and writings with certain Christian ones. At various points I highlight Orientalist aspects of previous translators and scholars as well. In addition, I have from the first owned up to my own location and interests as a scholar, always endeavoring to bring forward how these affect my interpretation. Most of all, I explicitly state that I am not giving the final word about Sengzhao, Liu, *prajñā* or Sagely Wisdom.

Let me be clear that I do not claim to have avoided all traces of Orientalism. The Orientalist practices of scholars have resulted in significant misunderstanding in the past. They have bequeathed us gross over-generalizations and distortions that remain enormous obstacles to cross-cultural understanding. To a large extent we contemporary scholars have all been affected by this; we are, all of us, "Orientalists" because we inevitably make generalizations and traffic in representations that we claim to be "true." We cannot overcome this legacy except through the constant and continuous self-criticism that hermeneutics calls for. There will always be obstacles in hermeneutic study. In my engagement with Sengzhao and Liu Yimin, I have striven to be mindful of these obstacles and to work through them. Ironically, even the scholar-monk and the gentry recluse speak of obstacles to understanding although neither dwells upon them at great length.[6] Similar problems based on initial difference and separation arise in all exchanges between parties, be they individuals within a family, leaders of communities, or scholars meeting through the medium of written words. Understanding and misunderstanding go hand in hand.

As scholars seeking a truer understanding we cannot change the past nor disown history's influence. We can, however, face the difficulties that arise in our interpretations and learn to work through them, much as Śākyamuni faced the forces of Māra under the Bodhi tree. By reminding ourselves of their presence, we allow ourselves to be honest and can more mindfully enter into dialogue with the text that is "Other," the "Other" that is text. And it is here that a text can help us. The Way of interpretation does not avoid problems, but flows into them by attending to the text. Words trace out the way to understanding; as Sengzhao notes, they not only are "a benefit for the present day but will serve as a ford and a bridge for many *kalpas* to come."[7] This offers no assurance of final success but it opens the way to self-critical and constructive engagement.

Interestingly, Sengzhao himself models such an interpretive approach. In "*Prajñā* is Not-knowing" Sengzhao sets out the problem of conflicting interpretations of *prajñā*, taking them seriously even as he aims towards a resolution. During the essay he looks to *prajñā* texts repeatedly and attempts to answer critical problems and possible objections opponents may raise. Most of all, he does not rest easy with his own interpretation–his use of "wild words" precludes him from providing a definitive description and he admits this from the essay's earliest sections. Similarly, in his reply to Liu Yimin, Sengzhao takes Liu's questions and objections seriously. His answers are both constructive and critical, and he attempts to show us the way when he urges that we go *through* his words to the truth of *prajñā*. Overall, Sengzhao offers an erudite interpretation that is both punning and playful while remaining faithful to the texts he interprets.

Liu provides another good example of a hermeneutic approach. Liu's letter, although shorter and evincing less technical Buddhist learning than Sengzhao's, offers a different interpretation yet demonstrates good hermeneutic techniques. Liu stays close to the text of "*Prajñā* is Not-knowing" and repeatedly asks questions in the midst of his criticisms. Both Sengzhao and Liu amply demonstrate the sort of hermeneutic "good will" that Gadamer often calls for. Both are also well aware of their differences and do not dismiss or ignore them. Rather, they strive for understanding despite differences, even if they ultimately misunderstand. Their exchange has much to teach us about hermeneutic encounters.

Interpreting Sengzhao allows us to "fuse horizons" with him and have our own perspective broadened. We simultaneously see that our perspective is informed by concerns which differ from Sengzhao's yet we can also see how his work casts new light on issues with which we have been struggling. One of the most significant issues that Sengzhao's writing brings up for scholars engaged in philosophical and religious studies concerns *prajñā* and "mysticism." I have already used the terms "mystical" and "mysticism" in discussing Sengzhao's work as if their meaning were self-evident, but this is adamantly *not* the case. If we are to move into a deeper understanding of Sengzhao and say something about what *prajñā* is for Sengzhao and for us, we now need to delve into this subject in more detail.

Prajñā and Mysticism

Mysticism is a highly charged subject in academic study. The terms "mysticism" and "mystical" both hearken back to the Ancient Greek word *muein*, "to close (eyes or lips)," and are connected to the "mystery religions" whose esoteric teachings (*mysteria*) were revealed only to the initiates (*mystikoi*). Such ideas inspired early Christians, who often referred to the *mystikos*, "hidden" or "secret" teachings about Christ. In this early Christian sense, "mysticism" had distinctly biblical, liturgical and spiritual/contemplative dimensions,[8] and these dimensions continued through the Middle Ages. Gradually, the latter dimension attained greater prominence and in current usage "mysticism" tends to have a more experiential meaning. Thus "mysticism" now denotes extraordinary experiences arising out of devotion or meditation as well as the cultivation of exercises designed to lead to such experiences. It also can include visions, spontaneous realizations or nearly anything thought to reveal the supernatural or sacred.

It would seem, then, that a concise definition of "mysticism" or "mystical" is well nigh impossible. As Louis Dupre observes:

> No definition could be both meaningful and sufficiently comprehensive to include all experiences that, at some point or other, have been described as mystical. In 1899 Dean W. R. Inge listed twenty-five definitions. Since then the study of world religions has considerably expanded, and new, allegedly mystical cults have sprung up everywhere.[9]

Mysticism is associated with paradox, altered states of consciousness, extremes of feeling and intuitions of cosmic unity. Much of mysticism transcends the normal and everyday, leaving one with the vague but powerful sense of inexpressible truths.

The rise of mysticism as a legitimate area for academic study is curious and illustrates how conflicting interpretations inevitably develop within scholarship. Although the study of mysticism goes back centuries, as a modern scholarly enterprise it begins with William James and his landmark work, *The Varieties of Religious Experiences*. In this book, a transcript of his 1901 Gifford Lectures, James takes a distinctly psychological approach to mysticism and provides a phenomenology of religious experiences based upon a four-fold scheme. For James, the "four marks" of mystical states include ineffability, noetic quality (a sense of "knowledge" being imparted), transience, and passivity.[10] James' work has met with much criticism but it has been extremely influential and is still cited by many scholars.

Another thinker whose work has greatly shaped the study of mysticism is Aldous Huxley. Huxley based his explorations of mysticism on James' assumptions about religious experience, his readings of various texts from the world's religions and his own experiments with mescaline. From his studies Huxley concluded that mystical experiences give direct knowledge of the single truth of all religions. This truth is beyond creeds and doctrines, and is the heart of reality itself. Various religions are founded on the same fundamental experience, although their outer forms may differ. Huxley presents this view most systematically in his book *The Perennial Philosophy*, drawing upon long-standing tendencies within European Romanticism as well as the writings of earlier thinkers.[11] In a real sense this work became a foundation for the perennialist view of mysticism. The "Perennial Philosophy" has claimed many advocates including Fritjof Schuon and Huston Smith, and has shaped many contemporary "New Age" movements.[12]

W. T. Stace is perhaps the foremost spokesperson for a perennialist position and his work has much in common with Huxley's views although Stace presents them in a more philosophical fashion.[13] According to Stace, mystical experiences are not of an "objective reality" but point to the "transubjective ground of consciousness" beyond the ego. In arguing this point, Stace distinguishes between experience and its interpretation. For Stace, mystical experiences ultimately provide evidence for a pantheist-monist reality that gets interpreted differently depending upon the mystic's religious tradition. In his view, theistic accounts of mystical experiences are distortions in which mystics are struggling to fit their experiences into theistic belief systems. Stace also groups mystical experiences into two broad categories: extrovertive (in which the self merges with "nature") and introvertive (in which the self is absorbed in the ground of reality). Stace generally regards introvertive experiences as "higher."[14]

R. C. Zaehner is another theorist of mysticism whose views stand in direct opposition to Stace but with whom he nonetheless shares many similarities. An Indologist and Roman Catholic convert, Zaehner was extremely critical of Huxley and the "Perennial Philosophy" in general, advocating instead a theistic point of view. In his book *Mysticism Sacred and Profane* Zaehner categorizes mystical experiences according to three types: nature mysticism (marked by pantheistic intuitions of oneness within nature), monistic (characterized by introvertive absorption into the One), and theistic (loving encounters with a Personal God climaxing in a permanent "marriage"). In Zaehner's view, the former two are profane while the latter is sacred, and only here is the mystic actually sanctified by her experiences.[15] Zaehner denies the ultimacy of the pantheist-monist view although he still believes all mystical experiences are the same. The difference lies in the fact that the profane mystic is misled by his beliefs into thinking that his experiences of quiet absorption constitute the final truth instead of progressing beyond such states to the loving relationship with God.

The study of mysticism was defined by these various competing ideas until the late 1970's and 1980's when Steven Katz published a collection of essays entitled *Mysticism and Philosophical Analysis*, a work that ushered in a new era. Katz in particular was stridently critical of James, Stace and Zaehner, and his own contribution to the volume still provokes controversy.[16] In his essay Katz makes a plea for the recognition of variety and differences between mystical experiences, a position that some call "constructivist" but which he terms "contextualist." For Katz, complex epistemological categories based upon our language and culture shape and even determine our experiences. Indeed, Katz declares that there are no pure experiences, be they "ordinary" or "mystical." Mystical experiences, like all experiences, are produced by the beliefs and dispositions derived from a mystic's own life and culture. Accounts of mystical experiences do not provide evidence of some basic hidden unity but point to genuine differences. Mystical experiences and their accounts are, in a word, "constructed" by ideas inherited from a mystic's tradition.[17]

Katz has not gone unchallenged. One of his staunchest critics is Robert Forman, who responds to Katz and other constructivists by arguing for a "pure conscious event" (PCE) within various mystical experiences.[18] The crux of Forman's view is a "forgetting model" of consciousness in which mystical experiences entail the dropping off of all culturally conditioned constructions.[19] This PCE, according to Forman, is common to many mystical experiences although it may not be present in all of them and certainly there is room to explore other areas.[20] Much of Forman's work is critical of Katz but he is not merely asserting a naïve perennialism. The work of Forman and Katz continues to fuel much scholarship on mysticism and the role language may (or may not) have in shaping accounts of mystical experiences.

The study of mysticism has by no means drawn to a close with the debates between the constructivists (Katz et al) and the advocates of pure consciousness (Forman et al). There have been numerous responses to their work and there are differing perspectives even among the advocates of either position. Recently, the 2000 annual meeting of the American Academy of Religion featured a panel entitled "Mysticism and its Contents" exploring these same ideas that included Ninian Smart, Robert Gimello, Katz, and Janet Gyatso.[21] Clearly these remain live issues. Certainly both the constructivists and the advocates of pure consciousness make good points and neither camp has decisively refuted the other. This standoff, though, may indicate larger philosophical problems with the study of mysticism up to this point. It may prove helpful to examine some of these before discussing how *prajñā* relates to mysticism.

Mysticism, as I have indicated, has always posed problems for followers of religious traditions as well as scholars of those traditions. Many of the problems with the study of mysticism stem from the tendency for scholars to make easy generalizations about religions that obscure real differences *within* these traditions.[22] Critics of mysticism studies argue that scholars cast their nets too widely, attempting to group too many diverse phenomena together under one topic.[23] The current debate between constructivists and advocates of pure consciousness is also hampered by the circularity within both positions. That is, the proponents of both positions beg the question by assuming at the outset the very position for which they argue.[24] Furthermore, both camps unquestioningly focus their efforts on *experience*, as if that were the end all and be-all of mysticism. This experiential focus owes much to Modern and Romantic assumptions about what "religion" is.[25] Needless to say, there are also lingering vestiges of Orientalism within this debate, particularly among proponents of perennialism, who often also share the hermeneutic views of Romantic thinkers such as Schleiermacher and Dilthey.[26] Simply put, debates concerning mysticism are carried out almost exclusively among Western scholars who draw on Orientalist and colonialist sources without questioning their accuracy or the political influences that have shaped them. Such uncritical assumptions must be challenged if we are to gain a fuller understanding of "mystical traditions" as well as our own scholarly practices.[27]

In light of these considerations, we may conclude that it would be best *not* to delve into the study of mysticism. The old adage that mysticism "begins in 'mist,' centers on 'I,' and ends in 'schism'" certainly seems born out in the scholarship on the subject. Hermeneutic approaches, though, offer ways of dealing with such difficulties by encouraging a dialogic engagement in which we question texts and our own initial ideas. Rejecting the study of mysticism because of various conflicts of interpretation is not a philosophically grounded move. Indeed, the fact that mysticism is such a contested topic and that so much scholarship on mysticism is based on problematic assumptions makes it all the more important to study it, albeit in a more self-conscious fashion. Moreover, mysticism, however ill-defined it may be, excites great interest in this age of increased interreligious contact. The renewed focus on "spirituality" in recent years in mainstream religions and the growth of "New Age" groups points to the fascination mysticism continues to hold. Mysticism is a vital concern for many people. Hermeneutics compels us to take such matters seriously and to explore them for deeper understanding.

What relationship then, does *prajñā* have with "mysticism" and where do Sengzhao and Liu Yimin fit into discussions of *prajñā* and mysticism? These are complicated questions, and it is best if we deal with them separately. *Prajñā* as "insight" or "wisdom," a skill or state one develops while following a religious path, certainly lends itself to study in the same way that Christian practices (e.g. hesychasm) or Sufi discussions of stages and states (*maqat* and *hal*) that

arise in spiritual cultivation do. The close connection between Buddhist cultivation and the Pan-Indian practice of yoga (which many consider synonymous
with "Indian mysticism") also inclines us to regard Buddhist practices under
the rubric of "mysticism." Discussions of *prajñā* as a "perfection" and a major
component of the Bodhisattva path would seem to fit here as well. However,
not every Buddhist discussion of *prajñā* may count as "mystical." In **Theravādin**
discussion of *prajñā* (*paññā*), for example, Buddhaghosa downplays the sort of
dramatic "states" or "powers" upon which many practitioners and scholars of
mysticism focus. According to Buddhaghosa such things may actually hinder
the development of *prajñā*,[28] an important fact to bear in mind when scholars
make blanket assertions about "Buddhist mysticism."

Mahāyāna discussions of *prajñā*, however, definitely seem to fit under
the rubric of "mysticism." In the **Mahāyāna** *prajñā* is almost invariably *prajñ
āpāramitā* (the "perfection" of *prajñā*) and it was the *prajñāpāramitā* texts
and commentaries that formed the basis for the Chinese *prajñā* schools. For
Sengzhao, *prajñā* is *prajñāpāramitā*, and he equates it with "Sagely Wisdom." It
is unclear that Liu is aware of any distinction between *prajñā*, *prajñāpāramitā*
or sageliness, and certainly his discussion has a somewhat different focus than
Sengzhao's.[29] As we have seen, Buddhist discussions of *prajñāpāramitā* are
paradoxical and overwhelmingly stress its transformative, "magical" aspects.
For example, in the *Aṣṭa* **Subhūti** (speaking from within the perspective of
prajñā) says even *nirvāṇa* is "like a magical illusion ... like a dream."[30] Many
prajñā texts also describe *prajñā* as non-dual realization, a "being/knowing"
in which "knower" and "known" cannot be separated.[31] *Prajñā* truly seems
to be a "mystical" way of knowing. Accounts and descriptions in *prajñā* texts
have great resonance with James' categories of noetic quality and ineffability,
although they may not fit well with his notions of transience and passivity. The failure of language to adequately convey *prajñā*, a theme repeatedly
stressed in the *prajñāpāramitā sūtras* and by later commentators, also fits well
with other scholarly studies of language and its role in mystical writings.[32]
Moreover, *prajñā* texts also speak of specific experiences of "insight," perhaps
most famously in the opening lines of the "Heart *sūtra*" where Avalokiteśvara
Bodhisattva perceives the emptiness of all phenomena in the midst of his
meditation.[33] This experiential aspect of *prajñā* certainly lends itself to the
general scholarly approach to mysticism taken in recent decades.

If *prajñā*, then, merits study as a sort of "mysticism" or "mystical knowing
and experiencing," what about Sengzhao and Liu Yimin's discussions of *prajñā*?
There has been little research on Liu in this regard although the accounts of

his visions and practices and his role in shaping worship on Lushan warrant further study. Liu was deeply involved in meditation and ascetic practices, and his visions had profound effect on his life. In this he resembles Christian mystics and visionaries such as Teresa of Avila (1515–1582), but such experiences stand in stark contrast to most discussions of *prajñā* in the *prajñāpāramitā sūtras* or Mādhyamika treatises which do not emphasize "visions" or devotion. On this basis we might question whether Liu is even speaking of *prajñā* or *prajñic* experiences. Forman and Stace might even deny that Liu is a true mystic since he does not seem to have been introvertive or to have experienced a PCE.

Sengzhao presents a different case. His writings clearly put him in line with the "*prajñā* Buddhism" of the *prajñāpāramitā sūtras*, their Mādhyamika commentators such as Nāgārjuna, and the various proponents of the *prajñā* schools. Unlike Liu, Sengzhao was not famous for practices or visions. His approach is more that of a "philosopher of *prajñā*." Even so, he is still of great interest to scholars of mysticism.

Both Liebenthal and Robinson dwell on the subject of Sengzhao and "mysticism" at great length. Liebenthal is especially keen on mystical experiences, refering in several passages to Sengzhao's "ecstasy," "visions," and "*samādhi*." According to Liebenthal, Sengzhao's work is part of a greater cultural quest during the Jin era for an awakening that would enable a person to transcend the human situation. Buddhist *sūtras* were understood to speak of this "secret" and Sengzhao's studies provoked certain "visions" that apparently prompted him to wonder if he had also gotten beyond such limits. Liebenthal maintains that this was what Indian practitioners saw in *samādhi*, citing as evidence a passage from Sengzhao's commentary on the *Vimalakīrti*:

> The followers of Hīnayāna enter a state of meditation called *nirodha-samāpatti* In this (trance) they resemble dry wood, being unable to move. The *Mahāsattvas* (followers of Mahāyāna) enter *bhūtalakṣana samādhi* (true reality trance). The flickering of their minds completely ceases and their bodies fill the eight directions (i.e. the universe). They respond harmoniously with the moving forces of nature, meeting the calls of innumerable Beings. Proceeding and receding in accordance with the circumstances, they [always] maintain appropriate action.[34]

For Liebenthal *samādhi* is a way Buddhist meditators in India amass spiritual "power," presumably for untangling their own karmic "knots" and aiding other sentient beings, although Liebenthal does not go into details.

Even more intriguing is how Liebenthal puts Sengzhao in the general category of those who enter *samādhi* while also calling attention to how

Sengzhao's *samādhi* differs from "Indian" *samādhi*. It seems that Sengzhao's *samādhi* is more "Chinese." Liebenthal writes:

> Seng-chao's *samādhi* might better be rated as an exalted state of mind in which the Saint felt himself in complete accord with nature. Cosmic life was the main problem of Chinese reasoning, union with cosmic life their religious goal. The state in which the Saint or poet felt himself in union with nature was the main theme of Chinese landscape painting, and, most probably, this was what Seng-chao experienced in his moments of *samādhi*.[35]

This is a remarkable passage for what it reveals about Liebenthal rather than Sengzhao. Liebenthal assumes Sengzhao not only attained *samādhi* but that it was an "experience" in which he felt "in complete accord with nature," and that apparently this was the "same experience" had by a poet or landscape painter. Such assumptions are, needless to say, highly problematic. Ironically, immediately after this passage Liebenthal even admits that Sengzhao himself never describes such an alleged state![36]

Robinson focuses even more extensively on Sengzhao's "mystical" side than does Liebenthal. In his article "Mysticism and Logic in Seng-Chao's Thought," Robinson writes "Liebenthal's opinion that Seng-chao is a mystic is virtually incontrovertible," and that "Seng-chao certainly presents a mystical philosophy,"[37] a theme to which he repeatedly returns in his book *Early Mādhyamika in India and China*. Unlike Liebenthal, however, Robinson also concentrates on Sengzhao's reasoning, taking great pains to diagram many of Sengzhao's arguments using logical notation.[38] Unfortunately Robinson never defines "mysticism," something quite surprising for a philosopher who goes out of his way to define key terms in the texts he analyzes. Even more troubling, Robinson never discusses the important scholarship on mysticism. Of all the major scholars of mysticism (e.g. James, Zaehner, Stace) Robinson only mentions Rudolf Otto. Although Otto's work, especially *The Idea of the Holy*, has contributed a great deal to the study of mysticism, he is not without his critics. The fact that Robinson fails to elaborate more on mysticism calls into question how much he really knows about the subject.

Robinson speculates that Sengzhao may have practiced methods prescribed in the *Bodhisattva-dhyāna*, a "Hīnayāna" text translated by Kumārajīva at the behest of his disciple Sengrui.[39] This is a reasonable suggestion based upon what we know of the Chang'an community and the fact that Buddhist monks almost universally engage in some sort of meditation practice but we cannot prove anything about Sengzhao's practices; we simply have no hard evidence.

Nonetheless, Robinson goes on to argue that Sengzhao most likely contemplated doctrines as a way of removing "wrong views" in order to attain realization, much like the followers of the later *Sanlun* school.[40]

As I say in Chapter Three, however, Robinson does at least hint at something else regarding Sengzhao and mysticism that seems quite promising. At one point Robinson suggests that Sengzhao may have considered the study and contemplation (and writing?) of texts to be a spiritual practice. After analyzing Sengzhao's arguments, Robinson concludes that the function of language in the writings of Sengzhao is not to argue for a specific position but to demonstrate the impossibility of true predication. He even writes that Sengzhao would agree with Wittgenstein's conclusion to the *Tractatus Logico-Philosophicus*:

> My propositions are elucidatory in this way; he who understands me finally recognizes them as senseless, when he has climbed out through them, on them, over them. (He must so to speak throw away the ladder, after he has climbed up on it.) He must surmount these propositions; then he sees the world right. Whereof one cannot speak, thereof one must be silent.[41]

Other scholars have picked up and developed this suggested parallel with Wittgenstein's views of language,[42] and it has strong echoes in passages from other Buddhist texts where the Buddha enjoins his disciples to discard his teachings after they attain *nirvāṇa*.[43] Robinson, however, does not elaborate further, adding only in regard to Sengzhao:

> It seems that in fifth century China, as in the modern world, at least one thinker saw an intimate connection between logical or dialectical forms and the mystery of reality, that he saw the road to *bodhi*, not in the practice of trances, but as a journey through, on, and over propositions about existence and inexistence.[44]

This suggestion of a textual meditation practice holds far more promise than searching for some alleged experience. It is also more in keeping with what we know of Sengzhao's scholarly bent and the philosophical climate of his times. I am unsure how to square such "textual mysticism" with Robinson's focus on logical exposition, an approach which entails translating Sengzhao's writings into propositions about "Reality" rather than using them as avenues to awakening. To his credit, though, Robinson explores both aspects of Sengzhao's work, and perhaps the tension between the logical and mystical poles mirrors Sengzhao's own dialectics.

Both Liebenthal and Robinson's studies are insightful but fraught with problems. Both scholars uncritically assume perrenialist views and this colors their interpretations of Sengzhao's texts.[45] Liebenthal and Robinson also grossly overgeneralize about mysticism, speaking of it as a simple universal phenomenon. For instance, Robinson writes that Sengzhao's notion of *prajñā* is "the well-known mystic vision of one in all and all in one."[46] Yet if anything has emerged from the study of mysticism, it is that there is no such thing as a single "mystical vision." The most problematic aspect of both Liebenthal and Robinson's discussions of Sengzhao and mysticism, though, is their overwhelming focus on experiences, for it leads both scholars to make questionable statements and reach rather tenuous interpretations. Simply put, nowhere in *"Prajñā* is Not-knowing," "The Correspondence" or the other essays in the *Zhaolun* does Sengzhao discuss his own experiences of awakening or insight. Indeed, he never mentions any specific practices in which he may have engaged.

We must beware, of course, of prematurely concluding that Sengzhao had no experience with meditation. As I indicate earlier, we have no evidence about Sengzhao's actual practices. He probably was familiar with basic *dhyāna* practices as these form a standard part of monastic regimen. We know from his letter to Liu that the meditation master Buddhabhadra had a large following in Chang'an,[47] and Sengrui and others among Kumārajīva's disciples were deeply interested in meditation.[48] However, Sengzhao's writings on *prajñā* are scholarly treatises and make little reference to meditation techniques. Although Sengzhao's later Chan commentators speak of their own experiences that were triggered from studying Sengzhao's works,[49] we are not warranted to assume that Sengzhao is reporting such experiences. What's more, even if Sengzhao based his discussion on his experiences, we still would not have those experiences to study. We only have his words. To understand Sengzhao's notion of *prajñā* we must stick to the words of his texts, as he himself says.

As we can see, both Liebenthal and Robinson base their interpretations of Sengzhao's work on certain ideas and assumptions about mysticism, experience and texts. These assumptions shape their interpretations in ways that differ from my own. I maintain that both Liebenthal and Robinson misinterpret Sengzhao, although it may be that they would argue the same about my view. We, thus, find ourselves once again facing a conflict of interpretations. This need not disturb us, though, for such conflicts can encourage further engagement and understanding by returning us again and again to the texts involved. Conflicting interpretations also force us to consider different, even opposing perspectives. It is interesting to note that Sengzhao once again serves as a model here, both in the section of *"Prajñā* is Not-knowing" where he addresses possible objections and throughout his letter to Liu Yimin. Hermeneutics is not about closure or resolution but finding and disclosing meaning using every means at hand. As David Tracy insightfully remarks, "there is no release for any of us from the conflict of interpretations if we would understand at all."[50]

The fact that we face conflicting interpretations of Sengzhao should come as no surprise. We are bound to find different meanings when interpreting texts because each interpreter brings his own concerns to a text and asks different questions. Moreover, we can learn from the different meanings other interpreters find and enrich our own understandings. Liebenthal and Robinson make many good points despite their shortcomings. Liebenthal, for instance, provides a wonderful discussion of Sengzhao's Chinese context, and does a masterful job with tracking down the many references and allusions Sengzhao employs. Robinson is better with Sengzhao's Buddhist side, showing how his work fits with the writings of Nāgārjuna, Kumārajīva and various members of the Chang'an translation bureau. Certainly both Liebenthal and Robinson have problematic notions of mysticism but clearly they are on to something when they speak of Sengzhao as a "mystic." Indeed, Robinson provides a key insight into Sengzhao's work when he suggests that the scholar-monk engaged in a type of "textual mysticism"—a notion that has prompted me to explore this avenue further.

Based upon these previous interpretations I that argue Sengzhao presents *prajñā* as a type of "wisdom" born of textual study. Such *prajñā* does not divide or discriminate but embraces all things. "Wild words" have a vital function in attaining this "wisdom" for they are the means for transforming ordinary discursive consciousness into the Mind of *prajñā*. Hence in *"Prajñā* is Not-knowing" Sengzhao replies to his second objector, "It (*prajñā*) is a nameless *dharma*, thus we are not dealing with speech and what can be spoken. Although it cannot be spoken of through words, yet it is not that words lack the means of conveying it. Therefore the Sage 'speaks night and day yet never speaks'."[51]

As I have indicated in Chapter Three, we find analogies to such "textual mysticism" in other cultures. Francis Clooney has demonstrated that the Indian tradition of Advaita Vedānta does not center on some vague intuition of "oneness" as proponents of the Perennial Philosophy assume but is a step-by-step training in proper textual understanding. Under the guidance of a *guru*, the student immerses himself in the *Upaniṣads* and various commentaries that instruct him on how to apprehend reality. "Mastery" is achieved when the student becomes conformed to the understanding encapsulated by such great sayings as *"Tat tvam asi."*[52] Similar types of textual training can be found among the medieval Kabbalists of Judaism, particularly those who studied the *Zohar* such as Isaac Luria (1534–1572), perhaps the greatest Kabbalist.[53] Generally speaking, the Kabbalists sought mystical insight through immersion in Scripture and esoteric commentaries. They regarded this as a dangerous process, open only to the most qualified and mature scholars. Once again, realization and insight came through regimented textual study.

However, it is probably the Neo-Confucian thinker Zhu Xi (1130–1200) who provides the closest parallel to Sengzhao's mystical cultivation through textual study. Zhu places the practice of *nian* ("reading/study") at the center of an intellectual and religious curriculum of education. *Nian* involves formal, repetitive recitation of sagely writings (*jing* and *zhuan*) as a way of internalizing the texts and making them part of one's being. *Nian* is a powerful technique; according to Master Zhu, *nian* brings one face to face with the Sages, and serves as the crucial first step in attaining realization.[54] Thus although *nian* has obvious practical applications (it trains students to memorize texts—a necessary skill for passing the civil service exams), it has a deeper purpose. *Nian* forms part of a textual Dao in which the words themselves trace out the path. The student tracks these traces through intense study but eventually ventures beyond them.

It is perhaps no surprise that Zhu Xi's practice of *nian* provides a particularly apt analogy to Sengzhao's use of "wild words" as both are premised on the deeply-rooted Chinese conviction that *wen* (writing, literature, culture) has a divine aura. In Chinese society of Sengzhao's time the mystique surrounding words was strong indeed. There were numerous folktales in which scholars had supernatural power because of their command of words and texts, and many viewed Neo-Daoist recluses and Buddhist scholar-monks as "holy men" with powers above and beyond those of ordinary people.[55] Words were powerful magic. To know, recite and especially write words placed one in the presence of the Sages and the Mysteries of Heaven and Earth. This remained the case even when words could not fully capture the essence of such Wisdom.

Several scholars have noted this wondrous power of words that we find in the writings of Sengzhao and other "mystical" thinkers, and they have explored its implications for the role of language in mysticism from a number of angles. Michael Sells has taken this discussion in a very promising direction, as I have indicated in Chapter Three. Sells focuses on "mystical languages of unsaying," the apophatic writings of several figures such as Plotinus, Ibn Arabi, Marguerite Porete, and Meister Eckhart. For Sells, apophasis is a cross-cultural mode of discourse in which a writer struggles with language's paradoxical power and failure to capture the transcendent.[56] At the heart of apophatic discourse is an "anarchic moment" (one without "principle" or "reason") that Sells describes as a "meaning event" in which language re-creates at the semantic level a sort of mystical awakening. Thus in Sells' analysis, apophasis proves to be both nonintentional (it does not refer to or assert "facts") and performative (it evokes an event in the reader analogous to the mystic's awakening).[57]

It seems clear, in light of Sells' findings, that Sengzhao's "wild words" also constitute an apophatic discourse, albeit of a *xuanxue* Buddhist type. His *prajñic* discourse of "wild words" defies clear, rational explanation or paraphrasing. It *unsays* definitive statements through a constant denial of positions (*dṛṣṭi*) and evokes an unsettled embracing of all the ten-thousand things. The result is a "not-knowing knowing," the Mind of the Sage.

It is in this regard that we can speak of "wild words" being similar to *Chan* and *Zen koans* (*gongan*). Sengzhao was not a *Chan* master and his writings predate the rise of any distinct *Chan* lineage by several centuries. Later *Chan* masters, of course, commented on his work, adopting him into the *Chan* fold posthumously. *Koans* are an integral part of most *Chan* and *Zen* training. They are serious proclamations that demand response. They are not logical and cannot be solved through discursive reasoning. *Koans* are perplexing, maddening, and take us to the edge of normal consciousness. Like "wild words," *koans* lie on the cusp of the relative and ultimate where words and concepts ("knowing") fail but Mind ("Wisdom") abides. *Koans* and "wild words" are rhetorical devices designed to provoke a truly "not-knowing knowing." However, Sengzhao draws on Mādhyamika and Neo-Daoist precedents for his "wild words" and not the examples of legendary *Chan* figures such as Bodhidharma or Huineng. "Wild words" are analogous to *koans*, and can even be used as *koans* in the hands of a skilled *Chan* master, but they are not the same. To equate the two types of discourse may lead to profound *misunderstanding* if we are not careful.

Revisiting Liu Yimin
and Sengzhao's Views of *Prajñā*

In the preceding section on mysticism we have seen how Liu Yimin and especially Sengzhao's writings on *prajñā* apply to an intriguing and controversial area of religious and philosophical studies. We have highlighted problematic assumptions concerning "experience" that scholars of mysticism have not always questioned, and we have also seen how Liebenthal and Robinson, two significant scholars of Sengzhao's writings, hold similar views. Our study has given us a different vantage point and has enabled us to suggest other ways to study mysticism, drawing on some more recent work. At this point, then, we need to turn back to Liu and Sengzhao's views of *prajñā* to see how our understanding of their views may change in light of our reflections on mysticism. Can theories of mysticism further our understanding of Liu and Sengzhao and open us to richer, more nuanced interpretations of their work?

Liu Yimin's Notion of Prajñā

As we have seen, Liu's view of *prajñā* arose out of and was informed by his devotional experiences. Liu practiced a form of meditation in which he "saw" Amitābha Buddha in the Pure Land. His reputation for such visions was so great that Huiyuan chose him to write the "Hymn to Amitābha" chanted by the Lushan community. We find hints of such practices in Liu's letter where he equates the way of the Sage/Bodhisattva with *samatha-vipassanā*.[58] All of this would seem to place Liu within Pure Land Buddhist tradition. Technically speaking, however, neither Liu nor his colleagues on Lushan were members of the Pure Land school (*qingtu zong*); Pure Land as a self-conscious lineage did not arise until the sixth century.[59] Still, Liu and his colleagues were members of an Amitābha cult, so investigating Pure Land practices and ideas may provide clues to understanding Liu's notion of *prajñā*.

Roger Corless describes Pure Land as a "mysticism of light" somewhat similar to what we find in the writings of the Christian mystic St. Augustine of Hippo as well as in other religious traditions such as Zoroastrianism.[60] Amita Buddha, alias Amitābha ("He of Immeasurable Light") and/or Amitāyus ("He of Immeasurable Life"), is a shining, enlightening being whose light symbolizes "Wisdom."[61] "Wisdom" or *prajñā* in this tradition is precisely the sort of vision of Amitābha that Liu experienced and the "insight" arising from such illumination. Such visions are also promises of rebirth in the Pure Land, a type of immortality in a heavenly realm that resembles Daoist religious ideas.[62] Although we might be tempted to consider such experiences as purely transcendent, they are also immanent in that they give access to the Pure Land while the devotee remains within the realm of birth-and-death. Moreover, these visions strongly influence a practitioner's view of life; a devotee apprehends the human realm as the Pure Land and vice-versa. *Saṃsāra* is *nirvāṇa*; *nirvāṇa* is *saṃsāra*. We should, thus, regard such visions as "gnostic" in the broadest sense of the word, for they impart "knowledge" of the ultimate nature of reality. The Pure Land is reality when we see it as it truly is.

Liu's views furnish a wealth of material for scholars of mysticism. On the surface, we can make a strong case for a constructivist view of Liu's notion of *prajñā*. Certainly his "devotional *prajñā*" is not "pure" in the sense of Forman's PCE but has a distinct Buddhist content. Moreover, it arises within a specific context that is informed by ideas and images derived from texts and practices. If we wish to follow Zaehner, we might consider Liu's experiences "true" (sacred) mysticism, for they seem to be "theistic" and would thus sanctify the devotee. By contrast, Stace would no doubt regard Liu's visions as "false" or at best misinterpretations of a monistic experience. Liu's experiences are of a distinct type, and perhaps some scholars would even dismiss them as mystical. Such considerations highlight something very important: Liu's view of *prajñā* does not appear to belong to the *prajñāpāramitā* tradition. In his letter to Sengzhao, Liu never refers to *prajñāpāramitā sūtras* or later commentaries (he only quotes Sengzhao's essay), and Liu only uses the term "*prajñā*" a few times, none of which evince any familiarity with the philosophy of *prajñā*. It is, thus, no wonder that he and Sengzhao do not understand each other.

All of this is not to say that Liu's Pure Land focus has nothing in common with *prajñā* Buddhism, for there are connections between these two traditions. Liu and his Lushan colleagues have picked up and amplified themes that were already present in Buddhism when it entered China. Certainly there are devotional aspects in some *prajñā* texts and the worship of *Prajñāpāramitā* as a "Goddess" played a major role in the spread of Mahāyāna. Furthermore, in the visions of Amitābha, a practitioner comes to realize that her mind and Amitābha are ultimately "non-dual," just like *saṃsāra* and *nirvāṇa* in *prajñā* texts.[63] We can find other connections between *prajñā* texts and Pure Land ideas as well. A good example occurs in the first chapter of the *Vimalakīrti sūtra*, where Śākyamuni demonstrates to Śāriputra that the human realm really is his Pure Land; the only difference is *how* beings perceive it based upon the purity of their own minds.[64] The *Vimalakīrti*, of course, was a great favorite among the Buddho-Daoist literati, and Sengzhao had a special fondness for it. Clearly these *prajñā* scholars were familiar with Pure Land themes. Moreover, we cannot divorce such ideas from their larger religious context. Those who studied and wrote these texts also engaged in meditation practices and rituals. The fact that scholars of mysticism such as Stace or Forman have tended to ignore or even dismiss "devotional mystics" throws into bold relief the limitations of the field thus far, and reveals a lot about assumptions of what counts as "mystical."[65]

Another consideration to bear in mind is that the visualization practices Liu and his fellow recluses engaged in were also based on texts. Early Chinese Buddhism centered on texts to a large extent and this was true even of its more devotional strands. We find, for example, important details regarding Pure Land visualizations and meditations and the rituals surrounding them in the *Panzhou sanmei jing*, a popular text that was well-known on Lushan. By contrast, as best as we can determine Sengzhao and his colleagues in the Chang'an translation bureau were not devotees of **Amitābha**, even though they were acquainted with Pure Land doctrines. Instead, Sengzhao speaks of the (*Chan?*) meditation master Buddhabhadra and his large following. This does not mean that Sengzhao and his colleagues sat *zazen* but it may indicate a different orientation to religious cultivation. At the very least, we can conclude that the two communities had distinct spiritual foci and probably engaged in different practices which, in turn, were based on disparate assumptions. Liu and his colleagues focus their energies on attaining a "wisdom" that is less scholarly, yet paradoxically both more sensual and ascetic (it involves intense preparation and deprivation). Sengzhao had more intellectual and ontological interests, for he speaks of a "not-knowing" that gives direct insight into reality beyond the intellect. For both communities, however, texts played a major role. In this sense, then, Liu's *prajñā* more closely resembles Sengzhao's textual mysticism of "wild words" than seems apparent at first glance.

Regardless of any connection to "*prajñā* Buddhism," however, Liu's "devotional *prajñā*" and what it reveals about the beliefs and practices of the Lu Shan community are intriguing. Obviously there were many trends in early Chinese Buddhism, with popular practices and cults having widespread appeal even among the elite classes. Such movements resemble Daoist religious sects and more than likely draw from them. Liu's "devotional *prajñā*" invites cross-cultural comparisons of monastic practices in particular, as these are often tied to communal worship and devotion. Certainly Liu's *prajñā* strikingly resembles discussions of visions found in the writings of Christian mystics such as St. Teresa or St. Francis of Assisi. For Liu, *prajñā* is "salvific" in an obvious sense, and forms part of an important dimension of Chinese religions as a whole. This area begs for further investigation than we can give it here.

Sengzhao's Notion of *Prajñā*

Sengzhao's view of *prajñā* differs considerably from Liu's. Sengzhao follows the more intellectual and scholarly approaches to Dharma we find in the "*prajñā*

Buddhism" of Mādhyamika thinkers (Nāgārjuna, Kumārajīva) as well as the
Buddho-Daoist adherents of the Chinese "*prajñā* schools." *Prajñā* constitutes
the very essence of the Buddhas and Bodhisattvas, a compassionate "being-
knowing" that clearly apprehends, understands, and identifies with all beings.
Among such thinkers, the primary way to attain such a state is by studying
texts. Reading Sagely words opens the path from the relative to the ultimate
which the scholar follows by tracing the tracks left by those who went before.
Prajñā is the Sagely Way of "not-knowing."

   Prajñā in this sense is "mystical" and lends itself to study by scholars of
mysticism. Sengzhao has been described as a "mystical philosopher" and with
good reason, for he writes of the mysterious way to Sagely awakening, and
such writings do seem to point to some sort of experience. As we have seen,
both Liebenthal and Robinson focus on Sengzhao's alleged "mystical" experiences although it is impossible to reach any definite conclusion about them.
Sengzhao's writings are not personal accounts, but are philosophical exegeses
of Buddhist *sūtras* in which he draws on Confucian and Daoist texts and even
debates certain points. Much of Sengzhao's discussion also amounts to an
extended description of the being-knowing of the Sage/Bodhisattva, the one
who embodies *prajñā*. Thus, for Sengzhao *prajñā* is less a matter of specific
"events" (PCE's) and more a lifelong process. Perhaps Sengzhao's *prajñā* is
akin to *sahaja samādhi*, a concept that Forman borrows from Hindu sources
but which he does not explore in any detail.[66]

   For Sengzhao *prajñā* is not tied to communal worship or devotion, although
his *prajñā* studies were carried out within a community of like-minded scholar-
monks. In some respects he seems closer to the more individualistic "shamanic"
strain within Chinese religion, an aspect of Chinese culture dating back to
the very beginnings of civilization. The mythic "Sage kings" who established
the social order by bequeathing the trappings of civilization to their subjects
were also shaman figures in touch with sacred powers; their political authority
was intertwined with religious authority.[67] This association of "kingship" and
"holiness" lent a sacred aura to the "gifts of civilization" these "Sage kings"
gave to posterity. Of these marks of civilization perhaps the most revered was
wen, "writing," "literature," the cultural arts. *Wen* was holy, sacred. In this
regard it is helpful to recall that many scholar-monks (e.g. Daoan and even
Kumārajīva) were "magicians," thaumaturges whose supernatural powers made
them valuable assets to their royal patrons. Sengzhao stands within their lineage and, although he himself was not a wonder-worker, he was noted for his
"brilliance"—his insight, intellectual ability, power in debate and facility with

language. Sengzhao was a man of *wen* and he would have exuded its supernatural aura. For him, *prajñā* came through *wen* as well.

Nonetheless, we need to be careful not to dismiss all points of contact between Sengzhao's notion of *prajñā* and Liu's "devotional *prajñā*." Daoan, the head of the Chang'an translation bureau before Kumārajīva and himself a great *prajñā* scholar, was devoted to Maitreya, the Buddha of the Coming Age.[68] The "holy man" aura surrounding Kumārajīva and other figures of his time, be they scholars or magicians, means that certain devotional aspects were present even among the most scholarly monks and literati. Even Zhi Dun, the great scholar-monk and head of the *jise* "*prajñā* school," was a devotee of Amitābha.[69] Although we have no evidence in Sengzhao's writings of the type of worship that we see among the Lu Shan community we cannot rule it out. Kumārajīva, for example, translated the so-called "Smaller *Sukhāvatīvyūha*" *sūtra* in 402 and his version remains the most commonly read Pure Land text to this day. The *Vimalakīrti* also discusses Pure Land ideas and there are passages on the Pure Land in the *Lotus sūtra*, one of the most important texts that Kumārajīva and his disciples translated. Finally, Sengzhao's veneration of Kumārajīva and Yao Xing as living Sages reminds us that making a clear-cut distinction between *prajñā* studies and devotionalism is not warranted and doing so may actually be imposing an alien view on Sengzhao's texts.[70] Devotionalism was not foreign to Sengzhao or his colleagues. The Chang'an community would not regard the Pure Land ideas and practices so prominent on Lushan as something divorced from *prajñā* studies. Perhaps the differences between the communities are matters of degree rather than kind.

The role of language is a key point in this difference. For Sengzhao, words are the Way to the "not-knowing" knowing of *prajñā*. His was a *scholarly* Dao and for him and many literati, scholarship was a religious vocation. The translation sessions presided over by Kumārajīva were also religious ceremonies, ritualized expositions and discussions of Dharma and these were well-attended by the public. Even the debates among the various scholars and Dharma masters probably partook of this religious or "holy" air. These were not purely intellectual exercises.

Seen in this light, Sengzhao's notion of *prajñā* forces us to reconsider what was going on in the Buddhist *xuanxue* circles of his time. These do not appear to be peopled by mere idle speculators. Certainly the Chang'an Buddhist community seems to have been fired by religious enthusiasm. From Sengzhao's letter to Liu Yimin we can see that Chang'an was a place where all aspects of Buddhism could be found. Study and translation formed an integral part of life in Chang'an, but so did meditation and attention to *vinaya* discipline. Chang'an was a holy center. Sengzhao speaks of **Kumārajīva** and Yao Xing with awe, and the veneration for the words of the Sages and Buddhas shines forth from his own texts. *Prajñā* is, perhaps, the true goal of all such Dharmic activities but especially those surrounding texts. This is why Sengzhao counsels those who read his words to go "through" them. Words point the Way, they form a Dao.

It is in this context that we must see Sengzhao's use of "wild words." As I have noted, Sengzhao borrows the phrase "wild words" (*kuangyan*) from an episode in chapter twenty-two of the *Zhuangzi*. This passage is intriguing and warrants close attention:

> Ah Hokan and Shen Nung were studying together under Lao Long Ji. Shen Nung sat leaning on his armrest, the door shut, napping when at midday Ah Hokan threw open the door and entered, saying, "Lao Long is dead!" Shen Nung, still leaning on his armrest, grabbed his walking staff and rose up. Then he dropped his staff with a clatter and laughed. He said, "Heaven knows I am cramped, mean, arrogant and willful, so [my master] abandoned me and died. My master died without leaving me any 'wild words' to open my mind!"
>
> Yan Gangtiao heard of this and said, "The one who embodies Dao has all the noble people in the world flocking to him. Now with respect to Dao, [Lao Long had not grasped] the tip of its hair, nor even a ten-thousandth part yet even he knew to store his 'wild words' and die [without saying]. How much more with someone who embodies Dao! Look for it, yet it has no form, listen, but is has no sound. Those who discuss it with others speak of it as "marvelous and wonderful" yet the Dao they discuss is not Dao."[71]

Like so much of the *Zhuangzi*, this apparently simple passage proves upon closer inspection to be puzzling, elliptical and pregnant with irony. Shen Nung bemoans (with joy!) the fact that his master Lao Long died without leaving him any "wild words" to open his mind. Yan Gantiao, another figure, learns of this event yet points out that Lao Long himself grasped only the merest fraction of Dao. Even so, he knew enough to keep his "wild words" to himself. The implication is that even the "wildest" of words cannot truly speak Dao (for Dao eludes description). Nonetheless, "wild words" do *something*—they furnish a map for our joyful wandering.

The *Zhuangzi*, along with the *Laozi* and the *Yijing*, was a vital text for Sengzhao. He and his fellow *xuanxue* thinkers regarded all three of these texts as providing the keys to understanding reality. For many *xuanxue* thinkers, Buddhist *sūtras* were in the same category. Indeed, for Sengzhao and others like him, the *sūtras* seem to have articulated the mysteries better than Daoist texts. The words of the *sūtras* could be baffling but they "darkly" pointed the way more clearly than the traces of Zhuang and Lao. Moreover, for Sengzhao the *sūtras* were not only the words of the Buddha, they came in his presence from the lips of his master **Kumārajīva**, a living Sage; their power would have truly been sacred, far-surpassing ordinary speech.[72] When Sengzhao uses the phrase "wild words," he is evoking an entire realm of discourse that defies our comprehension. "Wild words" comprise a Dao—a Dao (path) that can indeed be "Dao-ed" (spoken). Yet these "wild words" do not comprise the constant Dao. Rather, they lead us to the ultimate Dao, the Mystery of Mysteries, the Sagely Mind of Buddha, *Prajñā* itself.

"Wild words" expand our perspective beyond rational confines. They provide insight into the whole of reality as an ever-changing flux in which "things" and "ourselves" constantly arise, combine, and disintegrate. We no longer see the world as fixed and defined. More importantly, we understand that our words and concepts do not refer to fixed entities and do not limit their being. Words and concepts are part of the flux, part of our being and acting in the world. Like us, they roam and range, changing over time. Perhaps *all* words are "wild" though most of the time we are blind to this fact. We like things set and we like our words "tame." Sengzhao tells us, though, that this is not the Way to Sageliness. The Way to Sageliness, to *Prajñā*, cuts through the limits imposed by thought, by self and society. Sengzhao's "wild words" take us from convention through the gates of the Sages to the mystery where nothing (no thing) is real yet everything exists. Dwelling here amidst the changes, we truly understand all things and ourselves. Accepting all, rejecting none we realize the sameness of *dharmas*, the One Original *Qi*. Such realization, however, does not come in withdrawal to the mountains and forests but arises in the midst of the everyday. Ultimately it is through *prajñā* that we truly begin to live. In Buddhist terms, *prajñā* is *karuṇā*, compassion.[73]

This last point calls for special emphasis. Sengzhao was not a hermit but lived in a large community in the midst of Chang'an, a worldly and holy city, the Chinese equivalent of Rome. If he was not deeply involved in spiritual cultivation he did have insight into meditative states, as his letter to Liu attests. Sengzhao was a dedicated scholar but he was by no means a disinterested bystander. As a member of the translation bureau, Sengzhao held a political post and even before meeting **Kumārajīva** he rubbed elbows with various literati and officials. *Prajñā* studies and translation formed part of a public discourse on Dao that we can trace back to the time of Confucius. In early medieval China, the ideal figure around whom these discussions and debates centered, the Sage/Bodhisattva, was a cosmic ruler such as we find in the verses of the *Laozi*, or one of his ministers like the layman Vimalakīrti or even an "eminent monk" like Kumārajīva. Sengzhao was not removed from the political currents of the day and neither was his notion of *prajñā*. Perhaps, in the end, for Sengzhao *prajñā* is nothing other than "the way of inner sageliness and outer kingliness," that ever-elusive ideal sought by so many over the centuries. If Sengzhao emphasizes "inner sageliness" it nonetheless remains the case that such sageliness is never divorced from active involvement with all things.

It is interesting to note how my interpretation of Sengzhao compares with earlier scholars'. Tsukamoto, for example, takes Sengzhao to task for ignoring compassion in favor of the mystical "knowing" of *prajñā*:

> Depending on the absolute monarchial authority of Yao Hsing, the non-Chinese "Heavenly Prince," associating with a teacher who lived with court women and with the elders of Kumārajīva's school who received emoluments and contended for authority and advancement, the young Seng-chao, overwhelmed by the stimulus of doctrines from the continual new translations, let wider thoughts about the suffering of living beings be concealed and also tended to forget to examine the basis in actuality of himself and the people, who were profoundly separated from the Holy One. ...[74]

The puritanical streak coloring Tsukamoto's evaluation is unmistakable and it leads him to make illegitimate conclusions regarding Sengzhao's moral life.[75] Certainly Tsukamoto is profoundly incorrect about Sengzhao's failure to examine the situation of his age vis-à-vis the Buddha as his entire work was prompted by the hermeneutical crisis of Chinese Buddhism in his day.

We find similar misunderstandings of Sengzhao in the work of other scholars. Hsu offers a moral critique reminiscent of Tsukamoto's, albeit in a more generalized sense, placing Sengzhao in the company of the Chinese Nominalists (proponents of *mingjiao*), Śaṅkara and mainstream Mādhyamikas. In Hsu's view, all of these thinkers display an otherworldliness that overlooks present sufferings, adding "[such] high reasoning can be harmful and dangerous if indulged in."[76] Ming-wood Liu says that we find no evidence of compassion in Sengzhao's writings at all. "The one cardinal feature which distinguishes the Buddhist sage from the Taoist sage—the dedication to the mission of universal salvation founded on the heart of compassion—was, however, silently passed over."[77] Indeed, among previous scholarship on Sengzhao, Hashimoto Hōkei stands alone in maintaining that compassion is central to Sengzhao's writings.[78] From what we have seen in our present study, though, the interpretations of

Tsukamoto, Hsu, and Liu are all untenable. For Sengzhao, the Sage/Bodhisattva is active in his "not-knowing" knowing. His *prajñic* being is marked by *karuṇā*. In "Daoist" terms, we should describe "Sagely being" as *wei wuwei*, "non-acting acting."

Interestingly, my interpretation of Sengzhao's view of *prajñā* both resembles and differs from interpretations of *prajñā* put forth by two other Buddhist scholars, D. T. Suzuki and C. W. Huntington. In his landmark essay "Reason and Intuition in Buddhist Philosophy," Suzuki interprets *prajñā* as a mystical "intuition" that unites all of reality.[79] *Prajñā* cannot be analyzed into separate "things," or "subject" and "object," hence it cannot be spoken of rationally. Indeed, Suzuki says *prajñā* is incomprehensible, *acintya* (beyond understanding). Yet Suzuki also stresses that *prajñā* is a dynamic awareness, an activity, not a passive happening or "feeling." It involves the truest living, not quietistic gazing.[80] The person of *prajñā* is "Daoist" in the full sense of the word, like the wonderful characters in the *Zhuangzi* or the Sage of the *Laozi*. To live in *prajñā* is to live spontaneously, playfully, joyfully. As Suzuki says, in *prajñā* we engage in the *anābhoga-caryā* (purposeless activity) life of the Bodhisattva.[81]

Huntington's views provide an interesting contrast to Suzuki's. For Huntington, *prajñā* is not a vague "intuition" but a technical skill developed by following the Bodhisattva path. It begins in careful analysis (*hetubhūta-prajñā*, "wisdom as cause") and reaches its full actualization (*phalabhūta-prajñā*, "wisdom as effect") through long training in textual study, critical reflection, and meditation. *Prajñā* in this latter sense is *prajñā* "perfected," *prajñā-pāramitā*, the "nondualistic knowledge" (*advayajñāna*) that is *nirvāṇa* itself.[82] More importantly, Huntington stresses that *prajñā* arises from seeing emptiness (*śūnyatā*) and acting accordingly. In Huntington's view, *prajñā* is eminently practical, a sort of "know how" or "knowing-being" as opposed to a merely intellectual grasp of doctrine. Huntington states:

> Prajñā is not amassed through accretion of theoretical formulas or through reference to any sublime, metaphysical, or mystical reality. It is the essential clarity and flexibility of the mind revealed when, through the discipline of the path, the bodhisattva has completely rid himself of the tendency to cling to the contents of conceptualization and perception as though some or all of them were grounded in an a priori truth or reality. Prajñā is a matter both of intellectual understanding and of action.[83]

Prajñā is active, not passive. It is a transformed way of life but is not alienated from rational study and analysis nor daily comings and goings. *Prajñā* is the actualizing of the truth of *śūnyatā* in everyday existence. Intriguingly, although

Huntington is not dealing with Chinese texts, the notion of *prajñā* he proposes has great resonance with Chinese views of Buddhism and the views of
"wisdom" in other "Daoist" traditions.

Both Suzuki and Huntington's views of *prajñā* resemble Sengzhao's, even
though all three have different approaches to Buddhism and come from widely
differing backgrounds. I am not suggesting that we should equate them or
expect these thinkers to say "the same thing," but it is useful to note where
they overlap. For all three, *prajñā* is a transformative "cognition" that opposes
ordinary thinking yet remains very much a part of this world. One whose
mind is *prajñā* is not lost in *samādhi* or rapturous visions but fully aware and
responsive to all situations, and her actions are marked by compassion and concern. *Prajñā* is *karuṇā*. Despite this practical aspect, though, *prajñā* remains
a mystery for those stuck in dualistic thinking. Most interestingly, Sengzhao,
Suzuki and Huntington all attest to the fact that speaking of *prajñā* poses
immense difficulties. This is easiest to see with Sengzhao and Suzuki, who
often speak of *prajñā* in seemingly irrational or nonsensical ways. For Sengzhao
this is because we must use "wild words" to speak of *prajñā*. Suzuki, for his
part, maintains that *prajñā* appears baffling because *prajñā* is not rational; it
accepts contradiction and moves beyond it in its own "logic" of wholeness. [84]
Huntington, though, implies something similar when he argues that *prajñā*
overcomes the unenlightened perspective in which separate and independent
"things" (including our "selves") exist. For the unenlightened, language refers
to these separate things that we assume to be real. By contrast, those who
attain *prajñā* realize language is merely a system of conventions that do not
correspond to "reality."[85] Plainly, this perspective would be incomprehensible
to the unenlightened and well-nigh impossible to convey. Perhaps we should
say that for Sengzhao, Suzuki and Huntington *prajñā* is "mystical," as it denotes
a transformed way of perceiving and living that defies rational explanation,
confounds ordinary speech, yet is fully at home in the world. None of this, of
course, constitutes "proof" that Sengzhao or Suzuki or Huntington is "right."
Such comparisons, though, enrich our understanding of Sengzhao and give us
a better idea of the range of interpretations of *prajñā*.

From these considerations Sengzhao emerges as a thinker fully in line with
Buddhist and Chinese tradition whose writings on *prajñā* strongly resonate
with religious writings in other cultures. Moreover, Sengzhao's views, while
"ancient," seem strikingly contemporary in certain respects. He may be a "mystic" but he is also something of a pragmatist and even an anti-foundationalist,
as he is not trying to argue for an objectively certain truth. For Sengzhao,

prajñā offers a type of transcendence that is not divorced from this world or our socio-cultural context. The Sage/Bodhisattva does not really have an eternal, "God's eye view" but is a particular manifesting of clear, compassionate being. And it seems equally clear that Sengzhao's discussion of *prajñā* is prescriptive and even exhortatory. In Sengzhao's perspective, *prajñā*'s "not-knowing" is a distinct way of living, a Dao to which we should aspire.

Obviously this interpretation of Sengzhao is a product of my engagement, my "reading into" Sengzhao my own concerns. This does not make my interpretation merely "subjective" or "idiosyncratic," though. My entire study has involved a careful reading of Sengzhao and Liu's texts that critically draws on previous scholarship in order to disclose meaning. This disclosure of meaning is the heart of hermeneutics, and it requires us to take texts seriously, as saying something to us that we must make clear. In this perspective, a text can never be a simple "object." Sengzhao's texts are not "dead" but are very much alive. They speak to us across the centuries. In this sense, at least, Sengzhao joins the ranks of the Buddhas, Sages, and Bodhisattvas whose words will continue for ten thousand generations to come.

So it is that we have come full circle, back to our original question—what is *prajñā*? The question defies a simple answer and may even be confused. This is all right, however, for *prajñā* must confuse inquiry; it would not be *prajñā* if it were clear and straightforward. We can, though, venture to say some things. *Prajñā* is not a "thing" among other "things" nor an ordinary ability. *Prajñā* as a "perfection" may be more ideal than real, approachable but never fully attainable like the mathematical concept infinity. Better yet, *prajñā* resembles music or dance–a way of being or "knowing acting" governed by harmony and spontaneity. *Prajñā* is grace. There is no separation of "self" or "other" in *prajñā* and no sense of "time," just the fluid unfolding of reality. It is powerful, elusive, illusive, and allusive. *Prajñā* is mysterious but not otherworldly because we find *prajñā* here and now. *Prajñā* is "all-knowing" but this is not "knowing everything," for *prajñā* is, as Sengzhao tells us, "not-knowing." It is a way of living lightly but with concern for all being. *Prajñā* is Holy Wisdom, Divine Compassion.

Does this tell us anything? It seems the only way to speak truly of *prajñā* is to speak differently than the way in which we are accustomed. *Prajñā* is not ordinary and so calls for extraordinary speech. This is speech at the limit of speech, a different discourse that Sengzhao names "wild words." "Wild words" defy understanding, taking us beyond understanding to *prajñā* if we let them. "Wild words" are Sagely language, the language of the *sūtras* and it is these words that form the Way. Speaking "wild words" we hail *prajñā* as we come into its presence. Thus we speak *prajñā* in the "wild words" of the Sages and Bodhisattvas, those past, present, and future who have attained *prajñā* and live it. Perhaps, in the end, the nearest equivalent to "wild words" is a *mantra*, a holy syllable or phrase whose meaning is its sound, the sound of the Divine. So it is that we speak *prajñā* by means of a *mantra*–the Great Supernatural *mantra*, the Great Enlightening *mantra*, the Unsurpassed *mantra*, the Supreme *mantra* which can relieve all suffering and is Truly Real, not False. And so we repeat the words of the Sage Bodhisattvas, proclaiming the *Prajñāpāramitā Mantra* that says:

Gate gate, pāragate, pārasaṃgate, bodhi svāhā!

CONCLUSION:
UNDERSTANDING, HERMENEUTICS
AND *PRAJÑĀ*

"Is not the space between Heaven and Earth like a bellows?
It is empty without being exhausted:
The more it works the more comes out.
Too much speech leads inevitably to silence.
Better to hold fast to the void."

—Laozi, *Daode Jing 5*

To speak of a conclusion to a hermeneutic study is rather strange. By its very nature interpretation cannot end for meaning continually emerges every time we engage with a text. Interpretation is a conversation, creative and open-ended. The truth that emerges in interpretation is not "objective" and "certain" but is instead what the Greeks call *alētheia*, the process of disclosing the hidden mystery of being and thinking. Even when we draw interpretation to a close we do so with the understanding (and perhaps hope) that we are free to take it up again.

Over the course of the preceding pages I have examined the contested issue of *prajñā* during the period when Buddhism was being established in China. I have focused in particular on the role of Sengzhao in this process, and how he grapples with different views of *prajñā* in his essay "*Prajñā* is Not-knowing." In this essay Sengzhao critically examines various conceptions of *prajñā* that have been proposed but claims that all of these are mistaken. This is because all such notions treat *prajñā* as an ordinary type of "knowing."

Sengzhao, however, knows this is not the case. Citing scripture and drawing on his *xuanxue* heritage, Sengzhao asserts that *prajñā* is "not-knowing," a mysterious intuition that defies analysis. *Prajñā* cannot truly be spoken of in simple terms but requires a special language to convey its power and even provoke its occurrence. *Prajñā* calls for "wild words" to confound rational thinking and evoke the free and easy, non-dualistic coursing of the Sages and Bodhisattvas. In "*Prajñā* is Not-knowing" these "wild words" play off our set ideas and open us to the elusive nature of Dao.

The matter of *prajñā*, however, was not settled by Sengzhao's essay, and this becomes clear when we look at the correspondence between Sengzhao and his friend, Liu Yimin. Several things have emerged from our examination of their exchange. Although Liu and Sengzhao long to find common ground, they remain separated. Each thinker brings different presuppositions to the issue of *prajñā*, and these, in turn, are rooted in their respective communities. Liu never grasps the **Mahāyāna** spirit of Sengzhao's views, having little acquaintance with *prajñā* texts. In large part this was due to the fact that Liu and his fellow recluses had withdrawn from worldly life into a life of strict devotion. Their concerns were essentially religious and not scholarly. Sengzhao, on the other hand, lived in the urban setting of Chang'an as part of the greatest intellectual community of his day. By nature somewhat poetic and even "mystical," Sengzhao was drawn from an early age to Daoist and *prajñā* texts, and these deeply shaped his worldview. Moreover, he was devoted to the living Sages of his day (**Kumārajīva** and Yao Xing) and his writings are his attempts to explain how he saw these masters conducting themselves. It is little wonder, then, that Sengzhao and Liu never quite understand each other despite their shared cultural heritage and similar religious convictions. We might say they lack a common language, in this case the language of *prajñā*. Sengzhao speaks the "wild words" of *prajñā* but to Liu these seem to be the twittering of birds.

In my study I have translated both "*Prajñā* is Not-knowing" and "The Correspondence" into English but I do not claim that my translations supercede the earlier versions of Liebenthal, Robinson or Hsu. Instead, I offer an additional perspective to theirs and do not ask my readers to choose between them. This is in keeping with what Sengzhao himself does. Sengzhao does not choose among the various views of *prajñā* but works through them as a way to achieve insight. *Prajñā* does not take sides in debate but embraces all perspectives, accepting each as valuable albeit partial and limited. Above all, *prajñā* does not get ensnared in the concerns of ordinary life that result in *duḥkha*. The sagely "not-knowing knowing" of *prajñā* has no obstructions.[1]

Obviously "understanding" is a constant theme in this study. Understanding is the heart of hermeneutics—it is both process and goal. In "*Prajñā* is Not-knowing" Sengzhao's efforts aim at understanding *prajñā*. This same goal informs Liu and Sengzhao in "The Correspondence," where both thinkers probe each other's words, venture different interpretations, and ask questions in order to make sense of what the other says. Even though Liu and Sengzhao were unsuccessful, they clearly were reaching across geographical and philosophical distance to find some common ground.

By now the discerning reader has undoubtedly noticed that I have not fully defined the term "understanding," and perhaps at this point I should. "Understanding" is a complex cluster of related concepts, each of which has different connotations and associations. At the most generic level, "understanding" refers to a basic grasp of a specific matter or situation. Often, this has the sense of a power of comprehending, especially a power of clearly realizing relationships between general principles and particulars, or the capacity to apply concepts and categories in a way so as to make experience intelligible. More colloquially, "understanding" signifies a harmonious or friendly relationship, or an agreement of feelings and opinions. Finally, "understanding" has the more technical sense of explanation and interpretation.[2]

All of these senses of "understanding" have some bearing on what the term means and how it is used. Ultimately, though, it is the latter hermeneutic notion of understanding that most concerns us here. "Understanding" as explanation/interpretation deals with preserving, conveying and deciphering meaning. It is this quest for meaning that guides hermeneuts in any time or culture, from the priests at Delphi, to the commentators on the *jing*, to the missionaries spreading the Dharma through Central Asia, to the great thinkers of nineteenth century hermeneutics such as Schleiermacher. Philosophical hermeneutics bases itself squarely on such concerns and tries to bring this whole activity to light as much as possible. Indeed, Heidegger, Gadamer and Ricoeur devote much of their work to explicating the nature of understanding.

For Heidegger, understanding is not a cognitive faculty but the basic mode of our being-in-the-world. It is the basis for all our thoughts and actions, the structure through which our world is disclosed. Moreover, this basic understanding is historically formed and handed down to us, primarily through the medium of language. Thus for Heidegger, understanding is ontological, historical and linguistic. It is only on the basis of the primordially projected pre-understanding that we understand any specific thing.

Gadamer builds upon Heidegger's views of understanding as ontological, historical and linguistic by focusing on the hermeneutic encounter. For Gadamer, the model hermeneutic encounter is a conversation between two or more parties, hence it can apply to people or things ("texts"). Understanding here is a dialogical process, a back-and-forth between us and the "other" (person, text) that is initially informed by the prejudices imparted by our cultural tradition. However, this dialogue is a process of modification and testing, of going beyond first impressions towards a "fusion of horizons" in which our understanding changes. The "other" calls into question our prior horizon and pushes us to a newer, more encompassing understanding. It is only then that we have really "heard" what the "other" says.

Ricoeur echoes much of what Heidegger and Gadamer say yet has his own particular emphasis. For Ricoeur understanding is a dialectical process that starts from a naïve understanding and moves through explanation to a fuller understanding. Like Gadamer, Ricoeur stresses that understanding is a dialogic process of "play" between interpreter and text but unlike Gadamer, he reserves a place for method in the process. Explanation via some theoretical method (e.g. structural analysis and/or psychoanalysis) is an important step in this process. Ultimately, understanding culminates in the "appropriation" of the text's meaning in which the distance between text and interpreter is overcome. The modes of being that the text discloses then are given over to the subject who has a deeper, truer self-understanding.

From this brief synopsis of these thinkers' views we can pick out several important features of understanding. At its most comprehensive level, understanding constitutes our very way of being and is revealed in all our actions. Understanding develops though a dialectic that begins from the inherited prejudices of our tradition and progresses beyond them to a wider, richer way of living. Understanding, thus, presupposes community; we understand *with* others. Moreover, understanding also reaches out towards others, be they those who share our traditions or members of other communities. Understanding bridges the distance between ourselves and an "other" and so enables us to meet face to face. In this meeting, though, we let the other lead. Understanding, in the words of the *Daode jing*, "keeps to the role of the female."[3] Moreover, understanding is never final or absolute, but ranges along a continuum. As a result, it is always a work in progress. We can certainly use any number of methods and techniques in the process of understanding, but achieving understanding requires more than merely following set procedures to reach a definite goal.

One of the most important things to bear in mind here is the fact that understanding is a *shared* activity. The process of understanding may begin with a specific issue or event but ends in achieving community. As Gadamer writes:

> Understanding is, primarily, agreement. Thus people usually understand each other immediately, or they make themselves understood with a view toward reaching agreement. ... From language we learn that the subject matter is not merely an arbitrary object of discussion, independent of the process of mutual understanding, but rather is the path and goal of mutual understanding itself. And if two people understand each other independently of any topic, then this means that they understand each other not only in this or that respect, but in all the essential things that unite human beings.[4]

The mutuality of understanding can occur precisely because it is a joining of worlds, a "fusion of horizons." Understanding is the overcoming of distance and "otherness." This is the exact opposite of a theory of understanding such as the one Schleiermacher posits in which understanding is unilateral. For Schleiermacher understanding involves reconstructing the other while remaining apart. It is a striving for "truth" by assuming a subject-object scheme in which the text begins as and remains "other." In Gadamer's eyes, however, this is not really understanding at all. "Positing the alterity of the other is a symptom of the failure of understanding, not the principle of its success."[5]

If understanding always entails a meeting of minds, then what of its seeming opposite—*misunderstanding*? Misunderstanding would be an understanding that "misses" something, one in which we never quite meet the other. In the language of contemporary hermeneutics, to misunderstand would be to *not* appropriate the text's meaning, to refuse to enter the dialogue or perhaps to let one's preset agenda determine the outcome. Thus, misunderstanding is a type of privative understanding, one that is sadly impoverished. In misunderstanding we remain distant and aloof, and fail to be transformed. In a word, to misunderstand is to be stuck in one's own horizon and thus closed to fullness of a text's meaning(s). Of course, this misunderstanding does not come down to a few individuals who just happen to fail to see eye to eye, it includes their communities as well. Just as understanding is rooted in shared ideas and attitudes so is misunderstanding. Moreover, misunderstanding is not an all or nothing situation. As with understanding so, too, with misunderstanding there are various levels and grades. Like understanding, misunderstanding is a matter of degree.

We need to remember, though, that a misunderstanding is *still* an understanding. It is just an understanding that has missed something deemed by others as important. To dub an encounter a misunderstanding, as I have in the case of Liu Yimin and Sengzhao, is a judgment call, an interpretation based on a perceived disagreement. In a sense, misunderstanding is a case of conflicting language games. Those who misunderstand each other do not speak the same language because they do not play by same rules. The reasons for this being closed to the possibilities a text or another party offers may be due to mere personal obstinacy but they reach beyond the parties involved their own contexts. In the hermeneutic sense, misunderstanding (like understanding) has communal roots.

From these considerations, then, we might better think of misunderstanding as marking a *difference in understanding* between parties or text and interpreter. Misunderstanding occurs when different interpretive communities encounter each other. Misunderstanding is a conflict of interpretations. Such a difference may not be irreconcilable, for it is always possible at least in theory to find some agreement. Yet this raises more questions. If, as Gadamer maintains, all understanding is understanding differently, wherein lies the difference between understanding and misunderstanding? What is "missed" in the latter? In misunderstanding, there is no meeting, or at best meeting in passing but never a real knowing.[6] Note, however, that even in such misunderstandings, *some* understanding is reached. We may, for instance, be able to grasp the psychological motives and/or cultural factors that lie behind our different points of view and so understand each other as "other" on a certain level, but we do not reach a shared meaning on a topic of common concern. We find myriad examples of such "missed understanding" in literature and everyday life. Genuine hermeneutic understanding where both parties are transformed is exceedingly rare.

In Chapter One I note that scholars often trace the origins of hermeneutics to the Greek god Hermes. Such playful etymology provides important insights. Hermes is the most cunning and enigmatic of the Olympian gods. He presides over a motley array of professions: shepherds, merchants, travelers, thieves. Hermes has a particularly close relationship with those who speak for a living (politicians, priests) and those who write—in short, people who live by their wits and words. Hermes is the Divine messenger but also a trickster, a messenger of chaos. He is a liar and a cheat. As Gerald Bruns writes,

> Hermes was never simply our friendly postman but the granddaddy of tricksters, a figure of anarchy or misrule, of thievery, treachery and deceit, someone always a little out of control, the bringer of truth who doubles as the thief of reason and who therefore leaves you in perpetual hesitation as to what you have just heard or said, written or

read; in short, a polytropic figure, someone mischievous and untrustworthy, like the language we speak when we try to make sense of anything.[7]

Hermes is a magical fellow, perpetually crossing and recrossing boundaries as he flits between the divine and the human. Hermes knows no frontiers. He gives prophetic insights, brings dreams, and aids both heroes and gods in their endeavors. Hermes loves peace and promotes exchange. Perhaps most significant of all, unlike other gods Hermes is never cruel or fickle. He is friendly to mortals. Hermes guides us on our way (Dao) and even leads us on our final journey after death. Hermes always comes to meet us and never rejects us. Hermes has compassion. In Buddhist terms we could describe Hermes as a Bodhisattva; in Chinese terms, Hermes would be a Sage.

To be an interpreter is to be a devotee of this god, to be dedicated to achieving a "Hermes-like" point of view. It is this "Hermes perspective," a *hermeneutical* understanding, that Gadamer lifts up as the ideal and it is this ideal that I have striven for in interpreting Sengzhao and Liu Yimin. I will not claim complete success here. Certainly I have engaged in a great deal of reconstructive understanding of both thinkers in explicating their respective situations. But I have striven to see where they are coming from, to take on their perspectives to the extent I can, and to hear what their words say while remaining mindful of my own situation. In the end that is all an interpreter can do. *Prajñā* itself is another matter. As Sengzhao says, *prajñā* defies our understanding. *Prajñā* cannot be articulated in an ordinary fashion, and it always eludes our grasp. Perhaps, then, my failure here is my greatest success.

This last point is most interesting. Both *prajñā* and hermeneutic thinking are controversial topics that are maddeningly difficult to define. Might there be some relationship between them? My work with Sengzhao has convinced me that there is. Hermeneutic thinking at its best continually strives for insight. Interpretation, *real* interpretation, involves working towards discernment from within the give and take between "self" and "other." The thinking that guides hermeneutics does not feign objectivity in the sense of being abstract and indifferent but it is not merely "subjective" or idiosyncratic. Gentle yet critical, supple and flexible, a hermeneutic attitude is never stuck in one place for long as an interpreter always pushes towards a "perfection" that may never be fully achieved. This way to understanding is a painstaking process of patience and deliberation. Is this not also the way to *prajñā*?

I suggest, then, that to be a dedicated hermeneut is something of a "religious" vocation. A hermeneut must in some sense be a Bodhisattva, for the hermeneutic way calls for developing skills such as the *pāramitās* of generosity, virtue, patience, enthusiasm and concentration on the way to wisdom and insight. Such a project would seem to require at least three immeasurable *kalpas*. An ideal interpreter would be someone who dwells in the open by accepting (not rejecting) various perspectives while not settling within any one of them. Such a person abides at the very door to *nirvāṇa* while not leaving *saṃsāra*, dwelling at the intersection of the Two Truths without being ensnared by *kleśas*. From another point of view, we could say hermeneutics is a sagely way. The hermeneut strives to apprehend the fluctuations and combinations of *yin* and *yang* as they emerge from the source. In interpreting, the hermeneut follows the way, letting the source speak. She does not force, but acts without acting (*wuwei*) and so nothing is left undone. The interpreter steps into the center and, like the hinge, responds effortlessly by engaging with all perspectives that come her way.

There is another sense, moreover, in which the interpretative process resembles the arising of *prajñā* or Sagely Wisdom. In the philosophical hermeneutics of Heidegger, Gadamer and Ricoeur, the text leads and we follow. There is something very profound that often happens here, and it certainly happens when we engage with puzzling writings such as Sengzhao's: we are brought up short. Our normal expectations of meaning are dashed and, ironically, the text's words leave us at a loss for words. Gerald Bruns asks, "What would it be for a text to explode the conceptual world of the one who seeks to interpret it?"[8] It is precisely in this sort of transformative interpretive encounter that we see something similar to if not identical with *prajñā*. *Prajñā* breaks through our narrowly defined concepts as it brings us into a more open being-knowing. Whatever else it is, *prajñā* is a special understanding that, like Dao, works through reversal (*fan*). As we have seen, a genuine hermeneutic encounter works in the same way.

All of which brings us back to Sengzhao. Sengzhao was deeply involved in hermeneutic issues surrounding *prajñā* as he straddled religious and philosophic traditions. He was **Mādhyamika** and *xuanxue*, a simultaneous proponent of the Way of the Bodhisattva and the Sage. Using Zhuangzi's words we could say that Sengzhao walks two roads at once. For Sengzhao, *prajñā* is a "not-knowing knowing," an unbounded perspective within which we can take on other perspectives without becoming mired within them. *Prajñā* is the Sagely "not-knowing knowing" that knows it is this knowing and seeks to help others know. We may call this "mystical" if we wish, but it is not some otherworldly state divorced from ordinary life. To understand such a paradoxical being-knowing calls for a willingness to suspend discursive thought and remain open to the mysteries of Dao. Liu Yimin, although a believer in the saving grace of Amitābha, never reached this point. It may not have even occurred to him. Perhaps, though, we can at least approach this ideal through careful hermeneutic thinking that attends to the saying behind what a text says. We need only to stop clinging to our limited knowledge and let "wild words" show us the Way. The not-knowing of *prajñā* is open to us here and now, just as it was for Sengzhao and his contemporaries.

APPENDIX I:
NOTE ON TRANSLATION

"In any case, the hermeneutically enlightened consciousness seems to me to establish a higher truth in that it draws itself into its own reflection. Its truth, namely, is that of translation. It is higher because it allows the foreign to become one's own, not by destroying it critically or reproducing it uncritically, but by explicating it within one's own horizons with one's own concepts and thus giving it new validity. Translation allows what is foreign and what is one's own to merge in a new form by defending the point of view of the other even if it be opposed to one's own view."

—Hans-Georg Gadamer, "Semantics and Hermeneutics"

Translation is a constant theme in this study of Sengzhao and the Chinese search for *prajñā*. My analysis of Sengzhao arises out of my own engagement with "*Prajñā* is Not-knowing" and "The Correspondence," and I have translated both texts as part of my investigation. For these reasons I believe some more extensive reflection on translation is called for, if only to draw attention to an area that many scholars see as problematic.

Hermes has always been the translator *par excellence*, flitting between the Divine and human realms with ease. We mortals, however, lack his wondrous powers and so must proceed more laboriously. There have probably been translators since the earliest groups of people first encountered "strangers" in their wanderings. Most of the time translation emerges out of necessity—there needs to be some sort of common language (if only signs and gestures) for trading goods or settling disputes between communities. Only rarely have people thought through the processes involved in translating from one language to another. Translation is interpretation, and theories of translation have long been at the heart of hermeneutics.[1]

Scholars have proposed various theories of translation but all such theories, no matter their details, come down to attempts to understand how and to what extent meaning survives the movement from one language to another. This is a matter of great philosophic import. Whatever translation entails, it clearly is not a process of directly matching words in one language to words in another. Language is part of a communal system or network of relations between people, objects and practices. It is perhaps the most basic set of skills one learns as a member of a particular society. As W. V. O. Quine notes, language forms part of a larger conceptual framework in which "meaning" and "truth" are determined in terms of how things hang together.[2] Isolating individual pieces within such a system and then seeking their equivalents in another system will never allow us to use a language as native speakers do. Meaning is holistic, a matter of coherence within a larger framework rather than empirical content. Switching over to another language, then, would be switching over to another framework. It is doubtful that any two frameworks will square with one another, and this has great implications for translation. Translation will be in some part indeterminate; there will be no easy correspondence here and any number of "new" versions of the "original" may be possible.[3] In translating we are in a perpetually liminal state, always moving between different cultural and linguistic worlds in which nothing is firmly fixed.

George Steiner in *After Babel* describes translation as an interpretive process in terms very reminiscent of Ricoeur. For Steiner translation proceeds through a series of steps, from reconstructing a text's linguistic conventions to its "full intentional quality."[4] Ultimately, however, the translator-interpreter aims not at a grasp of the text but "the complete discovery and recreative apprehension of its life-forms."[5] Recovery and preservation of meaning is a delicate procedure, requiring a great deal of philological, historical and philosophic knowledge. It is also creative and calls for an almost poetic sensibility. Translation is an art, not a science.

Furthermore, translation is a powerful political act. Translators, like all interpreters, assume certain privileges. They take on the role of Hermes, the trader and thief who traffics in words and meanings, and all press for their own advantage. This assumption of discursive power often goes unacknowledged yet it has real effects beyond the scholar's study, as Asad and other critics rightly point out.

Aside from these more general points, however, there are also some specific points concerning my translations that warrant some explication. The
Chinese in which Sengzhao and his contemporaries wrote was never a "natural
language." It was highly artificial, somewhat mannered, rich in poetic and literary allusion. In large part this is because it was a *written* language, never spoken
in everyday dealings. Most certainly it was the province of a comparatively
small group of elites who were entrusted with China's Sagely heritage. Furthermore, it is now a "dead language," like classical Latin or Greek. As such, when
translating these texts we cannot help but be aware of the immense temporal
and cultural distance between Sengzhao's world and ours.[6]

In my translations I use masculine pronouns (he, his) when referring to
the Sage as part of my attempt to stay true to the assumptions of Sengzhao,
Liu and their colleagues. All of these figures were male and to the best of my
knowledge there were no women in the Chang'an translation bureau or on
Lushan. This situation is fully in keeping with the fact that historically men
have dominated the social and political spheres in China. Although this may
seem sexist from our perspective, to try to get around it by using inclusive
language would distort what the texts are saying. Indeed, such androcentric
assumptions are one of the marks of the distance between our world and
Sengzhao's. Moreover, the resulting clash between our assumptions as readers
and Sengzhao's assumptions as writer may provoke further questioning. Must
a Sage be masculine? Can a woman be a Sage? These questions may not have
even occurred to Sengzhao or Liu Yimin but by occurring to us, they open
up different avenues for thinking about Chinese culture and sageliness. Such
creative thinking is precisely the sort that should arise in interpretive work
and amply demonstrates how hermeneutic engagement can lead to important
philosophical inquiry.

In my translations I also capitalize key terms such as "Sage" and
"Bodhisattva." Chinese, of course, lacks letters let alone upper and lower cases
so the words themselves give no guidance. I choose to capitalize for emphasis,
to indicate in my actual words the difference between ordinary and Sagely
views. The Sage is set apart on some level but not wholly separate. The Sage/
Bodhisattva is awesome, even divine. There are obvious parallels with Western traditions here, where writers typically capitalize the names of important
figures (e.g. God, Christ). There is an important difference, however: in the
Chinese case, we can actually become "divine" and this is what Sengzhao is
urging. Capitalizing is a way to literally depict the "great understanding" to
which Sengzhao, Liu and their contemporaries aspired.

During my work I have often consulted previous English translations of Sengzhao's writings by Liebenthal, Robinson and Hsu. All three have been helpful although my own translations differ from theirs in ways too numerous to list. Generally I find Liebenthal too free in his work, so much so that he seems to read entire passages into the texts.[7] Robinson's translations strike me as better and more philosophically nuanced. He also evinces a real appreciation for the hermeneutic difficulties inherent in such work:

> The thoughts of men who lived fifteen centuries ago are imperceptible and only partially inferable. The only evidence for them is strings of written symbols representing a dead language for which only a limited corpus of texts now exists. This means that the writer's mood, his irony and humor, the triteness or novelty of his expressions, cannot be known with certainty, because the sample is defective. Not only are the lineaments of his literary mask discernible imperfectly, but the mental events that accompanied the composition of the text are even more inscrutable.[8]

Robinson is quite insightful here yet he betrays a view of interpretation that centers too much on authorial intentions for my comfort. Hsu's translations are the most problematic, largely due to his sparse annotations and the fact that he ignores Robinson and Tsukamoto's earlier work. Moreover, Hsu does not evince any awareness of the hermeneutic nature of translation, at times even shows disdain towards Sengzhao and even makes several factual errors.[9]

Despite my attempts to stick as close to the Chinese as possible I have at various places inserted additional words and phrases. I have in every case endeavored to indicate this with brackets. In some of the more problematic places I have supplied the Chinese in footnotes or provided Liebenthal or Robinson's translation as an alternative. This is my way of compensating for the telegraphic nature of Classical Chinese although sometimes it seemed the only way to make sense of texts in light of my overall interpretation. Often in such cases I have followed Sengzhao's commentators, especially Yuankang.

In the end I must admit that I do not think my translations are fully successful. They are somewhat clumsy and certainly lack the literary quality of the original Chinese. At best I have produced "partial translations," or perhaps, using a coinage inspired by Roland Barthes, "strong mistranslations." Much really is untranslatable in these texts and I have often found myself having to slip in and "feel" what they say when I cannot clearly spell it out. And in each case I have tried to follow the texts' lead, to let them teach me, for I truly believe this is the Dao of hermeneutics, the Way of translation.

There will always be gaps in translation and all translations are, in some sense, failures. This is particularly true when dealing with ancient texts. Some things are inevitably left out–the music of words in their original tongue, the deep connotations of a metaphor from another time and place, a sly allusion to some other text long since gone to dust. Translators of ancient texts must reconstruct laboriously what would have been obvious to original authors and their audience. Much must remain unknown and the result will always be based on conjecture. As usual, Gadamer, himself a translator of Ancient Greek, has to say about such cases and what the translator's role should be:

> Translation, like all interpretation, is a highlighting. A translator must understand that highlighting is part of his task. Obviously he must not leave open whatever is not clear to him. He must show his colors. Yet there are borderline cases in the original (and for the "original reader") where something is in fact unclear. But precisely these hermeneutical borderline cases show the straits in which the translator constantly finds himself. Here he must resign himself. He must state clearly how he understands. But since he is always in the position of not really being able to express all the dimensions of his text, he must make a constant renunciation. Every translation that takes its task seriously is at once clearer and flatter than the original. Even if it is a masterly re-creation, it must lack some of the overtones that vibrate in the original.[10]

A translator is always drawing our attention to the significance for him/her within his/her context. Yet this is always ambiguous and open to challenge.

Throughout my work I have endeavored to "show my colors" as well. I have come to understand that Sengzhao and Liu Yimin were both involved in deep existential issues of Sageliness and *prajñā*. For them struggling with these issues was not merely intellectual, and to understand them we must take at least entertain the idea that Sageliness is a real possibility for our own lives as well. If we have, in the end, to renounce final, definitive meaning then we must do so with sincerity, not out of despair.

Translation by definition presupposes understanding of what is being translated. As I have already noted in my conclusion, "understanding" is an ambiguous concept, a cluster of intertwined meanings and associations. Translating Sengzhao requires winding our way through this tangled skein to find the one thread that binds his work together. Ricoeur notes that in understanding we appropriate the meanings of the world the text opens up for us. In studying "*Prajñā* is Not-knowing" and "The Correspondence," we are *not* trying to understand Sengzhao but the meaning of his words. These words confront us not just with knowledge but Sagely Wisdom, a vision of world that challenges our views. Here we are led towards the great understanding of the *peng* bird—vast and joyful, rich in nuance. The small understanding of the little quail–*our* "knowing"—looks impoverished by comparison. Sengzhao's words present the Sagely Way in the enigmatic fashion of the Sage who smiles and extends an open hand while he lets his tail drag, turtle-like, in the mud. Clearly the texts invite us to take this hand and transform our world. What we do in light of this invitation is entirely up to us.

APPENDIX II:
PRAJÑĀ IS NOT-KNOWING
(ZHAOLUN, PART III)[1]

I. Introduction

I.1 (153a: 8–9)

Prajñā,[2] "void"[3] and "dark,"[4] is perhaps the beginning and end of the Three Vehicles.[5] It is truly One,[6] lacking all duality (*advaya*). [Yet] discussions of different teachings [of *prajñā*] have caused confusion for a long time.[7]

I.2 (153a: 9–15)

There is an Indian *śramaṇa,* **Kumārajīva,** who when young trod the "Great Square."[8] He investigated thoroughly the details[9] of this subject (e.g. *prajñā*) and alone rose beyond the surface of "words and symbols."[10] He was wondrously conformed to the "region of the unseen and unheard."[11] He harmonized the different teachings in Kapilivastu,[12] and stirred up the Pure Wind from the fans of the east.[13] He was about to bring light to the various regions when he was made to hide his glory in the land of Liang.[14] Therefore [we know] Dao does not vainly respond; its responses necessarily have their cause.[15] In the third year of *hung shi* (401 C.E.) under the zodiac sign of *xing ji,*[16] the kingdom of Jin took advantage of [Liang's] plan to invade the country[17] and mustered an army for the purpose of bringing him [to Chang'an]. So I think the prophecy concerning the north[18] was destined to come true.[19]

I.3 (153a: 15–20)

The Divine King of the Great [state of] Jin,[20] whose Way (Dao) rises above the principles of the hundred kings [of the past] and whose Virtue (de) will pervade a thousand generations to come, effortlessly manages the "ten thousand details" [of state][21] and so expands Dao night and day. I believe him to be like Heaven for the common people of this latter age,[22] and a [strong] support for Śākyamuni's Dharma. At this time he has gathered more than five hundred *śramaṇas* of proper learning[23] in the Xiaoyao monastery.[24] He personally holds the Jin text[25] and along with Kumārajīva takes part in translating the *vaipulya sūtras*.[26] What they have promulgated will not only be a benefit for the present day but will serve as a ford and a bridge for many *kalpas*[27] to come.[28]

I.4 (153a: 20–23)

I, although rather deficient [in ability and learning], was privy to this august assembly and considered what I heard to be strange and important. Truly Sagely Wisdom (*arya-jñāna, prajñā*) is subtle, deeply obscure,[29] difficult to fathom. It is without marks (*lakṣaṇas*)[30] and, being nameless,[31] [it] cannot be attained with words and symbols. [So it is that I] will use "deceiving symbols"[32] to [grasp] its inner essence by merely entrusting it to "wild words" (*kuangyan*).[33] How dare I say that the Sagely Mind can be analyzed! Yet I will attempt to discuss it.

II. Explanation and Exegesis

II.1 (153a: 24–26)

The *Fangguang* says, "*Prajñā* has no marks of being (*you*) nor birth-and-death (*udaya-vyaya*; i.e., *saṃsāra*)."[34] The *Daoxing* says, "[In] *prajñā* there is nothing that can be known and nothing that can be seen."[35] These [statements] describe Wisdom's[36] illuminating function yet they [also] speak of "having no marks" and "not-knowing." What is this? Ultimately there must be a knowing that has no marks and an illumination that does not know.

II.2 (153a: 27–b: 2)

Why is this? If there is that which is known, then there must be that which is not known. [However] since the Sagely Mind is "not-knowing," there is thus nothing that it does not know. This "not-knowing knowing" we call "all-knowing" (*sarvājñāta*).[37] Thus when the *sūtra* says, "As for the Sagely Mind, there is nothing known and nothing not-known,"[38] [we can] truly believe it.

Therefore, the Sage empties his mind yet "fills" his illumination.[39] Night and day he knows yet he [really] never knows. Thus he can darken his brightness and hide his brilliance.[40] His empty mind darkly mirrors [Heaven and Earth]. Closing up his Wisdom and blocking his hearing, [the Sage] thus alone awakens to the deep and profound.[41]

II.3 (153b: 2–8)

So it is that Wisdom is a mirroring that probes all secrets yet it has "not-knowing" in it. Spirit[42] has the function of responding to occasions yet there is no deliberation in it,[43] thus it alone can rule beyond the outer world. Wisdom's "not-knowing" is thus able to darkly illuminate external phenomena. Although Wisdom [darkly illuminates] external phenomena, it never lacks these phenomena. Although Spirit [rules beyond] the outer world, day and night it remains within the bounds [of reality].[44] Therefore, [the Sage] looks up [to Heaven] and down [towards Earth],[45] and so accords with the transformations. His responses endlessly touch [all things].[46] There is nothing secret that [he] does not see clearly yet his illumination is effortless. This then is what [the Sage's] not-knowing knows and what the Sage's Spirit meets.

II.4 (153b: 8–15)

So as for [the Sage's] existence, it is real and yet he does not exist [as a 'thing']. It is void and yet he is not [merely] non-being. That whose existence cannot be described—is this not Sagely Wisdom?

Why is this so? [We may] desire to speak of its existence but it lacks name and form. [We may also] desire to speak of its non-existence but the Sage becomes Divine through it.[47] Since the Sage becomes Divine through it, it thus is void but does not fail to illuminate. Lacking name and form, it thus illuminates but does not fail to be void. It illuminates while not failing to be void, thus it mixes [with the ten thousand things] yet does not change. It is void while not failing to illuminate, thus it moves and thereby contacts ordinary [things].

Therefore the function of Sagely Wisdom never begins or ceases even for a moment. We seek it among form and marks but it never for a moment can be attained. Thus **Ratnakūṭa** says, "Although [the Bodhisattva] lacks deliberation (*citta*) or concepts (*manas*) yet he manifests and acts."[48] The *Fangguang* says, "[The Tathāgata] does not move from Perfect Enlightenment (*sambodhi*) yet establishes all *dharmas*."[49] For this reason the Sage's traces[50] are myriad yet they all lead to a single end.

II.5 (153b: 15–18)

Therefore *Prajñā* can be considered void yet it illuminates. Ultimate Truth (*paramārtha*) can be forgotten yet [still] known. The ten thousand moving [things] can be considered identical in stillness.[51] The Sage's responses can be considered non-existent yet he acts. This then is not knowing [calculatively] but spontaneously knowing,[52] and not acting [deliberately] but spontaneously acting.[53] What more can it be said to know? What more can it be said to do?[54]

III. Questions and Answers

Question 1: (153b: 19–26)[55]

The True Mind of the Sage is unique in its brightness, illuminating thing after thing. Its responses effortlessly touch [all things] and its movements meet all phenomena. Since it illuminates thing after thing, in its "knowing" there is nothing neglected. Since its movements meet all phenomena, its meetings do not miss the cosmic workings. Because its meetings do not miss the cosmic workings, there necessarily is a "meeting" and "what can be met." Because in its "knowing" there is nothing neglected, there necessarily is a "knowing" and "what can be known." Since there necessarily is a "knowing" and "what can be known," the Sage does *not* vainly know. Since there necessarily is a "meeting" and "what can be met," the Sage does *not* vainly meet. So [the Sage] both knows and meets and yet you say, "he is one who has no knowing and no meeting." How can this be? If he is one who forgets his knowing and neglects his meeting, then the Sage lacks selfishness in his knowing and meeting and so merely perfects his own self-interest.[56] This then can be called "not having a self-reflexive knowing." On what basis, though, does this attain "no knowing"?

Reply: (153b: 26–c: 14)

The Sage's merit surmounts the Two Principles,[57] and yet he is not humane (*buren*).[58] His brightness exceeds the sun and moon yet he is all the darker.

How can we honestly speak of him being "blind" like wood or stone, and thus merely lacking knowing? That wherein [the Sage] truly differs from ordinary people in his Spiritual Understanding (*shenming*),[59] thus he cannot be sought through events and their marks. You wish it to be that the Sage does not *personally* have his knowing[60] whereas [in fact] the Sage never does not have [any] knowing. [In maintaining your view you] deviate from the Sagely Mind and miss the meaning of the texts.

Why? The *sūtras* say, "True *Prajñā*[61] is pure (*visuddhi*) like empty space (*ākāśa*), without knowing or seeing. There is nothing that arises [within it] and it lacks all conditioned objects (*ālambana*)."[62] *This* is a knowing that in itself has "no knowing."[63] How can you suggest that it relies on a "reversal of illumination" (*fan zhao*)[64] and only then has "not-knowing"? [On one hand,] if *prajñā* has knowing and yet because of its empty nature you declare it to be "pure" then it is not distinguished from deluded knowing. The Three Poisons[65] and the Four Misconceptions[66] would also be pure. Why should we only venerate *prajñā*?[67] [On the other hand,] if because of what is known you praise *prajñā* then what is known is not *prajñā*. What is known in itself is always pure thus *prajñā* [if it has knowing] is never pure. [Once again] there is no support for commending *prajñā* for being pure.[68]

So as for the *sūtras* saying, "*Prajñā* is pure,"[69] does it not mean *prajñā*'s essential nature (*svabhāva*) is absolutely pure, fundamentally lacking the knowing [characterized by] deluded grasping? Since it fundamentally lacks the knowing [characterized by] deluded grasping, it cannot be named "knowing." How can this lack of knowing[70] be called "no-knowing" when such knowing of itself is really no-knowing?[71]

Therefore the Sage, through *Prajñā*'s non-knowing, illuminates the Ultimate Truth [which is itself] markless. In Ultimate Truth there is no "falling short [such as we find with] the hare or the horse."[72] In *Prajñā* there is no mirroring that does not fully investigate [all Reality]. Because of this it meets and does not err, and matches [things with words] yet does not affirm [that words fully express truth].[73] Amazing in its stillness, it has "no-knowing" yet there is nothing it does not know.

Question 2: (153c: 15–22)

Since things lack the [conceptual] means of understanding themselves, we establish names by which we understand them. Although things are not names, in the end there are things that can be named and they really are "matched" by these names.[74] Therefore it is just through such names that we seek out things.

Things are not able to "hide" from them yet your treatise says "The Sage's Mind has no-knowing" and also "there is nothing that it does not know." In my opinion what we call "no-knowing" never knows and "knowing" never is "no-knowing." This is what is understood by the School of Names (*mingjiao*) as the basic idea of establishing [the meaning of] words. Now as regards your treatise, you wish [knowing and "no-knowing"] to be one in the Sagely Mind yet different in the meaning of the words. [However] when we examine the words and seek the reality [to which they refer], we do not see that they ever match. Why is this? If "knowing" refers to the Sagely Mind, then there is nothing to be distinguished by "not-knowing." If "not-knowing" refers to the Sagely Mind, then there is also nothing to be distinguished by "knowing." If neither[75] word refers, then we have nothing more that can be discussed.

Reply: (153c: 22–154a: 4)

The *sūtras* say, "As for the meaning of *prajñā*, it has no name nor explanation. It is neither being (*you*) nor non-being (*wu*), it is neither real nor empty."[76] Empty,[77] it does not fail to illuminate; illuminating, it does not fail to be empty. It is a nameless *dharma*, thus we are not dealing with speech and what can be spoken. Although it cannot be spoken of through words, yet it is not that words lack the means of conveying it.[78] Therefore the Sage "speaks night and day yet never speaks."[79]

Now I will attempt to distinguish it for you using "wild words."[80] The Sagely Mind is subtle and marvelous, lacking all marks [hence] it cannot be considered to exist. Its function is to be extremely active, thus it cannot be considered to not exist. Since it cannot be considered to not exist, Sagely Wisdom resides in it. Since it cannot be considered to exist, it is cut-off from the *mingjiao*.[81]

Therefore, when I say, "its knowing cannot be considered knowing" I desire to make clear its "mirroring." [And when I say,] "it is not the case that this not knowing is [really] not knowing," I desire to distinguish its marks. By distinguishing its marks we cannot consider it to not exist. By understanding its mirroring we cannot consider it to exist. Since it is not the case that it exists, it knows and yet has no-knowing. Since it is not the case that it does not exist, it has no-knowing and yet it knows.

Therefore its knowing is identical to its not-knowing and its not-knowing is identical to its knowing.[82] There is no reason to regard linguistic differences as creating differences within the Sagely Mind.

Question 3: (154a: 5–8)

Ultimate Truth is deep and "dark," but it is not that Sagely Wisdom does not fathom it. Sagely Wisdom's ability consists in this [fathoming] and this is how it manifests. Thus it is that the *sūtras* say, "[If you] do not attain *prajñā*, [you] do not perceive Ultimate Truth."[83] Ultimate Truth, then, is the object (*ālambana*) of *prajñā*. Since by means of an object [we can] seek out Wisdom, [we see that] Wisdom really is [ordinary] knowing.

Reply: (154a: 7–26)

[We can indeed] seek out Wisdom by means of its object, but it is not the case that Wisdom is [ordinary] knowing. Why?

The *Fangguang* says, "The consciousness (*vijñāna*) that is not conditioned by forms (*rūpa*) is called 'not seeing form'."[84] It also says, "Since the five *skandhas* are pure, *prajñā* is pure."[85] *Prajñā* is the knowing faculty. The five *skandhas* are what is known. What is known is the "object." Knowing and what-is-known combine and so mutually come into existence, and mutually go out of existence. Because they mutually go out of existence, things do not [really] exist. Because they mutually come into existence, things [at the same time] do not "not-exist."[86] Since things do not "not-exist", that which arises (knowing) is conditioned by its object. However, since things do not [really] exist, the object [of knowing] cannot itself be produced. As the object [of knowing] cannot itself be produced, [knowing] illuminates its objects yet is not a "knowing." Since what arises (i.e., knowing) is conditioned by its object, knowing and its object are produced[87] in mutual dependence.[88] Therefore knowing and "not-knowing" truly are produced from what-is-known. Why is this? Wisdom [arises] on account of "knowing" and "what-is-known," and since it grasps marks it we can call it [a type of] "knowing." But Ultimate Truth in itself lacks marks, so how can True Wisdom know?

As to why it is so, it is not the case that *this* what-is-known is what-is-known [in the normal sense]. In general, what-is-known arises from knowing. Since what-is-known arises from knowing, knowing also arises from what-is-known. [Knowing][89] and what-is-known mutually arise, and such mutually arisen [entities] are conditioned (*saṃskṛta*) *dharmas*. Conditioned *dharmas*, thus, are not Ultimate and not being Ultimate, thus they are not Ultimate truth.

So it is that the *Kārikās* say, "Things exist from causes and conditions, hence they are not Ultimate; they do not exist from causes (*hetu*) and conditions (*pratyaya*), thus they just are Ultimate."[90] Now then, if Ultimate Truth is called "Ultimate," then, being Ultimate, it is not conditioned. Since the Ultimate is not conditioned, there is nothing that is produced from conditions.[91] Thus the *sūtras* say, "[we] do not perceive among existing *dharmas* [any] that are not produced from conditions."[92] Therefore True Wisdom contemplates Ultimate Truth but never once grasps what-is-known. Since Wisdom does not grasp what-is-known, how is this Wisdom a "knowing"?

So it is that Wisdom [in fact] is not "Not-knowing."[93] [Moreover] just as Ultimate Truth is not what-is-known, so True Wisdom is also not a "knowing." Yet you desire to seek out Wisdom through conditions and so consider Wisdom to be a "knowing." But if conditions are in themselves not conditions, on what basis do you seek such a "knowing"?[94]

Question 4: (154a: 27–b: 1)

In your explanation you say, "It does not grasp." Is this because it is "not-knowing" that it does not grasp, or is it because it knows then afterwards does not grasp? If it is because it is "not-knowing" that it does not grasp, then is the Sage blind, like someone wandering at night who cannot distinguish between black and white? Or if it is because it knows and afterwards does not grasp, then [would not] its knowing differ from its not grasping?

Reply: (154b: 1–2)

It is not because it is "not-knowing" that it does not grasp nor is it the case that it knows and then afterwards does not grasp. Its knowing is identical to its not grasping, thus it is able to not grasp and yet know.

Question 5: (154b: 3–5)

In your explanation you say, "It does not grasp." Truly this is because the Sagely Mind does not regard things as things, thus it has no deluded grasping. If it has no grasping, then it has no affirming. If it has no affirming then it lacks matching [names with things].[95] Who then can match the Sagely Mind? And yet you say, "the Sagely Mind has nothing that is not known."

Reply: (154b: 5–8)

It is so. But as for "it has no affirming and no matching," if it has no matching then among things there is nothing not matched. If it has no affirming then among things there is nothing not affirmed. Since among things there is nothing not affirmed, it affirms and yet has no affirming. Since among things there is nothing not matched, it matches and yet has no matching. Hence a *sūtra* says "[The Bodhisattva] sees all *dharmas* in their entirety and yet there is nothing that is seen."[96]

Question 6: (154b: 9–12)

It is not the case that the Sagely Mind cannot affirm. In truth it is because it has no affirming that it can be said to affirm. Although it has nothing to affirm that can be affirmed, it thus matches and affirms in its affirming nothing. Therefore the *sūtras* say "Ultimate Truth has no marks thus *prajñā* is not-knowing."[97] In truth in *prajñā* there is actually no knowing of [things] that have marks. If it regards having no marks to be having no marks, why [even] bother with Ultimate Truth?

Reply: (154b: 12–18)

For the Sage there is nothing that lacks marks. Why is this? If he regarded having no marks to be having no marks, then having no marks just is a mark. But to reject being and go straight into non-being is just like fleeing from the mountain peaks and going into a ravine. Neither [way] avoids disaster. Therefore the *zhiren* abides in being yet does not exist, and dwells in non-being yet does not "not-exist". Although [the *zhiren*] does not grasp at being or non-being, so he also does not reject either being or non-being. For this reason he blends his brilliance into the "dust and toil"[98] and makes the circuit through the Five Destinies (*gatis*).[99] Silently he departs, shyly he comes. Serenely not-acting (*wuwei*) yet there is nothing he does not do.[100]

Question 7: (154b: 19–21)

Although the Sagely Mind is not-knowing, its way of responding and meeting does not err. Therefore it responds to what can be responded to, and reserves itself [when there is nothing] that can be responded to. So then the Sagely Mind has times when it arises and times when it ceases.[101] Can it really be like this?

Reply: (154b: 21–25)

The "arising and ceasing" [of which you speak] is arising and ceasing of mind (*citta*). Since the Sage has no mind, how could arising and ceasing come to be in it? Yet it is not the case that [the Sage] has no mind,[102] merely that [the Sage] has no discursive thinking.[103] Moreover, it is not the case that [the Sage] does not respond, merely that [the Sage] does not respond in responding. Therefore the Sage's way of responding and meeting is as trustworthy as the course of the Four Seasons. Plainly [we should] consider empty non-being as his substance,[104] hence he cannot arise and cannot cease.

Question 8: (154b: 26–27)

The "not" of Sagely Wisdom and the "not" of deluded "wisdom"[105] both are without arising and ceasing. How, then, do they differ?

Reply: (154b: 27–c: 14)

The "not" of Sagely Wisdom is "Not-knowing" while the "not" of deluded "wisdom" is "knowing nothing." Although their "nots" [seem] the same, what is "notted" differs. Why is this?

Sagely Wisdom, being void and still, is "Not-knowing" and so can be regarded as "nothing." [Although] it can be said to be "Not-knowing" it is not the case that this can be called "knowing nothing." Deluded wisdom has knowing, thus it has a knowing that can be regarded as "nothing." [Although] it can be called "knowing nothing," it is not the case that this is "Not-knowing."[106] "Not-knowing" is the "not" of *prajñā*; "knowing nothing" is the "not" of Ultimate Truth.[107]

Therefore, regarding *prajñā* and Ultimate Truth—when speaking of function [they] are similar yet different, and when speaking of stillness [they] are different yet the same. Since they are the same, they have no thoughts of "this and that." Since they are different, they do not fail in their power of illumination. For this reason those who distinguish their sameness regard them as the same in their difference while those who distinguish their difference differentiate them in their sameness. So then they cannot be considered different and cannot be considered the same.

Why is this so? Inside, there is the clarity of [the Sage's] solitary mirroring; outside, there is the reality of the ten thousand *dharmas*. Although the ten thousand *dharmas* are real,[108] it is not that illumination does not attain them. [Rather] inside and outside join together and so perfect [*prajñā*'s] power of illumination. These are functions that [even] the Sage cannot make the same. Although the inside illuminates, yet it is "not-knowing." Although the outside is real, yet it has no marks. [Since] inside and outside are still, they both together are "non-being." This is the stillness in which [even] the Sage cannot differentiate [them]. Therefore, a *sūtra* says, "All *dharmas* are not different."[109] How can this really be saying that [we must] "stretch the duck's [legs] and shorten the crane's,"[110] level the peaks and fill the valleys and only then is there no difference?! In the end [we] do not regard them as not different with respect to their differences and so although they are different, they do not differ.

Hence, a *sūtra* says "It is most wonderful, Bhagawan! In the midst of the not-different *dharmas* you preach those *dharmas* are different."[111] Moreover, it also says "*Prajñā* and the *dharmas* are neither united nor differentiated."[112] This is true indeed!

Question 9: (154c: 15–16)

In your explanation you say "[If we] speak of their function, then they are different; [while if we] speak of their stillness, then they are the same." It is not yet clear if inside *prajñā* there is a difference between function and stillness.[113]

Reply: (154c: 16–22)

Function is identical to stillness; stillness is identical to function. Function and stillness are in essence (*ti*) one. "They are the same but differ in name as they issue forth."[114] There is no functionless stillness that governs the function. Therefore, Wisdom is completely obscure but its illumination is exceedingly bright. Spirit is entirely still but its responses are exceedingly mobile. How can we really speak of the difference between bright and obscure, movement and stillness?

Thus the *Chengju* says, "[The Sage] does not act yet surpasses acting."[115] Ratnakūṭa says,[116] "[The Buddha] lacks mind and consciousness but has no unawakened knowing."[117] These [lines] probe Spirit and exhaust Wisdom; they discuss the Ultimate that is beyond symbols. [If you] go through and understand my words, the Sagely Mind can, indeed, be known.[118]

APPENDIX III:
SENGZHAO'S CORRESPONDENCE
WITH LIU YIMIN
(APPENDED TO *ZHAOLUN*, PART III)[1]

I. Liu Yimin's Letter to Sengzhao[2]

Cover Letter (154c: 25–27)[3]

Yimin sends his greetings.[4] Just recently I heard the good news [from your community].[5] I have so longingly awaited [such news] from afar. The year is almost over and the winter has been severe. How is your health?[6] [Since our] communication has been cut-off [for some time] I have had to store up my thoughts.[7] Your disciple[8] has been very ill in his wilderness retreat, constantly with a bad fever.[9] Since Brother Huiming[10] will be journeying north I have decided to communicate my feelings [to you].

Main Letter

Section I. Introduction (154c: 28–155a: 20)

In antiquity, people, even though separated in body, remained content; [if] they were aware of their connection then they felt near. So it is that although we are yet separated by rivers and mountains and will not meet this year, [I] reach in my anxious longing the fragrant air [of your presence][11] and my mind mirrors your traces.[12] The force of this much-anticipated joy has been truly strong. [Still, we are] far apart, and lack the means [of meeting]. [Instead] I gaze in awe at the distant rosy clouds[13] and perpetually sigh. Take care of yourself in accord with the season. I hope that since there will be official messengers [from now on], we can correspond [more] frequently.

I humbly desire that your great assembly (the Changan community) [continues in great] peace and harmony, and that the foreign Dharma Master (Kumārajīva) has good fortune. Master,[14] because of your famed ability of apprehension you participated in their "dark" and profound discussions. I think your powers of exegesis are more than equal to the *Tuanci* of the *Yijing*.[15] So it is that when I reflect upon our separation, my exasperation deepens [all the more].

The *śramaṇas* here on Lushan are perpetually pure and the precepts of Dao (*Dharma śīla*) are strictly enforced. When there is time left over from their solitary meditations, they either study or attend lectures. Their simplicity and reverence can be considered a great joy indeed. Your disciple [used] to follow an earlier [worldly] mind,[16] but now I contemplate the profundity of my [present] superior circle[17] and the sincerity of my gratitude at residing [here] is inscribed day and night [within my heart].

At this time Dharma Master Huiyuan continues to conduct himself with the utmost propriety. In meditation and instruction he makes great progress. [Truly he can be described as] "active all day long yet careful by night."[18] In him Dao does not flow in a hidden way. [He] regards Principle as his spirit's authority. Who else could, at over sixty years of age, have the vigor of such vast *qi*?[19] Therefore my confidence is profound and my thankfulness is beyond words.

At the end of last summer the venerable Daosheng[20] first showed me a copy of your essay "*Prajñā* is Not-knowing." It is written in a pure and refined style, and the meanings of its contents are deep and convincing. Your exposition of the words of the Sages is pleasant and it returns [the reader to the True meaning]. I savored your flourishing [prose] and could not put it down. Truly we can say you are one who has bathed your mind in the depths of the *vaipulya* [*sūtras*][21] and attained knowledge of the profound that is beyond [common] understanding. When this essay is published, then *prajñā*'s various currents will probably no longer be debated,[22] for [they] will be [fully] understood. How could this not bring such joy and happiness?

The obscurity of Principle is difficult to state. The lone singer [of such songs] has few respondents.[23] Truly, unless there is one who [can] make manifest what is beyond words and symbols, [those who] are led in accordance with symbols will end in error. I think the section of your reply on using the "object" (*ālambana*) to seek out Wisdom[24] is convincing and quite conclusive. Indeed, it is extremely clever and cannot be faulted. Nonetheless, one [such as myself] who is dull has difficulty understanding it all at once. I still have one or two doubts remaining. When you have time to study the subject [again] I hope that at your leisure you can once more give me a rough explanation.

Section II. Liu's First Question (155a: 20–27)

In your essay you say, "The essence of *prajñā* is neither being (*you*) nor non-being (*wu*),"[25] and "Empty, it does not fail to illuminate; illuminating, it does not fail to be empty."[26] Thus [the *Fangguang*] says, "[The **Tathāgata**] does not move from Perfect Enlightenment yet establishes all *dharmas*."[27] In a later section you say, "[That wherein the Sage truly] differs from ordinary people in his Spiritual Understanding (*shenming*), thus he cannot be sought through events and their marks."[28] Furthermore, you say [regarding the Sage] that "Function is identical to stillness; stillness is identical to function,"[29] and "Spirit is entirely still but its responses are exceedingly mobile."[30]

    Now then, the Sagely Mind is wondrously still. [It is] Principle, ultimately identical with non-being.[31] [Truly, we can speak of it as] "hurrying without haste"[32] [and] "sitting still yet racing around."[33] Therefore, in knowing it does not dispense with stillness and in stillness it does not dispense with knowing. Never is it *not* still; never is it *not* knowing.[34] Thus his Way of moving things to their perfection and transforming the world, although it abides in the midst of the Named yet is remote, [ultimately] identical with the Nameless.[35] The obscurity of such Principle defies comprehension! I remain obstinate in my perpetual dim-wittedness [regarding this theory].[36]

Section III. Liu's Second Question (155a: 28–b: 5)

Yet now [let us] discuss what [we on Lu Shan] doubt with respect to the meaning of your most excellent treatise. We wish to seek out the differences within the Sagely Mind.[37] Can we say that the probing of [the Sagely Mind] supernaturally[38] reaches the end of all items [in the cosmos], all the way to the "hidden tallies" [of our lives]?[39] Or is it that the Sage's Mind is in essence spontaneous (*ziran*), supernatural and perhaps alone[40] in influencing [all things]? If the probing of [the Sagely Mind] supernaturally reaches to the end of all items [in the cosmos], all the way to the "hidden tallies" [of our lives], then what you call "still illumination"[41] is in essence *śamatha-vipassanā*.[42] If the Sage's

Mind is in essence spontaneous, supernatural and alone in influencing [all things], then his responses to the multitudes of things will certainly thereby cease.[43] [The Sage's] mindfulness of the cosmic items is "dark" (*xuan*) yet he alone illuminates the revolving [of all things]. His Spirit is pure and outside of the transformations, yet the brightness of his wisdom remains [within]. We should have some profound proof [of this theory] that we can examine in order to distinguish them (i.e. the twin aspects of the Sage's Way–his knowing and acting).

Section IV. Liu's Third Question (155b: 5–18)

[Furthermore, we also have questions concerning the Sage's "existence."] Those who doubt [your treatise] think that a knowing that carefully meets and responds to the cosmic changes and that observes the transformations cannot really be said to be "not-existing." Yet your treatise says, "it (*prajñā*) fundamentally lacks the knowing [characterized by] deluded grasping."[44] But you never explain the principle of not-grasping on which [the Sage] relies. We think you ought to first determine the Way (Dao) of responding that the Sagely Mind relies upon. Is it that he matches [names with things] by only illuminating the markless (i.e. Ultimate Truth)? Or is it that he matches by fully observing the changes? If [he matches] by observing the changes, then this differs from [illuminating] the markless. If he only illuminates the markless, then he does not meet the cherished [things]. Since [you seem to say that the Sage] does not meet the cherished [things] yet has the power of cherishing and meeting, we do not apprehend your meaning. Please do us the favor of instructing us again.[45]

In your treatise you [also] say, "if it (*prajñā*) has no matching then among things there is nothing not matched. If it has no affirming then among things there is nothing not affirmed. Since among things there is nothing not affirmed, it affirms and yet has no affirming. Since among things there is nothing not matched, it matches and yet has no matching."[46] Now then, if [the Sage] has no matching and yet among things there is nothing not matched, then why [even] consider this as perfectly matching [all things with their proper names]? If [the Sage] has no affirming [of statements as Ultimately True] and yet among things there is nothing not affirmed, then why [even] regard this as truly affirming? How can it be that [the Sage] truly affirms [statements] while yet not affirming [them as Ultimately True] or perfectly matches [all things with their proper names] while yet not matching?[47] And still you say, "[the Sage] matches yet has no matching" and "affirms yet there is nothing affirmed"? If you mean that perfectly matching [all things with their proper names] is not constantly matching [them up] and truly affirming is not constantly affirming [statements as true], this [statement] simply speaks surreptitiously of the basic difference between understanding and ignorance.[48] In my stupidity I do not understand the meaning of what you say. I really desire that you instruct [me] once more and so disperse my ignorance.

Closing (155b: 18–21)

The day your treatise arrived I joined Dharma Master Huiyuan in examining it. The Master also regarded it as beautifully written,[49] and perceived your meaning. Yet it appears as if each [of us] has his own base [of understanding] and so perhaps our principles are not necessarily entirely the same.[50] At the present time we have distributed [your treatise throughout the community] and there are many who cherish it and frequently wrestle with its lines. We regret not being with your honored self at this time.

II. Sengzhao's Reply to Liu Yimin's Letter[51]

Cover letter (155b: 23–26)

[I have wanted] to meet you face to face for a long time but my hopeful thoughts have been frustrated. Brother Huiming arrived here and I obtained your comments[52] dated the twelfth month of last year together with your questions. I have unrolled and studied it again and again, and in my joy it was as if we suddenly were face to face. Cool winds have arrived with the Mid-autumn festival.[53] How are you faring now? I[54] am troubled by sickness,[55] and often not well.[56] I will be brief, as I believe that a messenger is returning to the South [soon].

The 15th day of the 8th month.
Śramaṇa Sengzhao's reply.

Main Letter

Section I.1 Introduction (155b: 26–c: 2)

Although our dress is different, our religious aspirations do not diverge.[57] Although separated by rivers and mountains, our principles agree and so we [truly] are neighbors. Therefore, when I gaze into the distance and reach out with my thoughts, my feelings are at rest. Sir, you demonstrate an uncommon beauty in following your inclinations [to live in] "noble retreat."[58] Alone and peaceful, away from outside affairs, joy fills your heart.[59] Every single word in your collection [of songs]—how could they ever stray?[60] They exemplify [the spirit] of the refined poems of the Worthies of the Bamboo Grove. Such high longings for perfection! I hope your purity will not be disturbed and affectionately [ask] that you take care of yourself. [Although] each [of us] must rely on messengers, [I hope we will] frequently exchange replies.

Section I.2 Sengzhao's praise for Huiyuan (155c: 2–7)

I wish the monks on your mountain perpetual well-being and the lay-followers of Dao all the best. I am pleased that Dharma Master Huiyuan is doing so well and consider this a great comfort. Although I have not yet undertaken such a pure [life] or submitted to such high regulations [as he has], my eagerness [to do so] grows stronger with each day. Your Lord (Huiyuan), although past the prime of ordinary people, has deep reserves of *qi* from his strict discipline. Watching over you in his secluded grotto, he "embraces the One in the empty valley."[61] From near and far people revere him and sing his praises–what beauty could there be like this? Each time I raise my thoughts in your direction, a bank of clouds hangs suspended over [your retreat].[62] Lacking the means to convey my reverence, I only reach my own deep regrets. Being in the presence of a gentleman of such purity everyday, [you should] rejoice and take pleasure in [his vast] understanding.

Section I.3 Portrait of the Chang'an community (155c: 7–156a: 4)

The great assembly [in Chang'an] continues as usual. Dharma Master Kumārajīva is well. The Way of the King of Jin (Yao Xing) is by nature spontaneous (*ziran*). [In his] heavenly workings he surpasses the ordinary people. He is a wall and a moat to the Three Jewels and regards extending the Way as his [most holy] duty.[63] Because of this he attracts eminent monks from various countries[64] to come from [the most] distant regions. [Truly it seems] the Divine Wind from Vulture's Peak draws together and condenses in this land.[65]

Master Ling[66] went abroad [to obtain Scriptures that will serve as] bridges and fords [to *nirvāṇa*] for a thousand years to come. He returned from the Western Regions having obtained more than two hundred volumes of new *vaipulya sūtras*.[67] [The King][68] invited a master of Mahāyāna meditation,[69] a *Tripiṭaka* master,[70] and two masters of the *Mahāvibhāṣa*.[71] Dharma Master Kumārajīva is in the Great Stone Monastery[72] expounding upon the newly arrived *sūtras*.[73] The treasure house of the Dharma is deep and far-reaching; daily it has different voices.[74]

The Meditation Master [Buddhabhadra] resides in the Palace Monastery[75] teaching the way (Dao) of meditation practice.[76] His disciples number several hundred. Night and day they are neither indolent nor careless. Such harmony and reverence is the ultimate joy and happiness. The *Tripiṭaka* Master [Buddhayaśas] is translating the *Vinaya*[77] in the Central Monastery.[78] From beginning to end it is entirely pure, as if one were seeing the law for the first time.[79] The masters of the *Vibhāśa* [Dharmayaśas and Dharmagupta] are in the Stone Sheep Monastery[80] translating a Central Asian copy of the *Śāriputra Abhidharma śāstra*.[81] Although they have not yet completed the transla-tion, questions about its contents give rise to new and wonderful words [and teachings].

As for myself, I have often participated in this most excellent turn of fate, joining in with this grand transformation [of learning]. Although I [have in the past] regretted not seeing Śākyamuni and his disciples in the Jeta Grove,[82] [at present] my only regret is that you gentlemen of highest purity have not joined our Dharma community.[83]

The venerable Daosheng was here only a short time ago, having stayed with us several years.[84] Whenever we had occasion for words, [he] always sang your praises. [I understand that] during his journey south you saw each other. I have not heard from him recently and am worried. What have you heard?[85]

Brother Wei[86] has arrived, bringing your song "Remembering the Bud-dha" (*nian fo*; in Japanese, *nembutsu*) and another song by Dharma Master Huiyuan along with his introduction.[87] These works are lofty and bring joy and elation. Such poems are perfectly pure and lovely, and all the literati praise their beauty. [They truly] can be called the songs of [one who has] wandered through the Gates of Wisdom and knocked at the Mysterious Portal.[88] Surely you and the Dharma Master have several other compositions. Why, then, do you send only a few?

In the year *wu*[89] Kumārajīva translated the *Vimalakīrti nirdeśa sūtra*. At that time I regularly attended [the translation sessions] and during the breaks I hastily recorded [the Master's] Perfect Words to make [my own] commen-tary. Although my composition is not literary, even so its meaning is based on the original.[90] So it is that today I entrust [to your] hands a copy which

I am sending south. You may examine it at your leisure and see if it merits consideration.[91]

Your questions are beautifully put and incisive. In replying to them I am like the Man of Ying.[92] My thoughts do not delve into the obscurities and I am clumsy when it comes to writing. Moreover, to reach our destination there are no words. Words will only divert [us] from our destination. [We] make statement after statement [yet it] does not end. And after all, what can be distinguished? So I will address your points with "wild words" instead.

Section II.1 First Reply to Liu's First Question (156a: 4–7)

In your comments you say, "the Sagely Mind is wondrously still. [It is] Principle, ultimately identical with non-being."[93] [You go on to say that,] "although it abides in the midst of the Named yet it is remote, [ultimately] identical with the Nameless."[94] [Finally confessing that,] "the obscurity of such Principle defies comprehension! I remain obstinate in my perpetual dim-wittedness [regarding this theory]."[95]

[I suggest that you] consider this [idea] as [something] to ponder in your heart of hearts. Attain it inwardly by "forgetting the words."[96] Take it up and fix your mind upon it. [Moreover, let me ask you something:] Why should it suffice to use the inconsistency of peoples' feelings to seek for the difference within the Sagely Mind?"[97]

Section II.2a. First Reply to Liu's Second Question (156a: 7–13)

[Returning to your] comments you say, "Can we say that the probing of [the Sagely Mind] supernaturally reaches the end of all items [in the cosmos], all the way to the 'hidden tallies' [of our lives]?"[98] In addition [you say] "what you call 'still illumination' is in essence *samatha-vipassanā*. If the Sage's Mind is in essence spontaneous, supernatural and alone in influencing [all things], then his responses to the multitudes of things will certainly thereby cease."[99]

[Yet] the idea spoken of by [the phrase] "all the way to the 'hidden tallies' [of our lives]" cannot be attained by the term "*samatha-vipassanā*," and [the phrase] "supernatural and perhaps alone in influencing [all things]" cannot be expressed [by saying] "[his responses to] the multitudes of things will certainly thereby cease." Although both statements seem contradictory, [in the Sage's] marvelous functioning they are always the same. Traces and the person [who makes them] proliferate but in the case of the Sage they do not differ.[100]

Section II 2.b Second Reply to Liu's First Question and Second Reply To Liu's Second Question (156a: 13–18)

Why is this? The Sage's dark (*xuan*) Mind darkly (*mo*) illuminates [the universe].[101] [But as you have said,] "[It is] Principle, ultimately identical with non-being."[102] [Now] since we have already spoken of the existence of this identity [and that regarding this] identity there is nothing not ultimate, how can [it] be identical with the Ultimate Non-being and yet have the name "*samatha-vipassanā*"? The term "*samatha-vipassanā*" is not identical with your declaration [of the Sage] being "outside" [the transformations].[103] If declaring [the Sage to be "outside" the transformations] is to produce identity [with a declaration about the Sage's] "inner" [illumination], then we have declarations that are not identical. If declaring [the Sage attains insight through meditation] is to produce identity [with your other declaration about the Sage] being "outside," then such declarations do not concern the [Sage's] "self."[104]

Furthermore, the Mind of the Sage is void and invisible, mysteriously cut-off, always alone. In his sympathy there is nothing [to which] he does not respond, and in his meeting there is nothing he does not penetrate. [The Sagely Mind] is the mysterious mechanism secretly revolving [Heaven]. It functions but does not move. In his responses to the innumerable multitudes, what "action" is there to cease?

Section II 2.c. First Reply to Liu's Third Question (156a: 18–b: 17)

Moreover, regarding this Mind's existence, [while we may] consider it to have existence, such 'existence' is not 'self-existence' (*svabhāva*). Thus, the Sagely Mind does not [really] have existence.[105] He does not [really] have existence, hence his "existence" [actually] lacks existence. Since his existence [actually] lacks existence, he [also] lacks non-existence. Because he lacks non-existence, the Sage neither exists nor not-exists. Neither existing nor not-existing, his Spirit is then void.[106]

What does [all of] this mean? [The concepts] 'existence' and 'non-existence' are [merely] images and sounds in our minds. Images and sounds support words and symbols. Since [the concepts] 'existence' and 'non-existence' have been discarded [when it comes to the Sage], our minds have no images or sounds [of him]. Since images and sounds have been destroyed, words and symbols cannot fathom [his nature]. As words and symbols cannot fathom [his nature], the [Sage's] Way is cut-off from our world of multiplicity.[107]

[The Sage's] Way is cut-off from our world of multiplicity, hence he is able to supernaturally probe the cosmic contents. Such supernatural probing we call "mysteriously exhausting." [The Sage's] Way of "mysteriously exhausting" is essentially lacking obstructions.

Now then, [since the Sagely Mind] lacks obstructions, he resides in hidden stillness. [In] hidden stillness he is cut-off [from our world of multiplicity], thus [we use the term] "void" in order to speak of him.[108] [The Sage] mysteriously exhausts the stores of the cosmic contents. [Since he mysteriously exhausts] the cosmic contents, [he knows] the contents and thereby responds to them. [As he knows] the contents and thereby responds to them, he thus moves along with the events he matches. [Since we use the term] "void" in order to speak of him, his Way extends outside the names. [The Sage's] Way extends outside the names, hence we speak of his "non-existence." He moves along with the events he matches, thus we speak of his "existence." Therefore, we speak of him as "existent" or more properly "truly existent," [yet even this] is merely to force a name on him, for how could he really be so?

So it is that a *sūtra* says, "Sagely Wisdom has neither knowing nor what is not known. [It] does not act (*wuwei*) yet there is nothing which is not done."[109] This is the Way of stillness and vanishing, without words or marks—[the Way of the Sage]. How can we speak of [him] as either "existing" or "not existing," as moving yet still or still and yet moving forth?

Those [of you] who discuss [my essay] lay too much emphasis on words to fix my meaning. [You] search the Great Square and seek for corners.[110] In your inner minds you foresee [events] and regard it as manifesting the Dark [Principles].[111] [You] hold on to the certain matches that you know. Therefore, when you hear that the Sage has "knowing" you take it to mean that he has a mind [like an ordinary person]. And when you hear that the Sage has "no knowing" you take it to mean that he is like a great void. [However], the ideas of "having" and "not having" are one-sided views that you hold. How can this be dwelling in the Way of Non-duality?

Why is it that the ten thousand things, although different, are in their essential nature always one? [In their nature they] cannot be "things" yet they cannot *not* be things. If [their nature] can be regarded as a thing among things, then various names and marks will proliferate. If it cannot be regarded as a thing among things, then things just are true [existence].[112] Therefore the Sage neither regards them as things among [other] things nor denies that they are things among [other] things. Since he does regard them as things among [other] things, he denies such "things" [really] exist. Since he does not deny that they are things among [other] things, he denies such "things" [really] do not exist. He denies their existence, hence he does not grasp. He denies their non-existence, hence he does not reject. He does not reject, thus his mysterious awareness is identical to Ultimate Truth. He does not grasp, thus he does not rely on names and marks. Since he does not rely on names and marks, we deny that he has knowing. Since his mysterious awareness is identical to the Ultimate Truth, we deny that he has "not knowing." Thus a *sūtra* says, "*Prajñā* neither grasps nor rejects *dharmas*. It neither knows nor not-knows."[113] This [Sage] rises up outside [existence and non-existence] to the region where mind is cut-off [from things]. Those who desire to restrain [*prajñā*] with "existence" and "non-existence"—have they not gone far astray?

Section II.2 d. Third Reply
to Liu's Second Question (156b: 17–c: 1)

Please ponder [this]: to expose [the fallacy of] "existence" and "non-existence" is the birth of Wisdom. Ultimately it [resides] within marks (i.e. among phenomena) yet *dharmas* essentially lack all marks. What [then] does Sagely Wisdom know? When the world speaks of "not knowing" it means the insentience of wood, stone, the void etc. [*Prajñā*, however,] supernaturally mirrors, darkly candles. Even when forms were not yet displayed, Dao had no hidden workings.[114] It is better to speak of such [knowing] as "not knowing."

Furthermore, [in *prajñā*] there is no knowing produced from not-knowing. It lacks not-knowing and lacks knowing.[115] Since it lacks knowing, we speak of it as "not existing." Since it lacks not-knowing, we speak of it as "not not-existing." Therefore [I have speak of it as] "void yet not failing to illuminate" and "illuminating while not failing to be void."[116] Perhaps it is perpetually silent, neither directing nor controlling. Who because of its ability to move dares command it to exist, or because of its stillness [dares] order it to not-exist? Thus a *sūtra* says, "True *prajñā* neither exists nor not-exists. It has no arising or destruction."[117] Yet this cannot be taught to ordinary people.

Why is this? [When I] speak of it (*prajñā*) as "not an existing [thing]," [my] words do not affirm it as "existing." [However], I do not mean to affirm it as "*not* existing [as a thing]." When I speak of it as "not a nothing," [my] words do not affirm it as "nothing," [yet] I do not mean to affirm it as "not a nothing." [*Prajñā*] is neither an existing [thing] nor is it not an existing [thing]. Neither is it nothing nor is it *not* a nothing.[118] So it is that [the *Fangguang* tells us] Subhūti expounded *prajñā* night and day yet said that he spoke of nothing.[119]

This is [truly] knowing the Dao that is cut-off from words but how can it be transmitted? I only hope that all you gentlemen versed in the mysteries will also meet it.

Section II.2e. Second Reply to Liu's Third Question (156c: 1–24)

Furthermore, you also say, "We think you ought to first determine the Way of responding that the Sagely Mind relies upon. Is it that he matches [names with things] by only illuminating the markless? Or is it that he matches by fully observing the changes?"[120] In your discussions you seem to consider the "markless" and the "changes" to refer to different things. [That is, you seem to think that the Sage's] observing the changes differs from his illuminating the markless. Or that if he illuminates the markless then he fails to carefully meet [all things]. If so then you are mistaken in your ideas of Truth. A *sūtra* says, "Form (*rūpa*) does not differ from emptiness (*śūnyatā*); emptiness does not differ from form. Form just is emptiness, emptiness just is form."[121] If [you were right] the *Tathāgata* would mean here that when meditating on form and emptiness, [the Sage] responds by seeing form with one mind, and emptiness with another mind. If he sees form with one mind, then it is only form and not emptiness. If he sees emptiness with one mind, then it is only emptiness and not form. If this were really so [however,] then emptiness and form would be two separate [things] and we could not determine their root.[122] [Clearly you are mistaken].

Therefore when the *sūtras* speak of "not-form" (i.e. *śūnyatā*) [we should] truly regard this as "not-form *qua* form" and not [consider it to be] "not-form *qua* not-form." [Otherwise] if it were "not-form *qua* not-form" then the Great Void would be not-form and then what could "not-form" be understood [to mean]? However, if we consider ["not-form"] to be "not-form *qua* form," then it just [means] "not-form does not differ from form." Since not-form does not differ from form, form just is not-form. Thus we know the changes just are the markless, and the markless just is the changes.[123] People's circumstances are not the same, thus the teachings wander and have their differences.[124]

Examine these abstruse[125] texts for the Sage's original idea. How could [you think the Sage] uses different minds for the "true" and the "false," or illuminates emptiness and existence differently? Therefore [the Sage] illuminates the markless yet does not fail in his ability to carefully meet [all things]. He observes the transformations and movements but does not stray from his affinity for the markless. From the first his being does not differ from non-being; from the first his non-being does not differ from being. Never once not existing, never once not not-existing. Hence [the *Fangguang*] says, "[The *Tathāgata*] does not move from Perfect Enlightenment (*sambodhi*) yet establishes all *dharmas*."[126] From this how can we infer that his stillness and functioning oppose each other? Similarly, how can [you] say [the Sage's] perception of the transformations differs from [his] illuminating of the markless? I fear that you discussants erroneously mean [the Sage has] two minds—one for emptiness, one for existence.[127] The quiescent and the turbulent differ [only] in their function, thus the words "perception of the transformations" cannot merely mean he does not exist.

If you are able to, abandon your one-sided mind confined within [existence] and seek the mysterious workings beyond external phenomena. All things exist from a single void. Those who realize that this perfect void is not nothing say that the *zhiren* responds night and day, joining with things [as they] move. Mounting the turns of fate [he] carefully tends the transformations.[128] Never has [he even] started to "exist." The Sagely Mind is like this. What "existence" can be grasped? And yet [you] say you have never understood the principle of not grasping.

Section II.2f Third Reply to Liu's Third Question (156c: 24–157a: 6)

Moreover, you say "if [the Sage] has no affirming [of statements as Ultimately True] then why [even] regard this as truly affirming?"[129] [and] "if [the Sage] has no matching then why [even] consider this as perfectly matching [all things with their proper names]?"[130] However, [these statements] are merely how *Tathāgata* can be spoken of.[131] If [you] are able, empty your mind (*wuxin*) with respect to [the Sage's] affirming and so consider his affirming as "not affirming [anything as real]." [If you are able,] empty your mind with respect to his matching and so consider his matching to be "not matching [anything real]." Then [you will understand when it comes to the Sage that] "night and day he affirms" yet [he] does not stray into "not affirming," [and also that] "night and day he matches" yet [he] does not fall into the error of "not matching."[132]

Yet I fear [you will think] there is a [real] affirming in [the Sage's] lack of affirming, or that there is a [real] matching in [the Sage's] lack of matching. Because of this, there will only be suffering. Why is this? If true affirmations can be affirmed and perfect matches can be matched, then [we will use] names and marks in order to [grasp] forms.[133] "Good" and "bad" will then be born, and this birth will quickly produce quarrels, and who then can stop them?[134]

Therefore the Sage has emptiness as his inner mind. He lacks [normal] consciousness (*vijñāna*) and has "no knowing." He dwells in the region of movement and function and yet remains settled in the territory of non-action (*wuwei*). He abides in the named things and yet rests in the district that is cut-off from words. Still and alone, void and empty, [he] can never be attained by words and symbols. Thus we should let our attempts [to do so] end.[135]

Still you say, "[With the Sage,] true affirming can be affirmed" and "perfect matching can be matched," [adding] "I have never understood your meaning."[136] I am afraid that [all this] producing of matching [things with names] and affirming [them as true] is just our calling things "so." [In reality] those things in themselves are not "so."[137]

Closing

So then, our words are an abundance of traces, the product of [many] different paths. And yet with words there is what is not worded, just as with traces there is what is not traced.[138] Therefore those skilled in wording words seek to word what they cannot word; those skilled in tracing traces seek to trace what they cannot trace. The Ultimate Principle (*prajñā*) is "void" and "dark."[139] To [attempt to] determine it by thinking is already to go astray. How much more [do we stray] by using words? I fear what I have transmitted is far from [your understanding]. [Perhaps] all you keen-minded gentlemen will, by using my words, anticipate (*qi*) [what lies] outside speech.[140]

NOTES

Introduction

1. In this study I use the terms "literati" or "gentry" to refer to the elite classes of Chinese society. Although not a homogenous group all shared the same classical literary education. For more details see Erik Zurcher, *The Buddhist Conquest of China: the Spread and Adaptation of Buddhism in Early Medieval China* (Leiden: E.J. Brill, 1959), 4–6.
2. The *"prajñā* schools" were comprised of Chinese literati-monks seeking to understand the teachings of the *Prajñāpāramitā sūtras* that had been translated into Chinese during the second and third centuries C.E. Since they rely heavily on Chinese philosophical categories, these schools bear little resemblance to Indian Buddhist schools. I deal with these schools in more detail in Chapter Two.
3. Liu was a "gentry recluse" who retired from his official post to become a lay leader at Lu Shan, a Buddhist community south of the Yangtze River founded by the renowned monk Huiyuan (334–417).
4. T.1858—153a: 8–9. Alternative translations in Richard H. Robinson, *Early Mādhyamika in India and China* (Madison, Milwaukee and London: The University of Wisconsin Press, 1967), 212 and Walter Liebenthal, *Chao Lun: The Treatises of Seng-chao*, 2nd revised edition (Hong Kong: Hong Kong University Press, 1968), 64.
5. I derive this idea a *hermeneutical* understanding from Martin Heidegger and Hans-Georg Gadamer but it has its roots in the work of Friedrich Schleiermacher, who tries to develop a universal hermeneutics in terms of an actual theory of understanding. See Jean Grondin, *Introduction to Philosophical Hermeneutics*, trans. Joel Weinsheimer (New Haven and London: Yale University Press, 1994), 64ff.

6. By "modernity" I mean the socio-historical era from the seventeenth century to the present which is characterized by the rise of the nation-state, capitalism, print, increasing reliance on technology to provide solutions to life's problems, and the loosening of communal ties. More specifically modernity is an epistemological concept marked by a way of knowing which is scientific, suspicious of faith and tradition, and alienated from nature and "old" ways.

Chapter 1

1. Gerald L. Bruns, *Hermeneutics Ancient & Modern* (New Haven: Yale University Press, 1992), 17.
2. Richard E. Palmer, *Hermeneutics* (Evanston: Northwestern University Press, 1969), 12–13.
3. Ibid., 67.
4. Ibid., 20–26.
5. Ibid., 31. Significantly, in *"Prajñā* is Not-knowing" Sengzhao describes Kumārajīva's translations in hermeneutic terms as serving "as a bridge and a ford for ages to come." See T.1858–153a: 20.
6. Jean Grondin, *Introduction to Philosophical Hermeneutics*, trans. Joel Weinsheimer (New Haven: Yale University Press, 1994), 28–32.
7. Kurt Mueller-Vollmer, "Introduction: Language, Mind, and Artifact: An Outline of Hermeneutic Theory since the Enlightenment," in *The Hermeneutics Reader: Texts of the German Tradition from the Enlightenment to the Present*, ed. Kurt Mueller-Vollmer (New York: The Continuum Publishing Company, 1985), 3–8.
8. Schleiermacher, "General Hermeneutics," 83.
9. Wilhelm Dilthey, "Draft for a Critique of Historical Reason," in *The Hermeneutics Reader: Texts of the German Tradition from the Enlightenment to the Present*, ed. Kurt Mueller-Vollmer (New York: The Continuum Publishing Company, 1985), 159.
10. Ibid., 154–156.
11. Martin Heidegger, *Being and Time*, trans. John Macquarrie and Edward Robinson (San Francisco: Harper & Row, Publishers, Inc., 1962), 189–193.
12. Ibid., 195.
13. Ibid., 188.
14. From a series of Heidegger's lectures from the early 1920's entitled "Hermeneutics of Facticity." Quoted in Grondin, *Introduction to Philosophical Hermeneutics*, 99 (italics in the original).
15. Heidegger, *Being and Time*, 200.
16. Ibid., 200–201.
17. Grondin, *Introduction to Philosophical Hermeneutics*, 101.
18. See, for example, Heidegger's essays in *Early Greek Thinking*, trans. David Farrell Krell and Frank A. Capuzzi (San Francisco: Harper & Row, Publishers, 1975) and *Poetry, Language, Thought*, trans. Albert Hofstadter (San Francisco: Harper & Row, Publishers, 1971).
19. Martin Heidegger, "A Dialogue on Language," in *On the Way to Language*, trans. Peter D. Hertz (San Francisco: Harper & Row, Publishers, 1971), 30.

20. Hans-Georg Gadamer, *Truth and Method*, 2nd revised ed., trans and revised by Joel Weinsheimer and Donald G. Marshall (New York: The Continuum Publishing Company, 1994), 476 and 483.

21. Paul Ricoeur, "Critique of Ideology," in *The Hermeneutic Tradition: from Ast to Ricoeur*, eds. Gayle L. Ormiston and Alan D. Schrift (Albany: State University of New York Press, 1990), 300.

22. Gadamer, *Truth and Method*, 101–110.

23. Ibid., 267.

24. Ibid., 383–389.

25. Hans-Georg Gadamer, "The Universality of the Hermeneutical Problem," trans. David E. Linge, in *The Hermeneutic Tradition: from Ast to Ricoeur*, eds. Gayle L. Ormiston and Alan D. Schrift (Albany: State University of New York Press, 1990), 151–152.

26. The term "tradition" is central to Gadamer's work but is rather ambiguous. For Gadamer, "tradition" is the historical chain of a text's explications, a definition that conveys both connection and temporal distance.

27. Gadamer, *Truth and Method*, 279.

28. Ibid., 311.

29. Ibid., *Truth and Method*, 302.

30. Ibid., 306. All understanding is a fusion of horizons according to Gadamer.

31. Ibid., 269.

32. Ibid., 311.

33. Ibid., 297.

34. Ibid., 298.

35. Hans-Georg Gadamer, "Reply to My Critics," trans. George H. Leiner, in *The Hermeneutic Tradition: from Ast to Ricoeur*, eds. Gayle L. Ormiston and Alan D. Schrift (Albany: State University of New York Press, 1990), 283.

36. Paul Ricoeur, *Interpretation Theory: Discourse and the Surplus of Meaning* (Fort Worth, TX: Texas Christian University Press, 1976) and *Hermeneutics and the Human Sciences*, trans. and ed. by John B. Thompson (Cambridge: Cambridge University Press, 1981).

37. Ricoeur, *Interpretation Theory*, 20–21.

38. Ibid., 30.

39. Ibid., 43.

40. Paul Ricoeur, "Between a Text and its Readers, " in *A Ricoeur Reader: Reflection and Imagination*, ed. Mario J. Valdes (Toronto: University of Toronto Press, 1991), 390–424.

41. For Ricoeur as well, texts can create their own open-ended audience, as more readers offer their differing interpretations. See Ricoeur, *Hermeneutics and the Human Sciences*, 208.

42. Ricoeur, *Interpretation Theory*, 92.

43. Ibid., 94.

44. Ricoeur, *Hermeneutics and the Human Sciences*, 178.

45. See "The Conflict of Interpretations: Debate with Hans-Georg Gadamer," in *A Ricoeur Reader: Reflection and Imagination*, ed. Mario J. Valdes (Toronto: University of Toronto Press, 1991), 216–241.

46. See Jurgen Habermas, "The Hermeneutic Claim to Universality," in *The Hermeneutic Tradition: from Ast to Ricoeur*, eds. Gayle L. Ormiston and Alan D. Schrift (Albany: State University of New York Press, 1990), 245–272.

47. Ricoeur, *Hermeneutics and the Human Sciences*, 94.

48. Ricoeur, "Habermas," in *A Ricoeur Reader: Reflection and Imagination*, ed. Mario J. Valdes (Toronto: University of Toronto, 1991), 163.

49. John E. Smith, "Interpreting across Boundaries," in *Understanding the Chinese Mind: the Philosophical Roots*, ed. Robert E. Allinson (Oxford: Oxford University Press, 1989), 42–43.

50. Paul Ricoeur, "The Creativity of Language," interview by Richard Kearney (Paris 1981), *Dialogues with Contemporary Continental Thinkers* (Manchester: Manchester University Press, 1984); reprint, *A Ricoeur Reader: Reflection and Imagination*, ed. Mario J. Valdes (Toronto and Buffalo: University of Toronto Press, 1991), 473 (page citation is to the reprint edition). Italics in the original.

51. For an in-depth discussion of Heidegger's lifelong interest in Eastern ways see Graham Parkes, ed., *Heidegger and Asian Thought* (Honolulu: University Press of Hawaii, 1987).

52. Hans-Georg Gadamer, Preface to W. Dilthey, *Grundriss der allgemeinen Geschichte der Philosophie* (Frankfort, 1949), 18; quoted in Wilhelm Halbfass, *India and Europe: An Essay in Understanding* (Albany: State University of New York Press, 1988), 164.

53. Wilhelm Halbfass, *India and Europe*, 165.

54. Elsewhere Gadamer suggests these differences have grammatical roots: "Eastern" (Chinese and Japanese) languages lack the subject-predicate structure of "Western" (Indo-European) languages and so do not gravitate toward a metaphysics of substance and accident. See Hans-Georg Gadamer, "Destruktion *and Deconstruction*," trans Geoff Waite and Richard Palmer in *Dialogue and Deconstruction: The Gadamer-Derrida Encounter*, ed. Diane P. Michelfelder and Richard E. Palmer (Albany: State University of New York Press, 1989), 104–105.

55. See, for example, D. A. Dilworth, *Philosophy in World Perspective: A Comparative Hermeneutic of Major Theories* (New Haven: Yale University Press, 1989); E. J. Sharpe, *The Universal Gita: Western Images of the Bhagavad Gita* (La Salle: Open Court Publishers, 1985); and Longzi Zhang, *The Tao and the Logos: Literary Hermeneutics, East and West* (Durham: Duke University Press, 1992).

56. Mary Ann Stenger, "Gadamer's Hermeneutics as a Model for Cross-Cultural Understanding and Truth in Religion," in *Religious Pluralism and Truth: Essays on Cross-Cultural Philosophy of Religion*, ed. Thomas Dean (Albany: State University of New York Press, 1995), 151–168.

57. Ibid., 162–166.

58. Karl H. Potter, "Metaphor as Key to Understanding the Thought of Other Speech Communities," in *Interpreting Across Boundaries: New Essays in Comparative Philosophy*, ed. Gerald James Larson and Eliot Deutsch (Princeton: Princeton University Press, 1988), 19–35.

59. Raimundo Panikkar, "What is Comparative Philosophy Comparing?" in *Interpreting Across Boundaries: New Essays in Comparative Philosophy*, ed. Gerald James Larson and Eliot Deutsch (Princeton: Princeton University Press, 1988), 119–136.

60. Henry Rosemont, "Against Relativism," in *Interpreting Across Boundaries: New Essays in Comparative Philosophy*, ed. Gerald James Larson and Eliot Deutsch (Princeton: Princeton University Press, 1988), 66.

61. *Zhuangzi*, chapter 33. *Zhuangzi*, SBBY 1411, *juan* 11, 13a; Burton Watson, trans., *The Complete Works of Chuang Tzu* (New York: Columbia University Press, 1968), 362.

62. Sarah Allen, *The Way of Water and Sprouts of Virtue* (Albany: State University of New York Press, 1997), 66–67.

63. *Laozi* 1, "The Dao that can be dao'ed (spoken) is not the eternal Dao. The name that can be named is not the eternal name." *Laozi Daodejing*, SBBY 1403, *shang pian*, 1a; D. C. Lau, trans, *Lao Tzu: Tao Te Ching*, (New York: Viking Penguin Inc., 1963), 57.

64. A. C. Graham, *Disputers of the Tao: Philosophical Argument in Ancient China* (La Salle: Open Court Publishing Company, 1989).

65. Feng Youlan (Fung Yu-lan), *The Spirit of Chinese Philosophy*, trans. E.P. Hughes (Boston: Beacon Press, 1962), 3–4.

66. Such sorting out of scholars (*shi*) into "schools" is a way of constructing intellectual lineages—something very important in China, where ancestral and familial lines are a significant social and political reality.

67. Benjamin Schwartz speaks of the "turbulent inner life" in Confucianism whereas John Berthrong has analyzed the Confucian tradition into six distinct epochs, all linked by enduring themes. See Benjamin Schwartz, "Some Polarities in Confucian Thought," in *Confucianism and Chinese Civilization*, ed. Arthur F. Wright (Stanford: Stanford University Press, 1975), 3–15 and John H. Berthrong, *Transformations of the Confucian Way* (Boulder: Westview Press, 1998), 7–11. Daoism is even more pluralistic. Indeed, it has never been a unified "religion" but is more a combination of teachings and traditions.

68. David L. Hall and Roger T. Ames, *Thinking from the Han: Self, Truth and Transcendence in Chinese and Western Culture* (Albany: State University of New York Press, 1998), 154–155.

69. Ibid.

70. *Zhuangzi*, SBBY 1411, *juan* 10, 13b–14a; Watson, *The Complete Works of Chuang Tzu*, 364.

71. Julia Ching, *Mysticism and Kingship in China: The Heart of Chinese Wisdom* (Cambridge: Cambridge University Press, 1997), 54.

72. Ibid., 134–137. Once again, we are in the realm of Hermes, mediator and patron god of hermeneuts.

73. Rodney L. Taylor, *The Religious Dimension of Confucianism* (Albany: State University of New York Press, 1990), 23–37. There are various groupings of *jing*, from the well-known "five *jing*" (*Yijing, Shijing, Shujing, Liji, Chunqiu*) to the "six *jing*" (the five plus the *Yuejing*). Although associated with Confucianism they were revered by all Chinese. Indeed, Daoists and Buddhists often called their own authoritative texts "*jing*" (e.g. the *Daode jing*).

74. *Analects* 7.19. *Lunyu*, SBBY 308, *juan* 4, 5a; Lau, *Confucius: The Analects*, 88. Lau numbers this passage 7.20.

75. *Analects* 2.11. *Lunyu*, SBBY 308, *juan* 1, 9a–b; Lau, *Confucius: The Analects*, 64.

76. *Analects* 7.1. *Lunyu*, SBBY 308, *juan* 4, 1a; Lau, *Confucius: The Analects*, 86.

77. *Analects* 15.28. *Lunyu*, SBBY 309, *juan* 9, 5b; Lau, *Confucius: The Analects*, 136 (15.29 by Lau's numbering).

78. Ching, *Mysticism and Kingship in China*, 137.

79. Roger T. Ames, "Knowing in the *Zhuangzi*: 'From Here, on the Bridge, over the River Hao," in *Wandering at Ease in the Zhuangzi*, ed. Roger T. Ames (Albany: State University of New York Press, 1998), 228.

80. The *Mahāparinibbāna sūtta* of the *Dīgha Nikāya*, translated by Henry Clark Warren in *Buddhism in Translation* (New York: Atheneum, 1984), 107.

81. For discussions see J. W. de Jong, "The Beginnings of Buddhism," *The Eastern Buddhist* N.S. 26/2 (1993): 11–30 and "The Buddha and His Teachings," in *Wisdom, Compassion, and the Search for Understanding: The Buddhist Studies Legacy of Gadjin M. Nagao*, ed. Jonathan A. Silk (Honolulu: University of Hawaii Press, 2000), 171–181.

82. Accounts of these councils differ, particularly between the Theravādins and the Sarvāstivādins. For details see David Snellgrove, *Indo-Tibetan Buddhism: Indian Buddhists and their Tibetan Successors*, vol. 1 (Boston: Shambhala Publications, Inc., 1987), 45–46.

83. Peter N. Gregory, *Tsung-mi and the Sinification of Buddhism* (Princeton: Princeton University Press, 1991), 94–95.

84. Quoted in Donald S. Lopez, Jr., "Introduction," in *Buddhist Hermeneutics*, ed. Donald S. Lopez, Jr. (Honolulu: The Kuroda Institute, University of Hawaii Press, 1987), 3.

85. Etienne Lamotte, "The Assessment of Textual Interpretation in Buddhism," in *Buddhist Hermeneutics*, ed. Donald S. Lopez, Jr. (Honolulu: The Kuroda Institute, University of Hawaii Press, 1987), 12.

86. Gregory, *Tsung-mi and the Sinification of Buddhism*, 95. *Nītārtha* (lit. "the meaning that has been led to") originally referred to teachings that were explicitly stated while *neyārtha* (lit. "the meaning that is to be led to") referred to teachings requiring further interpretation.

87. Jay L. Garfield, trans., *Fundamental Wisdom of the Middle Way: Nāgārjuna's Mūlamadhyamakakārikā* (New York/Oxford: Oxford University Press, 1995), 68.

88. Donald S. Lopez, Jr., "Interpretation of the Mahayana Sutras," in *Buddhist Hermeneutics*, ed. Donald S. Lopez, Jr. (Honolulu: the Kuroda Institute, University of Hawaii Press, 1987), 61–64.

89. Ibid., 98.

90. T.262–12b: 13–c: 17; Leon Hurvitz, trans., *Scripture of the Lotus Blossom of the Fine Dharma* (New York: Columbia University Press, 1976), 58–60.

91. As in the story from the *Lotus Sūtra* cited above: each child receives the same wonderful ox cart, despite the father's distinct promises. For a more detailed discussion of *upāya* see Michael Pye, *Skilful Means: A Concept in Mahāyāna Buddhism* (London: Duckworth, 1978).

92. Robert A. F. Thurman, "Buddhist Hermeneutics," *Journal of the American Academy of Religion* 46 (September 1978): 22.

93. Guifeng Zongmi, *Yuan ren lun* ("Inquiry into the Origin of Humanity"), T.1887–708a: 7–13. This translation comes from Peter N. Gregory, trans., *Inquiry into the Origin of Humanity: An Annotated Translation of Tsung-mi's Yuan jen lun with a Modern Commentary* (Honolulu: The Kuroda Institute, University of Hawaii Press, 1995), 44.

94. Arthur E. Link, "Shyh Daw-an's Preface to Saṅgharakṣa's *Yogācārabhūmisūtra*," *Journal of the American Oriental Society* 77 (1957): 1.

95. Gregory, *Tsung-mi and the Sinification of Buddhism*, 108.

96. Ibid., 297.

97. David W. Chappell, "Hermeneutical Phases in Chinese Buddhism," in *Buddhist Hermeneutics*, ed. Donald S. Lopez, Jr., (Honolulu: The Kuroda Institute, University of Hawaii Press, 1988), 175–205.

98. Ibid., 176–177.

99. Ibid.

100. "Critical Buddhism" challenges the very basis of most East Asian schools of Buddhism, particularly those that rely on *tathāgata-garbha* ("womb/embryo of Buddha") teachings. For details see Jamie Hubbard and Paul L. Swanson, ed., *Pruning the Bodhi Tree: the Storm over Critical Buddhism* (Honolulu: University of Hawaii Press, 1997).

101. See, for instance, Jonathan R. Herman, "To Know the Sages Better than They Know Themselves: Chu Hsi's 'Romantic' Hermeneutics" (paper presented at the annual meeting of the American Academy of Religion, Orlando, Florida, November 21–24, 1998); Matthew Kapstein, "Mi-pham's Theory of Interpretation," in *Buddhist Hermeneutics*, ed. Donald S. Lopez, Jr. (Honolulu: The Kuroda Institute, University of Hawaii Press, 1987), 149–174.and Thomas Kasulis, "Truth Words: The Basis of Kukai's Theory of Interpretation," in *Buddhist Hermeneutics*, ed. Donald S. Lopez, Jr. (Honolulu: The Kuroda Institute, University of Hawaii Press, 1987), 257–272.

102. On-cho Ng, "Negotiating the Boundary between Hermeneutics and Philosophy in Early Ch'ing Ch'eng-Chu Confucianism," in *Imagining Boundaries: Changing Confucian Doctrines, Texts, and Hermeneutics*, ed. Kai-wing Chow, On-cho Ng, and John B. Henderson (Albany: State University of New York Press, 1999), 167.

103. Lopez, "Introduction," 10.

104. John C. Maraldo, "Hermeneutics and Historicity in the Study of Buddhism," *The Eastern Buddhist* 19 (Spring 1986): 28.

105. Gadamer, *Truth and Method*, 361.

106. See Emilio Betti, *Die Hermeneutik als allgemeine Methodik der Gesisteswissenschaften*, Philosophie und Geschicte series, Pamphlet Nos. 78–79 (Tubingen: J.C.B. Mohr, 1962).

107. See E. D. Hirsch, Jr., *Validity in Interpretation* (New Haven and London: Yale University Press, 1967).

108. See Alasdaire MacIntyre, *Whose Justice? Which Rationality?* (Notre Dame: University of Notre Dame Press, 1988), 385 ff.

109. See Jean-Francois Lyotard, *The Postmodern Condition: A Report on Knowledge*, trans. Geoff Bennington and Brian Massumi (Minneapolis: University of Minnesota Press, 1979).

110. Ibid., 35.

111. Michel Foucault, "The Order of Discourse," in *The Archaeology of Knowledge*, trans. A. W. Sheridan Smith (New York: Harper & Row, 1972), 215–237.

112. Jacques Derrida, "Structure, Sign and Play in the Discourse of the Human Sciences," in *Writing and Difference* (Chicago: University of Chicago Press, 1978), 278–290.

113. David Tracy, *Plurality and Ambiguity: Hermeneutics, Religion, Hope* (Chicago: The University of Chicago Press, 1987), 83.

114. Edward W. Said, *Orientalism: Western Conceptions of the Orient* (New York: Random House, 1979), 202–203.

115. Ibid., 322.

116. For critical discussions of Said's work see Lisa Lowe, *Critical Terrains: French and British Orientalisms* (Ithaca: Cornell University Press, 1991), ix–x and J. J. Clarke, *Oriental Enlightenment: The Encounter between Asian and Western Thought* (New York: Routledge, 1997), 8–11.

117. Donald S. Lopez, ed., *Curators of the Buddha: The Study of Buddhism under Colonialism* (Chicago: University of Chicago Press, 1995).

118. Lauren Pfister, "Discovering Monotheistic Metaphysics: The Exegetical Reflections of James Legge (1815–1897) and Lo Chung-fan (d. circa 1850)," in *Imagining Boundaries: Changing Confucian Doctrines, Texts, and Hermeneutics*, eds. Kai-wing Chow, On-cho Ng, and John B. Henderson (Albany: State University of New York Press, 1999), 213–254.

119. As with Buddhist Studies so here the recent scholarship is too vast to list in toto. Some notable examples include Laurence G. Thompson, "What is Taoism? (with Apologies to H.G. Creel)," *Taoist Resources* 4 (December 1993): 9–22; Ames, *Wandering at Ease in the Zhuangzi*, 1998; and Livia Kohn and Michael LaFargue, *Lao-tzu and the Tao-te-Ching* (Albany: State University of New York Press, 1998).

120. Richard King, *Orientalism and Religion: Postcolonial Theory, India and 'The Mystic East'* (New York: Routledge, 1999), 135–142 and 156–160.

121. Arran E. Gare, "Understanding Oriental Cultures," *Philosophy East & West* 45 (July 1995): 309–328.

122. Ibid., 316.

123. Ibid., 317–319.

124. Hans-Georg Gadamer, "The Diversity of Europe," in Dieter Misgeld and Graeme Nicholson, eds., *Hans-Georg Gadamer on Education, Poetry, and History: Applied Hermeneutics* (Albany: State University of New York Press, 1992), 235–236.

125. King, *Orientalism and Religion*, 81, italics in the original.

Chapter 2

1. See Ben-Ami Scharfstein, "The Contextualist Fallacy," in *Interpreting Across Boundaries: New Essays in Comparative Philosophy*, ed. Gerald James Larson and Eliot Deutsch (Princeton: Princeton University Press, 1988), 84–97.

2. Tadeusz Skorupski, "*Prajñā*," in *The Encyclopedia of Religion*, ed. Mircea Eliade, Vol. 11 (New York: MacMillan Publishing Company, 1987), 477–481.

3. P. T. Raju, *The Philosophical Traditions of India* (Delhi: Motilal Banarsidass, 1992), 240.

4. Paul Williams, *Mahāyāna Buddhism: The Doctrinal Foundations* (London and New York: Routledge, 1989), 42.

5. See Christian Lindtner, *Nāgārjuniana: Studies in the Writings and Philosophy of Nāgārjuna* (Copenhagen, 1982), 270 and Ian Charles Harris, *The Continuity of Madhyamaka and Yogācāra in Indian Buddhism* (Leiden: E.J. Brill, 1991), 13–15.

6. Skorupski, "*Prajñā*," 481.

7. Snellgrove, *Indo-Tibetan Buddhism*, Vol. 1, 143, note 51.

8. Donald S. Lopez, Jr., *The Heart Sūtra Explained: Indian and Tibetan Commentaries* (Albany: State University of New York Press, 1988), 21–22.

9. *Kleśas* ("defilements") are afflictions marked by greed or desire and so lead to suffering. *Ăsravas* ("outflows") are specific types of *kleśas* which are said to "flow out" from the mind and affect other things. An awakened person is said to have exhausted all "outflows."

10. These powers were sometimes grouped with the "three-fold knowledge" and collectively referred to as the *sadabhijñā* (six "super-knowings").

11. I.B. Horner, trans., *The Collection of the Middle Length Sayings (Majjhima-nikāya)*, vol. 1, The First Fifty Discourses (*Mulapannasa*), the Pali Text Society (London: Luzac & Company, Ltd., 1954), 231.

12. Ibid., 120–121.

13. *Majjhima-nikāya* I.477 and the *Anguttara-nikāya* I.61, quoted in Harris, *The Continuity of Madhyammaka and Yogācāra*, 51–52.

14. *Digha-nikāya* III.219, quoted in Harris, *The Continuity of Madhyamaka and Yogācāra*, 141.

15. Louis de la Vallee Poussin, trans. *L' Abhidharmakośa de Vasubandhu*, Vol. 1 (Bruxelles: Institut Belge des Hautes Etudes Chinoise, 1971–80), 3–4.

16. Padmanabh S. Jaini, "*Prajñā* and *Dṛṣṭi* in the Vaibhāṣika Abhidharma," in *Prajñāpāramitā and Related Systems: Studies in Honor of Edward Conze*, ed. Lewis Lancaster, Berkeley Buddhist Studies Series (Berkeley: U.C. Berkeley Press, 1977), 404–407.

17. Sakurabe Hajime, "Abhidharma," in *Buddhist Spirituality I: Indian, Southeast Asian, Tibetan, Early Chinese*, ed. Takeuchi Yoshinori (New York: The Crossroad Publishing Company, 1995), 74.

18. Alfonso Verdu, *Early Buddhist Philosophy in the Light of the Four Noble Truths* (Delhi: Motital Banarsidass, 1985), 140ff. Such acts disassociate one from specific types of ignorance.

19. Jaini, "*Prajñā* and *Dṛṣṭi* in the Vaibhāṣika Abhidharma," 410.

20. For details see Hirakawa Akira, *A History of Indian Buddhism: from Śākyamuni to Early Mahāyāna*, trans and ed. Paul Groner (Honolulu: University of Hawaii Press, 1990), 270–274.

21. Subhūti means "foremost in peace," a hint that *prajñā* calms discursive thought and brings peace. Connections between Subhūti and *metta* ("loving kindness") in pre-Mahāyāna traditions could also indicate the Mahāyāna emphasis on compassion. See Williams, *Mahāyāna Buddhism*, 45 and 278 (note 4).

22. Some texts speak of a "counterfeit *prajñāpāramitā*" in which a Bodhisattva teaches impermanence and destruction of *dharmas*. See Edward Conze, trans., *The Perfection of Wisdom in Eight Thousand Lines & Its Verse Summary (Aṣṭasāhasrikaprajñāpāramitā-sūtra)* (Bolinas: Four Seasons Foundation, 1973), 19. Such verses refer to Sarvāstivāda analyses of *dharmas* into their arising, persisting, decay, and destruction.

23. Jaini, "*Prajñā* and *dṛṣṭi* in the Vaibhāṣika Abhidharma," 410–412.

24. Conze, *The Perfection of Wisdom in Eight Thousand Lines*, 274.

25. Edward Conze, trans., *The Large Sutra on Perfect Wisdom (with the divisions of the Abhisamayālankāra)* (Berkeley, Los Angeles, London: University of California Press, 1975), 92, 440–441.

26. Ibid., 126.

27. Ibid.

28. Ibid., 475.

29. Conze, *The Perfection of Wisdom in Eight Thousand Lines*, 257.

30. Ibid.

31. Conze, *The Large Sutra on Perfect Wisdom*, 651.

32. Ibid., 638.

33. Conze, *The Perfection of Wisdom in Eight Thousand Lines*, 97.

34. Ibid., 98–99.

35. Conze, *The Large Sutra on Perfect Wisdom*, 325.

36. Ibid., 501–504.

37. The original number of *pāramitās* was six but later texts put the number at ten, adding *upāya*, *praṇidhāna* ("resolution"), *bala* ("power"), and *jñāna*, with the final four being generally considered supplementary.

38. Conze, *The Perfection of Wisdom in Eight Thousand Lines*, 17.

39. Ibid., 100–101.

40. Conze, *The Perfection of Wisdom in Eight Thousand Lines*, 215. Ultimate Truth is "markless"; it cannot be grasped as it has no identifiying "marks" (*lakṣaṇa*—definitive features or characteristics) by which it is known.

41. Such "*prajñā* speak" had tremendous influence on Sengzhao's work, as we shall see.

42. Conze, *The Perfection of Wisdom in Eight Thousand Lines*, 137–138.

43. Jaini, "*Prajñā* and *dṛṣṭi* in the Vaibhāṣika Abhidharma," 403.

44. Garfield, *The Fundamental Wisdom of the Middle Way*, 76.

45. Ibid., 49.

46. Ibid.

47. Ibid., 2.

48. Ibid., 75.

49. Hsueh-li Cheng, trans., *Nāgārjuna's Twelve Gate Treatise* (*Dvādaśamukha śāstra*) (Dordrecht, Holland: D. Reidel, 1982), 54.

50. Garfield, *The Fundamental Wisdom of the Middle Way*, 69.

51. Nāgārjuna attained such mythic status that many works have been falsely attributed to him. The most notable example is the *Mahāprajñāpāramitā śāstra* (Chinese–*Dazhi du lun*), a commentary on the *Pañca*. Critical work by Lamotte and others has cast doubts on this attribution and although the treatise reflects genuine Mādhyamika teachings we cannot treat it as Nāgārjuna's work. See Etienne Lamotte, *Le Traite de la Grand Vertu de Sagesse de Nāgārjuna–Mahāprajñāpāramitāśāstra*, Vol. 1 and 2 (Louvain: Bureaux du Museon, 1944–49; reprint, Institut orientaliste, 1966–76), 491, 614, 734 (page citations are to the reprint edition); Paul Demieville, Review of Lamotte's *Traite*, tome II, *Journal Asiatique* (1950): 375–395; and Robinson, *Early Mādhyamika in India and China*, 34–39.

52. *Kārikā* 26, verses 10–11. See Garfield, *the Fundamental Wisdom of the Middle Way*, 78. Here *jñāna* has the same transforming power as *prajñā* does in the *Prajñāpāramitās* thus it seems to be another name for the same "wisdom."

53. Christian Lindtner, trans., *Bodhisambhāraka* in *Nāgārjuniana: Studies in the Writings and Philosophy of Nāgārjuna* (Copenhagen: Akademisk Forlag, 1982), 228–229, 235.

54. Ibid., 35.

55. See Mervyn Sprung, *Lucid Exposition of the Middle Way: the Essential Chapters from the Prasannapadā of Candrakīrti* (Boulder: Prajna Press, 1979), 32 and C. W. Huntington, Jr., with Geshe Namgyal Wangchen, *The Emptiness of Emptiness: an Introduction to Early Indian Mādhyamika* (Honolulu: University of Hawaii Press, 1989), 157.

56. This classic work of Buddhist literature describes the Bodhisattva path in verse form. Several Sanskrit and Tibetan versions survive. For an English translation see Shantideva, *The Way of the Bodhisattva*, translated by the Padmakara Translation Group (Boston & London: Shambhala Publications Inc., 1997).

57. One example is the *Ratnagotravibhāga*, a text of the *Tathāgata-garbha* ("Womb/embyro of Buddha") tradition, in which *prajñā* is the non-discriminative insight whereby we perceive the *tathāgata-garbha* in all beings. See Jikido Takasaki, *A Study on the Ratnagotravibhāga* (Rome: Instituto Italiano per il Medio ed Estremo Oriente, 1966), 175.

58. For details see Zurcher, *The Buddhist Conquest of China*, 30–80.

59. For a details see Jacques Gernet, *A History of Chinese Civilization*, trans. J. R. Foster (Cambridge: Cambridge University Press, 1982), 173.

60. Ch'en, *Buddhism in China*, 57–61. Together these texts were sometimes referred to as the *san xuan* ("Three Mysteries") for their metaphysical and mystical teachings.

61. Julia Ching, *Chinese Religions* (Maryknoll, NY: Orbis Books, 1993), 98–99.

62. *Qingtan* arose from the practice of *qing yi* ("criticism by the pure"), a method of finding suitable candidates for government posts by matching abilities with functions. For details see "Introduction," in Richard B. Mather, trans., *Shih-shuo Hsin-yu: A New Account of Tales of the World, by Liu I-ch'ing with commentary by Liu Chun* (Minneapolis: University of Minnesota Press, 1976), xxii–xxiii.

63. For profiles of their behavior and thought, see Donald Holzman, "Les sept sages de la foret des bambus et la societe de leur temps," *T'oung-pao* 44 (1956): 317–346; Mather, *Shih-shuo Hsin-yu*, 371ff. and Robert G. Henricks, *Philosophy and Argumentation in Third-Century China: The Essays of Hsi K'ang* (Princeton: Princeton University Press, 1983).

64. This despite the fact that Ge Hong disparaged the *qingtan* gentry as idlers given to "falsely quoting *Laozi* and the *Zhuangzi*." See Zurcher, *The Buddhist Conquest of China*, note 11, 347–348.

65. *Xuanxue* was *not* a-political. During the Eastern Jin, withdrawal for philosophic contemplation was often seen as proof of a person's worthiness to rule. See Charles Holcombe, *In the Shadow of the Han: Literati Thought and Society at the Beginning of the Southern Dynasties* (Honolulu: University of Hawaii Press, 1994), 125–134.

66. Xu Kangsheng, "A Brief Discussion of the '*Xuanxue*' School of the Wei-Jin Period," *Chinese Studies in Philosophy* 13 (Fall 1981): 58–59.

67. *Jinshu*, SBBY 525, *juan* 43, 8a–b.

68. Wang Bi served as a minor official for a time only to be dismissed in 249, dying soon after from some illness. For Wang's biography see the *Sanguo zhi*, *Weishu*, SBBY 510, *juan* 28, 30a. For detailed discussions of Wang's thought see Alan K. L. Chan, *Two Visions of the Way: A Study of the Wang Pi and the Ho-shang Commentaries on the Lao-tzu* (Albany: State University of New York Press, 1991), 15–44 and Marie-Ina Bergeron, *Wang Pi, Philosophe du Non-Avoir*, Varieties Sinologiques–Nouvelle Serie No. 69 (Paris: L'institut Ricci, 1986).

69. Wang Bi, *Laozi zhu*, SBBY 1403, *shang pian*, 1a–b and *xia pian*, 4a.

70. *Wu* could be considered "pure being" (potentia?) provided we remember that it refers to a state lacking concrete form (i.e. "no-thing") rather than Absolute Nothingness.

71. Alan K. L. Chan, *Two Visions of the Way*, 52–55.

72. Ibid., 65–67. Cf. Wang Bi, *Laozi zhu*, SBBY 1403, *shang pian*, 1b; Ariane Rump with Wing-tsit Chan, trans., *Commentary on the Lao-tzu by Wang Pi*, Monographs for the Society for Asian and Comparative Philosophy, no. 6 (Honolulu: The University of Hawaii Press, 1979), 109.

73. Alan K. L. Chan, *Two Visions of the Way*, 8.

74. Guo Xiang was regarded as "second to Wang Bi." For his biography see *Jinshu*, SBBY 526, *juan* 50, 5a–b and the biographical notice in Mather, *Shih-shuo Hsin-yu*, 545.

75. See Guo Xiang, *Zhuangzi zhu*, SBBY 1408–1411. For a partial English translation see Feng Youlan (Fung Yu-lan), "Appendix: Some Characteristics of the Philosophy of Kuo Hsiang," in *Chuang-Tzu: A New Selected Translation with an Exposition of the Philosophy of Kuo Hsiang*, 2nd ed. (New York: Paragon Book Reprint Corp., 1964), 145–157. Guo shaped the text of the *Zhuangzi* as we now have it, editing it down from 52 chapters to the present 33. According to some sources Guo plagiarized an earlier *Zhuangzi* commentary by Xiang Xiu, one of the Seven Worthies. See Mather, *Shih-shuo Hsin-yu*, 100.

76. Guo Xiang, *Zhuangzi zhu*, SBBY 1410, *juan* 7, 29a; Feng, *Chuang-Tzu*, 147.

77. Paul Demieville, "*La Penetration du Bouddhisme dans la tradition philosophique Chinoise*," in *Choix D'Etudes Bouddhiques* (1929–1970) (Leiden: E. J. Brill, 1973), 244.

78. T.2145–68b: 13–15; Feng Youlan, A *History of Chinese Philosophy*, vol. 2, 240. *Xuan pu* was a mythical abode of gods and immortals in the Kunlun Mountains. "Great Oneness" (*taiyi*) refers to the cause of all things, the *taiji* ("Supreme Ultimate"), which is prior to the differentiation into *yin* and *yang*.

79. This essay is now lost but is mentioned in the *Chu sanzang jiji*, T.2145–98a: 20–21.

80. T. 1464–851a: 11–14.

81. As recorded in the *Gaosengzhuan* ("Biographies of Eminent Monks"), T.2509–358a: 12ff. This text, compiled by the scholar Huijiao in 530, is one of our major sources for information on the early Chinese sangha. For details see Arthur Wright, "Biography and Hagiography: Hui-chiao's *Lives of Eminent Monks*," in *Silver Jubilee Volume of the Jimbun-Kagaku-Kenkyusho* (Kyoto: 1954); reprint in *Arthur F. Wright: Studies in Chinese Buddhism*, ed. Robert M. Sommers (New Haven and London: Yale University Press, 1990), 73–111 (page citations are to reprint edition).

82. Tang Yongtong, "On 'Ko-yi,'" the Earliest Method by which Indian Buddhism and Chinese Thought were Synthesized," in *Radhakrishnan: Comparative Studies in Philosophy presented in honour of his Sixtieth Birthday*, trans. M. C. Rogers (London: George Allen and Unwin LTD, 1951), 276–286.

83. Both versions are extant in the *Taishō*. Lokakṣema's version, translated in Loyang in 179, is located at T.224. Zhi Qian's version, translated in Liangzhou over the period from 223–253, is located at T.225.

84. Dharmarakṣa, the "Bodhisattva of Dunhuang," was the most important Buddhist transla-tor until Kumārajīva. For details on his work see Zurcher, *The Buddhist Conquest of China*, 65–70.

85. This *sūtra* was translated into Chinese seven times, six of which are preserved in the *Taisho* (T. 474–479). Of these, two were extant before Kumārajīva's arrival: Zhi Qian's *Weimo jie jing* (T.474, translated between 223–228) and another version by Dharmarakṣa (T.477, translated in 308).

86. Sengrui, a disciple of **Kumārajīva**, refers to "six houses" in a preface to a commentary on the *Vimalakīrti* (preserved in the *Chu sanzang jiji*, T.2145–59a: 1) but gives no information on names or tenets. Huida in his preface to the *Zhaolun* mentions "six or seven schools which then expanded into twelve" but gives no additional information. See T.1858–150b: 7. During the Liu-Song period (420–478) a figure named Tanji wrote a work entitled *Liujia qizong lun* ("Treatise of the Six Houses and Seven Schools") which seems to confirm the number of schools as six or seven but it is lost except for fragments quoted in other works. However, there may have been as many as thirteen or more schools in all.

87. See the *Zhong guan lun su*, ("Commentary on the Middle Treatise"), T.1824–29a: 4-b: 16, and the *Zhonglun su ji* ("Subcommentary on the Middle Treatise," ca. 801–806), T.2255–92c: 12f.

88. Excerpts of Jizang and **Anchō's** accounts are translated in Wing-tsit Chan, *A Source Book in Chinese Philosophy*, 336–342 and Feng Youlan, *A History of Chinese Philosophy*, Vol. 2, 243–258. For details on the schools see Tang Yongtong, *Han Wei liang Jin Nan Bei chao Fojiao shi* [History of Buddhism during the Han, Wei, Jin and Northern and Southern dynasties], Vol. 1 (Peking: 1938), 229–277.

89. Tang Yongtong holds that *benwu* may almost be considered to be a blanket term for Chinese *prajñā* study during this time and Lai regards it as the first and most basic school. See Tang, *History*, 238 and Whalen Lai, "The Early *Prajñā* Schools, especially 'Hsin-wu,' reconsidered," *Philosophy East and West* 32 (January 1983), 62.

90. T.1824–29a: 4–12.

91. T.2255–92c: 16–20.

92. Arthur E. Link, "The Taoist Antecedents of Tao-an's **Prajñā** Ontology," *History of Religions* 9 (1969–70): 200.

93. Kenneth Ch'en, "Neo-Taoism and the **Prajñā** School during the Wei and Chin Dynasties," *Chinese Culture* 1 (1957): 33.

94. Fatai composed several commentaries and corresponded with an official named Xi Chao (dates?) about *benwu*. See his biography at T.2059–354b: 29–355a: 17. Huiyuan's *benwu* views were similar to Daoan's. See Tang, *History*, 239 and Link, "The Taoist Antecedents of Tao-An's **Prajñā** Ontology," 192. Zhi Dun's *benwu* views can be found in his preface to a comparison of the *Aṣṭa* and *Pañca*, preserved in the *Chu sanzang j ji*, T.2145–55f. For an English translation see Leon Hurvitz, "Chih Tun's Notions of *Prajñā*," *Journal of the American Oriental Society* 88 (June 1968): 243–260.

95. Originally named Zhu (Dao) Qian, he was a member of the powerful Wang clan who became a prominent advisor at the Jin court and a great friend of Zhi Dun's. His biography is in the *Gaosengzhuan*, T.2059–347c: 12–348b: 7.

96. T. 1824–29a: 12–14.

97. T. 2255–93b: 1–6.

98. *Rūpa* (form-matter) is one of the five *skandhas* but in the context of this school probably is an abbreviation for all five. It is translated into Chinese as *se*, literally "color."

99. T.1824–29a: 19–21.

100. T.2255–94a: 7–13.

101. Presumably **Anchō** equates the fine "stuff" with the "underlying original nature" although since Jizang does not speak of "coarse" or "fine" he may be speculating. On the other

hand, Anchō may be drawing on Sarvāstivāda notions found in the *Abhidharmakośa* or Sautrāntika notions of two types of *skandhas*, the "gross" and "subtle" (i.e. "*skandhas* of a single flavor"). See Ming-wood Liu, *Madhyamaka Thought in China* (Leiden: E. J. Brill, 1994), 13

102. T. 1824–29a: 22–25.

103. T. 2255–94a: 21–27.

104. T.1824–29a: 25–28.

105. T.2255–94b: 16–21.

106. Zurcher, *The Buddhist Conquest of China*, 102 and Wing-tsit Chan, *A Source Book in Chinese Philosophy*, 341.

107. Zhi Mindu appears to have originated the theory which, according to the *Shishuo xinyu*, he concocted with several other monks as they were crossing the Yangtze (ca. 326–342). This story, though, is dubious. For an English version of the story see Mather, *Shih-shuo Hsin-yu*, 447. Daoheng proclaimed his *xinwu* theory in a debate against *benwu* theorists held in 365. See T.2059–345c: 13–20.

108. T.1824–29b: 3–7.

109. T.2255–94c: 21–25.

110. Fakai's biography is at T.2059–350a: 13–b: 12. He was a senior contemporary of Fashen and Zhi Dun. Wing-tsit Chan lists his "flourishing" as 364 but then says Fakai was a famous doctor during the Liu Song era. Clearly both cannot be correct since the Liu Song began in 420–a full fifty-six years after Fakai's supposed prime. Wing-tsit Chan, *A Source Book in Chinese Philosophy*, 341.

111. Wing-tsit Chan, *A Source Book in Chinese Philosophy*, 341–342; and Tang, *History*, 265.

112. T.2059–357a: 8–b: 17.

113. T.1824–29b: 8–10. Chan says that the scripture quoted is the *Daji jing*.

114. T.2255–95a: 3–7.

115. For his biography see T.2059–350b: 13–28. Like Fakai, Daosui, too, was a medical practitioner and accompanied his teacher Falan to India where he became ill and died.

116. T.1824–29b: 13–14.

117. T. 2255–95b: 1–4.

118. See Demieville, 'La Penetration du Bouddhisme dans la Tradition philosophique Chinoise," 248 and Leon Hurvitz, "The First Systematizations of Buddhist Thought in China," *Journal of Chinese Philosophy* 2 (1975): 370.

119. See Lai, "The Early *Prajñā* Schools," 65.

120. Jizang says that the *benwu*, *benwu yi*, *jise*, and *xinwu* schools all existed before Kumārajīva came to Chang'an (ca. 401) and the other schools were later in time. T.1824–92b: 1–3.

121. For details on "*wu* forms" see Hall and Ames, *Thinking from the Han*, 45–58.

122. Walter Liebenthal, "Chinese Buddhism during the 4th and 5th Centuries," *Monumenta Nipponica* 11 (1955): 77–78. Similar problems also plagued Indian Buddhism. See Edward Conze, *Buddhist Thought in India: Three Phases of Buddhist Philosophy* (London: George Allen & Unwin Ltd., 1962), 122–131.

123. *Benwu* is the most obvious example. Wang Qia (323–358), an educated layman, expresses great confusion over the various *benwu* teachings in a letter to Zhi Dun preserved in the *Guang hengming ji*, T.2103–323a: 7–13.

124. Wing-tsit Chan, A Source Book in Chinese Philosophy, 343.

125. The most detailed biography of Kumārajīva is in the Gaosengzhuan (T.2059–330a–333a: 12), which has been translated into German and English. See Johannes Nobel, "Kumārajīva," Sitzungsberichte der Preussischen Akademie der Wissenschaften, Philosophische-Historiche klasse (Berlin, 1927): 206–233 and Paul Robert Quinn, "The Biography of Kumārajīva, 350–409 A.D.," (M.A. thesis, University of California at Berkeley, 1961), 3–47. Other accounts of Kumārajīva's life are in the Chu sanzang ji ji (T.2145–100a: 23–102a: 13) and the Weishu (Weishu, Seng Lao zhi, SBBY 591, juan 114).

126. Weishu, Seng Lao zhi, SBBY 591, juan 114, 4a; Leon Hurvitz, trans., Wei Shou Treatise on Buddhism and Taoism, an English translation of the Original Chinese text of the Wei-shu CXIV and the Japanese Annotation of Tsukamoto Zenryu, reprinted from Yun Kang, the Buddhist cave-temples of the Fifth century A.D. in North China, Volume 16 Supplement (Kyoto University, Jimbunkgaku Kenkyusho, 1956), 50.

127. Robinson, Early Mādhyamika in India and China, 73–76. Yao Xing requested a new translation of the Pañca while Sengzhao seems to have requested a new version of the Vimalakīrti.

128. Zenryu Tsukamoto, A History of Early Chinese Buddhism: from its Introduction to the Death of Hui-yuan, Volume 1, trans. Leon Hurvitz (Tokyo, New York, San Francisco: Kodansha International Ltd., 1985), 374–375.

129. Zurcher, The Buddhist Conquest of China, 321, note 1.

130. Early translations usually involved only one or two foreign monks who recited the text and their Chinese collaborators who produced the written document. This basic technique prevailed until the fourth century until Daoan established more systematic methods. See Ch'en, Buddhism in China, 365–367.

131. Daoan himself notes this, relating how his chief secretary Huichang at one point remonstrated against making certain changes that deviated from the original Sanskrit. See T.2145–80b: 14ff.

132. T.2145–53a: 29. The "five deviations and three difficulties" refer to the translation guidelines Daoan devised for this translation bureau.

133. T.2145–364b: 2–6; Robinson, Early Mādhyamika in India and China, 80.

134. T.2145–76a: 29–b: 2; Robinson, Early Mādhyamika in India and China, 204.

135. Paul Demieville, "Review of Lamotte's Traite, tome II," Journal Asiatique (1950): 385.

136. J.W. de Jong, "Buddha's Word in China," in Buddhist Studies, ed. Gregory Schopen (Berkeley: Asian Humanities Press, 1979), 89.

137. K. Venkata Ramanan, Nāgārjuna's Philosophy as presented in the Mahā-Prajñāpāramitā Śāstra (Rutland: Charles E. Tuttle Company, 1966; reprint Delhi: Motilal Banarsidass, 1975), 15 (page citations are to the reprint edition).

138. This text, the Dacheng dayi zhang ("Chief Ideas of the Mahāyāna") is located at T.1856. Portions are translated by Richard Robinson in Early Mādhyamika in India and China, 181–195.

139. T.1856–135c: 1; Robinson, Early Mādhyamika in India and China, 183.

140. T.1856–136c: 18–137a: 8; Robinson, Early Mādhyamika in India and China, 188–189.

141. T.1856–135c: 12–13; Robinson, Early Mādhyamika in India and China, 183.

142. T.1856–137a: 10–b: 2; Robinson, Early Mādhyamika in India and China, 189–190.

143. T.1856–135c: 11; Robinson, Early Mādhyamika in India and China, 183.

144. T.1856–138b: 10–14; Robinson, *Early Mādhyamika in India and China*, 195.

145. Robinson, *Early Mādhyamika in India and China*, 34–39.

146. T.1509–257a: 28–29; Lamotte, *Traite*, Vol. 3, 1714.

147. T.1509–197a: 12–13; Lamotte, *Traite*, Vol. 2, 1111.

148. T.1509–205b: 1–5; Lamotte, *Traite*, Vol. 3, 1203.

149. T.1509–250b: 26–28, Lamotte, *Traite*, Vol. 3, 1654.

150. T.1509–752a: 10–12.

151. T.1509–288a: 1–5; Lamotte, *Traite*, Vol. 4, 2066.

152. T.1509–190a: 14 ff.

153. T.1509–370a: 20–24.

154. T.1509–450a: 23–28.

155. T.2059–365a: 9–366a: 29. Portions of the *Gaosengzhuan* biography are translated by Liebenthal in *Chao Lun*, 6–7. Other accounts of Sengzhao's life can be found in the *Fozu lidai tongzai*, T.2036–529c: 25–530a: 13, and the *Lidai sanbao ji*, T.2034–80b: 17–81c: 2, but these add little to Huijiao.

156. Tsukamoto argues for these dates rather than the traditional dates of 384–414. See Tsukamoto Zenryū, "Bukkyō shijoni okeru jōron no igi" ["The Position of the *Zhaolun* in the History of Chinese Buddhism"] in *Jōron Kenkyū*, ed. Tsukamoto Zenryū (Kyoto: Hōzōkan, 1955), 120–121.

157. Liu Yimin likened Sengzhao to the *xuanxue* thinker He Yan. See T.2059–365a: 27.

158. See Ying-shih Yu, "Individualism and the Neo-Taoist Movement," in *Studies in Confucian and Taoist Values*, ed. Donald Munro (Ann Arbor: Center for Chinese Studies, The University of Michigan, 1985), 141–143.

159. Robinson describes him as fond of Neo-Daoism and Liebenthal says he knew Wang Bi's writings. See Robinson, *Early Mādhyamika in India and China*, 123 and Liebenthal, *Chao Lun*, 8. Fukunaga Kōji also speaks of *xuanxue* influence on Sengzhao, particularly Guo Xiang. See Fukunaga Kōji, "Sojō to Rosō shisō" ["Sengzhao and Lao-Zhuang Thought"] in *Jōron Kenkyū*, ed. Tsukamoto Zenryū (Kyoto: Hōzōkan, 1955), 252–271.

160. *Wei shu, Seng Lao zhi*, SBBY 591, *juan* 114, 4b; Hurvitz, trans., *Wei Shou Treatise*, 54.

161. Jizang acknowledges his kinship with Sengzhao in his *Erdi lun* ("Treatise on the Two Truths"), T.1854–92a.

162. See the list in Robinson, *Early Mādhyamika in India and China*, 125.

163. John Kieschnick, *The Eminent Monk: Buddhist Ideals in Medieval Chinese Hagiography*, Kuroda Institute Studies in East Asian Buddhism 10 (Honolulu: University of Hawaii Press, 1997) 112–130.

164. T.1858–153a: 9.

Chapter 3

1. T.2059–365a: 19–26.

2. T.2059–365a: 26–28. Indeed, the essay was so good that "all [in the community] read and savored [it], and each wanted to keep it longer." (365a: 28–29).

3. Hsu Fancheng says that Sengzhao has "nothing original in his thoughts." See Hsu Fancheng, trans., *Three Theses of Seng-Zhao* (Beijing: Chinese Social Sciences Publishing House, 1985), 8.

4. T.1858–153a: 9. The explicitly hermeneutic character of Sengzhao's work shows in his other writings. See "Emptiness of the Non-Absolute" (T.1858–152a: 13–23), "Things Do Not Shift" (T.1858–151a: 13–20) and his "Preface to the Hundred Treatise" (*Ba lun xu*, located at T.2145–77b: 11–19.)

5. Sengzhao explicitly refers to the *Kārikās* only a few times (T.1858–154a: 20–21, possibly 22–23) but is clearly influenced by Nāgārjuna's "neither–nor" approach and use of *prāsaṅga* arguments.

6. This work, the *Bailun* (T.1569, translated in 404) is a refutation of *tīrthika* teachings so it fits very well with Kumārajīva's and Sengzhao's concerns.

7. Robinson, *Early Mādhyamika in India and China*, 124.

8. "If there is that which is known, then there must be that which is not known. [However] since the Sagely Mind is not-knowing, [it] thus has nothing that is not known." (T.1858–153a: 27–28)

9. T.1858–153a: 23 ff.

10. See Whalen Lai, "The Three Jewels in China," in *Buddhist Spirituality: Indian, Southeast Asian, Tibetan, Early Chinese*, ed. Takeuchi Yoshinori (New York: The Crossroad Publishing Company, 1995), 284–289.

11. Henricks, *Philosophy and Argumentation in Third-Century China*, 109. Brackets in original.

12. This term is often a colloquial way of referring to Buddhist and Daoist priests.

13. Wang Bi, *Laozi zhu*, SBBY 1403, *xia pian*, 1b; Rump and Chan, *Commentary on the Lao-tzu by Wang Pi*, 109.

14. Wang Bi, *Zhouyi Lueli*, SBBY 1, *juan* 3, 4b; Feng, *A History of Chinese Philosophy, Volume 2*, 181.

15. When asked why Confucius did not speak of *wu* if he were a Sage while Laozi spoke of it endlessly, Wang replied that Confucius identified with *wu* so thoroughly that he knew it could not be taught. Thus he confined his talk to *you* (being). Laozi and Zhuangzi, on the other hand, were inferior and so spoke of that in which they were deficient. See Mather, *Shih-shuo Hsin-yu*, 96.

16. Guo Xiang, *Zhuangzi zhu*, SBBY 1408, *juan* 5, 13b; Feng, *Chuang-Tzu*, 152.

17. Guo Xiang, *Zhuangzi zhu*, SBBY 1408, *juan* 1, 5a.

18. Guo Xiang, *Zhuangzi zhu*, SBBY 1408, *juan* 3, 17b; Feng, *Chuang Tzu*, 139–140.

19. T.2145–43c: 5–12; Arthur Link, "The Taoist Antecedents of Tao-An's Prajñā Ontology," 204–205.

20. T.2102–16b: 19–20; Liebenthal, *Chao Lun*, 17 (note 76).

21. Guo Xiang, *Zhuangzi zhu*, SBBY 1408, *juan* 2, 17b and 20a.

22. Lai, "The Three Jewels in China," 282–283.

23. T.2059–348b: 20–24. This debate took place in 342.

24. Mather, *Shih-shuo Hsin-yu*, 109.

25. *Weishu*, SBBY 591, *juan* 114, 4b; Hurvitz, *Wei Shou Treatise on Buddhism and Taoism*, 54.

26. T.2059–332c: 8–10; Liebenthal, *Chao Lun*, 3.

27. Lai, "The Three Jewels in China," 284–298. Examples of such "holy men" were Fotudeng and Dharmarakṣa, both of whom gained great fame in the early fourth century for their magical powers.

28. Lu Guang apparently forced Kumārajīva to drink wine, have sexual relations with women, and even ride oxen and horses for his own amusement (!) See Ikeda, *The Flower of Chinese Buddhism*, 45.

29. Yao Xing desired to maintain a lineage of Sages like Kumārajīva and to that end coerced the Kuchean master into having his own harem of ten women. T.2059–332c: 10–15. Although Kumārajīva sired several offspring there is no record of his founding a "Sagely line".

30. T.1858–153a: 9–15.

31. It is unclear what this prophecy is. Both the *Aṣṭa* and the *Pañca* refer to the *prajñā* teachings coming north. See Conze, *The Large Sutra on Perfect Wisdom*, 327–328. Whalen Lai has suggested, however, that this passage may refer to Pre-Han Chinese prophecies concerning the rise of a "Black Messiah" in the North which continued to resurface through the fifth and sixth centuries C.E. For details see Whalen Lai, "The Age of Aquarius: Tsou Yen on the Beginning and the End," (paper presented at the IRFWP conference, Washington D.C., 25–29 November 1997).

32. T.1858–153a: 15–20.

33. For example, Sengzhao speaks of Yao Xing's "Dao" and "de," which seem to be obvious references to the title and text of the *Laozi* (*Daode jing*).

34. Aśoka (274–232 B.C.E.) was the legendary Mauryan emperor credited with spreading Buddhism throughout the India and has long been held up as the ideal Buddhist ruler. See N.A. Nikam and Richard McKeon, ed. and trans., *The Edicts of Aśoka* (Chicago: The University of Chicago press, 1959). Yao Xing may have fancied himself as a latter-day Aśoka, since he named his main translation center the Xiaoyu ("Aśoka") compound.

35. Robinson, *Early Mādhyamika in India and China*, 124.

36. See also the first section of "*Nirvāṇa* is Nameless," a veritable dedication to Yao Xing in which Sengzhao praises the king's insight and virtue while emphasizing his closeness to Kumārajīva. Sengzhao says that together they were able to "kindle the flame of dark [learning] in order to enlighten our period of decay." T.1858–157a: 26–27; Liebenthal, *Chao Lun*, 102.

37. Both versions were retranslated by Kumārajīva but although Sengzhao was inspired by his master's new translation and exposition of the *Pañca* (the *Moho panruo polomi jing*, T.223) and does quote it in "*Prajñā* is Not-knowing," he seems to prefer the earlier *Fangguang*.

38. T.1858–153c: 12. Robinson notes the same reference may also be to the *Mahāparinirvāṇa sūtra* or the *Upasaka śīla sūtra*. See Robinson, *Early Mādhyamika in India and China*, 308 (note 62).

39. Robinson lists twenty-four references to Chinese texts (versus nineteen to Buddhist ones) in "*Prajñā* is Not-knowing" whereas Liebenthal lists eighteen references to Chinese texts and seventeen to Buddhist texts.

40. T.1858–153b: 2–8.

41. Guo Xiang, *Zhuangzi zhu*, SBBY 1408, *juan* 3, 10b.

42. Specifically at T.1858–153b: 2. See Liebenthal, *Chao Lun*, 67 (note 265).

43. T.1859–175c: 1–6. The line from *"Prajñā* is Not-knowing" is T.1858–153a: 10–11.

44. DNZ 2.B 23.4—434b: 15–16. The line from Sengzhao is T.1858–153b: 11–12.

45. T.1858–152a–153a: 6. This essay, the second in the *Zhaolun*, was written in 409, a few years after *"Prajñā* is Not-knowing," and reflects greater familiarity with Mādhyamika thought.

46. T. 1858–152a: 15–23.

47. Both Jizang and Anchō argue that Sengzhao's views are the same as the *benwu* and *jise* views of Daoan and Zhi Dun. See T.1824–29a: 11–12 and T.2255–94a: 27–28. Liebenthal, though says that Sengzhao is criticizing Zhi Dun. See Liebenthal, *Chao Lun*, 55 (note 184).

48. Huida considers the first objection (T.1858–153b: 19–26) to be a reference to the views of Zhi Dun. See DNZ 2.B 23.4—435c: 7. Liebenthal, however, believes that the eighth objection (T.1858–154b: 27–26) to be an allusion to Zhi Dun. See Liebenthal, *Chao Lun*, 78 (note 328).

49. T.2145–47a: 13–15.

50. T.1858–153a: 20–23.

51. Kumārajīva and Sengzhao have been considered the "founders" of the *Sanlun* ("Three Treatise", Chinese Mādhyamika) school, although they have no direct connection to later *Sanlun* thinkers. Jizang's claims that there was a "school of Kumārajīva and Sengzhao" (T.1824–29a: 12) is a retrospective fiction.

52. Guo Xiang, *Zhuangzi zhu*, SBBY 1408, *juan* 2, 7b; Watson, *The Complete Works of Chuang Tzu*, 58.

53. This plagued the transmission and translation of Buddhist texts into Chinese for many years. The *Dacheng qixin lun* ("Awakening of Faith in the Mahāyāna," T.1666), a sixth century text, notes that many Chinese "looked upon the wordiness of extensive discourses as troublesome, but their minds took pleasure in comprehensive, tersely worded [discourse] which held much meaning." T.1666–575c: 14–15; Yoshito S. Hakeda, trans., *The Awakening of Faith* (New York & London: Columbia University Press, 1967), 27.

54. These divisions are not in either the *Taishō* or *Dai Nihon Zokuzōkyō* but are based on the commentaries by Huida (DNZ 2.B 23.4–432b: 12–17) and Yuankang (T.1859–174c: 22ff). Liebenthal and Robinson's earlier English translations preserve them and I follow their lead.

55. T.1858–153a: 8–9.

56. T.1858–153a: 21 and 23 respectively.

57. T.1858–153a: 27–b: 2.

58. T.1858–153b: 2–8.

59. T.1858–153b: 8–15.

60. Scripture is not a valid source of knowledge in Mahāyāna circles. Since the time of Dignāga (400–485) the only valid forms of knowledge have been direct sense perception (*pratyakṣa*) and inference (*anumāna*). See Richard P. Hayes, *Dignāga on the Interpretation of Signs* (Dordrecht and Boston: Kluwar Academic Publishers, 1988), 178–183. However, as Cabezon notes, in practice scriptural authority has not been questioned and is upheld as a definitive authority. See Cabezon, *Buddhism and Language*, 91.

61. T.1858–153b: 15–18.

62. See George Makdisi, "The Scholastic Method in Medieval Education: an Inquiry into its Origins in Law and Theology," *Speculum* 497 (1974): 640–661.

63. Cabezon, *Buddhism and Language*, 85–86.

64. T.1858–153b: 8.

65. *Zhuangzi*, SBBY 1408, *juan* 1, 15a–b; Watson, *The Complete Works of Chuang Tzu*, 40.

66. As per Heidegger, I mean "work" here as "working," the opening/disclosing power of *alētheia* ("truth").

67. *Matthews Chinese-English Dictionary*, rev. American ed., entry 3601, line 38.

68. *Giles' Chinese-English Dictionary*, second ed., revised and enlarged, entry 6409. *Giles'* lists *dian*, "to fall, overthrow; bungling, confusion" (entry 11, 193) as a synonym. Interestingly, Giles' entry 6411, combines the phrase *kuangyan* into one character *kuang*, defining it as "lies, falsehood, to deceive."

69. *Zhongwen da cidian*, 1962 ed., entry 20729.13.

70. *The New Nelson Japanese-English Character Dictionary*, revised ed., s.v. , entry 3562. *Nelson* also lists three additional compounds which include *kyōgen: kyōgen jisatsu* ("faked suicide"), *kyōgen sakusha* ("dramatist, playwright"), and *kyōgenshi* ("Noh comedian").

71. *Zhuangzi*, SBBY 1410, *juan* 7, 27a–b; Watson, *The Complete Works of Chuang Tzu*, 242.

72. T.1858–153a: 9–15.

73. T.1856–135c: 11. This *kuang* is the form that contains both characters in the phrase *kuangyan*; it is the same character as *Giles'*, entry 6411. **Kumārajīva's** exchange with Huiyuan took place in 405, after Sengzhao had written "*Prajñā* is Not-knowing." Is **Kumārajīva** borrowing his disciple's phrasing?

74. Martin Palmer, trans., *The Book of Chuang Tzu* (London and New York: Arkana, Penguin Books Ltd., 1996), 194.

75. Robinson, *Early Mādhyamika in India and China*, 213 and 216.

76. Victor H. Mair, *Wandering on the Way: Early Taoist Tales and Parables of Chuang Tzu* (New York: Bantam Books, 1994), 218–219.

77. James Legge, trans., *The Texts of Taoism: the Sacred Books of China*, Vol. 2 (New York: Dover Publications, Inc., 1962), 68.

78. Liu, *Madhyamaka Thought in China*, 46.

79. Liebenthal, *Chao Lun*, 66 and Fang-cheng Hsu, *Three Theses of Seng-Zhao*, bilingual ed. (Beijing: Chinese Social Sciences Publishing House, 1985), 48.

80. The basic inadequacy of language in ultimate matters is a common theme in religious traditions, and I speak of this in more detail later in this chapter.

81. See Jordan Paper, *The Spirits are Drunk: Comparative Approaches to Chinese Religion* (Albany: State University of New York Press, 1995), 52–60.

82. N. J. Girardot, *Myth and Meaning in Early Taoism: The Theme of Chaos (hun-tun)* (Berkeley/Los Angles/London: University of California Press, 1974), 270–271.

83. Liebenthal borrows this description from Kant to speak of Sengzhao's "true language" (*zhenyan*) in the other essays in the *Zhaolun*.

84. Zurcher, *The Buddhist Conquest of China*, 89.

85. Alan K. L. Chan, *Two Visions of the Way*, 22–24. This movement has its roots in Pre-Han Confucian, Legalist and Moist views, and was quite strong in the Wei-Jin era. Even *xuanxue* thinkers such as Guo Xiang were deeply influenced by *mingjiao* concerns.

86. Quoted in Chad Hanson, *Language and Logic in Ancient China* (Ann Arbor: The University of Michigan Press, 1983), 84–85.

87. Ibid., 87.

88. *Zhou Yi, Xuanci shang*, SBBY 3, *juan* 7, 1b and 2b–3a; Richard Wilhelm and Cary F. Baynes, trans., *The I Ching, or Book of Changes* (New York: Bollingen Foundation Inc., 1950; reprint, Princeton: Princeton University Press, 1990), 287 and 293–294 (page citations are to the reprint edition).

89. The extent to which Sengzhao was familiar with the *mingjiao* is difficult to determine, although he clearly argues against their views in Part 3 of his essay. For details see Sohei Ichimura, "The Sino-Indian Trans-Cultural Method of Mādhyamika Dialectic: Nāgārjuna to Seng-chao to Chi-ts'ang," in *Buddhist Heritage in India and Abroad*, ed. G. Kuppuram and K. Kumudamani (Delhi: Dundeep Prakashan, 1992), 239–266.

90. As Zhuangzi says, "The fish trap exists because of the fish; once you've got the fish you can forget the trap. The rabbit snare exists because of the rabbit; once you've got the rabbit, you can forget the snare. Words exist because of the meaning; once you've gotten the meaning, you can forget the words." *Zhuangzi*, SBBY 1411, *juan* 9, 6a; Watson, *The Complete Works of Chuang Tzu*, 302.

91. T.1858–153a: 23 and 153c: 27. These are the only places where Sengzhao actually uses the term "wild words."

92. *A Dictionary of Literary Terms and Literary Theory*, 4th ed., s.v. "Allusion."

93. T.1858–153b: 6.

94. *Laozi Daode jing*, SBBY 1403, *shang pian*, 13b–14a; Lau, *Lao Tzu: Tao Te Ching*, 82.

95. This is to a passage in the *Da Zhuan* ("Great Commentary"), a.k.a. the *Xici*. See Wang Bi, *Zhou Yi Xici shang*, SBBY 3, 3a; Wilhelm and Baynes, *The I Ching*, 294–295.

96. Both Huida (DNZ 2.B 23.4—434d) and Yuankang (T.1859–177c: 16–18), who generally are very good at picking up allusions, insist on this Buddhist point.

97. T.1858–153c: 24–26.

98. *Kārikās* 24: 9–10; Garfield, *The Fundamental Wisdom of the Middle Way*, 68.

99. *Zhuangzi*, SBBY 1411, *juan* 9, 7a; Watson, *The Complete Works of Chuang Tzu*, 304.

100. T.312–719b: 21–24. See Robinson, *Early Mādhyamika in India and China*, 309 (note 72). The *Taishō* version of this *sūtra* dates to the eleventh century but includes the earlier translation completed by Dharmarakṣa in 280.

101. T.1858–153c: 27.

102. T.1858–154b: 15–18.

103. *Laozi Daode jing*, SBBY 1403, *shang pian*, 2b–3a and *xia pian*, 12a–b; Lau, *Lao Tzu: Tao Te Ching*, 60 and 117.

104. *Laozi Daode jing*, SBBY 1403, *shang pian*, 21a and *xia pian*, *zhang* 48, 7b; Lau, *Lao Tzu Tao Te Ching*, 96 and 109.

105. *Zhuangzi*, SBBY 1408, *juan* 3, 1b–4a; Watson, *The Complete Works of Chuang Tzu*, 77–80. Technically Zhuangzi is speaking of the "true person" (*zhenren*) in this passage.

106. Arthur Waley, *The Way and its Power: A Study of the Tao Te Ching and its Place in Chinese Thought* (New York: Grove Weidenfeld, 1958), 175. Waley cites *Laozi* 25 as a prime example.

107. T.1858–153b: 9–13.

108. Robinson, *Early Mādhyamika in India and China*, 131.

109. T.1858–153b: 19–26.

110. Robinson, *Early Mādhyamika in India and China*, 132.

111. T.1858–154a: 10–16. Note that I leave out Sengzhao's citations from the *Fangguang*.

112. Robinson, *Early Mādhyamika in India and China*, 133. My outline differs from Robinson's slightly.

113. Robinson, *Early Mādhyamika in India and China*, 135.

114. Contradiction and paradox differ considerably. A contradiction is a denial or direct opposition of a statement. A paradox embraces what *appear* to be contradictory ideas but asserts their truth.

115. *Hamlet*, Signet Classic edition, ed. Edward Hubler (New York: The New America Library, Inc., 1963), 3.4.179.

116. *A Dictionary of Literary Terms and Literary Theories*, 4th ed., s.v. "paradox."

117. Sohei Ichimura speaks of Sengzhao's approach as a "paradoxical method." See Sohei Ichimura, "On the Paradoxical Method of the Chinese **Mādhyamika**: Seng-Chao and the *Chao-Lun* Treatise," *Journal of Chinese Philosophy* 19 (1992): 51–71.

118. T.1858–153a: 27–28.

119. T.1858–153b: 1.

120. T.1858–153c: 27–28.

121. T.1858–154a: 3.

122. Robinson, *Early Mādhyamika in India and China*, 133–134.

123. *A Dictionary of Literary Terms and Literary Theories*, 4th ed., s.v. "metaphor."

124. Lakoff and Johnson, *Metaphors We Live By*, 3 ff.

125. In India, knowing is described as a kind of light in the *Upaniṣads* and the central act of worship (*darśan*–to see and be seen), which is how one knows the gods, requires light and nearness. In China, the basic organic worldview encourages notions of the Sage as participating in Dao by "touching" the myriad transformations. Moreover, terms often used for types of knowing (e.g. *ming*, *zhao*) are based on light.

126. As, for example, in descriptions of *prajñāpāramitā* as both a light and as *ākāśa* (pure all-embracing space).

127. T.1858–153a: 8.

128. T.1858–153a: 29–b: 1.

129. T.1858–153b: 1–2.

130. T.1858–153b.

131. T.1858–154c: 6–10.

132. Charles Dickens, *A Christmas Carol*, a facsimile edition of the autograph manuscript in the Pierpont Morgan Library (New York: The Pierpont Morgan Library, 1993), 12.

133. *A Dictionary of Literary Terms and Literary Theories*, 4th ed., s.v. "puns."

134. T.1858–154b: 27–28.

135. Cf. the Buddhist idea of *āśraya parāvṛtti* ("reversal of the basis") and Daoist notion of *fan* ("return," the way Dao moves.) Sengzhao speaks of something similar when he says that *prajñā*'s "not-knowing" is a "reversal of illuminating." T.1858–153c: 4.

136. Sengzhao sprinkles this pun at various places throughout the treatise. See T.1858–153b: 3 and 4–5, 154a: 8, 24–26 and c: 20–21.

137. Hurvitz, *Scripture of the Lotus Blossom of the Fine Dharma*, 110 and 115. Kumārajīva's version (T.262) lacks this passage but Dharmarakṣa's version uses the same image. See T.263–85c: 20.

138. Michael A. Sells, *Mystical Languages of Unsaying* (Chicago and London: The University of Chicago Press, 1994), 63. Do Sufis attain *prajñā*?

139. See Philip B. Yampolsky, trans., *The Platform Sutra of the Sixth Patriarch: the Text of the Tun-Huang Manuscript* (New York: Columbia University Press, 1967), 130–132. For mirror imagery in Buddhism see Alex Wayman, "The Mirror as a Pan-Buddhist Metaphor-Simile," *History of Religions* 13 (1974): 251–270.

140. *Zhuangzi*, SBBY 1408, *juan* 3, 19a; Watson, *The Complete Works of Chuang Tzu*, 97.

141. T.1858–153b: 2.

142. T.1858–153b: 3.

143. T.1858–154c: 6.

144. Sells, *Mystical Languages of Unsaying*, 63.

145. Kristofer Schipper, *The Taoist Body*, trans. Karen C. Duval (Berkeley and Los Angeles: University of California Press, 1993), 171.

146. Ibid., 172.

147. Harold H. Oshima, "A Metaphorical Analysis of the Concept of Mind in the *Chuang-tzu*," in *Experimental Essays on Chuang-tzu*, ed. Victor H. Mair (Honolulu: The University of Hawaii Press, 1983), 74–75, 79.

148. As Heidegger notes, "objects" only appear when *dasein* assumes a particular attitude towards the world, an attitude that he calls "thematizing." See Heidegger, *Being and Time*, 414–415.

149. T.1858–154c: 19–22.

150. As Demieville observes, neither Liebenthal nor Tsukamoto note that Sengzhao borrows the phrase from Zhuangzi. Paul Demieville, Review of *Jōron Kenkyū* by Tsukamoto Zenryū, *T'oung Pao* 45 (1957): 229.

151. T.1858–153a: 23.

152. *Zhuangzi*, SBBY 1408, *juan* 2, 10b; Watson, *The Complete Works of Chuang Tzu*, 61.

153. Roger J. Corless, *The Vision of the Buddha: the Space under the Tree* (New York: Paragon House, 1989), 217.

154. Steven T. Katz, "Mystical Speech and Mystical Meaning," in *Mysticism and Language*, ed. Steven T. Katz (New York and Oxford: Oxford University Press, 1992), 7.

155. Ibid., 7.

156. Francis X. Clooney, *Theology After Vedānta: an Experiment in Comparative Theology* (Albany: State University of New York Press, 1993), 198–199.

157. Kuang-ming Wu, *Chuang Tzu: World Philosopher at Play* (New York: The Crossroad Publishing Company & Scholars Press, 1982), 33.

158. Ibid., 34–35.

159. In "Emptiness of the Unreal" Sengzhao says "Ultimate Truth is Alone and Pure, outside [the reach] of *mingjiao*. How can it be distinguished by words!" (T.1858–152a: 26–27) and in "Things Do Not Shift" he reminds us that "the Ultimate of stillness and motion is never easy to put into words." (T.1858–151a: 15). Both essays are also replete with paradoxes and puns, and Sengzhao continues to use "chain arguments" in them, although not as

frequently. "*Nirvāṇa* is Nameless" poses more problems, as it is at least partly spurious but the title suggests Sengzhao is still operating on the same basic view of language.

160. T.1858–151a: 14 and 152c: 29 respectively.

161. As Sengzhao says in "Emptiness of the Unreal," "This phenomenon is one yet is explained dually. The words look as if not the same but if you understand where they are the same then they have no differences even though they are not the same." T.1858–152c: 13–15.

162. *Gongan* (lit. "public cases") are various anecdotes, dialogues, or paradoxical statements and questions (e.g. "What is the sound of one hand clapping?"). Typically, a master assigns a *gongan* to a student in order to push the student to a deeper level of insight. In the earliest stages of Chan history there were no set koans but during the Song dynasty particularly famous stories and sayings of great masters were collected and systematized in large volumes. For details see Heinrich Dumoulin, *Zen Buddhism: A History—Volume 1, India and China*, trans. James W. Heisig and Paul Knitter (New York: Macmillan Publishing Company, 1988), 245–261.

163. Steven T. Katz, "Mystical Speech and Mystical Meaning," 6–7.

164. Liebenthal, *Chao Lun*, vii.

165. DNZ 2.1.4: 294b; Liebenthal, *Chao Lun*, 40–41.

166. Dumoulin, *Zen Buddhism: A History. Volume 1*, 73.

167. Ibid. Dumoulin uses Wade-Giles romanization and does not italicize *prajñā* nor use diacritics.

168. Sells, *Mystical Languages of Unsaying*, 2.

169. William James regards ineffability as a defining mark of mystical states of consciousness. See William James, *The Varieties of Religious Experience: a Study in Human Nature* (Longmans, Green, and Co., 1902; reprint, New York: Viking Penguin Inc., 1982), 380 ff. (page citations are to the reprint edition). For a more recent discussion see Bimal Krishna Matilal, "Mysticism and Ineffability: Some Issues of Logic and Language," in Steven T. Katz, ed. *Mysticism and Language* (New York and Oxford: Oxford University Press, 1992), 143.

170. T.1858–153a: 21.

171. *Zhuangzi*, SBBY 1408, *juan* 1, 14a; Watson, *The Complete Works of Chuang Tzu*, 40.

Chapter 4

1. T.1858–154c: 24–157a: 11 and DNZ 2.1.1 315c–317c.

2. Schleiermacher, "General Hermeneutics," 82.

3. Liebenthal, *Chao Lun*, 41.

4. Sengzhao himself remarks on this fact in his reply to Liu, T.1858–155b: 26–27.

5. See *Zhuangzi*, SBBY 1408, *juan* 3, 8a–b; Watson, *The Complete Works of Chuang Tzu*, 83–84.

6. Kieschnick, *The Eminent Monk*, 122–123.

7. The exchange between Huiyuan and Kumārajīva took place over the period from 405 or 406 to 409 and was later collected under the title *Dacheng dayi zhang* ("Chief Ideas of

the Mahāyāna"), T.1856. For a good scholarly overview see R. G. Wagner, "The Original Structure of the Correspondence between Shih Hui-yuan and Kumārajīva," *Harvard Journal of Asiatic Studies* 31 (1971): 28–48.

8. Liu and Sengzhao's letters appear in the *Taishō* and the *Dai Nihonzokuzōkyō* and in the commentaries under separate titles. I follow Liebenthal, however, in treating the letters as two parts of a single text.

9. "*Interpretation, we will say, is the work of thought which consists in deciphering the hidden meaning in the apparent meaning, in unfolding the levels of meaning implied in the literal meaning.*" Paul Ricoeur, "Existence and Hermeneutics," in *The Conflict of Interpretations*, ed. Don Ihde (Evanston: Northwestern University Press, 1974), 13. Italics in the original.

10. Huiyuan himself was in awe of Lushan, noting that it was home to a Daoist immortal in antiquity and a great healer in the Han. According to legend An Shigao had visited Lushan where he converted a *naga* to Buddhism—a tradition commemorated in Huiyuan's day by a cult and a chapel. See Zurcher, *The Buddhist Conquest of China*, 208.

11. T.2059–361a: 28–29.

12. Huiyuan was a great defender of his Buddhist faith, as witnessed by his famous essay *Shamen bujing wangzhe lun* ("On the *Śramaṇa* not Offering Obeisance to the King"), T.2102–29c–32b.

13. Zurcher, *The Buddhist Conquest of China*, 211–212.

14. Ch'en, *Buddhism in China*, 105–106.

15. Zurcher, *The Buddhist Conquest of China*, 330.

16. His epithet *Yimin* ("to leave behind the masses" or "remnant") was often given to those who refused to accept office under a new dynasty. It is perhaps best translated at "Liu the Recluse." Sometimes it is prefaced with the additional title *yinshi*–"retired scholar."

17. T.2103–304a: 18–b: 16.

18. Liu's retirement was occasioned by the activities of Huan Xuan (369–404), a powerful military leader from the central regions who led various armed uprisings during the late fourth century in his quest to found a new dynasty. See Zurcher, *The Buddhist Conquest of China*, 154 ff.

19. Zurcher, *The Buddhist Conquest of China*, 217. Some sources say Liu dwelt on Lushan for twelve/thirteen years.

20. T.1858–155a: 5–8.

21. This practice is detailed in the *Pratyupanna-buddha-saṃmukhāvasthita-samādhi sūtra*, an early Mahāyāna text that contains some of the first known references to the cult of Amitābha. Lokakṣema translated it in 179 and it was this version (*Panzhou sanmei jing*, T.417) that was known on Lushan.

22. Zurcher, *The Buddhist Conquest of China*, 220–221.

23. T.2103–304b: 8 ff; Zurcher, *The Buddhist Conquest of China*, 221.

24. T.1858–155c: 23–27.

25. The text of this vow is preserved in Huiyuan's biography in the *Gaoseng zhuan*, T.2059–358c: 22–359a: 21; Zurcher, *The Buddhist Conquest of China*, 244–245.

26. T.1858–154c: 27.

27. Liu does, however, struggle with several hermeneutic difficulties in his letter to Sengzhao.

28. The Lushan community included many lay disciples but Liu seems to have been the first and foremost among them. Huiyuan consistently singled him out, personally appointing Liu to compose the community's vow to **Amitābha**.

29. T.1858–155a: 10–11.

30. T.1858–155c: 21–22.

31. For details of his life see his biography in the *Gaosengzhuan*, T.2059–366b: 20–367a: 28.

32. This date is controversial. Most scholars agree that it was 408 but Mano **Senryū** maintains that Daosheng showed Sengzhao's essay to Liu in 407 while Seiichi Kiriya says that this occurred in 410. See Mano **Senryū**, "Chronology of the History of Ideas in the Eastern Tsin," appendix in *Jōron Kenkyū*, ed. Tsukamoto **Zenryū** (Kyoto: **Hōzōkan**, 1955), 11 and Seiichi Kiriya, "On the Date and Composition of Seng-chao's '*Da Liu Yi-min Shu*'," *Indogaku Bukkyōgaku Kenkyū* 15 (December 1966): 180–181.

33. T.2059–365a: 26–29.

34. T.1858–155a: 11–15.

35. T.1858–155b: 18–21.

36. For instance, T.1858–155a: 18–20 and 27, and 155b: 21.

37. Mano **Senryū** holds that Liu wrote Sengzhao in 408 while Seiichi Kiriya maintains that Liu wrote his letter in 410. See Mano **Senryū**, "Chronology of the History of Ideas in the Eastern Tsin," 11 and Seiichi Kiriya, "On the Date of Composition of Seng-chao's '*Da Liu Yi-min Shu*',' 181.

38. Liebenthal, *Chao Lun*, 41.

39. T.1858–154c: 28–155a: 20.

40. T.1858–155a: 16.

41. T.1858–155a: 27.

42. T.1858–155a: 17–18.

43. T.1858–155a: 14.

44. T.1858–155a: 5–6 and 8–10.

45. T.1858–155b: 2.

46. T.1858–155a: 29–b: 1. Liebenthal says that Liu's phrasing here borrows from Huiyuan's description of the Pure Land in a document now preserved in the *Chu sanzang jiji*, T.2145–65c (the phrases Liebenthal cites from 55b are actually from Zhi Dun's preface to translations of the *Aṣṭa* and the *Pañca*). See Liebenthal, *Chao Lun*, 86 (note 372).

47. T.1858–155a: 18–20.

48. "*Prajñā* is Not-knowing" section II.4, T.1858–153b: 8 and 11.

49. T.221–140c: 15. Cited by Sengzhao at T.1858–153b: 14–15.

50. Sengzhao seems to address his reply to this question to Liu alone while his replies to the other questions seem to be aimed at the entire Lushan community. See T.1858–156a: 8 ff. and b: 5 ff.

51. T.1858–155a: 28.

52. We might contrast Liu's tone in this passage with that of Sengzhao's fourth "opponent" in "*Prajñā* is Not-knowing." See T.1858–154a: 28–b: 1. In each instance Sengzhao's opponent is challenging him by proposing two alternative explanations but Liu is less deferential.

53. He refers to them as "those who doubt [your treatise]." T.1858–155b: 5.

54. Sengzhao's reply to Question 1 in "*Prajñā* is Not-knowing," T.1858–153c: 9.

55. From Sengzhao's reply to Question 5 in *"Prajñā* is Not-knowing," T.1858—154b: 6–7.
56. T.1858–155b: 17–18.
57. T.1858–155b: 18.
58. T.1858–155b: 19–20.
59. Some traditions claim Huiyuan was an adherent of the *faxing* ("Dharma-nature") school while Sengzhao was an adherent of the *Shixiang* ("True Mark") school. However, these schools did not arise until later.
60. T.1858–155b: 20.
61. More literally: "[we] regret not attaining along with [your] honored self sameness [at this time]." I read this as Liu's expression of regret at both the geographical and philosophical distance between Sengzhao and himself.
62. See, for instance, Sengzhao's reply to the Third "Objection", T.1858–154a: 7–26.
63. For details see Graham, *Disputers of the Tao*, 167–170 and Hanson, *Language and Logic in Ancient China*, especially Chapters Three and Four.
64. Liebenthal translates this line as "I confess to having never been able to understand this abstruse theory." See Liebenthal, *Chao Lun: the Treatises of Seng-Chao*, 84.
65. It seems clear that for the practitioners of *buddhānusmṛti* on Lushan, Sukāvatī was a real place of future rebirth but to which they could also be transported when in *samādhi*.
66. Guo Xiang, *Zhuangzi zhu*, SBBY 1408, *juan* 1, 5b and 6b.
67. T.1858–155a: 29–b: 5.
68. This idea seems to be based on the Daoist image of a judge in the nether world deciding the fate of the "soul." Yet a passage in Liu's "Vow" describes the same idea in terms of the principles of causality (*pratītya-samutpāda*?) and karma. See T.2059–358c: 27 and Liebenthal, *Chao Lun*, 86 (note 373).
69. T.1858–154c: 16–18.
70. T.1858–155b: 5–11.
71. T.1858–155b: 11–18.
72. The "Four Treatises" (*Kārikās*, "Twelve Topic Treatise," "Hundred Treatise" and *Dazhi du lun*) form the core of Chinese **Mādhyamika**, which is known either as the "Four Treatise School" (*Silun zong*) or "Three Treatise School" (*Sanlun zong*) depending upon whether the *Dazhi du lun* is accorded primary status.
73. T.1858–155c: 7–18.
74. T.1858–155b: 23–26.
75. Mano Senryū, "Chronology of the History of Ideas in the Easter Tsin," 12; Robinson, *Early Mādhyamika in India and China*, 135 and Liebenthal, *Chao Lun*, 88.
76. Seiichi Kiriya, " On the Date of Composition of Seng-chao's '*Da Liu Yi-min shu*'," 181.
77. See note 6 above.
78. T.474–521a: 26 ff. and T.475–539b: 25ff. This allusion foreshadows Sengzhao's announcement that he is sending a copy of his *Vimalakīrti* commentary along with his reply. See T.1858–155c: 29–156a: 1.
79. T.1858–155c: 7.
80. *Nianfo sanmei yong*. This is actually the name of an entire collection of songs written by members of the Lushan community and seems to have been directly related to their worship of **Amitābha**.

81. T.1858–155b: 29–c: 1. This is Sengzhao's way of reassuring Liu of their closeness as "friends in Dao."

82. T.1858–153a: 14–15.

83. Further evidence of Sengzhao exerting his authority can be found in his comparing Chang'an to Vulture Peak and expressing his wish that those on Lushan might join the Chang'an community. T.1858–155c: 10 and 20–21 respectively. Although Lushan was a holy mountain there is no doubt that Vulture Peak was holier (more powerful) and it is generally the case that in social situations, the one who invites another to join is the "superior" party.

84. T.1858–156a: 15–16.

85. T.1858–156c: 6–8.

86. T.1858–154a: 24–26.

87. T.1858–156b: 7–8 and 156c: 28.

88. T.1858–156b: 25–28.

89. Robinson, *Early Mādhyamika in India and China*, 135–137.

90. T.1858–156a: 6–7.

91. T.1858–156b: 5.

92. T.1858–157a: 5–6.

93. T.1858–157a: 6–11.

94. T.1858–156a: 2–4.

95. T.1858–156a: 6–7.

96. See Guo Xiang, *Zhuangzi zhu*, SBBY 1410, *juan* 9, 6a; Watson, *The Complete Works of Chuang Tzu*, 302 and Wang Bi, *Zhou Yi lueli*, SBBY 3, *juan di shi*, 9a–b.

97. T.1858–156a: 17–18.

98. See *Zhuangzi*, SBBY 1409, *juan* 5, 19a; Watson, *The Complete Works of Chuang Tzu*, 154.

99. T.1858–156b: 5.

100. T.1858–156b: 5–8.

101. "The Great Square has no corners," and "Forseeing is the flowery embellishment of Dao and the beginning of folly." See *Laozi Daodejing*, SBBY 1403, *xia pian*, 4a–b and 1a–b; Lau, *Lao Tzu: Tao Te Ching*, 102 and 99.

102. "When I point out one corner of a square to someone and yet [he] does not come back with the other three, then I do not point it out to him again." *Analects* 7.8. *Lunyu*, SBBY 309, *juan* 4, 2a; Lau, *Confucius: The Analects*, 86.

103. T.1858–156a: 26–b: 1.

104. T.1858–156b: 11–15.

105. T.1858–154a: 24.

106. T.1858–156a: 4–157a: 6.

107. T.1858–156a: 10–13.

108. T.1858–156c: 14–17.

109. T.1858–157a: 1–3.

110. T.1858–156a: 15–16.

111. T.1858–156b: 18–20.

112. T.1858–157a: 9–10.

113. There are several small puns in Sengzhao's cover letter, the most obvious being his mention of his illness (T.1858–155b: 25), a punning allusion to both the *Zhuangzi* and

Vimalakīrti. Although Sengzhao most likely was ill, he is also playing off Liu's report of his own sickness by contrasting both their cases with those of the Masters in *Zhuangzi* and Vimalakīrti.

114. T.1858–156a: 13.
115. Perhaps significantly, the character *mo* combines two radicals, the character *hei* ("black," "dark") and the character *quan* ("dog"). Etymologically *mei* is truly a "wild word."
116. This would also be another example of Sengzhao playing with metaphors.
117. T.1858–156b: 28–c: 1.
118. Note that in true Mādhyamika fashion Sengzhao here is also affirming "nothing".
119. T.1858–157a: 10–11.
120. T.1858–156b: 25–28.
121. See D. S. Ruegg, "The Uses of the Four Positions in the Catuṣkoṭi and the Problem of the Description of Reality in Mahāyāna Buddhism," *Journal of Indian Philosophy* 5 (1977): 1–71.
122. T.1858–156c: 9–10.
123. T.1858–156b: 25–27.
124. T.1858–156c: 12–13.
125. "[The Sage's] Way extends outside the names, hence we speak of his 'non-existence.' He moves along with the events he matches, thus we speak of his 'existence.' Therefore, we speak of him as 'existent' or, more properly, 'truly existent,' [yet even this] is merely to force a name on him, for how could he really be so?" T.1858–156a: 29–b: 2.
126. Stanley Fish, "Interpreting the *Variorum*," in *Is There a Text in This Class: The Authority of Interpretive Communities* (Cambridge and London: Harvard University Press, 1980), 168–169.
127. Ibid., 172.
128. Fish refers to the phenomena of "institutional nesting" to account for examples of people being able to interpret texts in two or more fashions. See Stanley Fish, "Is There a Text in This Class?" in *Is There a Text in This Class: The Authority of Interpretive Communities* (Cambridge and London: Harvard University Press, 1980), 308.
129. Fish, "Interpreting the *Variorum*," 173.
130. It might be more accurate to say that their local interpretive communities (Chang'an and Lushan respectively) exert more authority over Sengzhao and Liu than their larger shared community of "Buddho-Daoist" gentry.
131. My claim here is based on Sengzhao's statement in "*Prajñā* is Not-knowing" that the time was ripe for Dharma to spread (the prophecies were coming true) and his advice to Liu in his letter to "let his understanding naturally grow." Although struggling with a hermeneutic crisis concerning *prajñā*, Sengzhao evinces a basic trust in Dao's workings.
132. As portrayed in Chapter 3 of this *sūtra*, especially in the persons of Śāriputra and Rāhula. See Robert A. F. Thurman, trans., *The Holy Teaching of Vimalakīrti: a Mahāyāna Scripture* (University Park: The Pennsylvania State University Press, 1976), 24–33. For the Chinese, see T.474–521b: 28–523c: 13 (Zhi Qian's version) and T.475–539c: 14–542a: 25 (Kumārajīva's version).
133. T.1858–155a: 14 and 20 respectively.
134. T.1858–155a: 13 and 21–22 respectively.

Chapter 5

1. I agree with Stanley Fish that in a sense we are "writing" (more accurately "re-writing") the text we interpret when we construe its meaning. This does not mean that "original author" or "original text" do not exist or have disappeared, only that author and text are continually re-born as they are read and discussed.

2. It is interesting to consider how Yao Xing continues to exert influence here, as witnessed by the fact that to this day many Chinese prefer **Kumārajīva's** translations to those of later translators such as Xuanzang.

3. Subaltern Studies deals with India in particular, focusing on the "subaltern classes" (commoners) whose lives tend to be ignored by the dominant elite (Western colonists and missionaries as well as upper class Indians.) For details see King, *Orientalism and Religion*, 190–196.

4. All three thinkers use blanket terms such as "Eastern traditions" to draw contrasts between European thought and the thinking found in India, China or Japan, implying a homogeneity that in fact does not exist.

5. Liebenthal relies heavily on German Idealism for his notions of philosophy and religion. He also holds an essentialist view of Buddhism. Robinson is less informed by Idealism but still uses a discourse of control by abstracting a "system" from various texts (those attributed to **Nāgārjuna**, **Candrakīrti** and **Kumārajīva**) which he then claims to be "**Mādhyamika**" and employing this system in investigating other texts (those written by Sengzhao and his colleagues). Robinson's implicit insistence on definitive meaning and complete texts run counter to the philosophical hermeneutics of Heidegger, Gadamer and Ricoeur that I draw upon in reading Sengzhao.

6. In "*Prajñā* is Not-knowing" Sengzhao not only acknowledges *prajñā* as a source of conflicting interpretations (T.1858–153a: 9) but also speaks of language's inherent inability to convey it. Only then does he switch to a different language of "wild words" (a type of translation) that he says still cannot describe *prajñā* (T.1858–153a: 23). He also argues that his "first opponent" misunderstands the meaning (intention) of the *sūtras* (T.1858–153c: 1–2), making the same argument against Liu Yimin in "The Correspondence' (T.1858–156c: 8 and 13). Liu, for his part, admits at one point that he cannot grasp Sengzhao's intention (T.1858–155b: 17–18) and observes that their misunderstanding is due in part to their different presuppositions (T.1858–155b: 19–20), a reference to the fact that he and Sengzhao have different contexts informing their understandings of *prajñā*.

7. T.1858–153a: 19–20.

8. Louis Boyer, "Mysticism: an essay on the history of the word," in Richard Woods, ed., *Understanding Mysticism* (London: Athlone Press, 1980), 42–55.

9. Louis Dupre, "Mysticism," in *The Encyclopedia of Religion*, ed. Mircea Eliade (New York: Macmillan, 1987), 10: 245.

10. James, *The Varieties of Religious Experience*, 379–429. James argues that ineffability and a noetic quality characterize all mystical states whereas most (but not all) are transient and involve a passive experiencer.

11. See Aldous Huxley, *The Perennial Philosophy* (London: Harper & Row, 1944). Explicitly perennialist views, for instance, inform Antequil-Duperron's *Oupnek'hat*, a Latin translation

of a Persian compilation of selections from the *Upaniṣads* published in 1801–02. This work proved extremely influential in shaping European notions of Indian thought and culture. See King, *Orientalism and Religion*, 119–120.

12. See Fritjof Schuon, *The Transcendent Unity of Religions* (Wheaton: Quest, 1984) and Huston Smith, *Forgotten Truth: The Common Vision of the World's Religions* (San Francisco: Harper Collins, 1976).

13. See W. T. Stace, *Mysticism and Philosophy* (New York: The Macmillan Press Ltd., 1960).

14. Ibid., 41–133.

15. R.C. Zaehner, *Mysticism, Sacred and Profane* (Oxford: Oxford University Press, 1961).

16. See Steven T. Katz, "Language, Epistemology and Mysticism," in *Mysticism and Philosophical Analysis*, ed. Steven Katz (New York: Oxford University Press, 1978), 22–74.

17. Katz' views are heavily informed by Post-Kantian philosophy and have great resonance with Heidegger, Gadamer and Ricoeur's views concerning the power of traditions in determining our basic understanding of the world.

18. See Robert K. C. Forman, "Introduction: Mysticism, Constructivism, and Forgetting," in *The Problem of Pure Consciousness: Mysticism and Philosophy*, ed. Robert K. C. Forman (Oxford/New York: Oxford University Press, 1990), 3–49.

19. Ibid., 30–42.

20. Ibid., 8–9. Forman makes this point explicitly but critics often overlook it.

21. Robert Gimello, Janet Gyatso et al, "Mysticism and its Contents" (Panel presented at the annual meeting of the American Academy of Religion, Nashville, Tennessee, 18–21 November 2000).

22. For example, we may speak of "Christian mysticism" as a singular phenomenon when in fact the term covers a vast range of writings, practices, and accounts from various thinkers and schools (the Desert Fathers, Medieval Scholastics, Rhineland mystics etc.) which can differ tremendously. To speak of "Christian mysticism" in this sense obscures the great differences within Christian mystical traditions.

23. Such ideas seem to lie behind the criticisms leveled at scholars of mysticism by Hans Penner, who argues that what we label "mysticism" is actually "an illusion, unreal, a false category which has distorted an important aspect of religion." See Hans H. Penner, "The Mystical Illusion," in *Mysticism and Religious Traditions*, ed. Steven T. Katz (New York: Oxford University Press, 1983), 89.

24. Forman discusses the circular nature of Katz' arguments, particularly as exemplified in Katz's bold rhetorical statements that "there are NO pure (i.e. unmediated) experiences." See Forman, "Introduction," 9–19. Forman, however, assumes that PCE's do occur and that they are unconstructed, when this is precisely the issue that needs to resolved. He also narrowly defines "mysticism" to fit certain parameters (see his discussion on pages 5–8) and his account is heavily biased towards introvertive experiences which lend themselves to a pantheist-monist ontology. He thus overlooks or plays down visions and experiences reported by devotional mystics.

25. James' focus on experiences owes much to Schleiermacher, who defined "religion" as a *feeling* of absolute dependence. This focus on an experience tames mysticism by locating it within the "private sphere" rather than the communal practices and teachings of traditions, which are often politically charged and highly critical of officially sanctioned authority.

For a discussion see Mark A. McIntosh, *Mystical Theology: the Integrity of Spirituality and Theology* (Malden: Blackwell Publishers, Inc., 1998), 136–145.

26. See especially King, *Orientalism and Religion*, 161–186. The relationship between perennialism and Orientalism is complex. The Romantic interest in "the Orient" for its alleged pantheism fed into Orientalist scholarship that defined the various "Eastern" religious traditions as objects of legitimate scholarship. These scholarly fictions were then appropriated by Western-trained "Orientals" such as Swami Vivekananda, Sarvepelli Radhakrishnan (Neo-Vedanta), and D. T. Suzuki (Zen Buddhism) and reasserted as the timeless wisdom at the heart of their traditions over and against the "secular West." Huxley and other perennialists devised their notions of the *philosophia perennis* from reading the English translations and popularized presentations of these "Occidentalized Orientals."

27. Grace Jantzen, who notes how the academic discourse of "mysticism studies" has been shaped by the unexamined modern bourgeois assumptions of many scholars, presents a far more developed version of this critique. See Grace Jantzen, *Power, Gender and Mysticism, Cambridge Studies in Ideology and Religion* 8 (Cambridge: Cambridge University Press, 1995).

28. Denise Lardner Carmody and John Tully Carmody, *Mysticism: Holiness East and West* (New York/Oxford: Oxford University Press, 1996), 76.

29. Significantly, Liu only mentions *prajñā* (*pan ruo*) by name twice in his letter to Sengzhao: once when expressing his hope that the essay will clarify *prajñā* once and for all (T.1858–155a: 14), and once when quoting Sengzhao's own words (T.1858–155a: 20). There are, of course, places where Liu implies *prajñā* without explicitly mentioning it, as for example when he repeats the title of Sengzhao's treatise (T.1858–155a: 11) or quotes Sengzhao's essay in the first section of his letter (T.1858–155a: 21 ff.). Nonetheless, this fact raises the distinct possibility that Liu is not concerned with *prajñā* in the same way Sengzhao is.

30. Conze, *The Perfection of Wisdom in Eight Thousand Lines*, 99.

31. Sengzhao speaks of *prajñā* in precisely these terms in his answer to the third objection in "*Prajñā* is Not-knowing." See T.1858–154a: 7–26.

32. Stace devotes an entire chapter to the relationship between mysticism and language but it is a constant theme in his work. See Stace, *Mysticism and Philosophy*, 277–306.

33. T.250–847c: 6–7.

34. T.1775–344c: 14ff.; quoted in Liebenthal, *Chao Lun*, 40; alternative translation in Richard H. Robinson, "Mysticism and Logic in Seng-Chao's Thought," *Philosophy East and West* 8 (1958): 103.

35. Liebenthal, *Chao Lun*, 40.

36. Ibid.

37. Robinson, "Mysticism and Logic in Seng-Chao's Thought," 102 and 108 and *Early Mādhyamika in India and China*, 155.

38. Robinson, *Early Mādhyamika in India and China*, 131–133, 136, 151–153.

39. Robinson, "Mysticism and Logic in Seng-Chao's Thought," 108–109.

40. Ibid. Recall that Sengzhao is regarded as a founder of the *Sanlun* school.

41. Ludwig Wittgenstein, *Tractatus Logico-Philosophicus* (London: Routledge and Kegan Paul, 1922), 188–189; cited in Robinson, "Mysticism and Logic in Seng-Chao's Thought," 120.

42. See, for example, Chris Gudmunsen, *Wittgenstein and Buddhism* (London: Macmillan press, 1977).

43. Cf. the *Majjhima-nikāya*, where the Buddha compares his teachings to a raft that should be discarded once one has crossed a great flood. See E. A. Burtt, ed., *The Teachings of the Compassionate Buddha* (New York: Penguin Books USA Inc., 1982), 118–120.

44. Ibid., 120.

45. Liebenthal, *Chao Lun*, xii. Liebenthal finds Sengzhao comparable to Nicolas of Cusa.

46. Robinson, "Mysticism and Logic in Seng-Chao's Thought," 108.

47. T.1858–155c: 14–16.

48. Kumārajīva translated several works on meditation and Daoxuan comments on the role of meditation in the Chang'an community in the *Xu Gaosengzhuan*. See T.2060–596a: 8–13. For scholarly discussions see Liu, *Madhyamaka Thought in China*, 188; Muranaka Yūshō, "Chūgoku Nambokuchō jidai no zenkan ni tsuite," in *Tendai Kanmon no Kichō* (Tokyo, 1986), 324–327; and Sasaki Kentaku, *Kan Gi Rikuchō Zenkan Hattenshi Ron*, 2nd revised ed., (Tokyo, 1978), 101–132.

49. As I note in Chapter Three, a well known report of such an experience belongs to Deching (1546–1623). Deching's report seems to relate a real experience and has all the trappings of a stereotypical Chan story (suddenness, a graphic and even earthy context, shocking humor.) Nonetheless, this report does not constitute evidence of *Sengzhao's* experiences so much as the later *Chan* co-optation of his work.

50. Tracy, *Plurality and Ambiguity*, 114.

51. T.1858–153c: 24–26.

52. "That (*Brahman*) thou (*ātman*) art." This line comes from the *Chāndogya Upaniṣad* (6.1–3, 12–14 *passim*) and serves as one of the four "great sayings" that Śaṅkara selects as containing the crucial insight of Advaita tradition. For details of Vedānta as a textual training, see Clooney, *Theology after Vedānta*.

53. The *Zohar* ("Book of Splendor") was probably written by Moses de Leon (1240–1305), a leading Jewish intellectual of his day. The *Zohar* draws upon long-standing traditions and practices stretching all the way back to the Hebrew Scriptures and became the core text of medieval Kabbalah (lit. "what is received"). It centers especially on doctrines of Creation and the ten *sefirot* ("numbers," mathematical entities that form the basis of all reality).

54. For details on *nian* see Daniel K. Gardner, trans., *Learning to be a Sage: Selections from the Conversations of Master Chu, Arranged Topically* (Berkeley/Los Angeles: University of California Press, 1990), 128–162.

55. The post-Han era saw a tremendous rise in interest in the supernatural, with *xuanxue* intellectuals often at the forefront of paranormal activities and investigations. See Holcombe, *In the Shadow of the Han*, 96–108.

56. Sells presents a preliminary outline of how apophatic discourse works involving seven stages, although he does not claim that this is a universal formula. See Sells, *Mystical Languages of Unsaying*, 206–209.

57. Ibid., 9–10, 213–217. On page 210 Sells draws an analogy between apophatic discourse and a joke.

58. It seems likely that *samatha-vipassanā* was part of Liu's practice of *buddhānusmṛti*, possibly the preliminary exercises performed during the time of seclusion before being graced by a vision of Amitābha.

59. The historical founder of Pure Land tradition is generally considered to be Dharma Master Tan Luan (476–542) although devotion to Amitābha and other Buddhas goes back to the beginnings of Buddhism.

60. Roger Corless, "Pure Land Piety," in *Buddhist Spirituality: Indian, Southeast Asian, Tibetan, Early Chinese*, ed. Takeuchi Yoshinori et al (New York: The Crossroad Publishing Company, 1995), 243–246.

61. Hence Amitābha's name also sometimes means "He of Immeasurable Wisdom."

62. One of Amitāyus' Chinese epithets is *Da xian*, "Great Immortal."

63. Corless, "Pure Land Piety," 248.

64. T.475–538c: 4–5; Thurman, *The Holy Teaching of Vimalakīrti*, 18–19.

65. Stace dismisses experiences that might be considered "mystical" (e.g. voices, visions, raptures), singling out Teresa of Avila as an example of someone who is not a "true mystic." See Stace, *Mysticism and Philosophy*, 47–55.

66. Forman describes *sahaja samādhi* as "a state in which a silent level within the subject is maintained along with (simultaneously with) the full use of the human faculties. It is, hence, continuous through part or all of the twenty-four hour cycle of (nonmeditative) activity and sleep." Forman, "Introduction," in *The Problem of Pure Consciousness*, 8.

67. Ching, *Mysticism and Kingship in China*, 1–34.

68. Zurcher, *The Buddhist Conquest of China*, 204. Maitreya was the patron of translators and exegetes.

69. Chen, *Buddhism in China*, 343. In one of his works, Zhi Dun describes the Pure Land of Amitāyus and by some accounts he venerated an image of Amitābha and vowed to be reborn in the Western Paradise.

70. During the early middle ages, there was greater emphasis on devotional Buddhism in the north than in the south. This may have been due to closer contacts with Central Asia and the presence of Central Asian missionaries. See Lai, "The Three Jewels in China," 311–312.

71. *Zhuangzi*, SBBY 1410, *juan* 7, 27a–b; Watson, *The Complete Works of Chuang Tzu*, 242.

72. Recall that Kumārajīva also says that, "The *sūtras* delude (*kuang*) the eyes of worldly people." T.1856–135c: 11. The *sūtras* serve as "wild words" by venturing from the ordinary to the extraordinary, and in a very strange way.

73. Sengzhao praises compassion in his commentary to the *Vimalakīrti sūtra* as the foundation of all virtues and that which unifies Mahāyāna teachings. See T.1775–406b: 15–16 and 415c: 15–16.

74. Tsukamoto, in *Jōron Kenkyū*, 160; translated in Robinson, "Mysticism and Logic in Seng-Chao's Thought," 108.

75. Robinson, "Mysticism and Logic in Seng-Chao's Thought," 109.

76. Hsu, *Three Theses of Seng-Zhao*, 4.

77. Liu, *Madhyamaka Thought in China*, 81.

78. Hashimoto Hōkei, "Sojō ni okeru daihishin no mondai," *Indogaku Bukkyōgaku Kenkyū* 16 (1968): 542–546 and 17 (1969): 542–545.

79. D. T. Suzuki, "Reason and Intuition in Buddhist Philosophy," in *The Japanese Mind: Essentials of Japanese Philosophy and Culture*, ed. C. A. Moore (Honolulu: University of Hawaii, East-West Center Press, 1967), 66–109.

80. Ibid., 80–81.
81. Ibid., 80.
82. Huntington, *The Emptiness of Emptiness*, 90–92.
83. Ibid., 89–90.
84. Suzuki, "Reason and Intuition in Buddhist Philosophy," 94–97.
85. Huntington, *The Emptiness of Emptiness*, 88.

Conclusion

1. T.1858–156a: 26.
2. *Webster's New Collegiate Dictionary* (1974), s.v. "understanding."
3. *Laozi* 28. See *Laozi Daode jing*, SBBY 1403, *shang pian*, 18b; Lau, *Tao Te Ching*, 85.
4. Gadamer, *Truth and Method*, 180.
5. Joel C. Weinsheimer, *Gadamer's Hermeneutics: A Reading of Truth and Method* (New Haven and London: Yale University Press, 1985), 138–139.
6. Cf. the biblical sense of "knowing," a euphemism for sexual contact that implies deep and rare intimacy.
7. Bruns, *Hermeneutics Ancient & Modern*, 215.
8. Ibid., 183.

Appendix I

1. Mueller-Vollmer, "Language, Mind and Artifact," 3.
2. W. V. O. Quine, *Word and Object* (New York: Oxford University Press, 1960), 26–30.
3. W. Haas, "The Theory of Translation," *Philosophy* 37 (1962); reprint in *The Theory of Meaning*, ed. G. H. R. Parkinson (Oxford: Oxford University Press, 1968), 101 (italics in the original, page citation is to reprint edition).
4. George Steiner, *After Babel: Aspects of Language and Translation* (Cambridge: Oxford University Press, 1975), 5.
5. Ibid., 25.
6. MacIntyre makes a similar point regarding "classical Latin" and "early modern Irish." Until fairly recently most languages marked off communities of shared belief and tradition. Yet with the rise of internationalized languages such as English, Spanish, Japanese etc. we have come to view languages as potentially open to persons from *any* community or background. See MacIntyre, *Whose Justice? Which Rationality?*, 373 ff.
7. Robinson agrees on this point. See Robinson, *Early Mādhyamika in India and China*, 4.
8. Ibid., 15.
9. For example, he reports that Sengzhao died at thirty-one and implies that Sengzhao knew Sanskrit. See Hsu, *Three Theses of Seng Zhao*, 7. Both of these claims are factually incorrect.
10. Gadamer, *Truth and Method*, 386.

Appendix II

1   T.1858–153a: 7–154c: 23 and DNZ 2.1.1–33–35. Japanese translation in Tsukamoto et al, *Jōron Kenkyū*, 22–36. Previous English translations in Liebenthal, *Chao Lun*, 64–80; Robinson, *Early Mādhyamika in India and China*, 212–221; Hsu, *Three Theses of Seng-Zhao*, 44–79. The title of this essay is an allusion to a line from chapter four of the *Zhuangzi*, in which Confucius says to his disciple Yan Hui, "You have heard of the knowing that knows but you have not yet heard of the knowing that is 'not-knowing'." See *Zhuangzi*, SSBY 1408, *juan* 2, 7b; Watson, *The Complete Works of Chuang Tzu*, 58.

2.   The Chinese term 般若 *panruo* is the most common transliteration of the Sanskrit *prajñā*.

3.   虛 *xu* ("empty," "void," "vacuity.") Commonly used in the Daoist sense of the primordial void from which being emerges but sometimes equated with the Buddhist notion of *śūnyatā* ("emptiness") by *xuanxue* Buddhists. Sengzhao at times does this as well. The *Dai Nihonzokuzōkyō* versions of Sengzhao's essay and Huida's commentary typically use a variant character,   , but the meaning is the same.

4.   玄 *xuan* (as in *xuanxue*), "dark," "profound," "abstruse."

5.   We could paraphrase this sentence as "*Prajñā* is the *alpha* and *omega*." Sengzhao is saying *prajñā* encompasses the entirety of the Buddhist path.

6.   Most likely a reference to Ultimate Truth (*paramārtha satya*). See Liebenthal, *Chao Lun*, 64 (note 236).

7.   *Analects* 2.16, "The Master said, 'The study of different strands brings harm indeed." *Lunyu*, SBBY 308, *juan* 1, 10a. Lau translates this as "The Master said, 'To attack a task from the wrong end can do nothing but harm.'" See Lau, *Confucius: The Analects*, 65.

8.   *Laozi* 41, "The Great Square has no corners." *Laozi Daode jing*, SBBY 1403, *xia pian*, 4a–5a; Lau, *Lao Tzu: Tao Te Ching*, 102. Yuankang says the phrase "the Great Square" refers to Mahāyāna in general (T.1859–175b: 7) and also India (T.1859–175b: 17), where Kumārajīva studied in his youth.

9.   Allusion to the *Da zhuan* ("Great Treatise") of the *Yijing*, 7.8a, "The *Book of Changes* is what the Sages used to reach the ultimate depths and grasp the details [of the universe]." *Zhou Yi, Xici shang*, SBBY 3, 8a; Wilhelm and Baynes, *The I Ching*, 315.

10.   *Yijing*, 7.10a, "The Master said: ... Words cannot express thoughts completely ... the Sages set up the symbols to express their thoughts completely ..." *Zhou Yi, Xici shang*, SBBY 3, 10a; Wilhelm and Baynes, *The I Ching*, 322. In his commentary (T.1859–175c: 1–10) Yuankang quotes Wang Bi's commentary on the *Yijing* here. See Wang Bi, *Zhouyi lueli*, *zhuan di shi*, SBBY 3, 9a–b.

11.   *Laozi* 14, "Look for it [and you] do not see it; its name is Formless. Listen for it [and you] do not hear it; its name is Soundless. Feel for it [and you] do not touch it; its name is Untouchable." *Laozi Daode jing*, SBBY 1403, *shang pian*, 8b–9a; Lau, *Lao Tzu: Tao Te Ching*, 70.

12.   Śākyamuni Buddha's country of origin, but in this case it stands for India as a whole. This phrase probably refers to Kumārajīva's victories over the tīrthikas of north India in his youth.

13.   According to Yuankang (T.1859–175c: 25) the wind is Dharma and the east is China.

14.   A reference to Kumārajīva's years of captivity in Liang.

15. Sengzhao means that **Kumārajīva's** captivity and his ensuing "rescue" by Yao Xing were "fated." Cf. his mention of the prophecy below.

16. This is the second year of the "earth branch" in a sixty-year cycle. See Hsu, *Three Theses of Seng-Zhao*, 76 (note 1). Yuankang (T.1859–176b: 5) observes that this sign of the month stands for that of the year 丑 chou.

17. Yuankang (T.1859–176b: 19) explains that Lu Guang feared an invasion from Northern and Southern Liang and so surrendered to Yao Xing.

18. The *Pañca* prophesizes that *prajñāpāramitā* teachings will first appear in the south, then spread west and north. See Conze, *The Large Sūtra on Perfect Wisdom*, 327–328 and Yuankang's remarks at T.1859–176c: 3.

19. Compare Sengzhao's description of **Kumārajīva** in his "Preface to the *Hundred Treatise*": "There is an Indian *śramaṇa*, **Kumārajīva**, whose talent is deep and broad, whose superb spirit far surpasses [ordinary people]. Although I have studied with him for years yet I cannot fathom him completely." T.2145–77b: 27–28; Robinson, *Early Mādhaymika in India and China*, 211. The last line is a reference to the *Analects* 9.10. Sengzhao is likening **Kumārajīva** to Confucius here, perhaps even alluding to Wang Bi's description of Confucius as embodying *wu* (non-being). See *Sanguo zhi*, SBBY 510, *juan* 28 (Wang Bi *juan*), 30a.

20. Yao Xing, who adopted the title 天王 Tian wang.

21. Probably an allusion to the skillful and easy "Dao" of Cook Ding as related in *Zhuangzi*, chapter 3. See *Zhuangzi*, SBBY 1408, *juan* 2, 1b–2b; Watson, *The Complete Works of Chuang Tzu*, 50–51.

22. Perhaps a reference to Sengzhao's era as the period of the Dharma's decay (*mo fa*; Japanese, *mappo*), one of the three periods of the Dharma spoken of in the *Lotus Sūtra*. This period was alleged to begin after the age of the "Counterfeit Dharma," approximately one thousand years after the Buddha's *parinirvāṇa*. Liebenthal, however, notes that this interpretation is unlikely since in Sengzhao's day it was not yet thought that the period of *mo fa* had begun. See Liebenthal, *Chao Lun*, 65 (note 250). Other possibilities are that Sengzhao is speaking of his day as "latter" in the sense of it being the fulfillment of the prophecies, or is alluding to the temporal distance separating his age from that of the Buddha and the Sages.

23. These were the scholar-monks of the Chang'an academy. The full number of monks was three thousand.

24. The Aśoka compound located outside the walls of Chang'an, where **Kumārajīva** did much of his translating. See Liebenthal, *Chao Lun*, 91 (note 408).

25. The previous Chinese translations.

26. The Mahāyāna *sūtras*, specifically the *Pañca*.

27. A *kalpa* is an immensely long cycle of time (traditionally said to be 8,640,000,000 years) comprised of various lesser periods (*yugas*). One *kalpa* is the equivalent of one "day" (day and night) of Brahma.

28. There are echoes of this passage in other sections of Sengzhao's work. In the dedicatory introduction of *"Nirvāṇa* is Nameless" (T.1858–157a: 14–19, a: 27–b: 9), Sengzhao lavishly praises Yao Xing for his virtue and wisdom, and especially the insight he demonstrates in a letter to his younger brother Yao Song. Sengzhao similarly praises Yao Song in his "Preface to the *Hundred Treatise*" (T.2145–77c: 1–7).

29. 陰 yin ("hidden," "obscure.") Also the "feminine" and/or "negative" principle of Daoist cosmology (versus *yang*). As the treatise demonstrates, the Sage's being comprises both the deepest of *yin* (*prajñā*) and the most expansive of *yang* (his effortless and compassionate responses). Cf. the two "wings" of the Bodhisattva, Wisdom (*prajñā*) and Compassion (*karuṇā*).

30. A characteristic feature ("mark") by which something is known. The mind ordinarily knows "things" by grasping their characteristic *lakṣaṇa*.

31. *Wuming*, 無名, possibly an allusion to He Yan's treatise *Wuming lun* ("Treatise on the Nameless").

32. A reference to the tale of the Yellow Emperor retrieving the pearl of wisdom. See *Zhuangzi*, SBBY 1409, *juan* 5, 2b–3a; Watson, *The Complete Works of Chuang Tzu*, 128–129. The word-play in this story is impossible to capture in English. The emperor's servant who succeeds in getting the pearl (after "Knowledge," the clear-sighted Li Zhu, and "Wrangling Debate" all fail) is named 罔象 *wang xiang*, which can mean "lacking images," "deceitful semblance," or even "mindless." The individual terms can also mean "net" and "image." I believe we should consider all of these associations to be at work here. Sengzhao is saying that the net of symbols (language) *can* retrieve wisdom from its hidden depths but this net can be tricky and deceitful, entrapping us if we are not careful. This is, of course, Sengzhao's Buddho-Daoist "take" on **Nāgārjuna**'s point that we only attain *paramārtha* by going through *saṃvṛti*, and foreshadows Sengzhao's announcement in the next line that he will be using "wild words."

33. *Zhuangzi*, chapter 22. *Zhuangzi*, SBBY 1410, *juan* 7, 27b; Watson, *The Complete Works of Chuang Tzu*, 242.

34. T.221–97c and 354a.

35. T.224–428a: 20.

36. To distinguish *prajñā* for ordinary knowing, I translate 智 zhi as "Wisdom" and 知 zhi as "knowing." Sengzhao plays these two terms off each other throughout the treatise.

37. "Omniscience." Sengzhao elaborates upon this "all-knowing" of *prajñā* in his commentary to the *Vimalakīrti*: "As for 'all-knowing,' it is the Ultimate of knowing. [It is] bright like morning light, when all obscurities are fully illuminated. [It is] clear like the still depths [of water], when the multitudes of images are mirrored together. As for 'not-knowing and yet having nothing not-known,' isn't this just he all-knowing [of the Buddha]? Why? [If] one has [deliberate] mind, then there are restrictions. [If] there are restrictions then [one's knowing] has limits. Since restrictions and limits are formed, one's wisdom has bounds. [If] one's wisdom is bounded, then what is illuminated is not universal. The *zhiren* [by contrast] has no [deliberate] mind. Since [the *zhiren*] has no [deliberate] mind, he has no restrictions. [If] there are no restrictions then there are no limits. Since [the *zhiren*] has no restrictions and no limits, his Wisdom is boundless. Since his Wisdom is boundless, what he illuminates is limitless. Because of this [the *zhiren*] can with one thought instantly know all *dharmas* in full." T.1775–365a: 8–15.

38. A reference to the *Viśeṣacintā -brahma paripṛcchā sūtra*, T.586–39b: 11.

39. *Laozi* 3, "Hence in governing the people the Sage empties their minds but fills their bellies." *Laozi Daode jing*, SBBY 1403, *shang pian*, 2a–b; Lau, *Lao Tzu: Tao Te Ching*, 59. Sengzhao substitutes "illumination" for "belly."

40. *Laozi* 41, "The Dao that is bright seems dull." *Laozi Daode jing*, SBBY 1403, *xia pian*, 4a; Lau, *Lao Tzu: Tao Te Ching*, 102.

41. *Zhuangzi*, chapter 12, "He sees in the darkest dark, hears where there is no sound. In the midst of darkness, he alone sees the dawn; in the midst of the soundless, he alone hears harmony." *Zhuangzi*, SBBY 1409, *juan* 5, 2b; Watson, *The Complete Works of Chuang Tzu*, 128.

42 神 shen, "consciousness" or "awareness" but also "spirit" in the sense of animating force. The "spiritual essence" refined through the practices of Daoist alchemy to achieve immortality and something of an undying "soul" in the writings of the Buddho-Daoists. *Shen*, however, is never considered a "thing" among other things. For Sengzhao, *shen* is the Sage's active aspect, *prajñā* in action, i.e. *karuṇā*.

43. Cf. the Chinese notion of 感應 *gan ying*, "sympathetic response." Heaven responds appropriately to all occasions. For Sengzhao, this idea also describes the Way of the Sage, the one who has attained *prajñā*. Sengzhao describes this more explicitly in his commentary to the *Vimalakīrti*. See T.1775—413c.

44. *Laozi* 25, "There are four great things within the bounds [of reality] …" *Laozi Daode jing*, SBBY 1403, *shang pian*, 13b–15a; Lau, *Lao Tzu: Tao Te Ching*, 82.

45. *Yijing* 8.2a, "When in early antiquity Fu Xi ruled the world, he looked up and observed the images in Heaven; he looked down and observed the patterns on Earth." *Zhou Yi*, *Xici xia di ba*, SBBY 3, 2a; Wilhelm and Baynes, *The I Ching*, 328. Both Huida (DNZ 2.B 23.4–434d) and Yuankang (T.1859–177c: 16) speak of this in *Buddhist* terms, however, as referring to the Bodhisattva appearing wherever needed to spread the Dharma.

46. Just as the Sage resides in "the hinge of the Way" in *Zhuangzi*, chapter 2. See *Zhuangzi*, SBBY 1408, *juan* 1, 15a; Watson, *The Complete Works of Chuang Tzu*, 40.

47. *Laozi* 39, "Spirits attained the One and became Divine [through it]." See *Laozi Daode jing*, SBBY 1403, *xia pian*, 3a–4a; Lau, *Lao Tzu: Tao Te Ching*, 100. I translate 靈 *ling* ("numinous") as "Divine."

48. T.474–519c: 21. The same passage is also in **Kumārajīva**'s version of this *sūtra* at T.475–537c: 18.

49. T.221–140c: 15.

50. 跡 *ji*, "traces" or "footsteps." Here it means *written* traces, the texts that mark out the Sagely Way.

51. Yuankang (T.1859–178a: 24) says that Sengzhao identifies motion and stillness (non-motion). Sengzhao further explores this thesis in "Things Do Not Shift," T.1858–151a: 8–c: 29.

52. The text as preserved in Yuankang's commentary has 即 ji instead of 則 ze. See T.1859–178a: 25.

53. Reference to the knowing and acting of the *zhenren* in *Zhuangzi*, chapter 6. See *Zhuangzi*, SBBY 1408, *juan* 3, 1a–1b; Watson, *The Complete Works of Chuang Tzu*, 77.

54. Compare the portrait of *prajñā* Sengzhao has just given with the introductory section of "Emptiness of the Unreal" (T.1858–152a: 2–13): "The perfectly void and birthless is the wondrous goal of *prajñā*'s dark mirroring. It is the origin and ultimate end of existing things. Thus if oneself does not attain Sagely Understanding, how can you fit your Spirit to the space between being and non-being? Therefore the *zhiren* pushes his Spirit and mind

through into the limitless and cannot be impeded by any limits. He takes his ears and eyes to the limits of sight and hearing and so cannot be constrained by forms and sounds. How can this not be due to his identity with the self-emptiness of the ten thousand things? Thus things cannot fetter his Spiritual Intelligence.

Therefore the Sage mounts the True Mind [of *prajñā*], conforms to Principle, and so has no obstacles and no not passing-through. He discerns the One [Original] *Qi* and thereby contemplates the transformations, thus he accords with what he meets. Since he has no obstacles and no *not* passing-through, he can mix with the confusion and reach simplicity. Since he accords with what he meets, he touches all things and unites [with them]. So, although the ten thousand forms differ, yet they cannot in themselves be [truly] different. Because they cannot in themselves be [truly] different, [the Sage] knows forms are not True Forms. Since forms are not True Forms, although they are forms yet they are not forms.

So it is that things and myself have the same root. Affirming and denying are of the One [Original] *Qi*. The apprehension of the hidden, subtle, abstruse and secret cannot be exhausted by our multitudes of feelings."

55. Both the *Taishō* and the *Dai Nihonzokuzōkyō* note that the *Yuan* version of the text has 問 wen instead of 難 nan here. Yuankang has *wen* in his commentary as well. See T.1859–178b: 1.

56. *Laozi* 7, "Therefore the Sage puts himself last yet finds himself first. *Laozi Daode jing*, SBBY 1403, *shang pian*, 4b; Lau, *Lao Tzu: Tao Te Ching*, 63.

57. The two primordial forms of creation as expounded in the *Yijing*–*yin* and *yang* or Heaven and Earth.

58. *Laozi* 5, "Heaven and Earth are not humane; they treat the ten-thousand things as straw dogs. The Sage is not humane; he treats the people as straw dogs." *Laozi Daode jing*, SBBY 1403, *shang pian*, 3b; Lau, *Lao Tzu: Tao Te Ching*, 61.

59. Most likely a reinterpretation of Wang Bi's view of the Sage (Confucius).

60. The opponent holds that the Sage does not *selfishly* "know" in the manner of unenlightened people.

61. This probably means *prajñāpāramitā* versus the "lower" analytic types of *prajñā* such as we find in the "Hīnayāna" schools. In his essay Sengzhao does not distinguish among various types of *prajñā* as do the Abhidharmists. For him *prajñā* = *prajñāpāramitā* = Sagely Wisdom.

62. T.223–262c: 24.

63. T.223–302a: 19.

64. Cf. "Reversal of the basis" (*paravṛtti*).

65. *Rāga* (lust), *dveṣa* (hatred) and *moha* (stupidity).

66. Mistaking the impermanent (*anitya*) for the permanent, suffering (*duḥkha*) for bliss, that which lacks a "self" (*anatta*) as having a "self" and that which is "empty" (*śūnya*) as having its "own-being" (*svabhāva*).

67. Since all "things" are "empty," emptiness cannot be a logical basis for praising *prajñā* as "pure."

68. Praising *prajñā* as "pure" on the basis of it having a "pure" object makes a distinction between subject and object. *Prajñā* does not admit to any such distinctions.

69. The *sūtras* in general.

70. Huida (DNZ 2.B 23.4–435c) has 智 (Wisdom) here instead of 知 (knowing).

71. According to Huida (DNZ 2.B 23.4–435c), Sengzhao is arguing against Zhi Dun in this passage.

72. Cf. A Buddhist proverb on the Three Vehicles. The *śrāvaka* (hare) and the *pratyekabuddha* (horse) are too short to "touch bottom" in crossing the stream (*saṃsāra*) but the Bodhisattva (elephant) is large enough to cross easily. Possibly alluding to the *Lalitavistara sūtra* (T.186–488b: 20 f), or the *Mahāvibhāṣā śāstra* (T.1547–445c: 9).

73. 當而無是 "Match" here means matching some "thing" with an appropriate word. "Affirm" means to "affirm (as fully existent)." *Prajñā* unerringly comprehends all events in the everyday world, speaks of them with appropriate words but considers such words "pragmatic fictions" and not the full truth.

74. The basic position of the "School of Names" (*mingjiao*), one of the various movements within "Neo-Daoism." Its roots go back to the Confucian notion of "rectification of names" and the Dialecticians (Huishi, Gongsun Long) of the Warring States era.

75. Both the *Taishō* and the *Dai Nihonzokuzōkyō* note that the *Yuan* version of the text has 俱 ju instead of 都 du here. Yuankang in his commentary has *ju* as well. See T.1859–179b: 20.

76. Probably referring to the Mahāyāna *sūtras* in general.

77. *Xu*. Probably *not* a reference to *śūnyatā* (usually translated 空 kong) although technical terminology was not set at this time and in any case Sengzhao freely plays with various linguistic conventions.

78. Language cannot express *prajñā* in the way it does ordinary truth but language is the only means to reach Ultimate Truth. Cf. *Kārikās* 24: 9–10.

79. *Zhuangzi*, chapter 27, "With words that are not-words you can speak all your life yet never say anything." *Zhuangzi*, SBBY 1411, *juan* 9, 7a; Watson, *The Complete Works of Chuang Tzu*, 304.

80. See note 33 above. Sengzhao is allerting us to the fact that he is using a special language to convey the *prajñic* perspective.

81. The *mingjiao* only deals with definite things ("what has names and marks") i.e. the things of being (*you*). Sagely Wisdom, though, spans both being and non-being (*you* and *wu*).

82. Cf. the "*Heart sūtra*": "Form just is Emptiness, Emptiness just is form." (T.250–847c: 10). Kumārajīva may have already translated this *sūtra* or it could be that Sengzhao is borrowing the basic structure of the phrase from the *Pañca* (T.223–223a: 13) or perhaps Zhi Dun's *jise* treatises.

83. Unknown. According to Sengzhao's commentator Wen Cai (1241–1302), the reference is to the *Dazhidu lun* (T.1509–190c: 20). See Wen Cai's commentary, the *Zhaolun xinxu*, T.1860–217a: 21.

84. T.221–67a: 7 and 78a: 27.

85. T.221–67a: 7.

86. Ordinary "things" are not "real" (i.e. permanent and unchanging) but they can be said to exist in the conventional sense. From a Sagely perspective, then, they share in "being" and "non-being" yet are neither one nor the other.

87. Both the *Taishō* and the *Dai Nihonzokuzōkyō* versions note that the *Yuan* version of the text includes 以 yi here. Yuankang's commentary includes *yi* as well. See T.1859–180a: 9.

88. This passage is a basic explanation of the conditioned nature of perception, and an example of *pratītya-samutpāda*. Awareness arises out of the confluence of subjective and objective conditions. When either "side" is no longer present, neither is awareness.

89. The text as preserved in Yuankang's commentary includes the 知 ("knowing") that I include in brackets. All other versions lack this *zhi*. See T.1859–180a: 18.

90. Both the *Taishō* and the *Dai Nihonzokuzōkyō* note that the Yuan version of the text lacks 有 *you*. This passage is a direct quotation from Kumārajīva's translation of the *Kārikās*, although probably an early draft since the final version was not completed until 409. According to Tsukamoto et al, this is a reference to a line in the twenty-fourth chapter of the *Taishō* version (the *Zhong lun*, "Middle Treatise"), T.1564–33b: 11–12. See Tsukamoto, *Jōron Kenkyū*, 99 (note 108). For an English translation of the line see Garfield, *The Fundamental Wisdom of the Middle Way*, 69 (verse 18). This line of Sengzhao's essay is extremely important for its use of the technical terms *yin-yuan* (*hetu* and *pratyaya*, "causes and conditions"), a strong indication that Sengzhao was familiar with the finer points of Mādhyamika and Sarvāstivāda philosophy.

91. Robinson says Sengzhao is playing on the double meaning of 緣 *yuan* here–*ālambana* (object) and *pratyaya* (condition). See Robinson, *Early Mādhyamika in India and China*, 309 (note 93).

92. 不見有法無緣而生 Liebenthal, following Yuankang, says this merely quotes the general contents of the scriptures. See Liebenthal, *Chao Lun*, 76 (note 313). However Robinson believes it is a reference to the *Kārikās* 24: 19 (T.1564–33b: 13). See Robinson, *Early Mādhyamika in India and China*, 309–310 (note 94).

93. Is Sengzhao contradicting his thesis (as per the title of the treatise) that *prajñā* is "not-knowing?" From another perspective it may be that Sengzhao is making the point that when it comes to *prajñā*, no thesis–even an allegedly correct one–is ultimately true; *prajñā* cannot be defined, even by a negative definition.

94. An example of a *prasaṅga* argument. Sengzhao catches his opponent in a dilemma based upon his own assumptions that *prajñā* is a "knowing" and that what it knows (*paramārtha*) is an object.

95. That is, the Sage does not affirm what he perceives as a "this" or "that" and does not put a definitive label on it. The Sage is not stuck in the discursive demarcating of reality that informs ordinary experience.

96. T.221–12c: 4.

97. The source of this quotation is unknown. Possibly Sengzhao is referring to the message of the *sūtras* in general.

98. *Laozi* 4, "It blends with the dust and toil." *Laozi Daode jing*, SBBY 1403, *shang pian*, 3a; Lau, *Lao Tzu: Tao Te Ching*, 60.

99. The realms of rebirth (*gatis*): hell beings, *pretas* ("hungry ghosts"), animals, human beings, *devas*. This is a description of the Bodhisattva continually being reborn wherever needed. Hsu has *dhātu* ("realms") here but his translation does not make sense in this context. See Hsu, *Three Theses of Seng-Zhao*, 70.

100. *Laozi* 37, "Dao never acts yet nothing is left undone," and 48, "When one does not act, there is nothing left undone." *Laozi Daode jing*, SBBY 1403, *shang pian*, 21a and *xia pian*, 7b; Lau, *Lao Tzu: Tao Te Ching*, 96 and 109.

101. The idea seems to be that at times the Sage is as if asleep and at other times is awake.

102. 然非無心.

103. 無心心. The Sage does not get caught up in the proliferation of thoughts that characterizes existence in *saṃsāra*.

104. Yet another allusion to Wang Bi's description of Confucius.

105. Such worldly "wisdom" is not *true* Wisdom (i.e. *prajñā*), thus I put it in quotes.

106. Sagely Wisdom and deluded "wisdom" are exactly opposite. To get from the latter to the former requires a "conversion," a turning around of perspective.

107. Yuankang says *prajñā* does not apprehend marks so it is "Not-knowing." Deluded wisdom is empty of own-being (is "nothing") so it is "knowing nothing." Being "empty" is the mark of Ultimate Truth. T.1859–181a: 25.

108. The text as preserved in Yuankang's commentary reads "萬法雖異." See T.1859–181b: 7.

109. T.223–382c: 23.

110. *Zhuangzi*, chapter 8, "The duck's legs are short but to stretch them would worry him; the crane's legs are long but to shorten them would make him sad." *Zhuangzi*, SBBY 1409, *juan* 4, 2b–3a; Watson, *The Complete Works of Chuang Tzu*, 99–100.

111. T.223–390a: 4.

112. T.223–382c: 23.

113. The text as preserved in Yuankang's commentary has 即 *ji* here instead of 則 *ze*. See 1859–181b: 26.

114. *Laozi* 1, "The two are the same but differ in name as they issue forth." *Laozi Daode jing*, SBBY 1403, *shang pian*, 1b; Lau, *Lao Tzu: Tao Te Ching*, 57.

115. T.630–452b: 29.

116. Both the *Taishō* and the *Dai Nihonzokuzōkyō* note that the *Yuan* version of the text has 曰 yue for 云 yun.

117. T.475–537c: 18.

118. Yuankang (T.1859–181c: 10–11) says that Sengzhao is referring both to "*Prajñā* is Not-knowing" and to the two *sūtras* just quoted. Huida (DNZ 2.B 23.4–437b) says that Sengzhao's words can cause us to know not just his treatise but also *prajñā*. Compare Sengzhao's closing words in "Emptiness of the Unreal": "So then, is Dao far? It touches [all] phenomena yet is True. Is the Sage far? Embodying him, [you] are identical to his Spirit." (T.1858–153a: 4–5) and "Things Do Not Shift": "If you can conform your spirit to identify with [all] things, then [Truth] is not far and can be known." (T.1858–151c: 27–28).

Appendix III

1. T.1858–154c: 24–157a: 11 and DNZ 2.1.1–35–38. Japanese translation in Tsukamoto et al, *Jōron Kenkyū*, 36. Previous English translation in Liebenthal, *Chao Lun*, 81–100. This title is my own invention to combine both letters into a single text.

2. 劉遺民書問附 "Liu Yimin's appended Questions." Huida has the title as 隱士劉遺民書問無知論 "The retired scholar Liu Yimin's questions on the essay '[*Prajñā*] is Not-knowing'."

3. I follow Liebenthal in separating the cover letter from the main letter and in subdividing the text of the latter, making only minor changes. Liebenthal himself follows the commentaries of Huida and Yuankang.

4. The text has 和南 *he nan*, the Chinese rendering of the Sanskrit *vandanam*.

5. Referring to the letter that Daosheng brought to Lushan with a copy of "*Prajñā* is Not-knowing," in 408.

6. Yuankang does not have these last two sentences.

7. The hostilities that led to the collapse of the Jin dynasty centered in the Yangtze region just north of Lushan. See Liebenthal, *Chao Lun*, 81 (note 348).

8. Liu refers to himself as Sengzhao's "disciple" even though they are of different lineages.

9. The character 瘵 *zhai* today means tuberculosis.

10. 慧明道人, "Huiming, man of Dao." His identity is unknown.

11. Possibly a reference to the notion of *vāsanā* ("perfuming"), in which the Buddhas and Bodhisattvas exercise a pervasive spiritual influence upon those they encounter.

12. According to Yuankang (T.1859–182a: 21–22) the "traces" are the words of "*Prajñā* is Not-knowing," which have illuminated Liu's mind.

13. 霞, rose-colored clouds of mist. Distant, mysterious place, suggesting Daoist associations.

14. Sengzhao.

15. As per Huida (DNZ 2.B 23.4–38a and b) and Yuankang (T.1859–182b: 7–11). *Tuanci* (lit. "decisions and judgments") refers to the explanations of the various hexagrams of the *Yijing* attributed to King Wen of Zhou (ca. 1150 B.C.E.), or possibly the *Tuan Juan* ("Commentary on the Decision"), the commentary on the *Yijing* traditionally attributed to Confucius which comprises the "first and second wings" of this work.

16. Liebenthal translates this phrase as "past incarnations" (Liebenthal, *Chao Lun*, 82) but that seems unwarranted. Liu is referring to his life in the world prior to his "retirement."

17. Liu's current life on Lushan.

18. An allusion to the third line of the hexagram 乾 *qian* ("the Creative") in the *Yijing*: "All day long the noble person is creatively active. At night his mind is still beset with cares." See *Zhou yi*, SBBY 1, *juan* 1, 1a; Wilhelm and Baynes, *The I Ching*, 8.

19. Yuankang (T.1859–182c: 2–4) quotes the *Analects* 2.4, "The Master said, 'At fifteen, I set my mind on learning. At thirty, I was established. At forty, I had no doubts. At fifty, I knew the Mandate of Heaven. At sixty, my ear was attuned. At seventy, I could follow what my heart desired without transgressing what was right." *Lunyu*, SBBY 308, *juan* 1, 7a–b; Lau, *Confucius: The Analects*, 63.

20. Zhu Daosheng (360–434), one of Zhu Fatai's disciples. He came to Lushan in 397 to study before venturing north to Chang'an. He returned to Lushan in 408 with a copy of Sengzhao's treatise.

21. The Mahāyāna *sūtras*, especially the *Pañca*.

22. The various *prajñā* schools.

23. Yuankang (T.1859–182c: 29–183a: 1) says the singer is Sengzhao and the song is "*Prajñā* is Not-knowing."

24. See Sengzhao's reply to Question 3 in "*Prajñā* is Not-knowing," III, T.1858–154a: 7–27.

25. Liu is paraphrasing the first line of Sengzhao's reply to Question 2 in "*Prajñā* is Not-knowing," III, T.1858–153c: 23. This phrase, however, is Sengzhao's summary "quotation" of the Mahāyāna *sūtras*.

26. These are Sengzhao's own words following the "quotation" that Liu cites at T.1858–153c: 24.

27. T.221–140c: 15. Quoted by Sengzhao at T.1858–153b: 14–15.

28. From Sengzhao's reply to Question 1 in *"Prajñā* is Not-knowing," III, T.1858–153b: 28–29.

29. From Sengzhao's reply to Question 9 in *"Prajñā* is Not-knowing," III, T.1858–154c: 16.

30. From Sengzhao's reply to Question 9 in *"Prajñā* is Not-knowing," III, T.1858–154c: 18–19.

31. Cf. Wang Bi's description of the Sage (Confucius) as identical to non-being (*wu*) in his essence.

32. *Yijing* 7.8b, "Only through the Divine can one hurry without haste ..." *Zhou yi Xici shang,* SBBY 3, 8b; Wilhelm and Baynes, *The I Ching,* 316.

33. *Zhuangzi,* chapter 4, "If you do not keep still, this is what is called sitting but racing around." *Zhuangzi,* SBBY 1408, *juan* 2, 8a; Watson, *The Complete Works of Chuang Tzu,* 58.

34. Liu is trying to understand Sengzhao but he gets him wrong here. Sengzhao explicitly says the Sagely Mind (*prajñā*) is always "not-knowing."

35. Cf. He Yan's *Wuming lun* ("Treatise on the Nameless"). Recall that Liu compared Sengzhao to He Yan.

36. Liebenthal translates this line as "I confess to having never been able to understand this abstruse theory." See Liebenthal, *Chao Lun,* 84. Although a gloss, Liebenthal's translation conveys Liu's point that he simply does not understand the paradoxical nature of the Sagely Mind.

37. Yuankang (T.1859–183b: 15–16) writes that the following alternatives that Liu proposes concern the Sage as knowing and not-knowing.

38. 靈 *ling* ("numinous," "divine").

39. 冥符 *mingfu.* The "tally" is like the two portions of a bamboo slip used for identification. In this case it has a religious (Daoist) meaning, referring to the record of the "soul" kept by the judge of the underworld who, based upon it, determines the dead person's fate. Liu is asking if we can conceive of the Sage's wisdom as encompassing all phenomena in the universe, even our individual destinies, which are normally hidden from view.

40. *Laozi* 20, "The multitudes are joyful, as if partaking of the *tai lao* offering or ascending a terrace in spring. I alone practice non-action (*wuwei*) and reveal no signs..." See *Laozi Daode jing,* SBBY 1403, *shang pian,* 12a; Lau, *Lao Tzu: Tao Te Ching,* 76.

41. 寂照 *jizhao.* Liu misquotes Sengzhao here since Sengzhao speaks of 寂用 ("stillness and function").

42. 定慧, "fixing (one's) awareness," the basic style of meditation in almost all schools of Buddhism.

43. *Yijing* 7.10b, "If there were no more changes to see, the effects of the Creative and the Receptive would also gradually cease." *Zhouyi Xici shang,* SBBY 3, 10b; Wilhelm and Baynes, *The I Ching,* 323. Liu is saying that the Sage's Mind will be pure and still thus when there is nothing to respond to, the Sage will not be or know. There will be no Sagely knowing or acting.

44. From Sengzhao's reply to Question 1 in *"Prajñā* is Not-knowing" III, T.1858–153c: 9.

45. Liu and his colleagues on Lushan have confused the levels of truth, separating the Ultimate from the relative as if they were two spheres of being. In fact, the Sage knows there is no such separation.

46. From Sengzhao's reply to Question 5 in "*Prajñā* is Not-knowing" III, T.1858–154b: 6–7.

47. Liu is troubled by the way in which Sengzhao speaks of the Sage as one who uses language (matches "things" with "words") but does not regard the expressions so formed as true. For Sengzhao the Sage "matches [things with words] yet does not affirm [that words fully express truth]." See Sengzhao's reply to Question 1 in "*Prajñā* is Not-knowing" III, T.1858–153c: 13.

48. Liu's point is pure common sense. Ignorant people use words incorrectly and make statements that are not true. Those who have understanding, on the other hand, use words correctly and make true statements. For Liu this distinction seems obvious. He does not see how in "*Prajñā* is Not-knowing" Sengzhao is playing off the two levels of truth in the fashion of **Vimalakīrti** and **Nāgārjuna**.

49. 好相 *hao xiang*, literally "good marks." Huiyuan approved of Sengzhao's words.

50. A perceptive hermeneutic insight on Liu's part. He and Sengzhao have different presuppositions informing how they understand Sageliness and how they read the texts.

51. Both the *Taishō* and *Dai Nihonzokuzōkyō* merely have 答劉遺民書 "Reply to Liu Yimin's Letter."

52. Liu's letter.

53. The Harvest Festival, 15th day of the 8th month.

54. In the *Taishō* text, Sengzhao refers to himself as 貪道 - lit. "desiring Dao." The *Dai Nihonzokuzōkyō*, though, has 貧道 - "poor (man) of Dao," which has a more humilific sense. Both epithets are fitting.

55. 病 *bing*. Although Sengzhao was no doubt ill, this is the same character denoting the feigned illness of the Bodhisattva **Vimalakīrti** (T. 474–521a: 26; T.475–539b: 25) and to Master Yu's sudden illness in Chapter 6 of the *Zhuangzi* (SBBY 1408, *juan* 3, 8a–b).

56. Following Liebenthal (*Chao Lun*, 88, note 391) and Yuankang (T.1859–184b: 10) I read 住 zhu as 佳 jia. Liebenthal's reference to Huida's commentary here is mistaken.

57. Sengzhao is a monk while Liu is a layman but both follow the Sagely Way. My translation follows Liebenthal's gloss. Sengzhao actually writes 妙期不二("[our] wondrous aspirations are not two.")

58. 嘉遯 *jia dun*, an allusion to hexagram 33 (*dun*) of the *Yijing*: "The Judgment: Retreat. Success. In what is small perseverance furthers. The Image: Mountain under Heaven: the image of retreat. Thus the noble person keeps the petty person at a distance, not angrily but with reserve." *Zhou yi*, SBBY 3, *juan* 4, 3a–b; Wilhelm and Baynes, *The I Ching*, 129–130.

59. 方寸 *fang cun* ("square inch"), the heart but also a focus of Daoist "inner alchemy."

60. Allusion to Ruan Ji and the Seven Worthies of the Bamboo Grove, who never strayed from their Daoist lifestyle. The former Emperor Sima Zhao said of Ruan Ji, "Whenever I talk with him, all his talk is about the abstruse and the remote. I have never heard him pass any judgment on personalities." See Mather, *Shih shuo Hsin-yu*, 9.

61. *Laozi* 10, "When carrying your perplexed bodily soul, can you embrace the One and not let go?" *Laozi Daode jing*, SBBY 1403, *shang bian*, 6a; Lau, *Lao Tzu: Tao Te Ching*, 66. "Embracing the One" is a common form of Daoist meditation.

62. *Analects* 7.8, "The Master said, 'When I reveal one corner (一 yi yu) of a subject to anyone and he does not get the other three, I do not repeat it.'" *Lunyu*, SBBY 308, *juan* 4, 2a–b; Lau, *Confucius: The Analects*, 86. Here Sengzhao seems to be referring to himself anxiously

gazing in the direction (*yi yu*) of Lu Shan and regretting his separation, emphasizing the gulf and the feeling of remoteness through the image of the bank of clouds or mist. Simultaneously, however, Sengzhao is also admitting to his inability to grasp the profundity of Huiyuan's wisdom. Thus the sentence can just as easily read, "Each time I lift my thoughts to one corner (*yi yu*) [of his teaching it is as if] I hang suspended in a bank of clouds."

63. *Analects* 15.28, "The Master said, 'Humanity is able to enlargen Dao, it is not that Dao enlargens humanity." See *Lunyu*, SBBY 309, *juan* 9, 5b; Lau, *Confucius: The Analects*, 136. Lau's numbering differs slightly from the original. He has this passage as 15.29.

64. I follow Yuankang (T.1859–185a: 25) in reading 國 *guo* instead of 典 *dian*.

65. Gṛddhakūta Mountain, said to be where the *Lotus* and other Mahāyāna *sūtras* were preached.

66. Zhi Faling, a disciple of Huiyuan sent by to Central Asia to obtain Buddhist scriptures in 392. He spent some time in Khotan collecting various texts including an abbreviated version of the *Avataṁsaka sūtra*.

67. The exact date of Faling's arrival in Chang'an is uncertain but it was most likely between 406 and 408.

68. Both the *Taishō* and *Dai Nihonzokuzōkyō* versions of the text lack a specific subject. Grammatically one could read this as implying that Zhi Faling invited the monks mentioned below but this makes no sense. Yao Xing, after all, made concerted efforts to attract prominent monks from all over Central Asia.

69. Buddhabhadra (d. 429), a disciple of the Sarvāstivāda master Buddhasena who came to Chang'an to study with Kumārajīva only to be expelled in 411 over disputes between himself and other members of the Chang'an community. He eventually made his way to Lushan where Huiyuan received him warmly.

70. Buddhayaśas, a great teacher of Mahāyāna. He was the teacher from whom Kumārajīva first learned Mahāyāna teachings in Kashgar and he received royal treatment when he came to Chang'an. Several commentaries hold that this teacher was actually Dharmaruci, another foreign monk, but this seems untenable. See Liebenthal, *Chao Lun*, 90–91 (note 406).

71. Dharmayaśas and Dharmagupta, both of whom were from Kashmir and arrived in Chang'an in 407.

72. A.k.a. "The Great Monastery," one of the two main large compounds which housed the translation bureau along with the "Aśoka compound."

73. Kumārajīva was translating the texts brought by Faling and the other monks mentioned above.

74. A significant passage involving a pun on the word 藏 *zang* ("treasury," "store-house"). Sengzhao is speaking both of Dharma in the broadest sense as the repository of Buddhist teachings (the Truth reaching throughout the cosmos) and Dharma in the form of the *Tripiṭaka*, the actual collection of written texts (growing ever larger as more texts arrive for translation). The latter clause is most intriguing. Literally it reads 日有異"D ("daily it has different sounds"). Sengzhao is untroubled by apparent contradictions between various texts; all are authentic teachings. Dharma is plurivocal–it speaks in many voices.

75. The "Aśoka compound."

76. In each instance the word I translate as "meditation" is the Chinese term 禪 c *han*, although it would be a mistake to see this as a reference to a distinct *chan* lineage.

77. The *Dharmaguptaka vinaya*, T. 1428, translated from 410–412.

78. This monastery was located inside the city walls.

79. A reference to the famous story of **Buddhayaśas'** recitation of the entire text (some 447 pages in the *Taishō*) from memory without any mistake. The Chinese doubted this could be done but he proved himself first by reciting a medical manual that the Chinese could check from a written copy.

80. Another compound for monks of the translation bureau.

81. *Sheli fo abitan lun*, T.1548. A text of the Dharmagupta sect, this copy was taken down in 407–408 but the Indian monks needed to learn more Chinese to translate it. It was finally finished in 414. See Liebenthal, *Chao Lun*, 91, note 412.

82. Jetavana, a park near **Śrāvast** that once belonged to Prince Jeta. It was obtained by the elder **Anāthapiṇḍada**, a wealthy Buddhist patron, and became a favorite site for **Śākyamuni** and his followers.

83. This last phrase is ambiguous but it appears Sengzhao is expressing his desire for joining with Liu and his colleague in the Chang'an community. Perhaps a subtle invitation?

84. The dates of Daosheng's sojourn in Chang'an are a matter of dispute but the consensus seems to be that he was there from 407–408 or 409.

85. Sengzhao actually writes 何言 he yan–"what's the word?"

86. Otherwise unknown.

87. The collection of devotional songs used by the Lushan community.

88. A statement pregnant with Daoist association, refering both to the notion of "free and easy wandering" (*Zhuangzi* chapter 1) and the legend of Laozi's departure from China through the gates of the west.

89. 406 C.E.

90. Sengzhao has a double meaning here. First and most obviously, he means that his commentary is based on the original text (and **Kumārajīva's** exposition) and thus should be considered authoritative. Yet Sengzhao's use of the term 本 *ben* ("root," substance") points to a deeper, ontological meaning for *xuanxue* thinkers. Sengzhao is saying his commentary, despite its lack of literary merit (he is appropriately humble), is based on the Truth of Reality itself.

91. This paragraph is one of the few passages of "The Correspondence" that Robinson translates. See Robinson, *Early Mādhyamika in India and China*, 137.

92. An allusion to a famous parable in chapter twenty-four of the *Zhuangzi*. As he is passing the grave of Huizi, Zhuangzi relates to his followers the story of a plasterer and a carpenter (mason?) who worked together. When the plasterer got a speck on his nose his friend would wield his hatchet so skillfully that he would slice off the speck without hurting the man. When later called by a lord to perform the same feat the carpenter sadly tells him he can longer do it as friend has since died. In what is probably the most touching scene in the entire work, Zhuangzi then addresses Huizi, lamenting that since his passing he (Zhuangzi) no longer has anyone with whom he can speak. See *Zhuangzi*, SBBY 1410, *juan* 8, 16a; Watson, *The Complete Works of Chuang Tzu*, 269. This allusion is one of our most important clues to the depth and sincerity of the friendship between Sengzhao and Liu Yimin.

93. See Liu's first question, T.1858–155a: 24. Note that Sengzhao is quoting Liu's letter here wherein he (Liu) misquotes Sengzhao.

94. T.1858–155a: 26–27.
95. T.1858–155a: 27.
96. A major theme in the *Zhuangzi* and an essential part of cultivation. See especially the exchange in Chapter 6 between Yan Hui and Confucius where the former improves by "forgetting" everything. *Zhuangzi*, SBBY vol. 1408, *juan* 3, 14a–b; Watson, *The Complete Works of Chuang Tzu*, 90–91.
97. T.1858–156a: 6–7. This last sentence is Sengzhao's response to Liu's declaration that he and his colleagues are seeking the differences within the Sage's Mind (T.1858–155a: 28). For Sengzhao such a statement indicates that Liu and his friends are already in error.
98. T.1858 –158a: 29.
99. T.1858–158b: 1–3.
100. T.1858–156a: 10–13.
101. T.1858–156a: 13.
102. T.1858–155a: 24.
103. T.1858–155b: 4.
104. T.1858–156a: 15–16. Note that the "self" of which Sengzhao speaks here is not a permanent "soul" or *ātman* but the "true self" of the Sage, who embodies Principle or non-being.
105. 不有有, lit. "not existingly exists".
106. Sengzhao's point here is both Daoist and Buddhist: the Sage's Mind is not a "thing" among the myriad things for the Sage is in essence "non-being". Similarly, this Mind is not a real permanent entity, i.e. an *ātman*. Thus although we may speak of the Sage as "existing," he is really "void" of such description.
107. I follow Yuankang (T.1859–187a: 11–13) in reading this sentence as contrasting the mind of the Sage to our rational and discriminating consciousness. Since the Sage's Mind cannot be said to exist or not-exist, it is perpetually cut-off from the world of separate "things."
108. Reading 謂 *wei* for 通 *tong*, following Yuankang, T.1859–187a: 19.
109. Cf. Kumārajīva's translation of the *Pañca*, T.223–292c: 15.
110. *Laozi* 41, "The Great Square has no corners." *Laozi Daode jing*, SBBY 1403, *xia pian*, 4a–5a; Lau, *Lao Tzu: Tao Te Ching*, 102. Also *Analects* 7.8. See note 62 above.
111. *Laozi* 38, "Foresight is merely the flowery embellishment of Dao, and the beginning of folly." *Laozi Daode jing*, SBBY 1403, *xia pian*, 1a–b; Lau, *Lao Tzu: Tao Te Ching*, 99.
112. All things are "one" in that they all are essentially "empty" of own-being. There are, thus, no real, true "things" and this fact is true reality. Yet this "empty nature" all things share is itself not a "thing."
113. Cf. The *Fangguang*, T.221–61c: 6.
114. *Prajñā* discerns even the most hidden mysteries, apprehending all possibilities before they come to be.
115. 且無知生於無知無知知也無有知也.
116. Sengzhao is quoting "*Prajñā* is Not-knowing," T.1858–153b: 11.
117. Unknown. According to Yuankang (T.1859–188a: 4), this is the main idea of the *Pañca*, although he actually refers by name to Kumārajīva's version (the *Da pin jing*, T.223) of this text, and not to the earlier *Fangguang*, T.221, as Liebenthal indicates.

118. 非有非非有非無非非無. Here Sengzhao is using the *catuṣkoṭi*, an indication of his growing awareness of the technical side of Nāgārjuna's philosophy.

119. T.221–39c: 20ff.

120. Sengzhao is quoting Liu's third question, T.1858–155b: 7–8.

121. Cf. The *Pañca* (T.223–223a: 13) and/or the "Heart *Sūtra*", T.250–847c: 10–11.

122. A *xuanxue* adaptation of a *prasaṅga* argument. Sengzhao equates "the changes" with form (*rūpa*) and "the markless" with emptiness (*śūnyatā*) and then demonstrates how these are not separate (*pace* Liu and his colleagues). The Sage is not of two minds but perceives both form and emptiness all at once.

123. Once again Sengzhao restates in more familiar *xuanxue* terms the "thesis" of the *sūtras*.

124. A reference to *upāya*. The Buddha/Sage adopts his teachings to suit his audience.

125. 玄 xuan, "dark." A dig at Liu and his colleagues, *xuanxue* thinkers for whom the texts truly are "dark."

126. T.1858–156c: 14–17.

127. Sengzhao is referring to Liu's second question.

128. Yuankang (T.1859–189a: 7–8) considers this whole passage to be an allusion to the *Zhuangzi*.

129. T.1858–155b: 14–15. Sengzhao is quoting from Liu's third question but he omit several words.

130. T.1858–155b: 13–14. As with the previous quote, so here Sengzhao also omits some of Liu's words.

131. *Laozi* 1, "The Dao that can be dao'ed is not the eternal Dao; the name that can be named is not the eternal name." *Laozi Daode jing*, SBBY 1403, *shang pian* 1a; Lau, *Lao Tzu: Tao Te Ching*, 57.

132. An extremely interesting passage in which Sengzhao tells Liu how to interpret passages about the Sage/Buddha using both Daoist and Buddhist strategies. Liu must begin with an "empty mind" (i.e. lack preconceived "rational" ideas) and then understand the words as saying something different from what they appear to say (cf. *neyārtha* and *nītārtha*). When we read of the Sage "affirming" and "meeting" this does not mean that the Sage affirms things as *really existing* or meets *really existing* things. These are just ways of speaking, "wild words" that do not denote states of affairs but evoke the carefree life of the Sage.

133 形 xing ("figure," "for m," "appearance"). This differs from *rūpa* (usually translated into Chinese as *se*) as *xing* refers to the actual shape or figure of something rather than "materiality."

134. Sengzhao's point is subtle. Yuankang interprets this passage along Buddhist lines while Huida cites Zhuangzi. See T.1859–189a: 25–b: 1 and DNZ 2.B 23.4–442b: 7–16.

135. T.1858–157a: 1–3.

136. Sengzhao is making some interesting rhetorical moves here, paraphrasing Liu's statements in his third question (T.1858–155b: 11ff) and combining them with Liu's confession of ignorance (T.1858–155b: 10–11). Although Sengzhao has already addressed Liu's third question at the beginning of Section 2.E (T.1858–156c: 24–25) he is returning to it again.

137. T.1858–157a: 5–6. Yuankang says this sentence is about the Sagely Mind ("聖心," T.1859–189b: 13–14) but it may refer to the relationship between words and things, the truth which the Sage alone knows.

138. Allusion to an incident in Chapter fourteen of the *Zhuangzi* where Laozi explains to Confucius that the Six Classics are merely the words/traces of former Sages, not that which made the paths. *Zhuangzi*, SBBY 1409, *juan* 5, 26b; Watson, *The Complete Works of Chuang Tzu*, 166.

139. Sengzhao alludes to the opening lines of "*Prajñā* is Not-knowing," T.1858–153a: 8.

140. Yet another instance where Sengzhao informs his readers (Liu and his colleagues–"keen-minded gentlemen") how to understand his words. They should use his words ("wild words") to attain what is beyond words. The word 期 qi here is truly "wild," as it can mean "to fix, delimit" as well as "to hope" or "wait for." It is akin to "wu forms" of other words, in that it has both passive and active qualities, perhaps denoting the proper interpretive frame of mind in which to approach Sengzhao's work.

GLOSSARY

Anchō 安澄

Anpan shouyi jing 安般守一經

An Shigao 安世高

Bailun 百論

Bailun xu 百論序

Baopuzi 抱朴子

benwu 名無

Benwu yi 名無異

Binaiye xu 鼻奈耶序

bing 病

Biyan lu 碧巖錄

buren 不仁

buwu 不無

buyou 不有

Buzhenkong 不真空

Chan 禪

Chang'an 長安

Chengju guangming
    dingyi jing 成具光明定意經

Chusanzang jiji 出三藏記

Chunqiu 春秋

Dacheng dayi zhang 大乘大義章

Dacheng qixin lun 大乘起信論

Daji jing 大集經

Daming du jing 大明度經

dazhi 大智

Dazhi du lun 大智度論

Da Zhuan 大傳

Dao 道

Daoan 道安

Daode jing 道德經

Daoheng 道恒

daojia 道家

Daojiao 道教

Daosui 道邃

Daoxian lun 道仙論

Daoxing jing xu 道行經序

Daoxing panruo jing 道行般若經

Daoxuan 道宣

Daoyi 道噎

de 德

Deqing 得清

dian 顛

ding 定

Donglin si 東林寺

Erdi lun 二諦論

Fashen 法深

faxing 法性

fan 反

fanzhao 反照

Fangguang jing 放光經

fangwai 方外

Fang Xuanling 房玄齡

feiwu 非無

feiyou 非有

fen 分

Fotudeng 佛圖澄

Fozulidai tongzai 佛祖歷代通載

Fu Jian 符堅

Fu Xi 伏羲

ganying 感應

Gaosengzhuan 高嘎

Ge Hong 葛洪

geyi 格義

gongan 公案

Gongson Long 公孫龍

guannei 關內

Guanghongming ji 廣弘明

guoshi 國師

Guo Xiang 郭象

He Yan 何晏

hei 黑

huahu 化胡

Huainanzi 淮南子

Huan Xuan 桓玄

Huichang 慧常

Huida 慧達

Huideng 慧燈

huiming 慧明

Huineng 慧能

Huiyuan 慧遠

Huizi 惠子

ji 寂

jizhao 寂照

jise 即色

Jise youxuan lun 即色遊玄論

ji 跡

Jiankang 建康

Jin 晉

Jinshu 晉書

jing 經

kuang 狂

kuang (form Kumārajīva uses) 誑

kuangfu 狂夫

kuangyan 狂言

Laozi 老子

li (principle) 理

li (rites) 禮

Liji 禮記

Lidai sanbao ji 歷代三寶記

Liu Chengzhi 劉程之

Liu Qiu 劉虬

Liu Yimin 劉遺民

Liujia qizong lun 凹家七宗論

Lu Guang 呂光

Lushan 廬山

Lunyu 論語

ming (light, understanding) 明

ming (name, word) 名

mingjiao 名教

mingli 名理

mo 默

moyou 末有

Mozi 墨子

Moho panruo polomi jing 摩訶般若波羅蜜經

mu 母

Mumonkon 無門關 (Japanese)

nian 念

Nianfo sanmei yong 念佛三昧詠

Niepan wuming 涅槃無名

Panzhou sanmei jing 般舟三昧經

Panruo wuzhi 般若無知

Peng 鵬

Pengcheng 彭城

Pingshu 平叔

pu 樸

qi (energy) 氣

qi (to wait, anticipate) 期

qing 情

qingtan 清談

qingyi 清議

Qingtu zong 清土宗

quan 犬

rujia 儒家

Sanguo 三國

Sanlun zong 三論宗

se 色

Sengrui 寡

Sengyu 僧

Sengzhao 僧肇

*Shamen bujing wangzhe
    lun* 沙門不 敬王者論

Shanmen xuanyi 山門玄義

Shelifo apitan lun 舍利佛阿毗曇論

shen 訖

sheng 聖

shenming 訖明

Shenxiu 訖秀

shi (consciousness) 識

shihan 識含

shi (real) 實

shixiang 實

Shixiang lun 實量

shi (scholar) 士

Shijing 詩經

Shisi lun 釋私論

Shishuo xinyu 世說新語

Shujing 書經

Shun 舜

Silun zong 四論宗

Sun Cho 孫綽

taiji 太極

taiyi 太一

Tanji 曇濟

ti 體

Tiantai 天台

Wang Bi 王弼

Wang Qia 王

Wei 魏

Wei Shou 魏

Weishu 魏書

Weimo jie jing 維摩詰經

wen 文

wenhua 文化

wu 無

Wuming lun 無名論

wuwei 無

wuxin 無心

Wubuqian 俐不遷

wuxing 五行

xi 繫

Xiang Xiu 向秀

Xici 繫辭

xinwu 心無

Xi Kang 稀康

xu 虛

Xu Gaosengzhuan 續高嘎

xuan 玄

xuan junzi 玄君子

xuanming 玄明

Xuan pu 玄圃

xuanxue 玄學

Xunyang 尋

Yan Hui 顏回

yang **陽**

Yao 堯

Yao Song **姚嵩**

Yao Xing **姚興**

Yijing **易經**

yin 陰

yinyuan 因緣

yong 用

you 有

Yudao lun 喻道論

Yuankang 元康

Yuanren lun 元人論

Yu Fakai **于法開**

Yu Falan 于法蘭

yuanhui 緣會

Yuejing 樂經

zhao 照

Zhaolun **肇論**

zhenren 真人

zhenyan 真言

zhi (knowing) 知

zhi (Wisdom) 智

Zhi Dun 支遁

Zhi Mindu **支愍度**

Zhi Qian 支謙

zhiren 至人

zhiyan 卮言

Zhongguan lun su 中觀論疏

Zhonglun suji 中論疏記

Zhouli 周禮

Zhouyi Lueli **周易略例**

Zhu Daosheng 竺道生

Zhu Fatai 竺法汰

Zhu Fawen 竺法溫

Zhu Xi 江Q

zhuan **傳**

Zhuangzi 莊子

ziran 自然

WORKS CITED

Primary Texts in Classical Chinese

Texts from the Sibu beiyao (SBBY)

Confucius (Kong Fuzi) 孔夫子. *Lunyu* 論語 [The *Analects*].
Guo Xiang 郭象. *Zhuangzi zhu* 莊子註 [Commentary on the *Zhuangzi*].
Jinshu 晉書 [History of the Jin dynasty].
Laozi Daode jing 老子道德經 [Laozi's Classic of Dao and De].
Wang Bi 王弼. *Laozi zhu* 老子註 [Commentary on the *Laozi*].
———. *Zhouyi Lueli* 周易略例 [Commentary on the Book of Changes].
Weishu 魏書 [History of the Wei dynasty].
Yijing 易經 [The Book of Changes]. (N.B. Includes *Da zhuan*, "The Great Commentary"].
Zhuangzi 莊子 [Book of Master Zhuang].

Texts from the Taishō shinshū daizōkyō

Anchō 安澄. *Zhonglun su ji* 中論疏記 [Subcommentary on the Middle Treatise]. Vol. 65, No. 2255.
Āryadeva. *Bai lun* 百論 [Hundred Treatise]. Translated by Kumārajīva. Vol. 45, No. 1569.
Aśvaghoṣa, attr. *Da cheng qixin lun* 大乘起信論 [The Awakening of Faith in the Mahāyāna]. Translated by Paramārtha. Vol. 32, No. 1666.
Daoxing panruo polomi jing 道行般若波羅蜜經 [*Daśasāhasrikā prajñāpāramitā sūtra*]. Translated by Lokakṣema. Vol. 8, No. 224.
Daoxuan 道宣. *Guang hongming ji* 廣弘明集 [Further Collected Essays on Buddhism]. Vol. 52, No. 2103.
Fangguang panruo polomi jing 放光般若波羅蜜經 [*Pañcaviṃśatisāhasrikā prajñāpāramitā sūtra*]. Translated by Mokṣala. Vol. 8, No. 221.

Fei Changfang 費長房. *Lidai sanbao ji* 歷代三寶記 [Historical Dynastic Record of the Three Jewels]. Vol. 49, No. 2034.

Guifeng Zongmi 圭峰宗密. *Yuanren lun* 元人論 [Inquiry into the Origin of Humanity]. Vol. 45, No. 1887.

Huiyuan and **Kumārajīva**. *Dacheng dayi zhang* 大乘大義章 [Chief Ideas of the **Mahāyāna**]. Vol. 45, No. 1856.

Huijiao 慧皎. *Gaosengzhuan* 高僧傳 [Biographies of Eminent Monks]. Vol. 50, No. 2059.

Jizang 吉藏. *Erdi lun* 二諦論 [Treatise on the Two Truths]. Vol. 44, No. 1854.

———. *Zhong guan lun su* 中觀論疏 [Commentary on the Middle Treatise]. Vol. 42, No. 1824.

Kātyāyanīputra. *Shelifo apitan lun* 舍利佛阿毗曇論 [*Śāriputra Abhidharma*, a.k.a. *Jñānaprasthāna śāstra*]. Translated by **Dharmayaśas** and **Dharmagupta**. Vol., No. 1548.

Moho panruo polomi damingzhou jing 摩訶般若波羅蜜大明咒經 ["Heart Sūtra," a.k.a., *Prajñā pāramitā hṛdaya sūtra*]. Translated by **Kumārajīva**, Vol. 8, No. 250.

Moho panruo polomi jing 摩訶般若波羅蜜經 [*Pañcaviṃśātisāhasrikā prajñāpāramitā sūtra*]. Translated by **Kumārajīva**. Vol. 8, No. 223.

Nāgārjuna, attr. *Dazhidu lun* 大智度論 [Great Perfection of Wisdom Treatise]. Translated by **Kumārajīva**. Vol. , No. 1509.

Nianchang 念常. *Fozu lidai tongzai* 佛祖歷代通載 [Complete Historical Dynastic Account of the lineage of the Buddha]. Vol. 49, No. 2036.

Sengyou 僧祐. *Chusanzangji ji* 出三藏記集 [Collected records on the production of the *Tripiṭaka*]. Vol. 50, No. 2145.

Sengzhao 僧肇. *Zhu Weimojie jing* 註維摩詰經 [Vimalakīrti Commentary]. Vol. 38, No. 1775.

———. *Zhaolun* 肇論 [Treatises of Zhao]. Vol. 45, No. 1858. (Includes Introduction, Things Do Not Shift", "Emptiness of the Not-Ultimate", "*Prajna* is Not-Knowing", and "Correspondence with Liu Yimin").

Weimojie jing 維摩詰經 [*Vimalakīrtinirdeśa sūtra*]. Translated by Zhi Qian. Vol. 14, No. 474.

Weimojie suoshuo jing 維摩詰所說經 [*Vimalakīrtinirdeśa sūtra*]. Translated by **Kumārajīva**. Vol. 14, No. 475.

Wencai 文才. *Zhaolun xinsu* 肇論新疏 [New Commentary on the *Zhaolun*]. Vol. 45, No. 1860.

Yuankang 元康. *Zhaolun su* 肇論疏 [Commentary on the *Zhaolun*]. Vol. 45, No. 1859.

Texts from the Dai Nihonzokuzōkyō

Huida 慧達. *Zhaolun su* 肇論疏 [Commentary on the *Zhaolun*], 2.B 23.4

Sengzhao. *Zhaolun* [Treatises of Zhao], 2.1.1.

Secondary Sources and Texts in Translation

Sengzhao, Neo-Daoism, Chinese Buddhism

Bergeron, Marie-Ina. *Wang Pi, Philosophe du Non-Avoir*. Varieties Sinologiques–Nouvelle Serie No. 69. Paris: L'institut Ricci, 1986.

Cai, Zongqi. "Derrida and Seng-zhao: Linguistic and Philosophical Deconstructions." *Philosophy East and West* 43 (July 1993): 389–404.

Chan, Alan K. L. *Two Visions of the Way: A Study of the Wang Pi and the Ho-shang Commentaries on the Lao-Tzu.* Albany: State University of New York Press, 1991.

Ch'en, Kenneth K. S. *Buddhism in China: A Historical Survey.* Princeton: Princeton University Press, 1964.

———. "Neo-Taoism and the *Prajñā* School during the Wei and Jin Dynasties." *Chinese Culture* 1 (1957): 33–46.

De Jong, J. W. "Buddha's Word in China." In *Buddhist Studies,* ed. Gregory Schopen, 77–101. Berkeley: Asian Humanities Press, 1979.

Demieville, Paul. "La Penetration du Bouddhisme dans la tradition philosophique Chinoise." In *Choix D'Etudes Bouddhiques (1929–1970), par Paul Demieville,* 241–260. Leiden: E. J. Brill, 1973.

———. Review of *Jōron Kenkyū,* by Tsukamoto Zenryū. *T'oung Pao* 45 (1957): 229.

———. Review of Lamotte's *Traite, tome II. Journal Asiatique* (1950): 375–395.

Dumoulin, Heinrich. *Zen Buddhism: A History–Volume I, India and China.* Translated by James W. Heisig and Paul Knitter. New York: Macmillan Publishing Company, 1988.

Fukunaga Kōji 福永光司. "Sojō to Rōso shisō" 僧肇と老荘思想 [Sengzhao and Lao-Zhuang Thought]. In *Jōron Kenkyū* 肇論研究 [Zhaolun Studies], ed. Tsukamoto Zenryū, 252–271. Kyoto: Hozokan, 1955.

Gregory, Peter N. *Inquiry into the Origin of Humanity: an Annotated Translation of Tsung-mi's Yuan jen lun with a Modern Commentary.* Honolulu: The Kuroda Institute, University of Hawaii Press, 1995.

———. *Tsung-mi and the Sinification of Buddhism.* Princeton: Princeton University Press, 1991.

Hakeda, Yoshito S., trans. *The Awakening of Faith.* New York & London: Columbia University Press, 1967.

Hashimoto Hōkei 橋本芳契. "Sojō ni okeru daihishin no mondai." 僧肇における大悲心の問題 [Questions on *Mahākaruṇā* in Sengzhao's work]. *Indogaku Bukkyōgaku Kenkyū* 16 (1968): 542–546 and 17 (1969): 542–545.

Henricks, Robert G, trans. *Philosophy and Argumentation in Third-Century China: The Essays of Hsi K'ang.* Princeton: Princeton University Press, 1983.

Holcombe, Charles. *In the Shadow of the Han: Literati Thought and Society at the Beginning of the Southern Dynasties.* Honolulu: University of Hawaii Press, 1994.

Holzman, Donald. "Les Sept Sages de la Foret des Bambous et la Societe de leur temps." *T'oung Pao* 44 (1956): 317–346.

Hsu, Fang-cheng, trans. *Three Theses of Seng-zhao.* Bilingual ed. Beijing: Chinese Social Sciences Publishing House, 1985.

Hurvitz, Leon. "Chih Tun's Notions of *Prajñā.*" *Journal of the American Oriental Society* 88 (June 1968): 243–260.

———. "The First Systematizations of Buddhist Thought in China." *Journal of Chinese Philosophy* 2 (1975): 361–388.

———, trans. *Wei Shou Treatise on Buddhism and Taoism, an English translation of the original Chinese text of Wei-shu CXIV and the Japanese annotation of Tsukamoto Zenryu.* Reprinted from Yun Kang, the Buddhist cave-temples of the Fifth century A.D. in North China. Volume XVI Supplement. Kyoto University: Jimbunkgaku Kenkyusho, 1956.

Ichimura, Sohei. "On the Paradoxical Method of the Chinese *Mādhyamika*: Seng-Chao and the *Chao-lun* Treatise." *Journal of Chinese Philosophy* 19 (1992): 51–71.

———. "The Sino-Indian transcultural method of **Mādhyamika** Dialectic: **Nāgārjuna** to Seng-chao to Chi-ts'ang." In *Buddhist Heritage in India and Abroad*, ed. G. Kuppuram and K. Kumudamani, 239–266. Delhi: Sundeep Prakashan, 1992.

Ikeda, Daiseku. *The Flower of Chinese Buddhism*. Translated by Burton Watson. New York and Tokyo: Weatherhill, Inc., 1986.

Ikeda, Shūjo 池田宗讓. "Sojō no nichigi." 僧肇の二智義 [The meaning of Sengzhao's Two Types of 'Knowing'] *Taishō Daigaku Sōgō Bukkyō Kenkyūjo Nempō* 3 (1981): 1–14.

Kieschnick, John. *The Eminent Monk: Buddhist Ideals in Medieval Chinese Hagiography*. Honolulu: University of Hawaii Press, 1997.

Kiriya, Seiichi 桐谷征一. "Joron 'Do Ryu Yuimin Sho' no seiritsu jiki nitsuite." 肇論 '答 劉遺民書' の成立時期につて [On the Date and Composition of the *Zhaolun's* "Reply to Liu Yimin"]. *Indogaku Bukkyōgaku Kenkyū* 15 (December 1966): 180–181.

Koseki, Aaron K. "Seng-chao." In *The Encyclopedia of Religion*, Editor-in-chief, Mircea Eliade. New York: MacMillan Publishing Co., 1987.

Lai, Whalen W. "The Early *Prajñā* schools, especially '*Hsin-wu*,' reconsidered." *Philosophy East and West* 32 (January 1983): 61–76.

———. "The Three Jewels in China." In *Buddhist Spirituality: Indian, Southeast Asian, Tibetan, Early Chinese*, ed. Takeuchi Yoshinori, in association with Jan Van Bragt, James W. Heisig, Joseph S. O'Leary, and Paul S. Swanson, 275–342. New York: The Crossroad Publishing Company, 1995.

Liebenthal, Walter. *Chao Lun: The Treatises of Seng-chao*. 2nd rev. ed. Hong Kong: Hong Kong University Press, 1968.

———. "Chinese Buddhism during the 4th and 5th Centuries." *Mounmenta Nipponica* 11 (April 1955): 44–83.

Link, Arthur E. "Shyh Daw-an's Preface to Saṅgharakṣa's *Yogācārabhūmisūtra*." *Journal of the American Oriental Society* 77 (1957): 1–14.

———. "The Taoist Antecedents of Tao-An's *Prajñā* Ontology." *History of Religions* 9 (1969–1970): 181–215.

Liu, Ming-Wood. *Madhyamaka Thought in China*. Leiden: E.J. Brill, 1994.

———. "Seng-Chao and the **Mādhyamika** Way of Refutation." *Journal of Chinese Philosophy* 14 (March 1987): 97–110.

Mano Senryū 間野潛龍. "To Shin shisō shi nempyō" 東晉思想史年表 [Chronology of The History of Ideas in the Eastern Jin]. In *Jōron Kenkyū* 肇論研究 [Zhaolun Studies], ed. Tsukamoto Zenryū, 180. Kyoto: Hozokan, 1955.

Mather, Richard B., trans. *Shih-shuo Hsin-yu: A New Account of Tales of the World, by Liu I-Ching with commentary by Liu Chun*. Minneapolis: University of Minnesota Press, 1976.

———. "Vimalakīrti and Gentry Buddhism." *History of Religions* 8 (1968–69): 60–73.

Muranaka Yūshō 村中祐生. "Chūgoku Nambokuchō jidai no zenkan ni tsuite" 中國南北朝時代の禪觀について [On meditation in China during the period of the Northern and Southern dynasties]. In *Tendai Kanmon no Kichō*. 天台觀門の基調 Tokyo, 1986.

Robinson, Richard H. *Early Mādhyamika in India and China*. Madison: The University of Wisconsin Press, 1967.

———. "Mysticism and Logic in Seng-Chao's Thought." *Philosophy East and West* 8 (1958): 99–120.

Sasaki Kentaku 佐佐木憲徳. *Kan Gi Rikuchō Zenkan Hattenshi Ron* 漢魏六朝禪觀發埋史 [History of meditation during the Han, Wei and Six dynasties]. Second revised edition. Tokyo, 1978.

Somers, Robert M., ed. *Arthur F. Wright: Studies in Chinese Buddhism*. New Haven and London: Yale University Press, 1990.

Tang Yongtong 湯用彤. *Han Wei liangjin Nanbeichao fojiao shi* 漢魏兩晉南北朝佛教史 [History of Buddhism during the Han, Wei, Jin and Northern and Southern dynasties]. Volume 1. Peking, 1938.

———. "On 'Ko-yi,' the Earliest Method by which Indian Buddhism and Chinese Thought were Synthesized." In *Radhakrishnan: Comparative Studies in Philosophy Presented in honour of his Sixtieth Birthday*, 276–286. London: George Allen and Unwin Ltd., 1951.

Tsukamoto Zenryū . "Bukkyōshi ue ni okeru Jōron no igi." 佛教史上における [The Position of the *Zhaolun* in the History of Chinese Buddhist Thought]. In *Jōron Kenkyū* 肇論研究 [*Zhaolun* Studies], ed. Tsukamoto Zenryū, 113–166. Kyoto: Hozokan, 1955.

———. *A History of Early Chinese Buddhism: from its Introduction to the Death of Hui-yuan.* Translated by Leon Hurvitz. Vols. 1 and 2. Tokyo, New York, San Francisco: Kodansha International Ltd., 1985.

Wagner, R. G. "The Original Structure of the Correspondence between Shih Hui-yuan and Kumārajīva." *Harvard Journal of Asiatic Studies* 31 (1971): 28–48.

Wang Pi. *Commentary on the Lao Tzu.* Translated by Ariane Rump in collaboration with Wing-tsit Chan. Honolulu: The University of Hawaii Press, 1979.

Xu Kangsheng. "A Brief Discussion of the 'Xuanxue' School of the Wei-Jin Period." *Chinese Studies in Philosophy* 13 (Fall 1981): 57–86.

Yampolsky, Philip B., trans. *The Platform Sūtra of the Sixth Patriarch: the Text of the Tun-Huang Manuscript.* New York: Columbia University Press, 1967.

Zurcher, Erik. *The Buddhist Conquest of China: the Spread and Adaptation of Buddhism in Early Medieval China.* Leiden: E.J. Brill, 1959.

Chinese Philosophy—Confucianism and Daoism

Allen, Sarah. *The Way of Water and Sprouts of Virtue.* Albany: State University of New York Press, 1997.

Ames, Roger T. "Knowing in the *Zhuangzi*: From Here, on the Bridge, over the River Hao." In *Wandering at Ease in the Zhuangzi*, ed. Roger T. Ames, 219–230. Albany: State University of New York Press, 1998.

Berthrong, John H. *Transformations of the Confucian Way.* Boulder: Westview Press, 1998.

Chan, Wing-tsit, ed. and trans. *A Sourcebook in Chinese Philosophy.* Princeton: Princeton University Press, 1963.

Ching, Julia. *Chinese Religions.* Maryknoll, NY: Orbis Books, 1993

———. *Mysticism and Kingship in China: The Heart of Chinese Wisdom.* Cambridge: Cambridge University Press, 1997.

Fang Keli. "On the Categories of Substance and Function in Chinese Philosophy." *Chinese Studies in Philosophy* 17 (Spring 1986): 26–77.

Feng Youlan (Fung Yu-lan). *Chuang-Tzu: A New Selected Translation with an Exposition of the Philosophy of Kuo Hsiang.* Second edition. New York: Paragon Book Reprint Corp., 1964.

———. *A History of Chinese Philosophy. Volume II: the Period of Classical Learning (from the Second Century B.C. to the Twentieth Century A.D.).* Translated by Derk Bodde. Princeton: Princeton University Press, 1953.

———. *The Spirit of Chinese Philosophy.* Translated by E. P. Hughes. Boston: Beacon Press, 1962.

Gardner, Daniel K., trans. *Learning to Be a Sage: Selections from the Conversations of Master Chu, Arranged Topically.* Berkeley/Los Angeles: University of California Press, 1990.

Gernet, Jacques. *A History of Chinese Civilization*. Translated by J. R. Foster. Cambridge: Cambridge University Press, 1982.

Girardot, N. J. *Myth and Meaning in Early Taoism: The Theme of Chao (hundun)*. Berkeley/Los Angeles/London: University of California Press, 1983.

Graham, A. C. *Disputers of the Tao: Philosophical Argument in Ancient China*. La Salle: Open Court Publishing Company, 1989.

Hall, David L. and Roger T. Ames. *Thinking from the Han: Self, Truth and Transcendence in Chinese and Western Culture*. Albany: State University of New York Press, 1998.

Hanson, Chad. *Language and Logic in Ancient China*. Ann Arbor: The University of Michigan Press, 1983.

Kohn, Livia. *Daoism and Chinese Culture*. Cambridge, MA: Three Pines Press, 2001.

Lai, Whalen. "The Age of Aquarius: Tsou Yen on the Beginning and the End." Paper Presented at the IRFWP Conference, Washington, D.C., November 25–29, 1997.

Lau, D. C., trans. *Confucius: The Analects (Lun yu)*. New York: Penguin Books, 1979.

————, trans. *Laozi: Tao Te Ching*. New York: Viking Penguin Inc., 1963.

Legge, James., trans. *The Texts of Taoism: the Sacred Books of China*. Volume II. New York: Dover Publications, Inc., 1962.

Mair, Victor H. *Wandering on the Way: Early Tales and Parables of Chuang Tzu*. New York: Bantam Books, 1994.

Oshima, Harold. "A Metaphorical Analysis of the Concept of Mind in the *Chuang-tzu*." In *Experimental Essays on the Chuang-tzu*, ed. Victor H. Mair, 63–84. Honolulu: The University of Hawaii Press, 1983.

Palmer, Martin, trans. *The Book of Chuang Tzu*. London and New York: Arkana, Penguin Books, Ltd., 1996.

Paper, Jordan. *The Spirits are Drunk: Comparative Approaches to Chinese Religion*. Albany: State University of New York Press, 1995.

Schipper, Kristofer. *The Taoist Body*. Translated by Karen C. Duval. Berkeley and Los Angeles: University of California Press, 1993.

Smullyan, Raymond M. *The Tao is Silent*. New York: Harper & Row, Publishers, 1977.

Taylor, Rodney L. *The Religious Dimension of Confucianism*. Albany: State University of New York, 1990.

Thompson, Laurence G. "What is Taoism? (with Apologies to H. G. Creel)." *Taoist Resources* 4 (December 1993): 9–22.

Waley, Arthur. *The Way and its Power: A Study of the Tao Te Ching and its Place in Chinese Thought*. London: George Allen & Unwin, Ltd., 1934.

Watson, Burton, trans. *The Complete Works of Chuang Tzu*. New York: Columbia University Press, 1968.

Wilhelm, Richard and Cary F. Baynes, trans. *The I Ching, or Book of Changes*. New York: Bollingen Foundation, Inc., 1950; Reprint, Princeton: Princeton University Press, 1990.

Wright, Arthur F., ed. *Confucianism and Chinese Civilization*. Stanford: Stanford University Press, 1975.

Wu, Kuang-ming. *Chuang Tzu: World Philosopher at Play*. New York: The Crossroad Publishing Company Scholars Press, 1982.

Yu, Ying-shih. "Individualism in the Neo-Taoist Movement." In *Studies in Confucian and Taoist Values*, ed. Donald J. Munro, 121–155. Ann Arbor: Center for Chinese Studies, The University of Michigan, 1985.

Indian Buddhism—History and Philosophy

Burtt, E. A., ed. *The Teachings of the Compassionate Buddha*. New York: Penguin Books, 1982.

Cabezon, Jose Ignacio. *Buddhism and Language: A Study of Indo-Tibetan Scholasticism*. Albany: State University of New York Press, 1994.

Cheng, Hueh-li, trans. *Nāgārjuna's Twelve Gate Treatise (Dvādaśamukha śāstra)*. Dordrecht, Holland: D. Reidel, 1982.

Conze, Edward. *Buddhist Thought in India: Three Phases of Buddhist Philosophy*. Ann Arbor: The University of Michigan Press, 1967.

Conze, Edward, trans. *The Perfection of Wisdom in Eight Thousand Lines & Its Verse Summary (Aṣṭasāhasrikāprajñāpāramitā sūtra)*. Bolinas: Four Seasons Foundation, 1973.

———. *The Large Sūtra on Perfect Wisdom (with the divisions of the Abhisamayālaṅkāra)*. Berkeley, Los Angeles, London: University of California Press, 1975.

Corless, Roger J. " Pure Land Piety." In *Buddhist Spirituality: Indian, Southeast Asian, Tibetan, Early Chinese*, ed.Takeuchi Yoshinori et al, 242–271. New York: The Crossroad Publishing Company, 1995.

———. *The Vision of the Buddha: the Space under the Tree*. New York: Paragon House: 1989.

Dayal, Har. *The Bodhisattva Doctrine in Sanskrit Literature*. Reprint edition. Delhi: Motilal Banarsidass, 1970.

De Jong, J. W. "The Beginnings of Buddhism." *The Eastern Buddhist*. N.S. 26.2 (1993): 11–30.

Garfield, Jay L., trans. *Fundamental Wisdom of the Middle Way: Nāgārjuna's Mūlamadhyamakakārikā*. New York/Oxford: Oxford University Press, 1995.

Gudmensen, Chris. *Wittgenstein and Buddhism*. London: Macmillan Press, 1977.

Hayes, Richard P. *Dignāga on the Interpretation of Signs*. Dordrecht and Boston: Kluwar Academic Publishers, 1988.

Hirakawa, Akira. *A History of Indian Buddhism: from Śākyamuni to Early Mahāyāna*. Translated and edited by Paul Groner. Honolulu: University of Hawaii Press, 1990.

Harris, Ian Charles. *The Continuity of Madhyamaka and Yogācāra in Indian Mahāyāna Buddhism*. Leiden: E.J. Brill, 1991.

Horner, I. B., trans. *The Collection of the Middle Length Sayings (Majjhima-nikāya)*. Volume 1, *The First Fifty Discourses (Mulapannasa)*. The Pali Text Society. London: Luzac & Company, Ltd., 1954.

Hubbard, Jamie, and Paul L. Swanson, ed. *Pruning the Bodhi Tree: the Storm over Critical Buddhism*. Honolulu: University of Hawaii Press, 1997.

Huntington, C. W., Jr., with Geshe Namgyal Wangchen. *The Emptiness of Emptiness: an Introduction to Early Indian Mādhyamika*. Honolulu: University of Hawaii Press, 1989.

Hurvitz, Leon, trans. *Scripture of the Lotus Blossom of the Fine Dharma*. New York: Columbia University Press, 1976.

Jaini, Padmabh S. "Prajñā and dr̥ṣṭi in the Vaibhāṣika Abhidharma." In *Prajñāpāramitā and Related Systems: Studies in Honor of Edward Conze*, ed. Lewis Lancaster and Luis Gomez, 403–415. Berkeley Buddhist Studies Series. Berkeley: University of California Berkeley Press, 1977.

Kalupahana, David J. *Nāgārjuna: The Philosophy of the Middle Way*. Albany: State University of New York Press, 1986.

La Vallee Poussin, Louis de, trans. *L' Abhidharmakośa de Vasubandhu*. Volume 1. Bruxelles: Institut Belge des Hautes Etudes Chinoise, 1971–1980.

Lamotte, Etienne, trans. *Le Traite de la Grande Vertu de Sagesse de Nāgārjuna—Mahā-prajñ āpāramitāśāstra [traduit et annote de la traduction chinoise de Kumārajīva].* Louvain: Institute Orientaliste, 1966–1976.

Lindtner, Christian. *Nāgārjuniana: Studies in the Writings and Philosophy of Nāgārjuna.* Copenhagen, 1982.

Lopez, Donald S., Jr. *The Heart Sūtra Explained: Indian and Tibetan Commentaries.* Albany: State University of New York Press, 1988.

Nikam, N. A., and Richard McKeon, eds and trans. *The Edicts of A±oka.* Chicago: The University of Chicago Press, 1959.

Nobel, Johannes. "Kumārajīva." *Sitzungsberichte der Preussischen Akademie der Wissenschaften.* Philosophische-Historiche klasse, 206–233. Berlin, 1927.

Olson, Robert. "Whitehead, Mādhyamika, and the Prajñāpāramitā." *Philosophy East and West* 15 (1975): 449–464.

Pye, Michael. *Skillful Means.* London: Duckworth, 1978.

Quinn, Paul Robert. "The Biography of Kumārajīva, 350–409 A.D." M.A. thesis, University of California at Berkeley, 1961.

Raju, P. T. *The Philosophical Traditions of India.* Delhi: Motilal Banarsidass, 1992.

Ramanan, K. Venkata. *Nāgārjuna's Philosophy as presented in the Mahā-Prajñāpāramitā Śāstra.* Rutland: Charles E. Tuttle Company, 1966; reprint Delhi: Motilal Banarsidass, 1975.

Ruegg, D. S. "The Uses and the Four Positions in the Catuṣkoṭi and the Problem of the Description of Reality in Mahāyāna Buddhism." *Journal of Indian Philosophy* 5 (1977): 1–71.

Sakurabe Hajime. "Abhidharma." In *Buddhist Spirituality: Indian, Southeast Asian, Tibetan, Early Chinese,* ed. Takeuchi Yoshinori et al, 67–78. New York: The Crossroad Publishing Company, 1995.

Shantideva. *The Way of the Bodhisattva.* Translated by the Padmakara Translation Group. Boston and London: Shambhala Publications Inc., 1997.

Silk, Jonathan A., ed. *Wisdom, Compassion, and the Search for Understanding: The Buddhist Studies Legacy of Gadjin M. Nagao.* Honolulu: University of Hawaii Press, 2000.

Skorupski, Tadeusz. "*Prajñā,*" in *The Encyclopedia of Religion,* Editor-in-chief, Mircea Eliade. New York: MacMillan Publishing Co., 1987.

Snellgrove, David. *Indo-Tibetan Buddhism: Indian Buddhists and their Tibetan Successors.* Volume 1. Boston: Shambhala Publications, Inc., 1987.

Sprung, Mervyn. *Lucid Exposition of the Middle Way: the Essential Chapters from the Prasannapadā of Candrakīrti.* Boulder: Prajñā Press, 1979.

Suzuki, Daisetz Teitaro. "Reason and Intuition in Buddhist Philosophy." In *The Japanese Mind: Essentials in Japanese Philosophy and Culture,* ed. Charles A. Moore, 66–109. Honolulu: East-West Center Press, University of Hawaii, 1967.

Takasaki, Jikido. *A Study on the Ratnagotravibhāga.* Rome: Instituto Italiano per il Medio ed. Estremo Oriente, 1966.

Thurman, Robert A. F., trans. *The Holy Teaching of Vimalakīrti: a Mahāyāna Scripture.* University Park: The Pennsylvania State University Press, 1976.

Verdu, Alfonso. *Early Buddhist Philosophy in the Light of the Four Noble Truths.* Delhi: Motilal Banarsidass, 1985.

Warder, A. K. *Indian Buddhism.* Delhi: Motilal Banarsidass, 1970.

Warren, Henry Clark, trans. *Buddhism in Translation.* New York: Atheneum, 1984.

Wayman, Alex. "The Mirror as a Pan-Buddhist Metaphor-Simile." *History of Religions* 13 (1974): 251–270.

Williams, Paul. *Mahāyāna Buddhism: the Doctrinal Foundations.* New York: Routledge, 1989.

Sources on Interpretation and Mysticism

Betti, Emilio. *Die Hermeneutik als allegemeine Methodik der Geisisteswissenschaften*. Philososphie und Geschicte series. Pamphlet Nos. 78–79. Tubingen: J. C. B. Mohr, 1962.

Boyer, Louis. "Mysticism: an Essay on the History of the Word." In *Understanding Mysticism*, ed. Richard Woods, 42–55. London: Athlone Press, 1980.

Bruns, Gerald. *Hermeneutics Ancient and Modern*. New Haven and London: Yale University Press, 1992.

Carmody, Denise Lardner and John Tully Carmody. *Mysticism: Holiness East and West*. New York/Oxford: Oxford University Press, 1996.

Chappell, David W. "Hermeneutical Phases in Chinese Buddhism." In *Buddhist Hermeneutics*, ed. Donald S. Lopez, Jr., 175–206. Kuruda Institute Studies in East Asian Buddhism 6. Honolulu: University of Hawaii Press, 1988.

Clarke, J. J. *Oriental Enlightenment: The Encounter between Asian and Western Thought*. New York: Routledge, 1997.

Clooney, Francis X. *Theology after Vedānta: An Experiment in Comparative Theology*. Albany: State University of New York Press, 1993.

Derrida, Jacques. "Structure, Sign and Play in the Discourse of the Human Sciences." In *Writing and Difference*, 278–290. Chicago: University of Chicago Press, 1978.

Dickens, Charles. *A Christmas Carol*. Facsimile edition of the autograph manuscript in The Pierpont Morgan Library. New York: The Pierpont Morgan Library, 1993.

Dilthey, Wilhelm. "Draft for a Critique of Historical Reason." In *The Hermeneutics Reader: Texts of the German Tradition from the Enlightenment to the Present*, ed. Kurt Mueller-Vollmer, 148–164. New York: The Continuum Publishing Company, 1985.

Dilworth, D. A. *Philosophy in World Perspective: A Comparative Hermeneutic of Major Theories*. New Haven: Yale University Press, 1989.

Dreyfus, Hubert L. *Being-in-the-World: a Commentary on Heidegger's Being and Time, Division I*. Cambridge: The MIT Press, 1991.

Dupre, Louis. "Mysticism." In *The Encyclopedia of Religion*, Editor-in-chief, Mircea Eliade. New York: Macmillan Publishing Co., 1987.

Fairweather, Eugene R., ed and trans. *A Scholastic Miscellany: Anselm to Ockham*. Philadelphia: The Westminster Press, 1955.

Fish, Stanley Eugene. *Is there a Text in this Class?: the Authority of Interpretive Communities*. Cambridge: Harvard University Press, 1980.

Forman, Robert K. C. "Introduction: Mysticism, Constructivism, and Forgetting." In *The Problem of Pure Consciousness: Mysticism and Philosophy*, ed. Robert K. C. Forman, 3–49. New York/Oxford: Oxford University Press, 1990.

Foucault, Michel. *The Archaeology of Knowledge*. Translated by A. W. Sheridan Smith. New York: Harper & Row, 1972.

Gadamer, Hans-Georg. "Destruktion and Deconstruction." In *Gesammelte Werke*, Volume 2: *Hermeneutik II*, 361–372. Tubingen: J. C. B. Mohr, 1986. Reprint, trans. Geoff Waite and Richard Palmer. In *Dialogue and Deconstruction: The Gadamer-Derrida Encounter*, ed. Diane P. Michelfelder and Richard E. Palmer, 102–113. Albany: State University of New York Press, 1989.

———. "The Diversity of Europe." In *Hans-Georg Gadamer on Education, Poetry, and History: Applied Hermeneutics*, ed. Dieter Misgeld and Graeme Nicholson. Albany: State University of New York Press, 1992.

———. "On the Problem of Self-Understanding." In *Philosophical Hermeneutics*, trans. and ed. David E. Linge, 44–58. Berkeley/Los Angeles/London: University of California Press, 1976.

———. "On the Scope and Function of Hermeneutical Reflection," trans. G. B. Hess and R. E. Palmer. In *Philosophical Hermeneutics*, ed. David E. Linge, 18–43. Berkeley/Los Angeles/ London: University of California Press, 1976.

———. "Reply to my Critics." Translated by George H. Leiner. In *The Hermeneutic Tradition: from Ast to Ricoeur*, ed. Gayle L. Ormston and Alan D. Schrift, 273–297. Albany: State University of New York Press, 1990.

———. "Semantics and Hermeneutics." Translated by P. Christopher Smith. In *Philosophical Hermeneutics*, trans and ed. David E. Linge, 82–94. Berkeley/Los Angeles/London: University of California Press, 1976.

———. *Truth and Method*. 2nd revised ed. Translation revised by Joel Weinsheimer and Donald G. Marshall. New York: The Continuum Publishing Company, 1994.

———. "The Universality of the Hermeneutical Problem." In *Philosophical Hermeneutics*, ed. and trans. David E. Linge, 3–17. Berkeley/Los Angeles/London: University of California Press, 1976.

Gare, Arran E. "Understanding Oriental Cultures." *Philosophy East and West* 45 (July 1995): 309–325.

Grondin, Jean. *Introduction to Philosophical Hermeneutics*. Translated by Joel Weinsheimer. New Haven: Yale University Press, 1994.

Habermas, Jurgen. "The Hermeneutic Claim to Universality." In *The Hermeneutic Tradition: From Ast to Ricoeur*, ed. Gayle L. Ormiston and Alan D. Schrift, 245–272. Albany: State University of New York Press, 1990.

Halbfass, Wilhelm. *India and Europe: An Essay in Understanding*. Albany: University of New York Press, 1988.

Heidegger, Martin. *Being and Time*. Translated by John Macquarrie and Edward Robinson. San Francisco: Harper & Row, Publishers, Inc., 1962.

———. *Early Greek Thinking*. Translated by David Farrell Krell and Frank A. Capuzzi. San Francisco: Harper & Row, Publishers, 1975.

———. *On the Way to Language*. Translated by Peter D. Hertz. San Francisco: Harper & Row, Publishers, 1971.

———. *Poetry, Language, Thought*. Translated by Albert Hofstadter. San Francisco: Harper & Row, Publishers, 1971.

Heisig, James W., and John C. Maraldo, eds. *Rude Awakenings: Zen, the Kyoto School & the Question of Nationalism*. Honolulu: The Nanzen Institute, University of Hawaii Press, 1994.

Herman, Jonathan R. "To Know the Sages Better than They Know Themselves: Chu Hsi's 'Romantic' Hermeneutics." Paper presented at the annual meeting of the American Academy of Religion, Orlando, Florida, November 21–24, 1998.

Hirsch, E. D., Jr. *Validity in Interpretation*. New Haven: Yale University Press, 1967.

Huxley, Aldous. *The Perennial Philosophy*. London: Harper & Row, 1944.

James, William. *The Varieties of Religious Experience: a Study in Human Nature*. Longmans, Green, and Co., 1902; reprint, New York: Viking Penguin Inc., 1982.

Jantzen, Grace. *Power, Gender and Mysticism*. Cambridge Studies in Ideology and Religion 8. Cambridge: Cambridge University Press, 1995.

Kapstein, Matthew. "Mi-pham's Theory of Interpretation." In *Buddhist Hermeneutics*, ed. Donald S. Lopez, Jr., 149–174. Kuroda Institute Studies in East Asian Buddhism 6. Honolulu: University of Hawaii Press, 1988.

Kasulis, Thomas P. "Truth Words: The Basis of Kukai's Theory of Interpretation." In *Buddhist Hermeneutics*, ed. Donald S. Lopez, Jr., 257–272. Kuroda Institute Studies in East Asian Buddhism 6. Honolulu: University of Hawaii Press, 1988.

Katz, Steven T. "Language, Epistemology, and Mysticism." In *Mysticism and Philosophical Analysis*, ed. Steven T. Katz, 22–74. New York: Oxford University Press, 1978.

———. "Mystical Speech and Mystical Meaning." In *Mysticism and Language*, ed. Steven T. Katz, 3–41. New York and Oxford: Oxford University Press, 1992.

King, Richard. *Orientalism and Religion: Postcolonial Theory, India and 'The Mystic East.'* New York: Routledge, 1999.

Lamotte, Etienne. "The Assessment of Textual Interpretation in Buddhism," trans. Sara Boin-Webb. *Buddhist Studies Review* 2 (1985): 4–24. Reprint, In *Buddhist Hermeneutics*, ed. Donald S. Lopez, Jr., 11–27. Kuroda Institute Studies in East Asian Buddhism 6. Honolulu: University of Hawaii Press, 1988.

Lopez, Donald S., Jr., ed. *Curators of the Buddha: The Study of Buddhism under Colonialism.* Chicago: University of Chicago Press, 1995.

———. "Interpretation of the Mahayana Sutras." In *Buddhist Hermeneutics*, ed. Donald S. Lopez, Jr., 47–70. Kuroda Institute Studies in East Asian Buddhism 6. Honolulu: University of Hawaii Press, 1988.

———. "Introduction." In *Buddhist Hermeneutics*, ed. Donald S. Lopez, Jr., 1–10. Kuroda Institute Studies in East Asian Buddhism 6. Honolulu: University of Hawaii Press, 1988.

———, et al, eds. *On Method. Journal of the International Association of Buddhist Studies* 18 (Winter 1995). [Entire issue.]

Lowe, Lisa. *Critical Terrains: French and British Orientalisms.* Ithaca: Cornell University Press, 1991.

Lyotard, Jean-Francois. *The Postmodern Condition.* Translated by Geoff Bennington and Brian Massumi. Minneapolis: University of Minnesota Press, 1979.

MacIntosh, Mark A. *Mystical Theology: the Integrity of Spirituality and Theology.* Malden: Blackwell Publishers, Inc., 1998.

MacIntyre, Alasdaire. *Whose Justice? Which Rationality?* Notre Dame: University of Notre Dame Press, 1988.

Makdisi, George. "The Scholastic Method in Medieval Education: an Inquiry into its Origins in Law and Theology." *Speculum* 497 (1974): 640–661.

Maraldo, John C. "Hermeneutics and Historicity in the Study of Buddhism." *The Eastern Buddhist* 19 (Spring 1986): 17–43.

Matilal, Bimal Krishna. "Mysticism and Ineffability: Some issues of Logic and Language." In *Mysticism and Language*, ed. Steven T. Katz, 143–157. New York and Oxford: Oxford University Press, 1992.

Mueller-Vollmer, Kurt. "Introduction: Language, Mind, and Artifact: An Outline of Hermeneutic Theory Since the Enlightenment." In *The Hermeneutics Reader: Texts of the German Tradition from The Enlightenment to the Present*, ed. Kurt Mueller-Vollmer, 1–53. New York: The Continuum Publishing Company, 1985.

Ng, On-cho. "Negotiating the Boundary between Hermeneutics and Philosophy in Early Ch'ing Ch'eng-Chu Confucianism: Li Kuang-ti's (1642–1718) Study of the *Doctrine of the Mean* (Chung-yung) and *Great Learning* (Ta-hsueh)." In *Imagining Boundaries: Changing Confucian Doctrines, Texts, and Hermeneutics*, ed. Kai-wing Chow, On-cho Ng, and John B. Henderson, 165–193. Albany: State University of New York Press, 1999.

Palmer, Richard E. *Hermeneutics: Interpretation Theory in Schleiermacher, Dilthey, Heidegger, and Gadamer.* Evanston: Northwestern University press, 1969.

Panikkar, Raimundo. "What is Comparative Philosophy Comparing?" In *Interpreting Across Boundaries: New Essays in Comparative Philosophy*, ed. Gerald James Larson and Eliot Deutsch, 116–136. Princeton: Princeton University Press, 1988.

Parkes, Graham, ed. *Heidegger and Asian Thought*. Honolulu: University of Hawaii Press, 1987.

Parkinson, G. H. R., ed. *The Theory of Meaning*. Oxford University Press, 1968.

Penner, Hans. "The Mystical Illusion." In *Mysticism and Religious Traditions*, ed. Steven T. Katz. New York: Oxford University Press, 1983.

Pfister, Lauren. "Discovering Monotheistic Metaphysics: The Exegetical Reflections of James Legge (1815–1897) and Lo Chung-fan (d. circa 1850)." In *Imagining Boundaries: Changing Confucian Doctrines, Texts, and Hermeneutics*, ed. Kai-wing Chow, On-cho Ng, and John B. Henderson, 213–249. Albany: State University of New York Press, 1999.

Potter, Karl H. "Metaphor as Key to Understanding the Thought of Other Speech Communities." In *Interpreting Across Boundaries: New Essays in Comparative Philosophy*, ed. Gerald James Larson and Eliot Deutsch, 19–35. Princeton: Princeton University Press, 1988.

Quine, W. V. O. *Word and Object*. New York: Oxford University Press, 1960.

Ricoeur, Paul. "Between the Text and Its Readers." In *A Ricoeur Reader: Reflection and Imagination*, ed. Mario J. Valdes, 390–424. Toronto and Buffalo: University of Toronto Press, 1991.

———. "The Conflict of Interpretations: Debate with Hans-Georg Gadamer." In *A Ricoeur Reader: Reflection and Imagination*, ed. Mario J. Valdes, 216–241. Toronto and Buffalo: University of Toronto Press, 1991.

———. "The Creativity of Language." In *A Ricoeur Reader: Reflection and Imagination*, ed. Mario J. Valdes, 463–481. Toronto and Buffalo: University of Toronto Press, 1991.

———. "Existence and Hermeneutics." In *The Conflict of Interpretations: Essays in Hermeneutics*, ed. Don Ihde, 3–24. Evanston: Northwestern University Press, 1974.

———. "Habermas." In *A Ricoeur Reader: Reflection and Imagination*, ed. Mario J. Valdes, 159–181. Toronto and Buffalo: University of Toronto Press, 1991.

———. *Hermeneutics and the Human Sciences*. Translated and edited by John B. Thompson. Cambridge: Cambridge University Press, 1981.

———. *Interpretation Theory: Discourse and the Surplus of Meaning*. Fort Worth, TX: Texas Christian University Press, 1976.

Rosemont, Henry. "Against Relativism." In *Interpreting Across Boundaries: New Essays in Comparative Philosophy*, ed. Gerald James Larson and Eliot Deutsch, 36–72. Princeton: Princeton University Press, 1988.

Said, Edward W. *Orientalism: Western Conceptions of the Orient*. New York: Random House, 1979.

Scharfstein, Ben-Ami. "The Contextual Fallacy." In *Interpreting Across Boundaries: New Essays in Comparative Philosophy*, ed. Gerald James Larson and Eliot Deutsch, 84–97. Princeton: Princeton University Press, 1988.

Schleiermacher, Friedrich D. E. *Hermeutik und Kritik*. Translated by James Duke and Jack Frostman. Heidelberg: Carl Winter, 1974. Reprint, "General Hermeneutics" and "Grammatical and Technical Interpretation," in *The Hermeneutics Reader: Texts of the German Tradition from the Enlightenment to the Present*, ed. Kurt Mueller-Vollmer, 72–86 and 86–97.

Schuon, Fritjof. *The Transcendent Unity of Religions*. Wheaton: Quest, 1984.

Sells, Michael. *Mystical Languages of Unsaying*. Chicago and London: The University of Chicago Press, 1994.

Shakespeare, William. *Hamlet*. Signet Classics edition, edited by Edward Hubler. New York: The New American Library, Inc., 1963.

Sharp, E. J. *The Universal Gita: Western Images of the Bhagavad Gita*. La Salle: Open Court Publishers, 1985.

Smith, Huston. *Forgotten Truth: The Common Vision of the World's Religions*. San Francisco: Harper Collins, 1976.

Smith, John E. "Interpreting across Boundaries." In *Understanding the Chinese Mind: the Philosophical Roots*, ed. Robert E. Allinson, 26–47. Hong Kong: Oxford University Press, 1989.

Stace, W. T. *Mysticism and Philosophy*. New York: The Macmillan Press Ltd., 1960.

Steiner, George. *After Babel: Aspects of Language and Translation*. Cambridge: Oxford University Press, 1975.

Stenger, Mary Ann. "Gadamer's Hermeneutics as a Model for Cross-Cultural Understanding and Truth in Religion." In *Religious Pluralism and Truth: Essays on Cross-Cultural Philosophy of Religion*, ed. Thomas Dean, 151–168. Albany: State University of New York Press, 1995.

Tracy, David. *Plurality and Ambiguity: Hermeneutics, Religion, Hope*. Chicago: The University of Chicago Press, 1987.

Thurman, Robert. "Buddhist Hermeneutics." *Journal of the American Academy of Religion* 46 (January 1978): 19–39.

Weinsheimer, Joel C. *Gadamer's Hermeneutics: a Reading of 'Truth and Method'*. New Haven and London: Yale University Press, 1985.

Wittgenstein, Ludwig. *Tractatus Logico-Philosophicus*. London: Routledge and Kegan Paul, 1922.

Zaehner, R. C. *Mysticism, Sacred and Profane*. Oxford: Oxford University Press, 1961.

Zhang, Longzi. *The Tao and the Logos: Literary Hermeneutics, East and West*. Durham: Duke University Press, 1992.

Reference Works on Chinese, English and Japanese Language

A Dictionary of Literary Terms and Literary Theory. Fourth edition.

Giles' Chinese-English Dictionary. Second edition, revised and enlarged.

Matthews' Chinese-English Dictionary. Revised American edition.

The New Nelson Japanese-English Character Dictionary. Revised edition.

Webster's New Collegiate Dictionary. 1974 edition.

Zhongwen da cidian. 中文大辭典. 1962 edition.

INDEX